Surprise!

You may be reading the wrong way!

It's true: In keeping with the original Japanese comic format, this book reads from right to left—so action, sound effects, and word balloons are completely reversed. This preserves the orientation of the original artwork—plus, it's fun! Check out the diagram shown here to get the hang of things, and then turn to the other side of the book to get started!

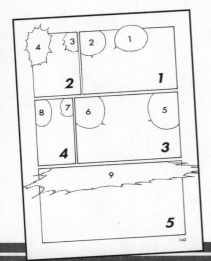

WELCOME to Imperial Academy: a private school where trying to become SUPERIOR can make you feel INFERIOR!

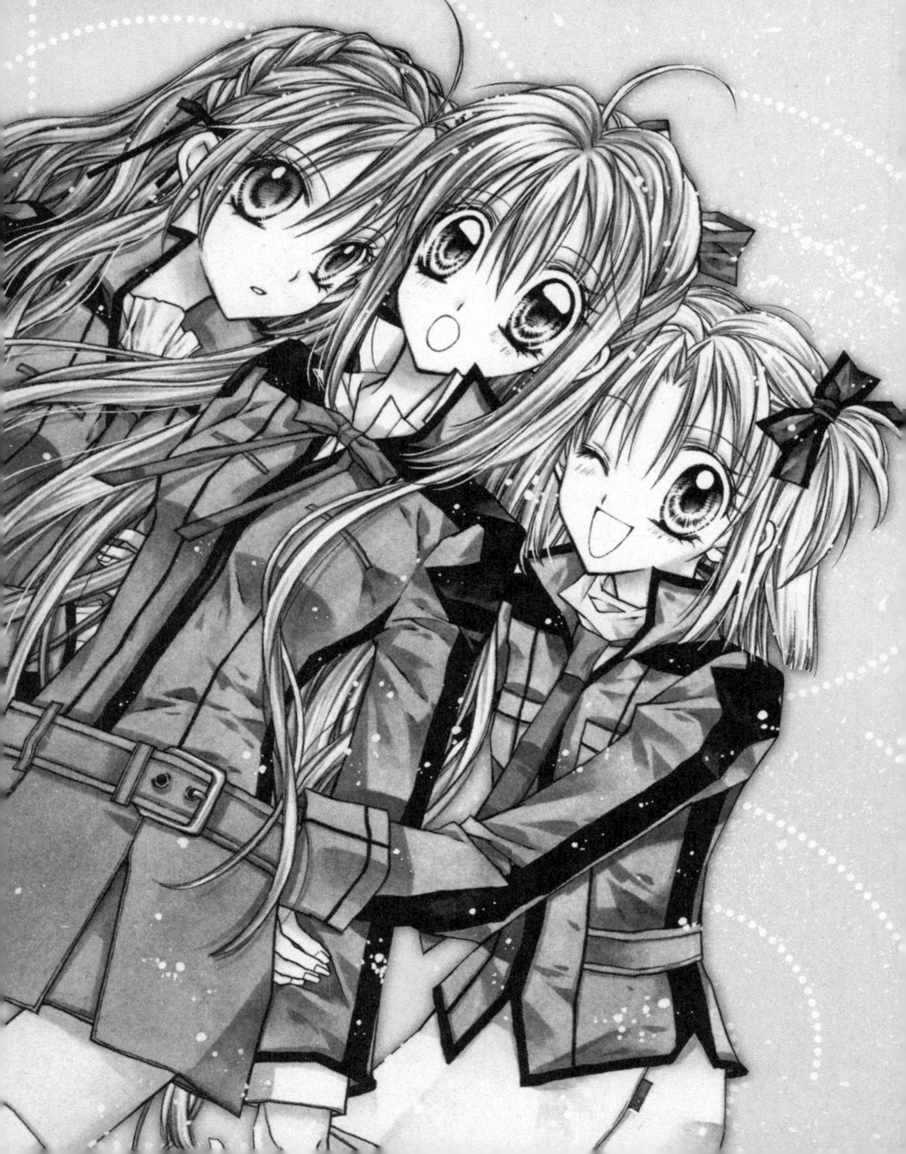

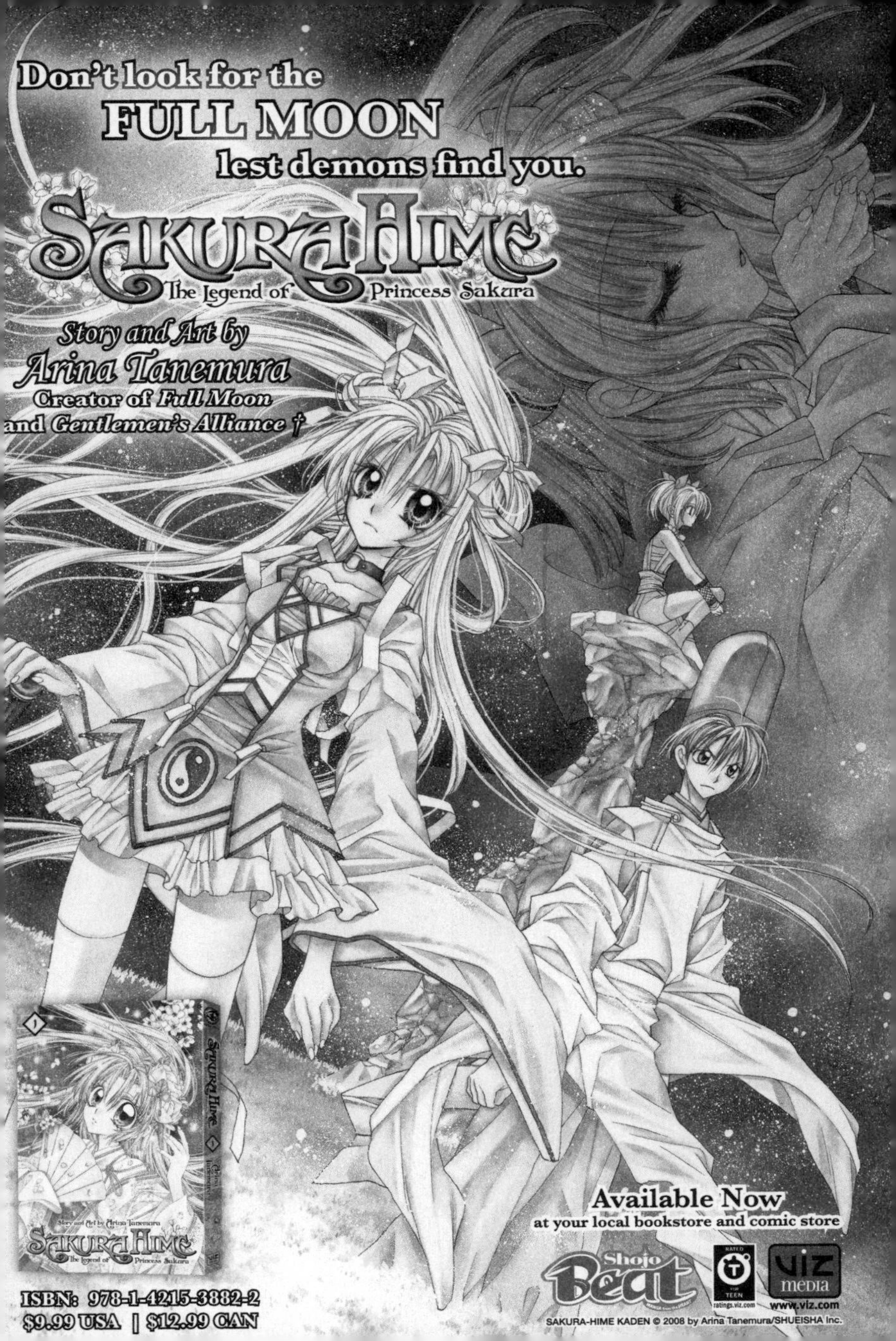

Is this girl a devil in disguise...
or a misunderstood angel?

A Devil and Her Love Song

Story and Art by Miyoshi Tomori

Meet Maria Kawai—she's gorgeous and whip-smart, a girl who seems to have it all. But when she unleashes her sharp tongue, it's no wonder some consider her to be the very devil! Maria's difficult ways even get her kicked out of an elite school, but this particular fall may actually turn out to be her saving grace...

Only $9.99 US / $12.99 CAN each!

Vol. 1 ISBN: 978-1-4215-4164-8
Vol. 2 ISBN: 978-1-4215-4165-5
Vol. 3 ISBN: 978-1-4215-4166-2
Vol. 4 ISBN: 978-1-4215-4167-9

Check your local manga
retailer for availability!

Shojo
Beat

VIZ
MEDIA
www.viz.com

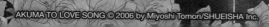

Kimi ni Todoke
VOL. 19

Shojo Beat Edition

STORY AND ART BY
KARUHO SHIINA

Translation/Ari Yasuda, HC Language Solutions, Inc.
Touch-up Art & Lettering/Vanessa Satone
Design/Nozomi Akashi
Editor/Hope Donovan

KIMI NI TODOKE © 2005 by Karuho Shiina
All rights reserved. First published in Japan in 2005 by SHUEISHA Inc.,
Tokyo. English translation rights arranged by SHUEISHA Inc.

Printed in the U.S.A.

Published by VIZ Media, LLC
P.O. Box 77010
San Francisco, CA 94107

10 9 8 7 6 5 4 3 2 1
First printing, June 2014

www.viz.com

www.shojobeat.com

There wasn't much snow during the year I was drawing the characters in their first-year winter, so I didn't put much in the manga either. And now in their second year, there's a ton of snow, so there's tons of snow in the manga too. Since manga and reality happen to be in sync, I decided to visit a shrine for New Year's this year and take some reference photos. There was a big snowstorm, though, and I almost didn't go. Also, I lost the lens cap to my camera and that almost grounded me too. Given the weather, I doubted anyone would show, but they did! Young people are so adventurous!

--Karuho Shiina

Karuho Shiina was born and raised in Hokkaido, Japan. Though *Kimi ni Todoke* is only her second series following many one-shot stories, it has already racked up accolades from various "Best Manga of the Year" lists. Winner of the 2008 Kodansha Manga Award for the shojo category, *Kimi ni Todoke* also placed fifth in the first-ever Manga Taisho (Cartoon Grand Prize) contest in 2008. In Japan, an animated TV series debuted in October 2009, and a live-action film was released in 2010.

Shojo Beat

kimi ni todoke

From Me to You

Vol. 19

Story & Art by

Karuho Shiina

Volume 19

Contents

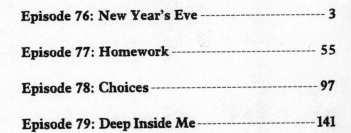

Story Thus Far

Sawako Kuronuma has always been a loner. Though not by choice, this
optimistic 16-year-old girl can't seem to make any friends. Stuck with
the unfortunate nickname "Sadako" after the haunting movie character,
rumors about her summoning spirits have been greatly exaggerated.
With her shy personality and scary looks, most of her classmates will
barely talk to her, much less look into her eyes for more than three
seconds lest they be cursed. Thanks to Kazehaya, who always treats her
nicely, Sawako makes her first friends at school, Ayane and Chizu.
Eventually, Sawako finds the courage to date Kazehaya.

On a school trip to Okinawa, poor Sawako and Kazehaya's attempt at a
first kiss is interrupted, leaving them stiff and awkward around each
other. Also during the trip, Ryu confesses his long-held romantic feelings
to Chizu, who turns him down. But during the Christmas party, Chizu
and Ryu end up exchanging gifts that bring them closer. Also during
the party, Ayane finally accepts Kento's feelings for her. After the party,
Sawako and Kazehaya walk home together, so uncomfortable around
each other that Sawako breaks down crying, thinking he no longer cares
for her. It is in that moment that Kazehaya finally kisses her!

On Christmas Day, Sawako and her friends gather at Sawako's house
for girl talk, and the gathering turns into a full-blown party with all the
guys. Sawako's parents are happy to see how their daughter has grown
now that she is halfway through high school.

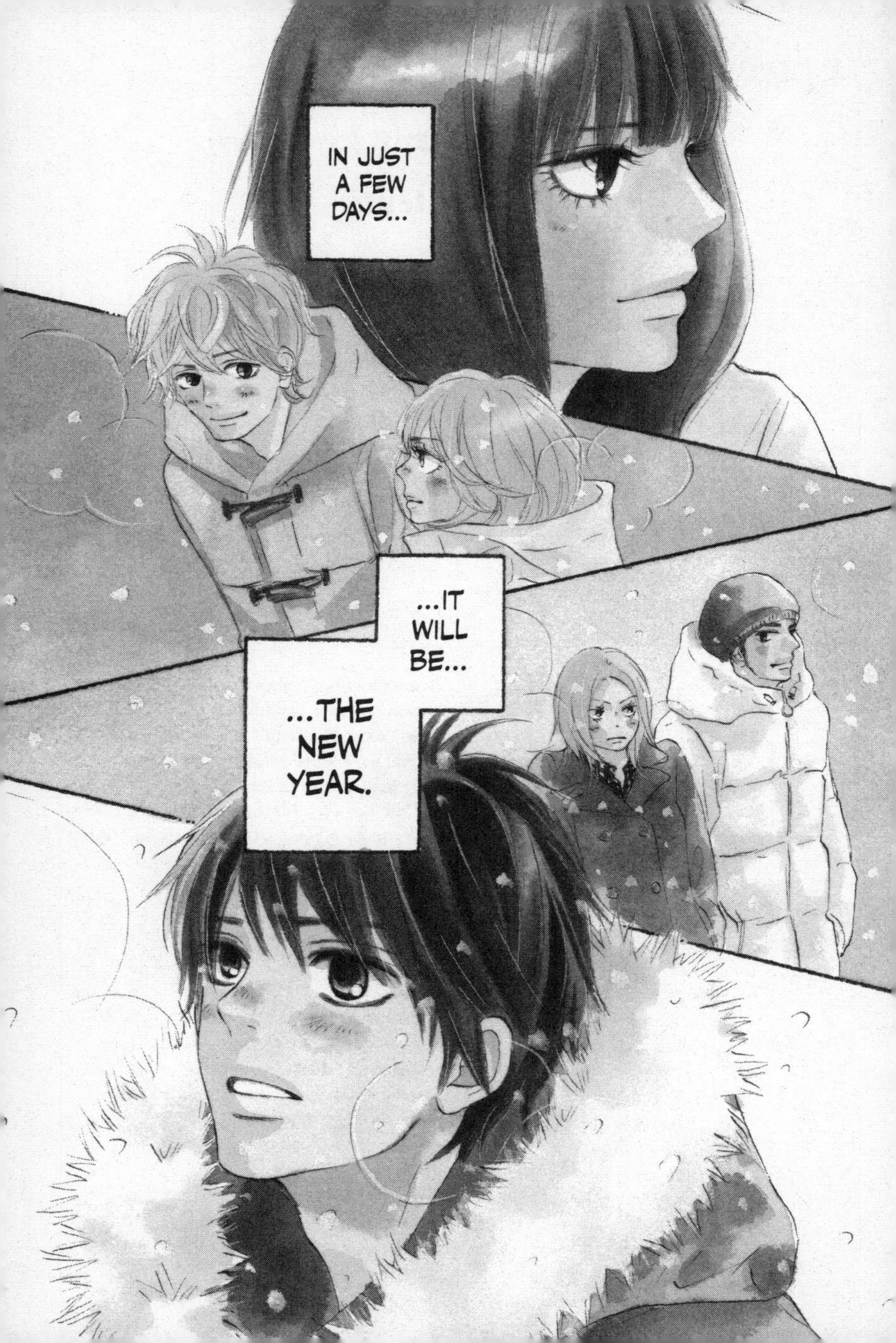
IN JUST A FEW DAYS...
...IT WILL BE...
...THE NEW YEAR.

Episode 76: New Year's Eve

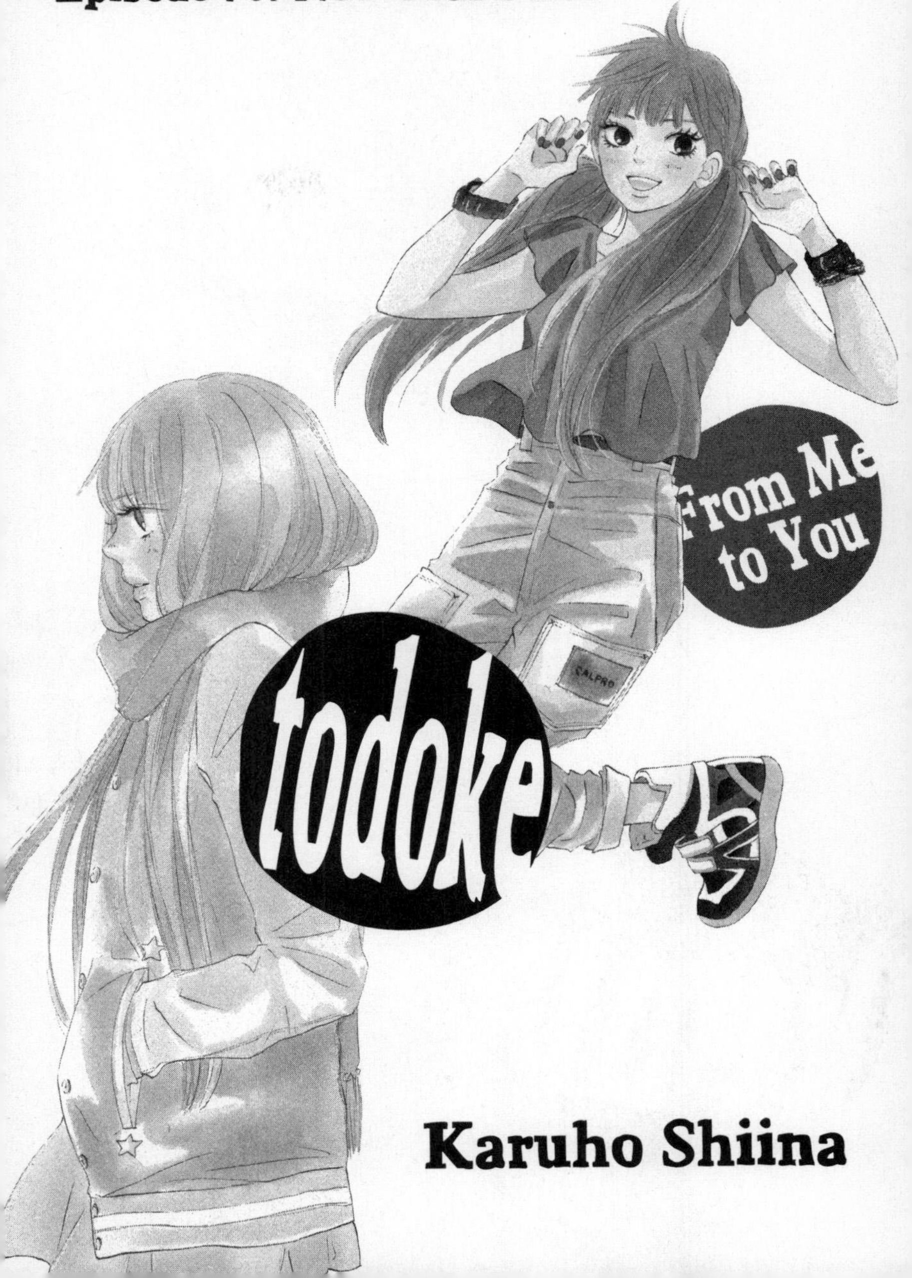
From Me to You
todoke
CALPRO

Karuho Shiina

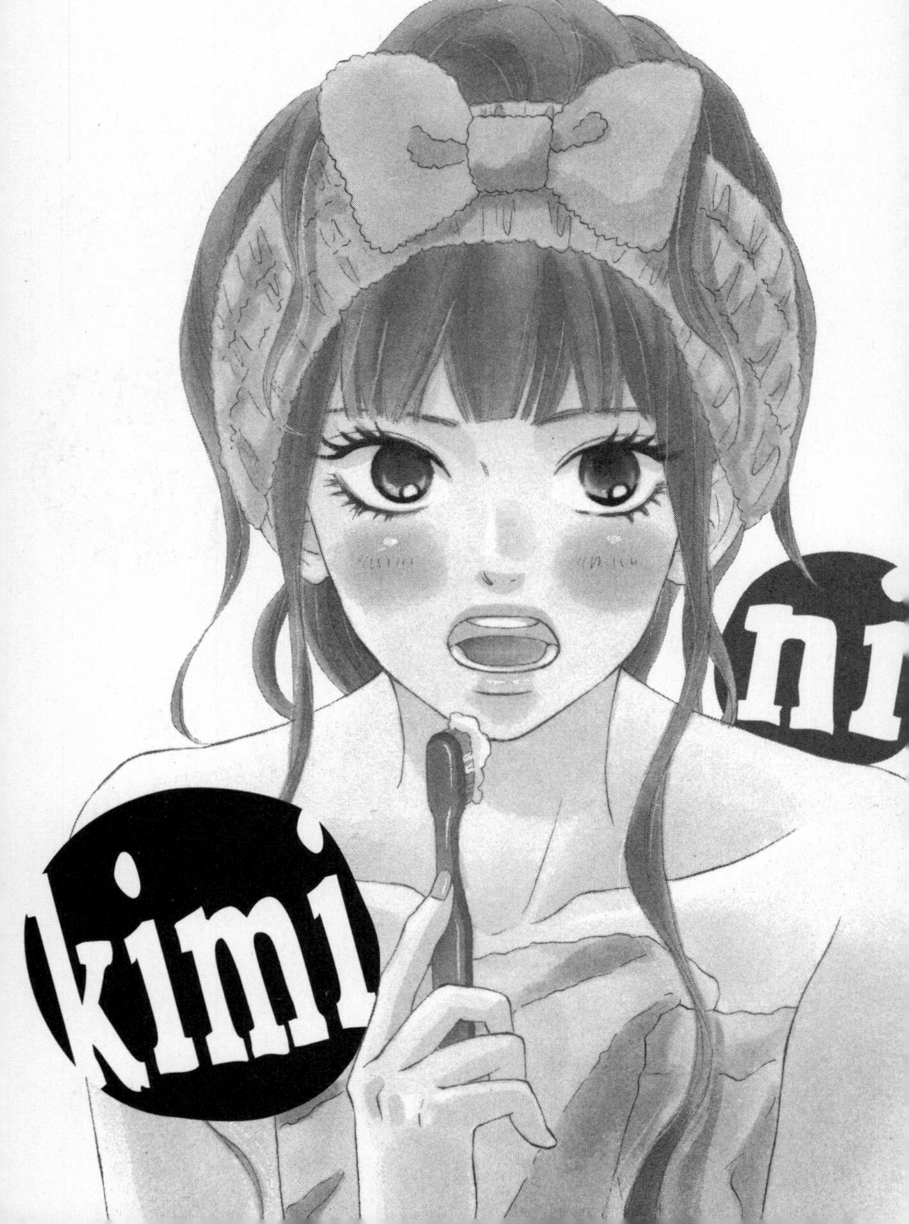
ni
kimi

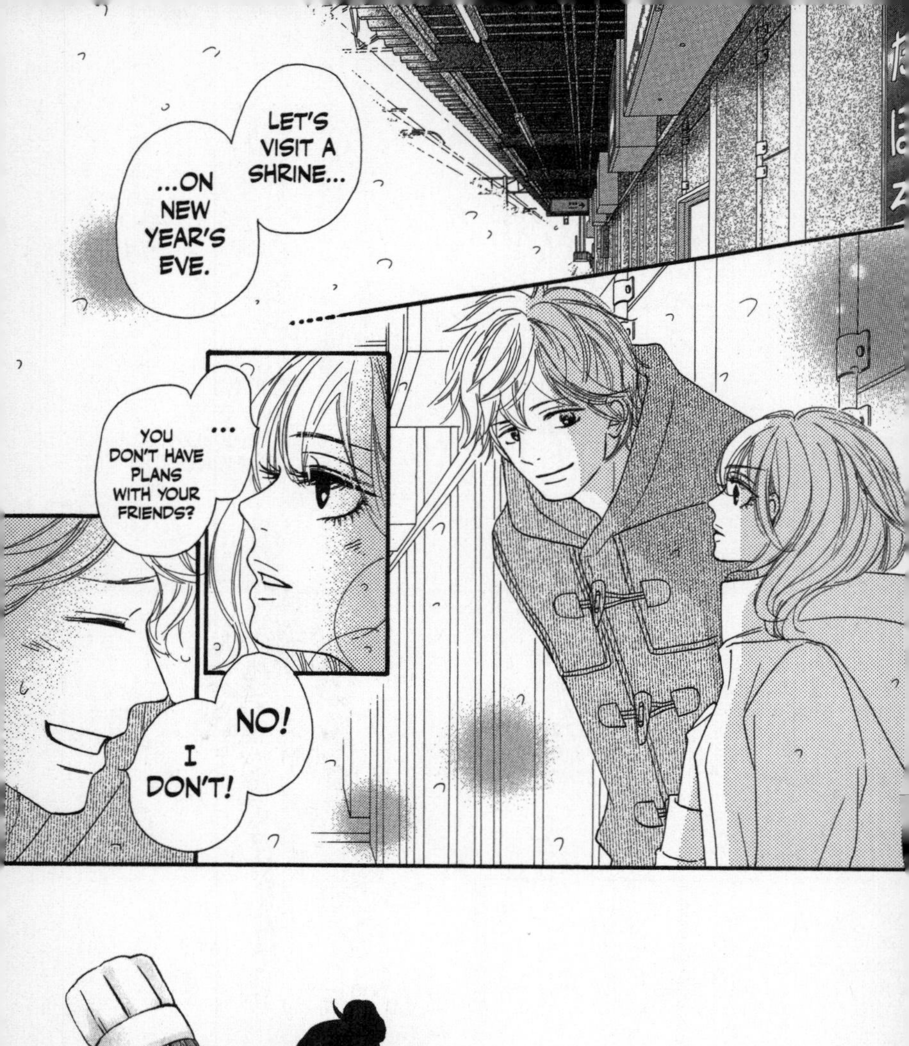
LET'S VISIT A SHRINE...
...ON NEW YEAR'S EVE.
.....
...
YOU DON'T HAVE PLANS WITH YOUR FRIENDS?
NO! I DON'T!

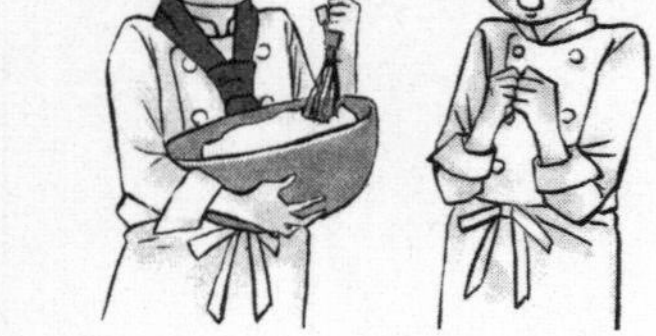

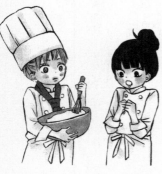

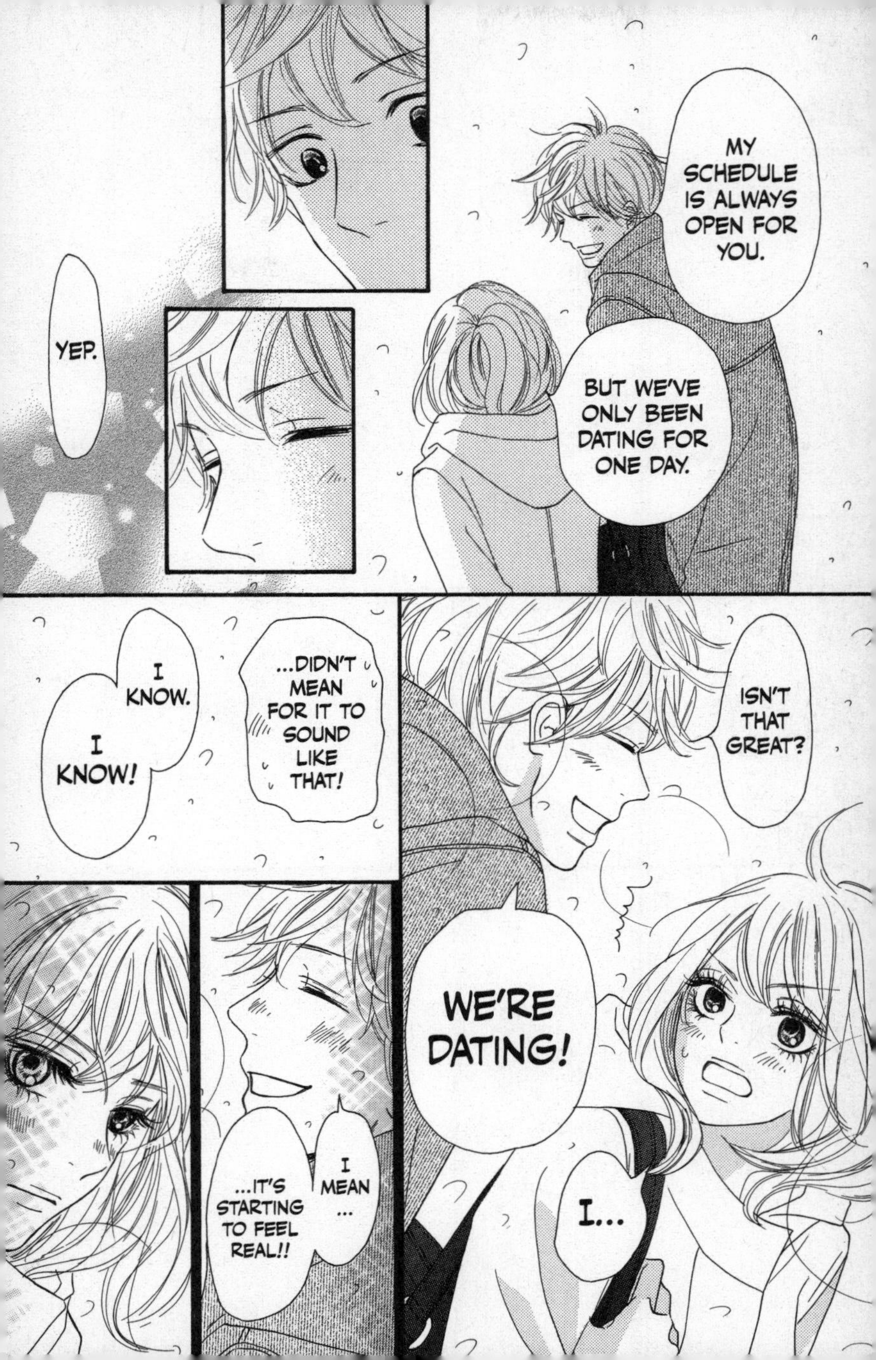
MY SCHEDULE IS ALWAYS OPEN FOR YOU.
BUT WE'VE ONLY BEEN DATING FOR ONE DAY.
YEP.
ISN'T THAT GREAT?
WE'RE DATING!
I...
...DIDN'T MEAN FOR IT TO SOUND LIKE THAT!
I KNOW.
I KNOW!
I MEAN ...
...IT'S STARTING TO FEEL REAL!!

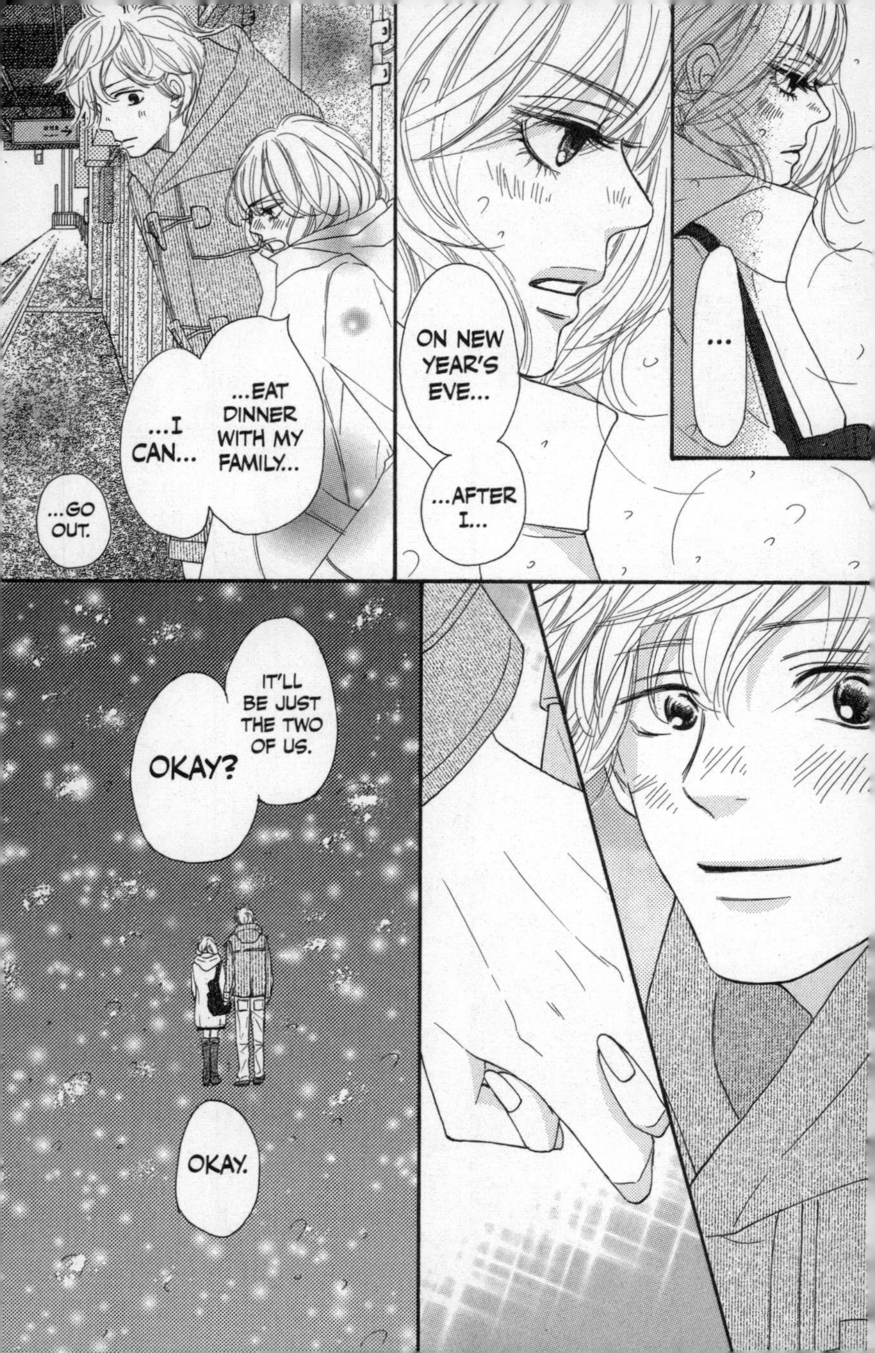
...
ON NEW YEAR'S EVE...
...AFTER I...
...EAT DINNER WITH MY FAMILY...
...I CAN...
...GO OUT.
IT'LL BE JUST THE TWO OF US.
OKAY?
OKAY.

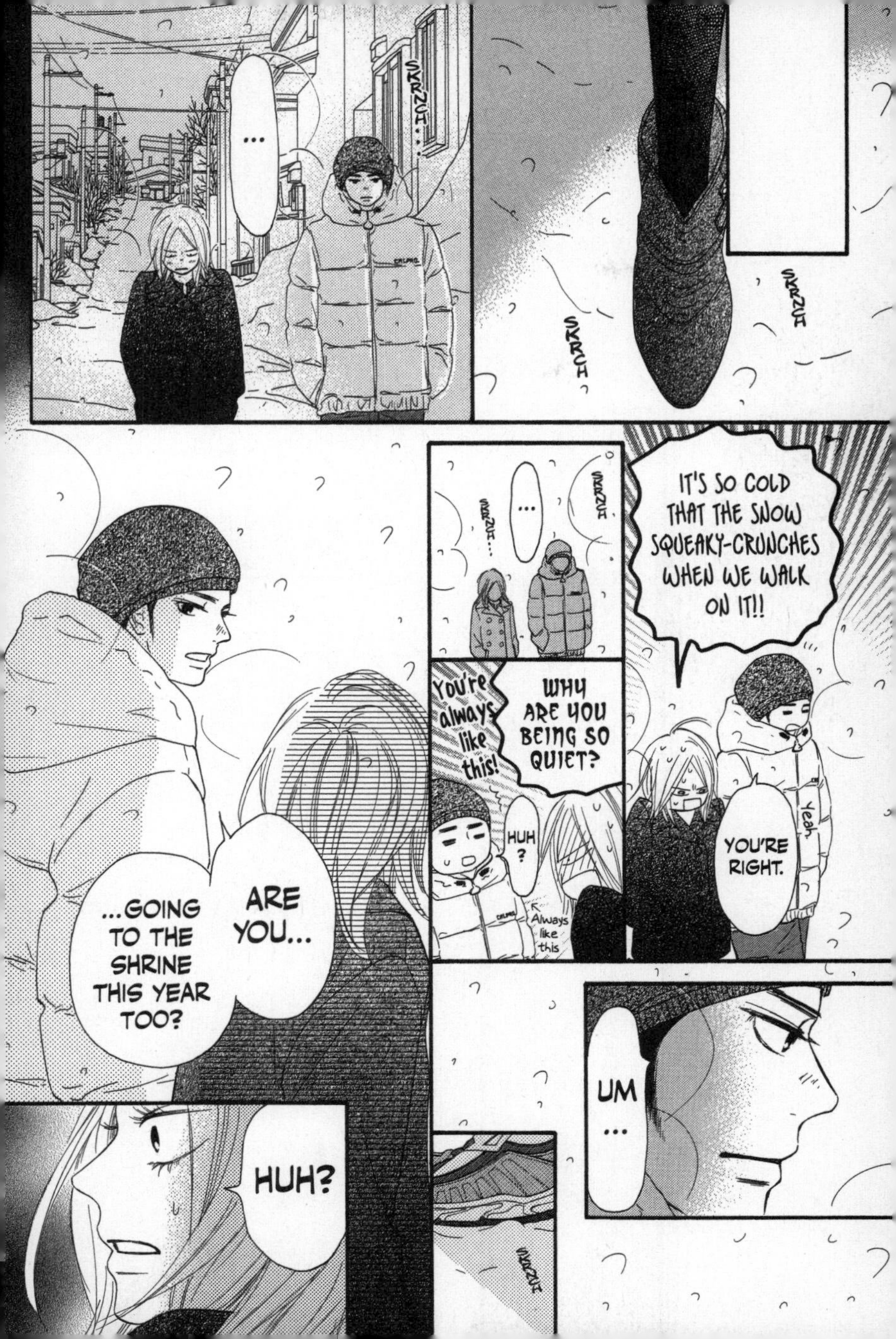
SKRNCH
SKRCH
SKRNCH...
...
IT'S SO COLD THAT THE SNOW SQUEAKY-CRUNCHES WHEN WE WALK ON IT!!
YOU'RE RIGHT.
Yeah.
...
SKRNCH
SKRNCH...
WHY ARE YOU BEING SO QUIET?
You're always like this!
HUH?
Always like this
ARE YOU...
...GOING TO THE SHRINE THIS YEAR TOO?
UM...
SKRNCH
HUH?

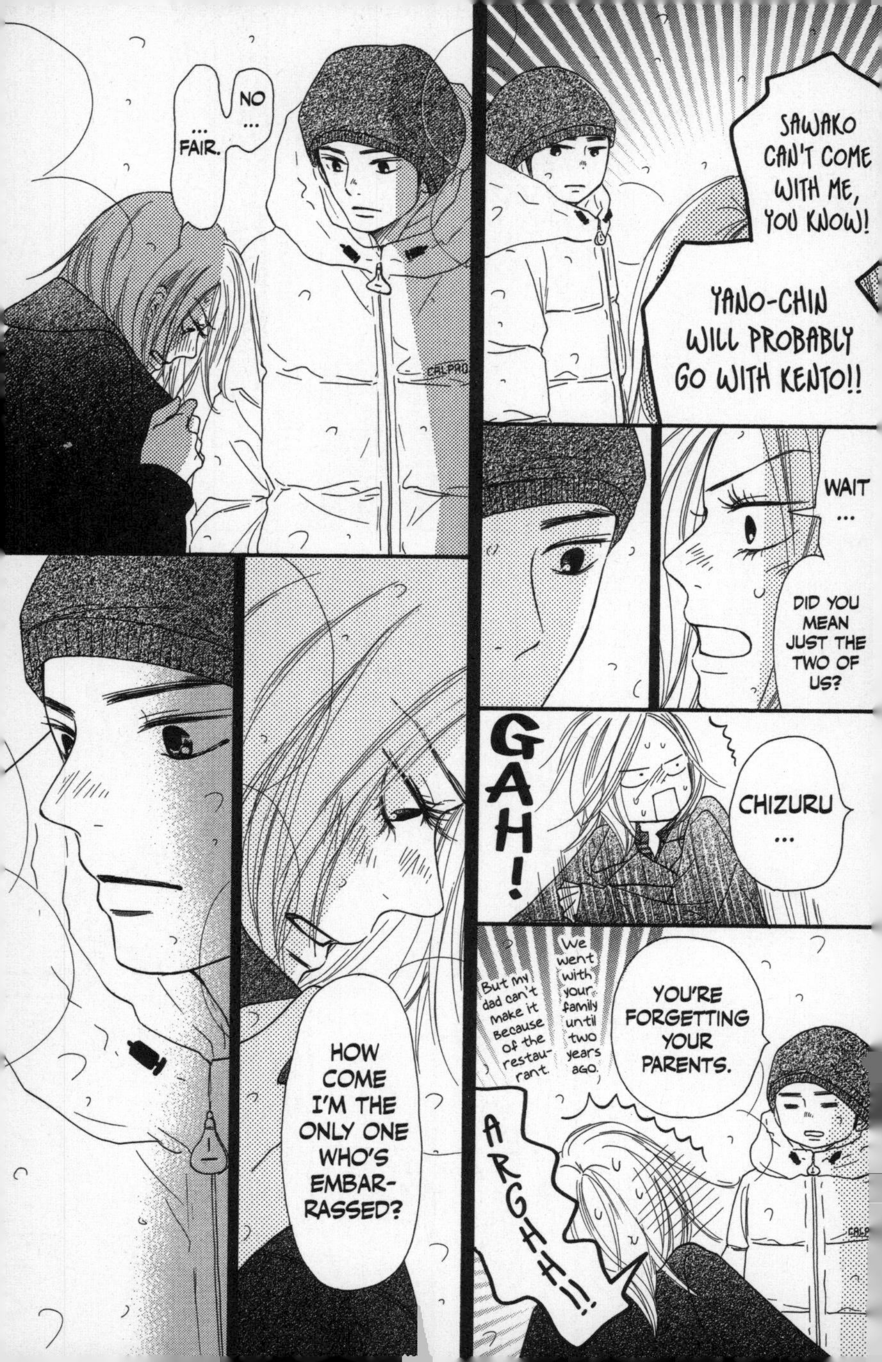
SAWAKO CAN'T COME WITH ME, YOU KNOW!
YANO-CHIN WILL PROBABLY GO WITH KENTO!!
NO ... ... FAIR.
WAIT ...
DID YOU MEAN JUST THE TWO OF US?
GAH!
CHIZURU ...
YOU'RE FORGETTING YOUR PARENTS.
We went with your family until two years ago.
But my dad can't make it because of the restaurant.
ARGHH!!
HOW COME I'M THE ONLY ONE WHO'S EMBARRASSED?

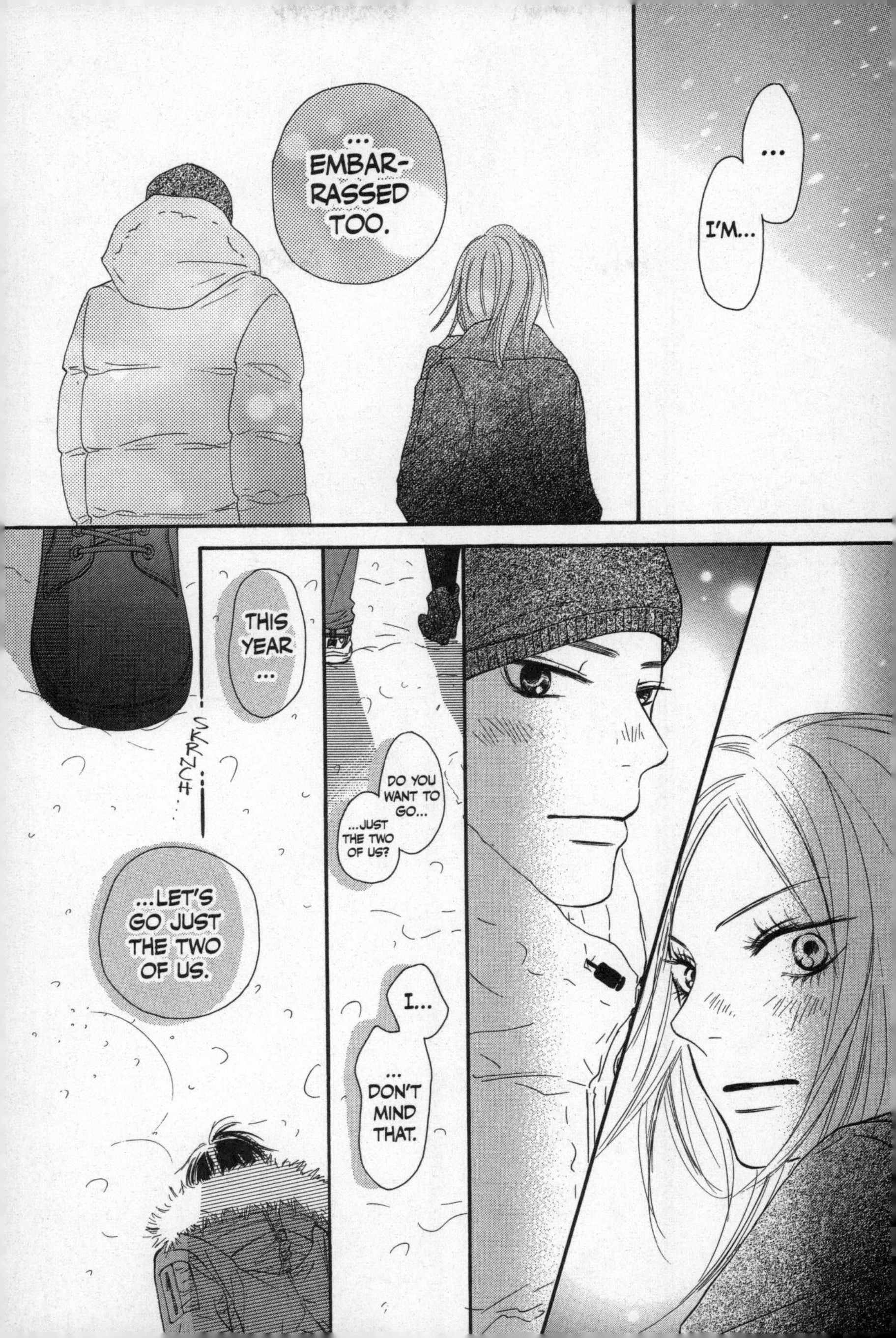
... I'M...
... EMBAR-RASSED TOO.
DO YOU WANT TO GO... ...JUST THE TWO OF US?
I... ...DON'T MIND THAT.
THIS YEAR ...
SKRNCH...
...LET'S GO JUST THE TWO OF US.

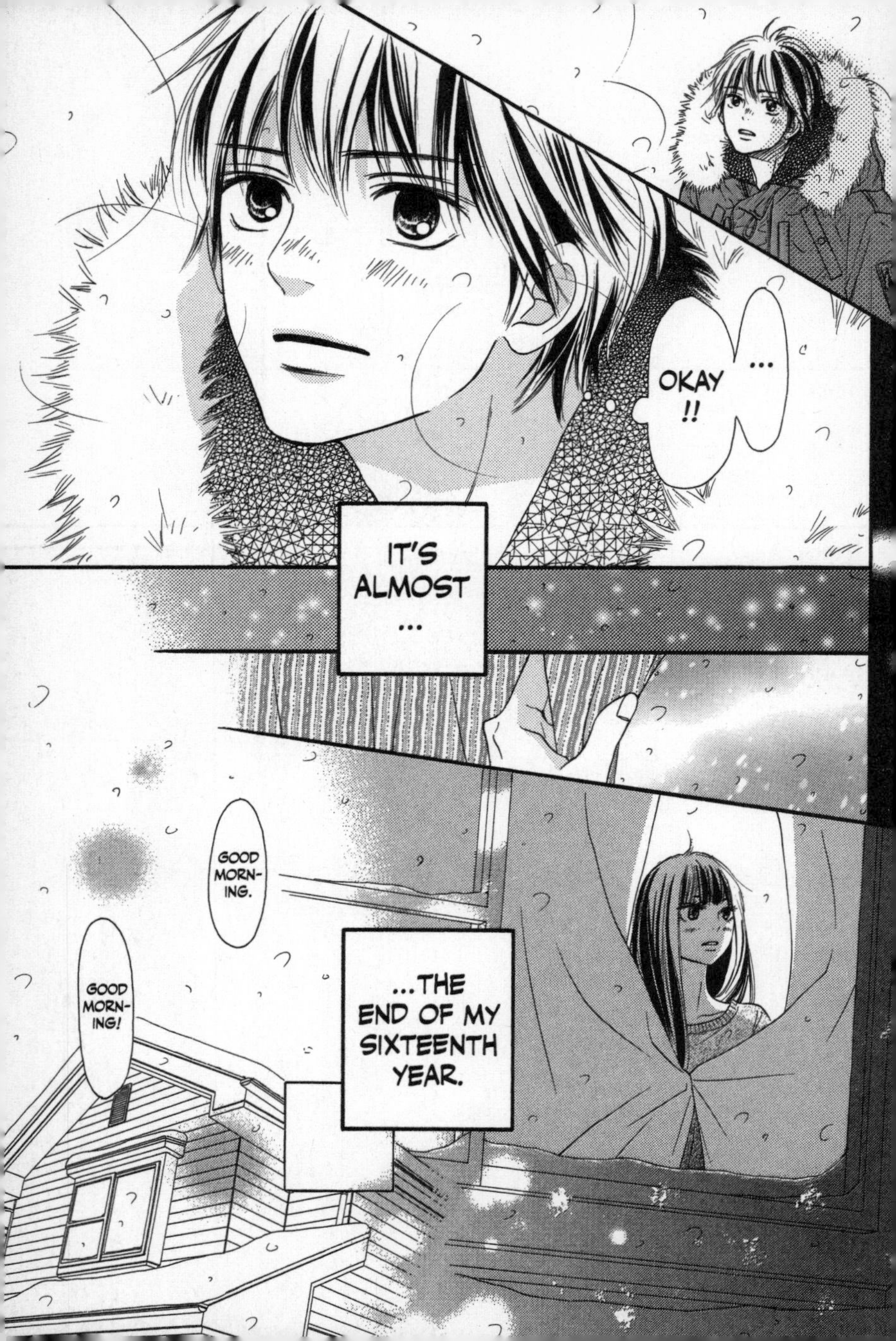
... OKAY !!
IT'S ALMOST ...
...THE END OF MY SIXTEENTH YEAR.
GOOD MORNING.
GOOD MORNING!

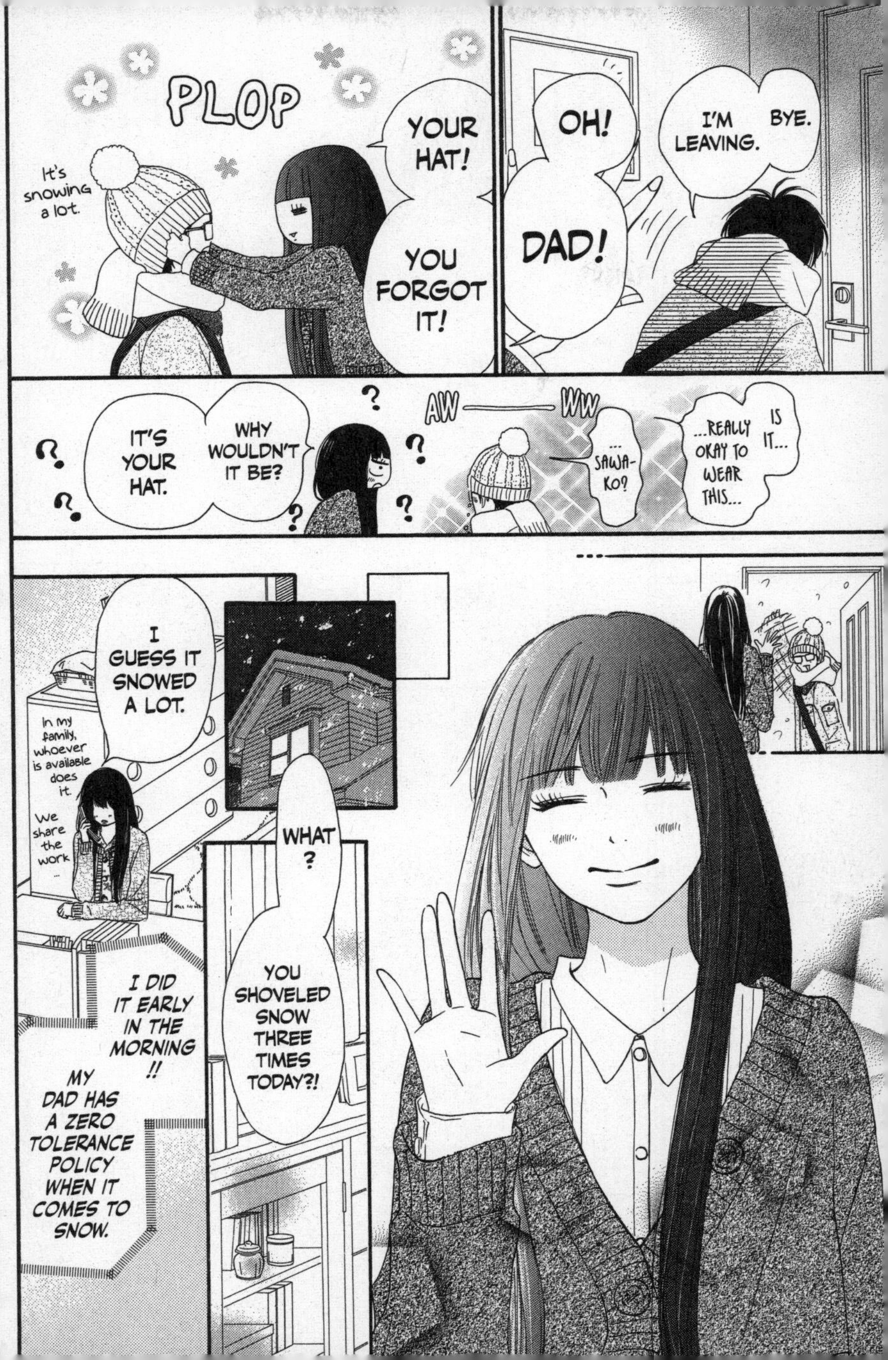
I'M LEAVING. BYE.
OH! DAD!
YOUR HAT! YOU FORGOT IT!
PLOP
It's snowing a lot.
IS IT... ...REALLY OKAY TO WEAR THIS...
... SAWAKO?
AW——WW
WHY WOULDN'T IT BE?
IT'S YOUR HAT.
I GUESS IT SNOWED A LOT.
WHAT?
YOU SHOVELED SNOW THREE TIMES TODAY?!
I DID IT EARLY IN THE MORNING!!
MY DAD HAS A ZERO TOLERANCE POLICY WHEN IT COMES TO SNOW.
In my family, whoever is available does it.
We share the work...

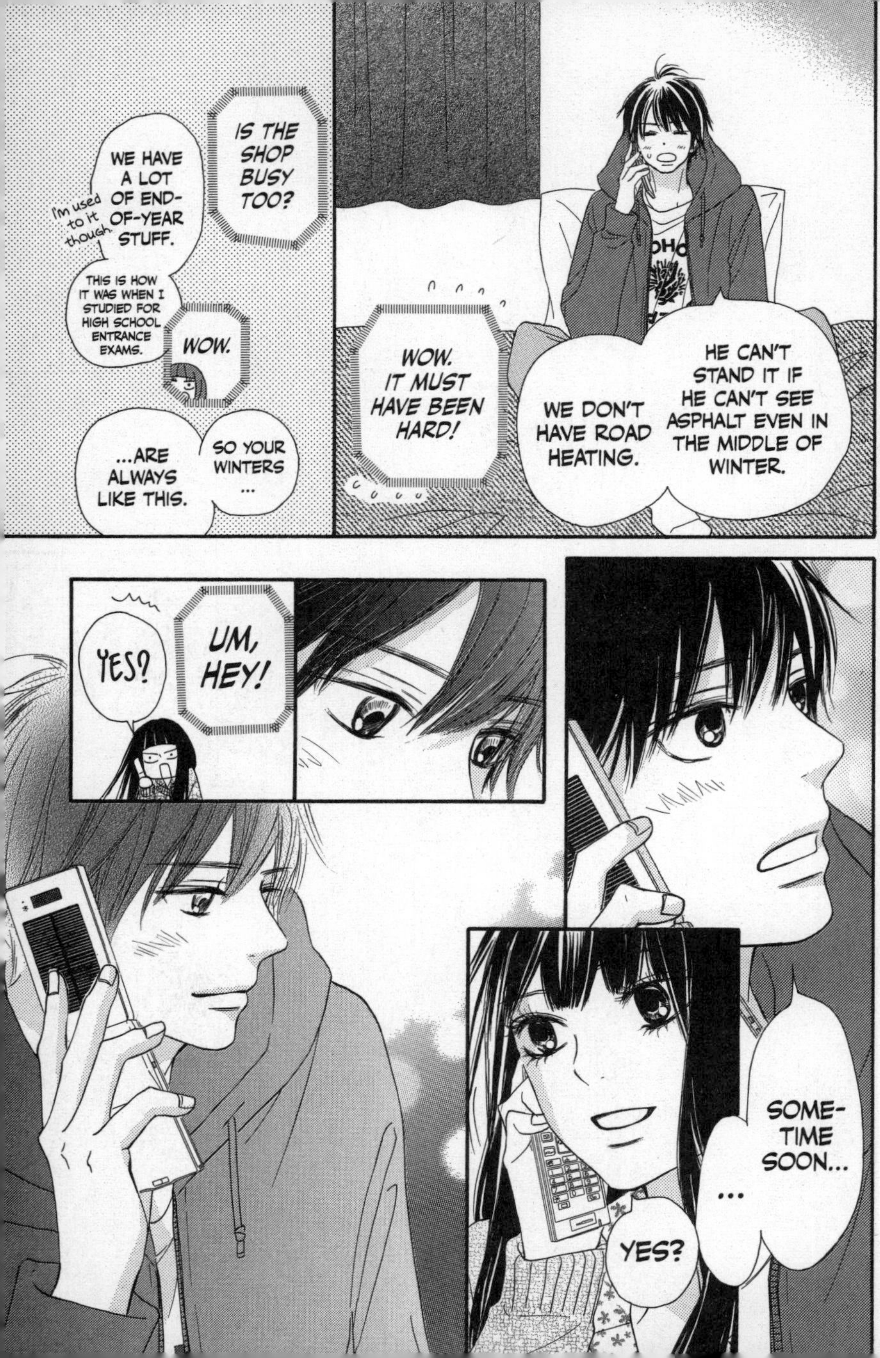
HE CAN'T STAND IT IF HE CAN'T SEE ASPHALT EVEN IN THE MIDDLE OF WINTER.
WE DON'T HAVE ROAD HEATING.
WOW. IT MUST HAVE BEEN HARD!
IS THE SHOP BUSY TOO?
WE HAVE A LOT OF END-OF-YEAR STUFF.
I'm used to it though.
THIS IS HOW IT WAS WHEN I STUDIED FOR HIGH SCHOOL ENTRANCE EXAMS.
WOW.
SO YOUR WINTERS ...
...ARE ALWAYS LIKE THIS.
UM, HEY!
YES?
SOME-TIME SOON...
...
YES?

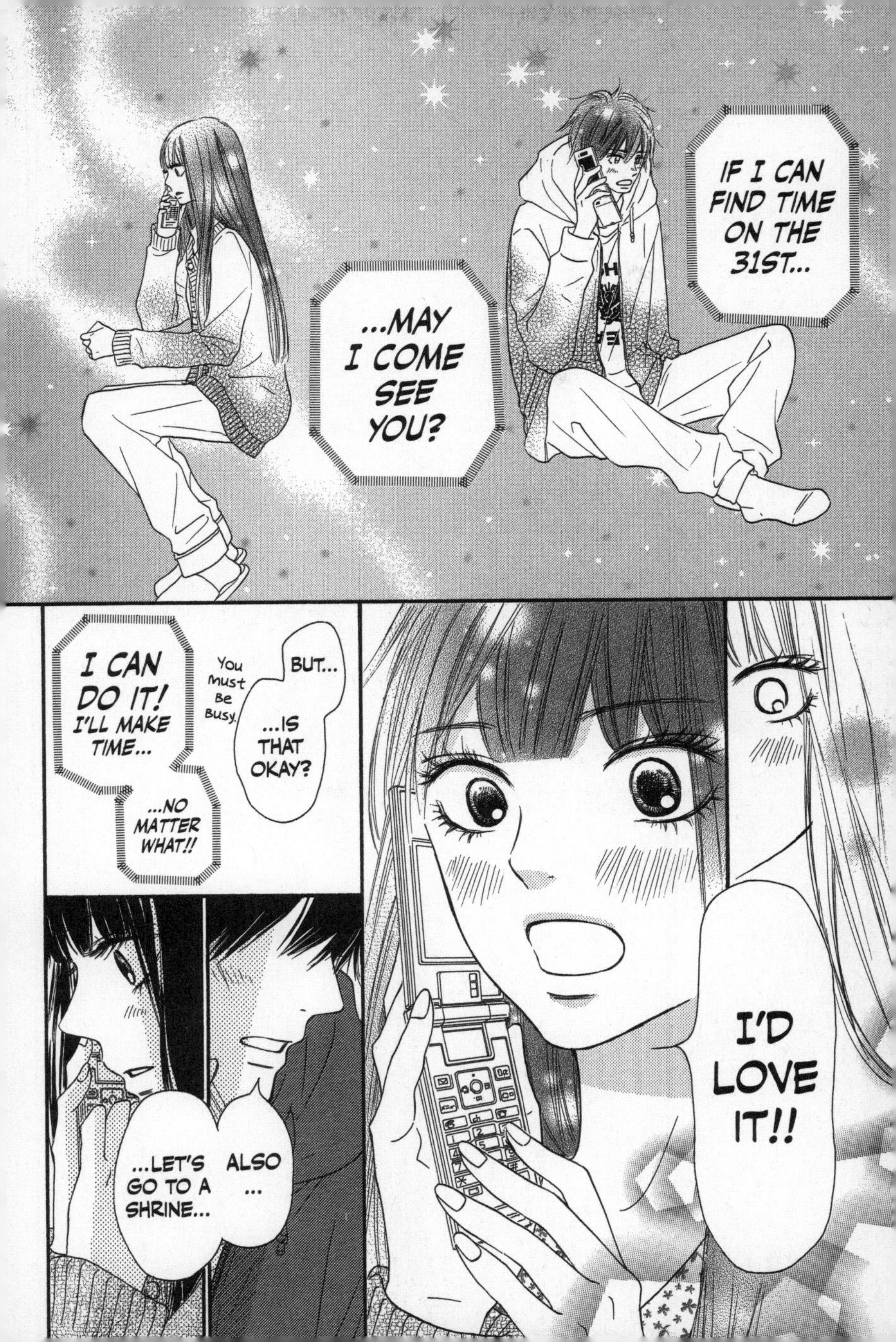
IF I CAN FIND TIME ON THE 31ST...
...MAY I COME SEE YOU?
I'D LOVE IT!!
BUT...
...IS THAT OKAY?
You must be busy.
I CAN DO IT! I'LL MAKE TIME...
...NO MATTER WHAT!!
ALSO...
...LET'S GO TO A SHRINE...

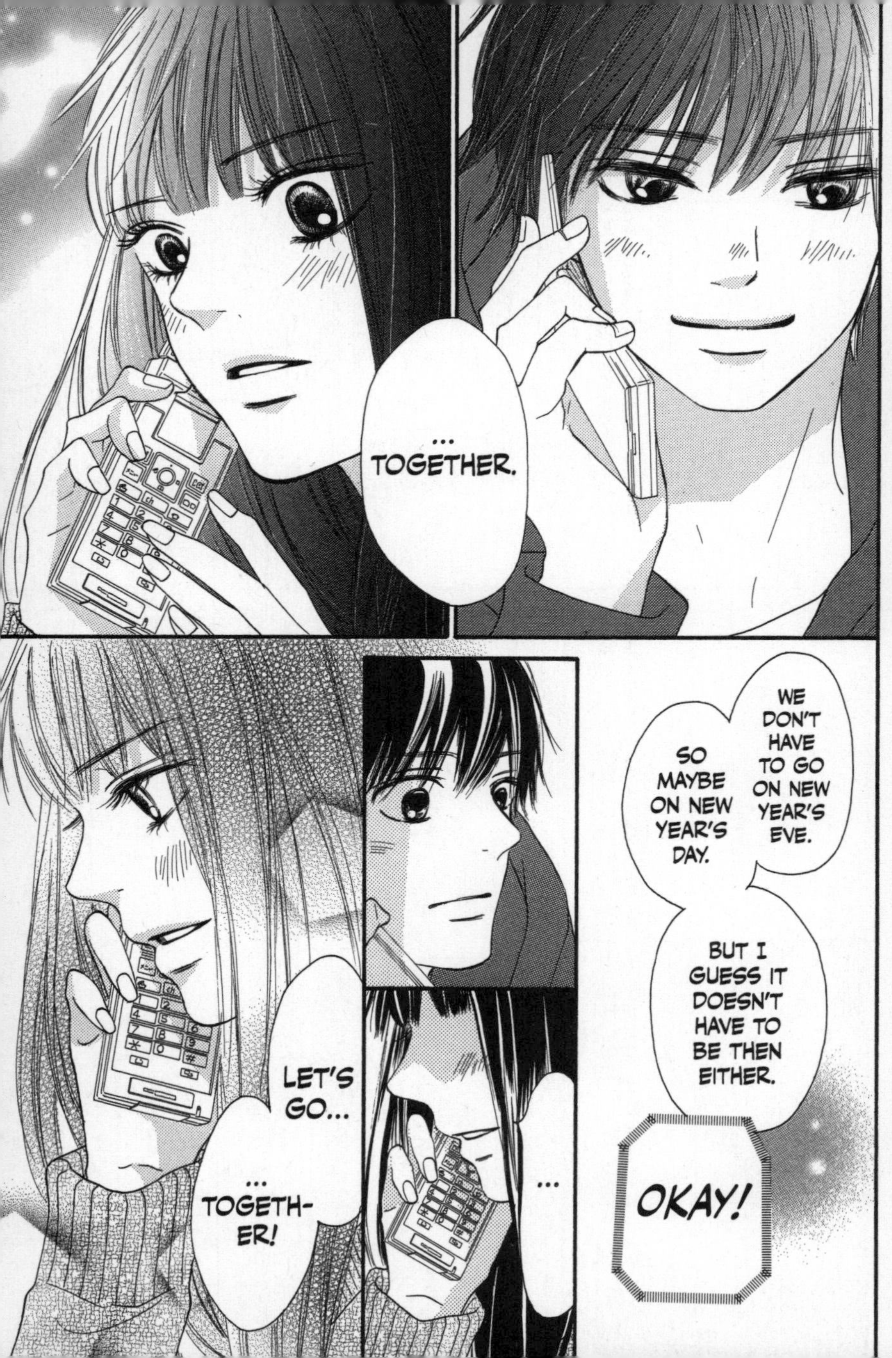
... TOGETHER.
WE DON'T HAVE TO GO ON NEW YEAR'S EVE.
SO MAYBE ON NEW YEAR'S DAY.
BUT I GUESS IT DOESN'T HAVE TO BE THEN EITHER.
OKAY!
...
LET'S GO...
... TOGETH-ER!

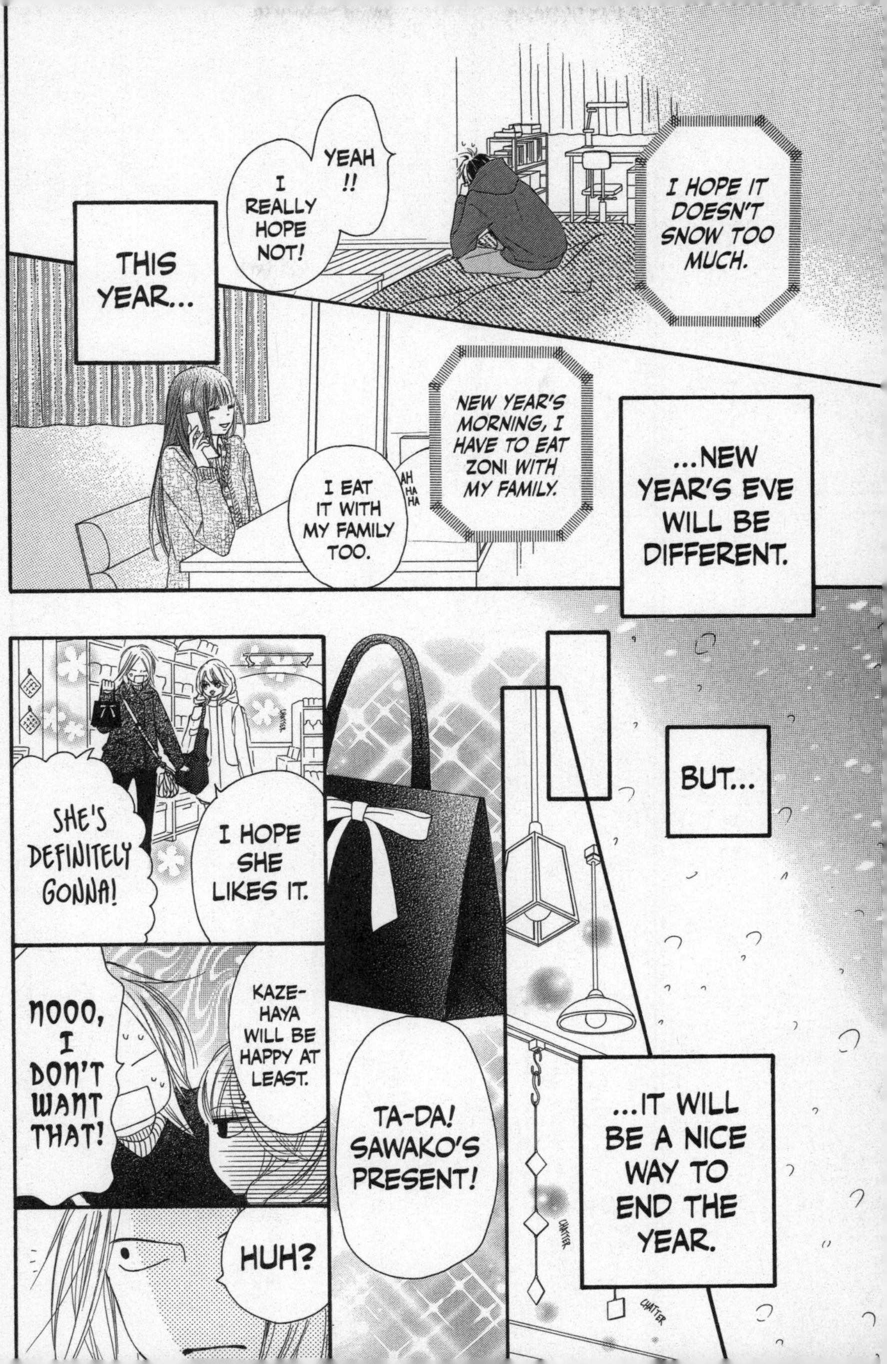
I HOPE IT DOESN'T SNOW TOO MUCH.
YEAH!! I REALLY HOPE NOT!
THIS YEAR...
...NEW YEAR'S EVE WILL BE DIFFERENT.
NEW YEAR'S MORNING, I HAVE TO EAT ZONI WITH MY FAMILY.
AH HA HA
I EAT IT WITH MY FAMILY TOO.
BUT...
...IT WILL BE A NICE WAY TO END THE YEAR.
CHATTER
CHATTER
I HOPE SHE LIKES IT.
SHE'S DEFINITELY GONNA!
CHATTER
KAZE-HAYA WILL BE HAPPY AT LEAST.
NOOO, I DON'T WANT THAT!
TA-DA! SAWAKO'S PRESENT!
HUH?

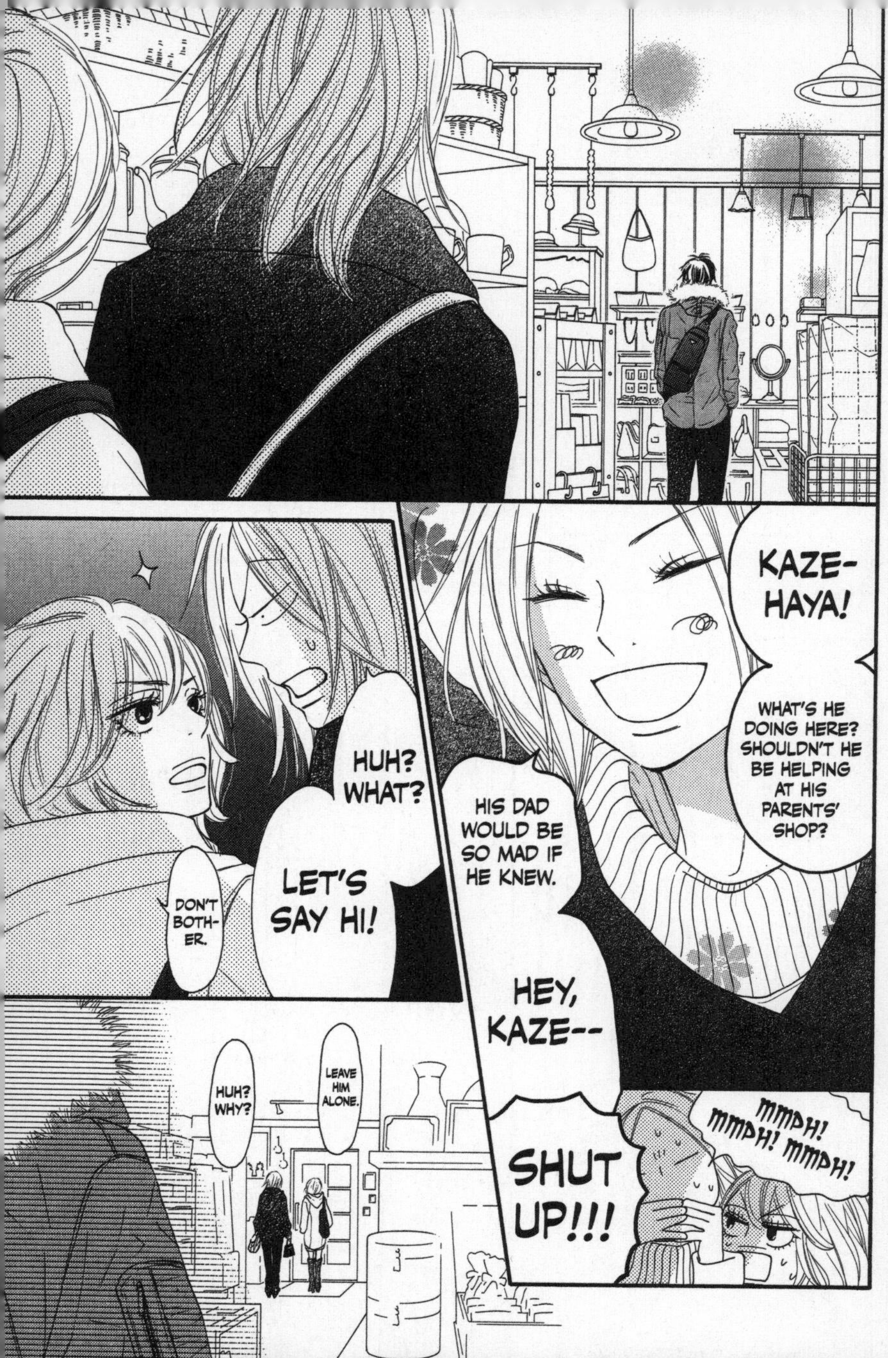

KAZE-HAYA!
WHAT'S HE DOING HERE? SHOULDN'T HE BE HELPING AT HIS PARENTS' SHOP?
HIS DAD WOULD BE SO MAD IF HE KNEW.
HUH? WHAT?
LET'S SAY HI!
DON'T BOTH-ER.
HEY, KAZE--
SHUT UP!!!
MMPH! MMPH! MMPH!
LEAVE HIM ALONE.
HUH? WHY?

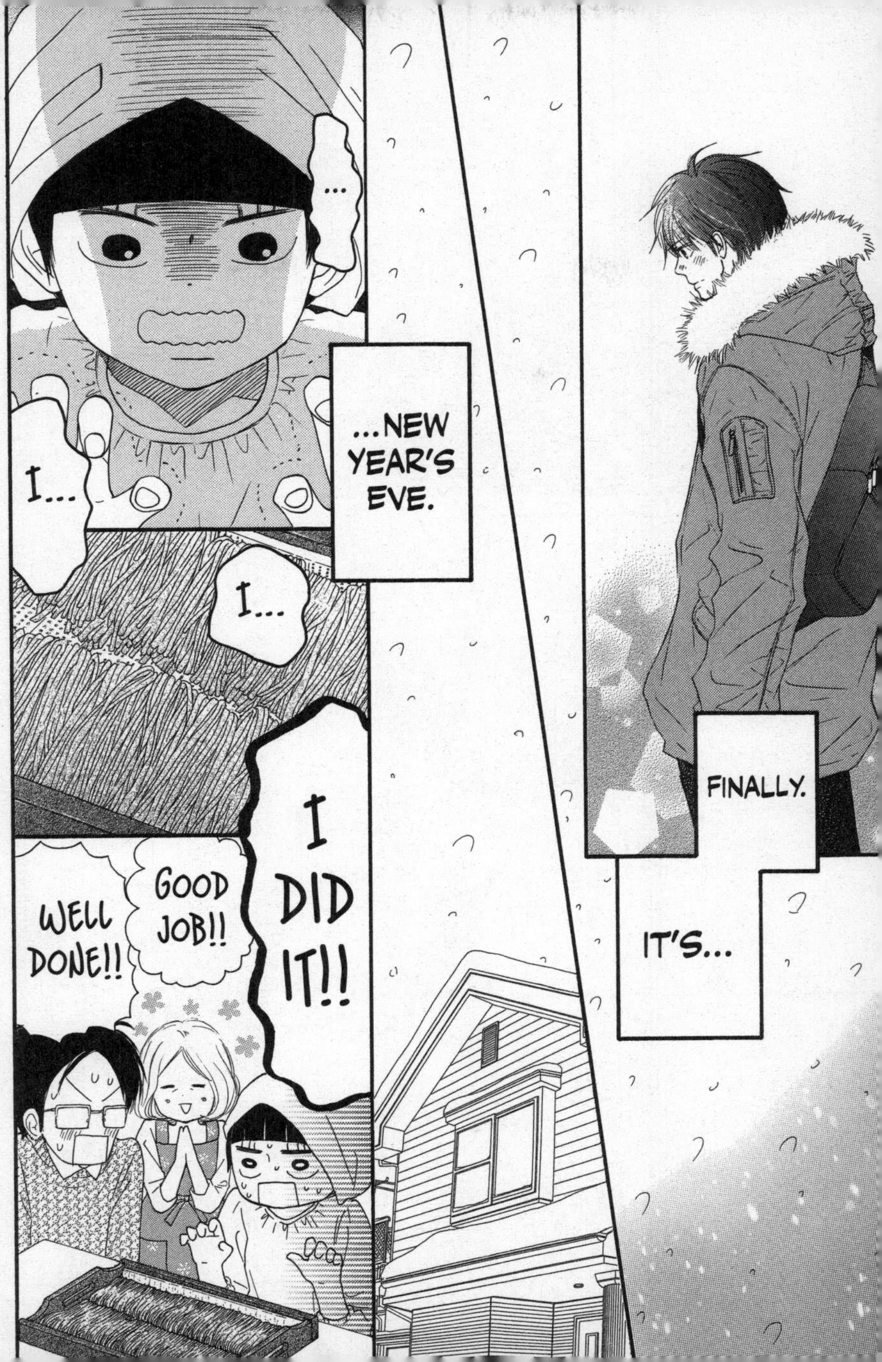
FINALLY.
IT'S...
...NEW YEAR'S EVE.
...
I...
I...
I DID IT!!
GOOD JOB!!
WELL DONE!!

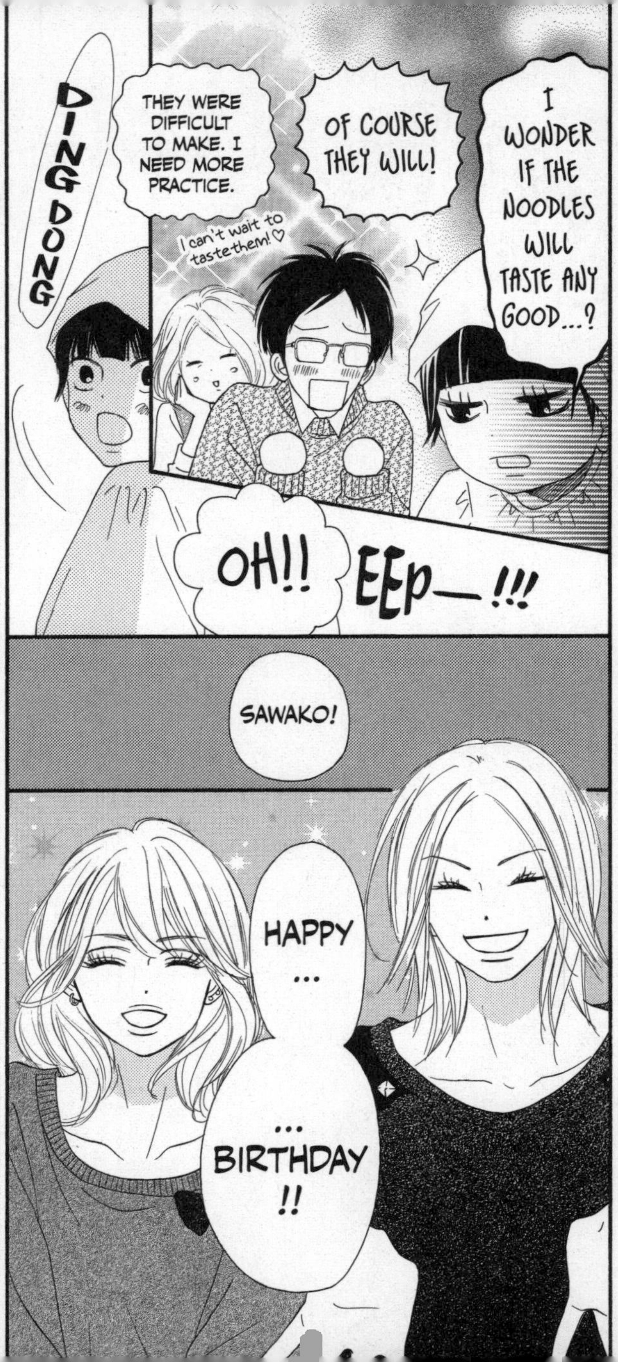
I WONDER IF THE NOODLES WILL TASTE ANY GOOD...?
OF COURSE THEY WILL!
THEY WERE DIFFICULT TO MAKE. I NEED MORE PRACTICE.
I can't wait to taste them!♡
DING DONG
EEp—!!!
OH!!
SAWAKO!
HAPPY ...
... BIRTHDAY !!

KARUPIN on JAPAN 1

Hello! How are you? This is Shiina. Nice to meet you. I'm the author of this manga.

As I get older, my scribbly handwriting gets even scribblier. What's up with that?

Am I setting a poor example for my daughter?

In general, I don't write very neatly. I can't write...

I'm especially bad at writing addresses on letters. I start off writing neatly, but it doesn't last past the first line:

東京都千代田区一ツ橋
2-5-10
集英社
別冊マーガレット*

↑The address for Bessatsu Margaret always turns out like this.

Awful! Even the end of the first line gets bad...

*Tokyo Prefecture, Chiyoda Ward Hitotsubashi 2-5-10 Shueisha Bessatsu Margaret

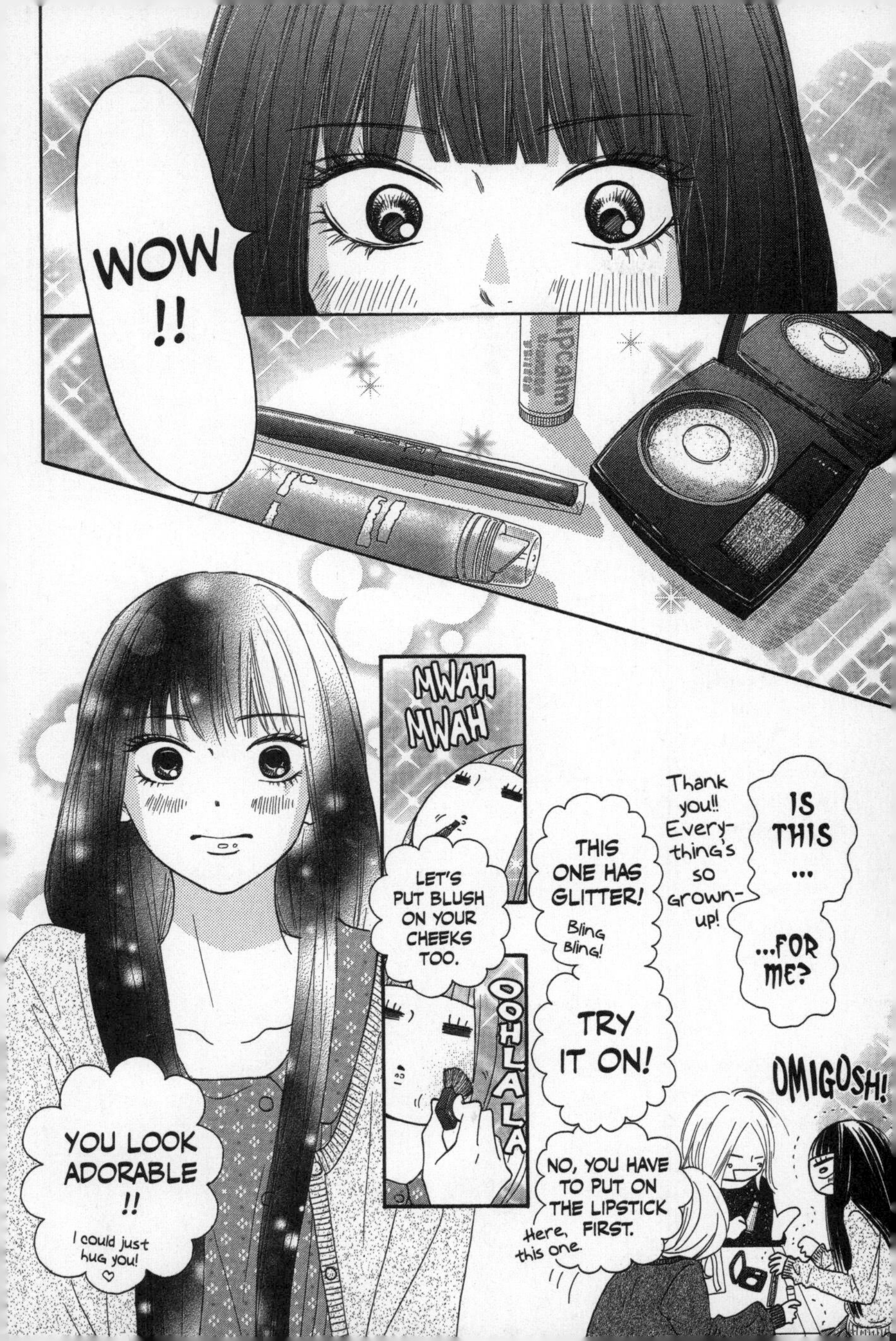
WOW !!
IS THIS ... ...FOR ME?
Thank you!! Every-thing's so grown-up!
THIS ONE HAS GLITTER!
Bling Bling!
TRY IT ON!
OMIGOSH!
NO, YOU HAVE TO PUT ON THE LIPSTICK FIRST.
Here, this one.
MWAH MWAH
LET'S PUT BLUSH ON YOUR CHEEKS TOO.
OOHLALA
YOU LOOK ADORABLE !!
I could just hug you! ♡

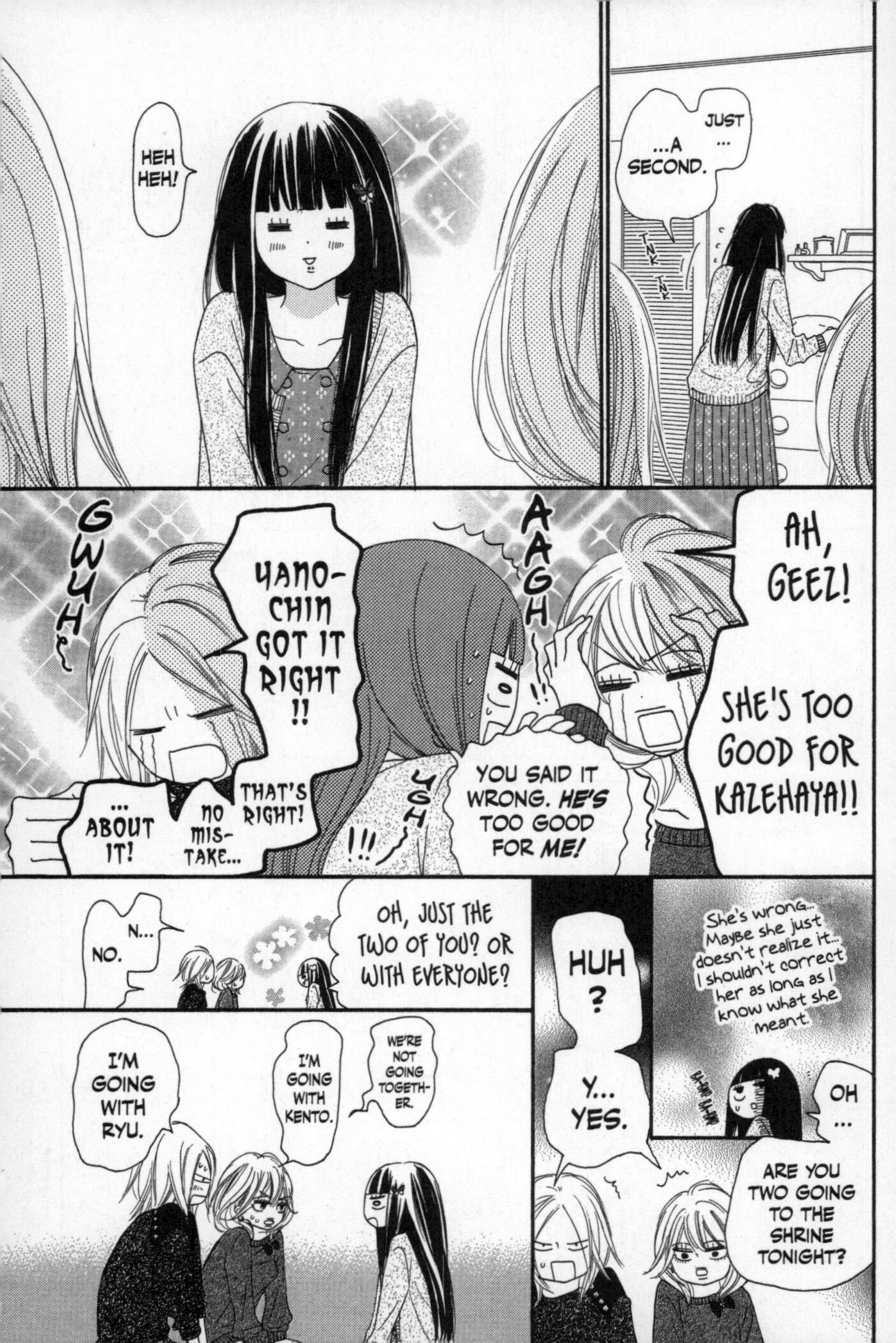
JUST ...
...A SECOND.
TNK TNK
HEH HEH!
AH, GEEZ!
SHE'S TOO GOOD FOR KAZEHAYA!!
AAGH
YOU SAID IT WRONG. HE'S TOO GOOD FOR ME!
UGH
!!!
YANO-CHIN GOT IT RIGHT!!
GWUH
THAT'S RIGHT!
NO MIS-TAKE...
... ABOUT IT!
She's wrong... Maybe she just doesn't realize it... I shouldn't correct her as long as I know what she meant.
OH ...
ARE YOU TWO GOING TO THE SHRINE TONIGHT?
HUH?
Y... YES.
OH, JUST THE TWO OF YOU? OR WITH EVERYONE?
N... NO.
WE'RE NOT GOING TOGETHER.
I'M GOING WITH KENTO.
I'M GOING WITH RYU.

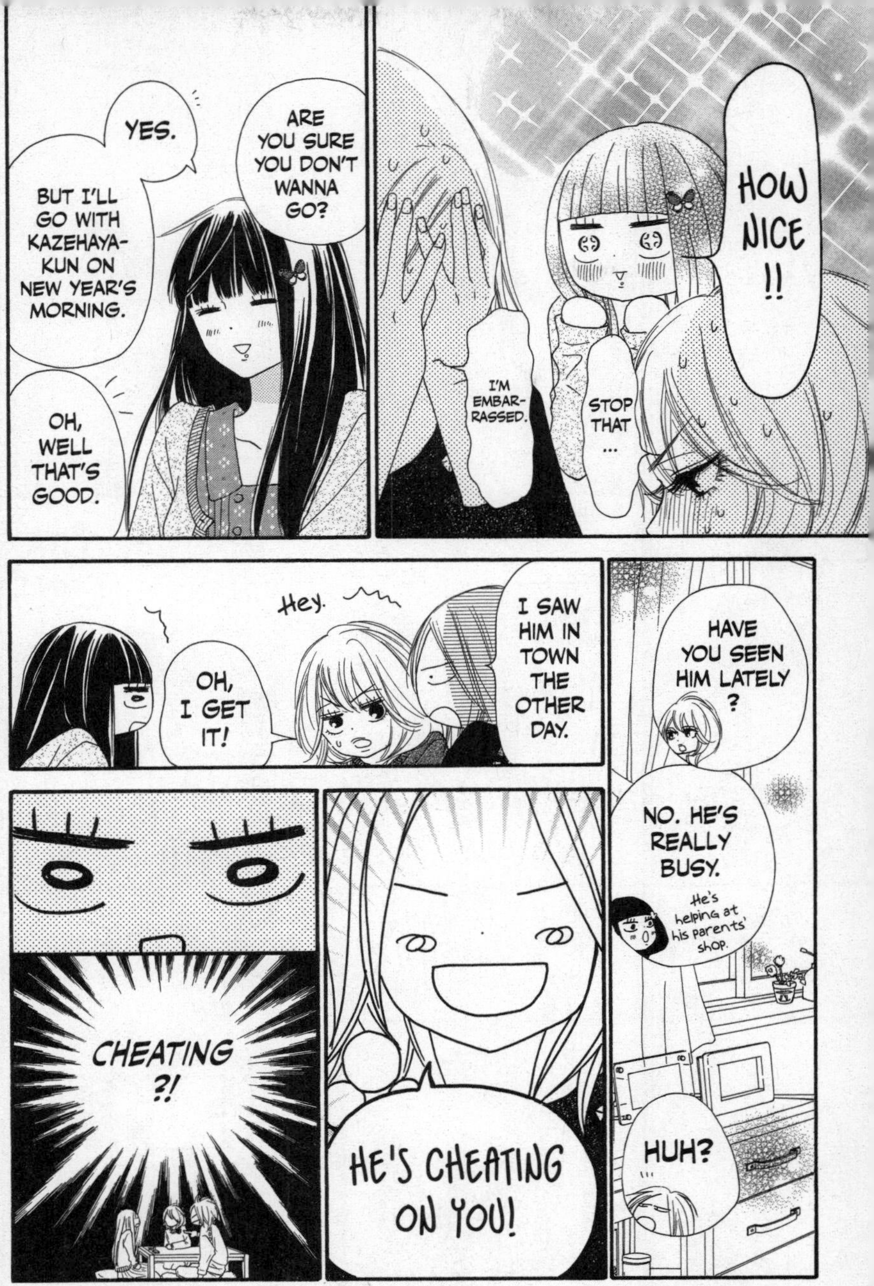
HOW NICE !!
STOP THAT ...
I'M EMBARRASSED.
ARE YOU SURE YOU DON'T WANNA GO?
YES.
BUT I'LL GO WITH KAZEHAYA-KUN ON NEW YEAR'S MORNING.
OH, WELL THAT'S GOOD.
HAVE YOU SEEN HIM LATELY ?
NO. HE'S REALLY BUSY.
He's helping at his parents' shop.
HUH?
I SAW HIM IN TOWN THE OTHER DAY.
Hey.
OH, I GET IT!
HE'S CHEATING ON YOU!
CHEATING ?!

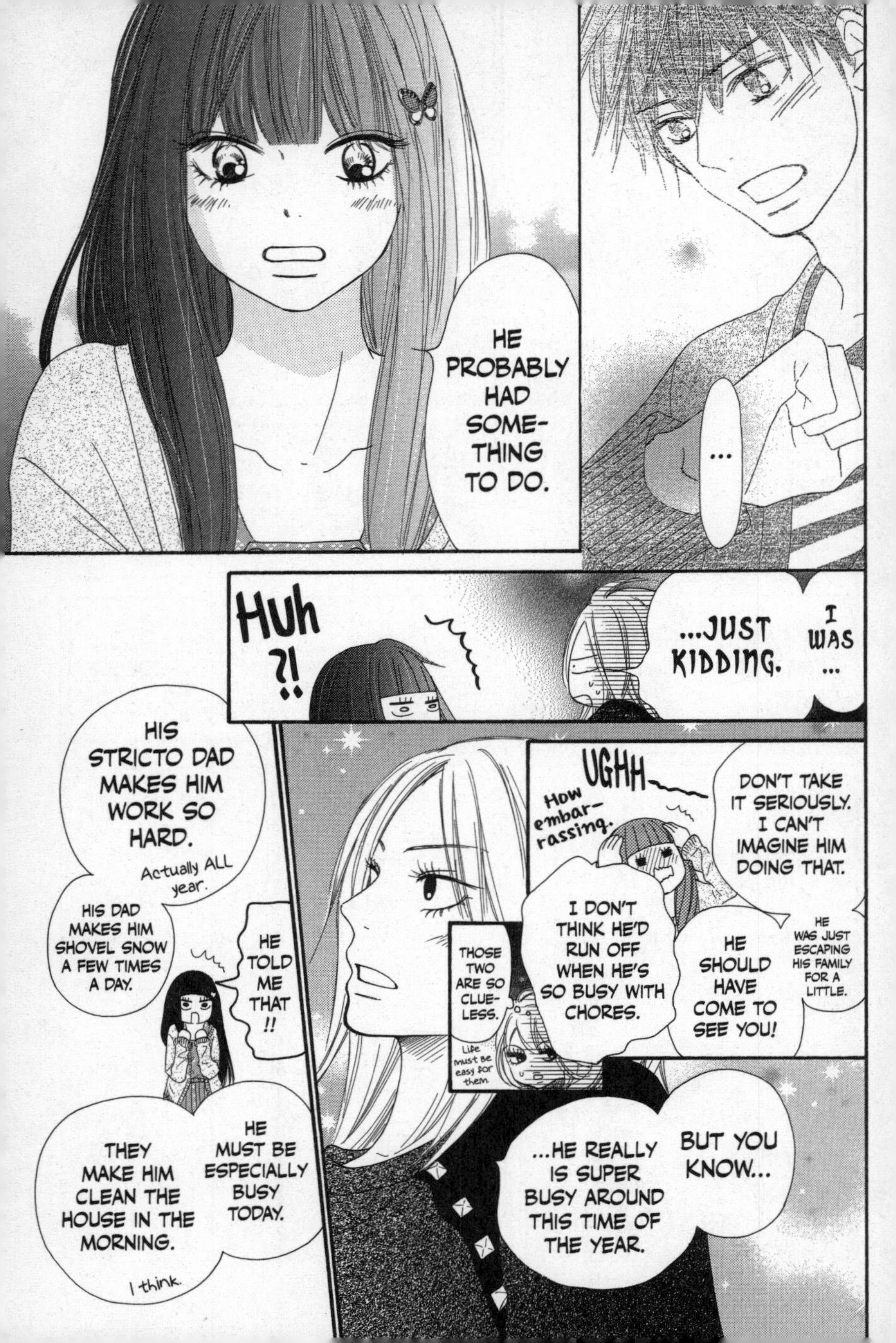
...
HE PROBABLY HAD SOMETHING TO DO.
I WAS...
...JUST KIDDING.
Huh ?!
UGHH—
How embarrassing.
DON'T TAKE IT SERIOUSLY. I CAN'T IMAGINE HIM DOING THAT.
HE WAS JUST ESCAPING HIS FAMILY FOR A LITTLE.
HE SHOULD HAVE COME TO SEE YOU!
I DON'T THINK HE'D RUN OFF WHEN HE'S SO BUSY WITH CHORES.
THOSE TWO ARE SO CLUELESS.
Life must be easy for them.
BUT YOU KNOW...
...HE REALLY IS SUPER BUSY AROUND THIS TIME OF THE YEAR.
HIS STRICTO DAD MAKES HIM WORK SO HARD.
Actually ALL year.
HIS DAD MAKES HIM SHOVEL SNOW A FEW TIMES A DAY.
HE TOLD ME THAT !!
HE MUST BE ESPECIALLY BUSY TODAY.
THEY MAKE HIM CLEAN THE HOUSE IN THE MORNING.
I think.

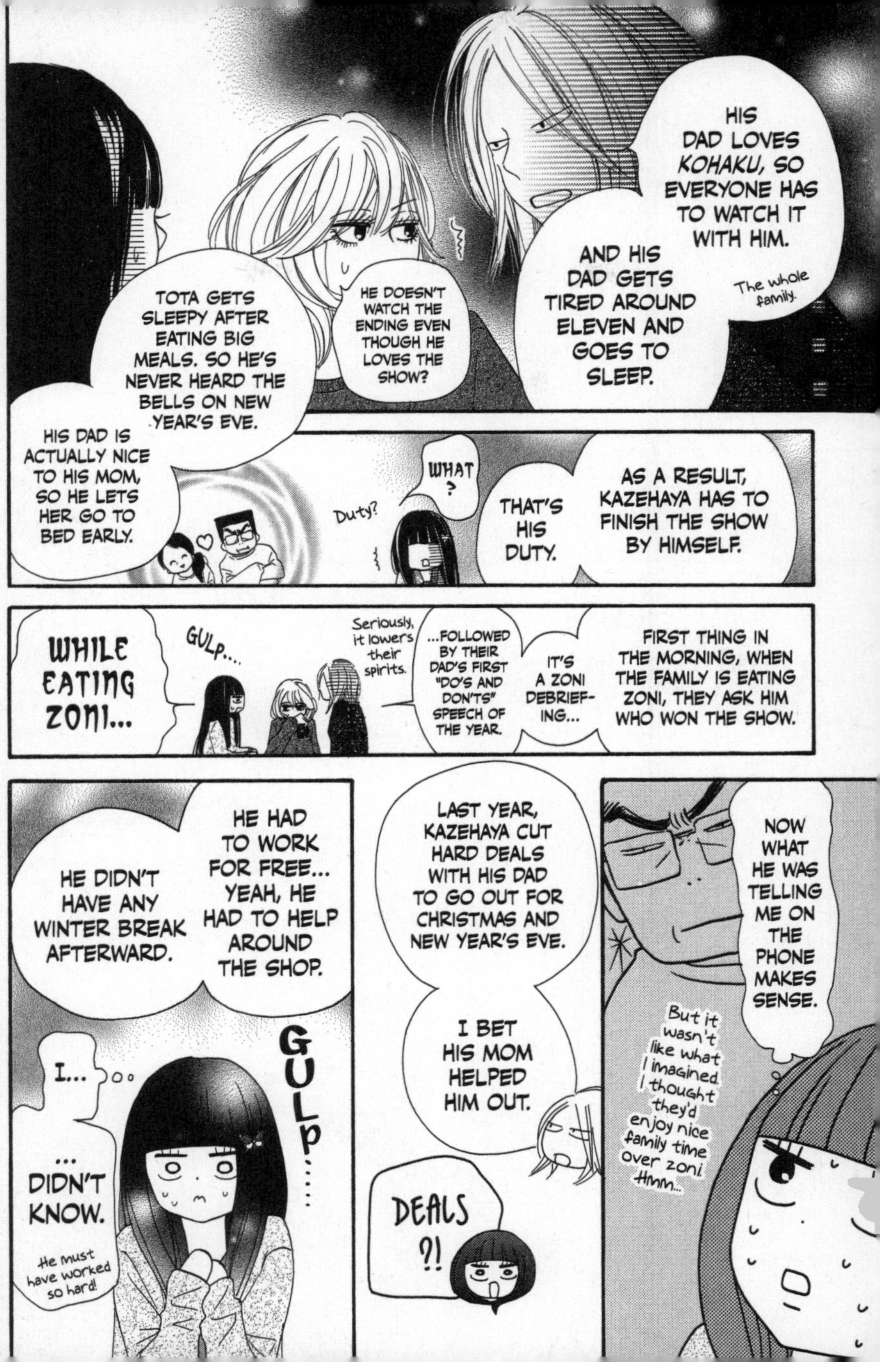
HIS DAD LOVES KOHAKU, SO EVERYONE HAS TO WATCH IT WITH HIM.
The whole family.
AND HIS DAD GETS TIRED AROUND ELEVEN AND GOES TO SLEEP.
HE DOESN'T WATCH THE ENDING EVEN THOUGH HE LOVES THE SHOW?
TOTA GETS SLEEPY AFTER EATING BIG MEALS. SO HE'S NEVER HEARD THE BELLS ON NEW YEAR'S EVE.
HIS DAD IS ACTUALLY NICE TO HIS MOM, SO HE LETS HER GO TO BED EARLY.
AS A RESULT, KAZEHAYA HAS TO FINISH THE SHOW BY HIMSELF.
THAT'S HIS DUTY.
WHAT?
Duty?
FIRST THING IN THE MORNING, WHEN THE FAMILY IS EATING ZONI, THEY ASK HIM WHO WON THE SHOW.
IT'S A ZONI DEBRIEFING...
...FOLLOWED BY THEIR DAD'S FIRST "DO'S AND DON'TS" SPEECH OF THE YEAR.
Seriously, it lowers their spirits.
GULP....
WHILE EATING ZONI...
NOW WHAT HE WAS TELLING ME ON THE PHONE MAKES SENSE.
But it wasn't like what I imagined. I thought they'd enjoy nice family time over zoni. Hmm...
LAST YEAR, KAZEHAYA CUT HARD DEALS WITH HIS DAD TO GO OUT FOR CHRISTMAS AND NEW YEAR'S EVE.
I BET HIS MOM HELPED HIM OUT.
DEALS ?!
HE HAD TO WORK FOR FREE... YEAH, HE HAD TO HELP AROUND THE SHOP.
HE DIDN'T HAVE ANY WINTER BREAK AFTERWARD.
GULP....
I...
...DIDN'T KNOW.
He must have worked so hard!

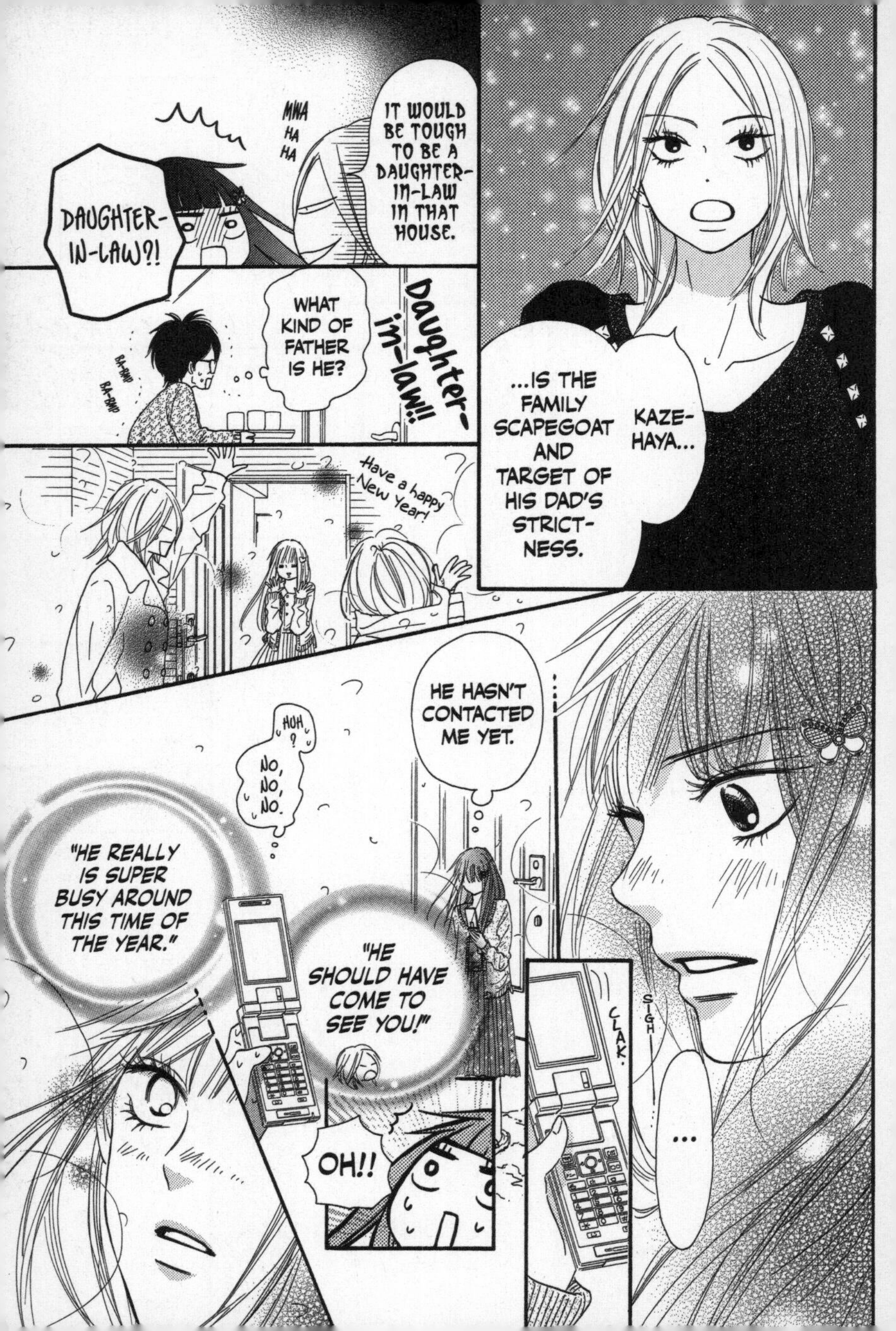
KAZE-HAYA...
...IS THE FAMILY SCAPEGOAT AND TARGET OF HIS DAD'S STRICT-NESS.
IT WOULD BE TOUGH TO BE A DAUGHTER-IN-LAW IN THAT HOUSE.
MWA HA HA
DAUGHTER-IN-LAW?!
Daughter-in-law!!
WHAT KIND OF FATHER IS HE?
BA-BUMP BA-BUMP
Have a happy New Year!
...
SIGH
CLAK.
HE HASN'T CONTACTED ME YET.
HUH?
NO, NO, NO.
"HE REALLY IS SUPER BUSY AROUND THIS TIME OF THE YEAR."
"HE SHOULD HAVE COME TO SEE YOU!"
OH!!

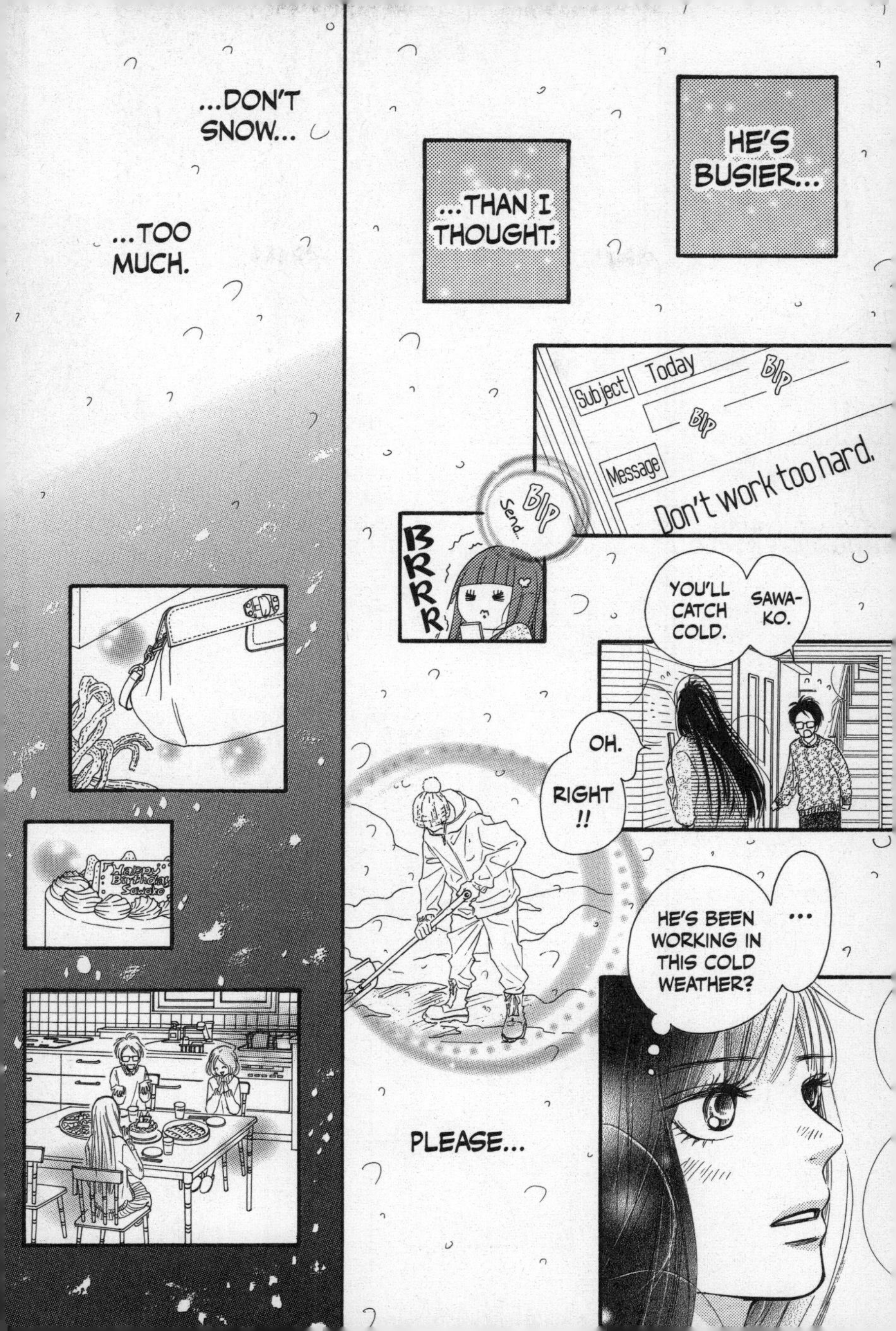
HE'S BUSIER...
...THAN I THOUGHT.
Subject
Today
BLIP
BLIP
Message
Don't work too hard.
BLIP
Send...
BRRR
SAWA-KO.
YOU'LL CATCH COLD.
OH.
RIGHT!!
...
HE'S BEEN WORKING IN THIS COLD WEATHER?
PLEASE...
...DON'T SNOW...
...TOO MUCH.
Happy Birthday Sawako

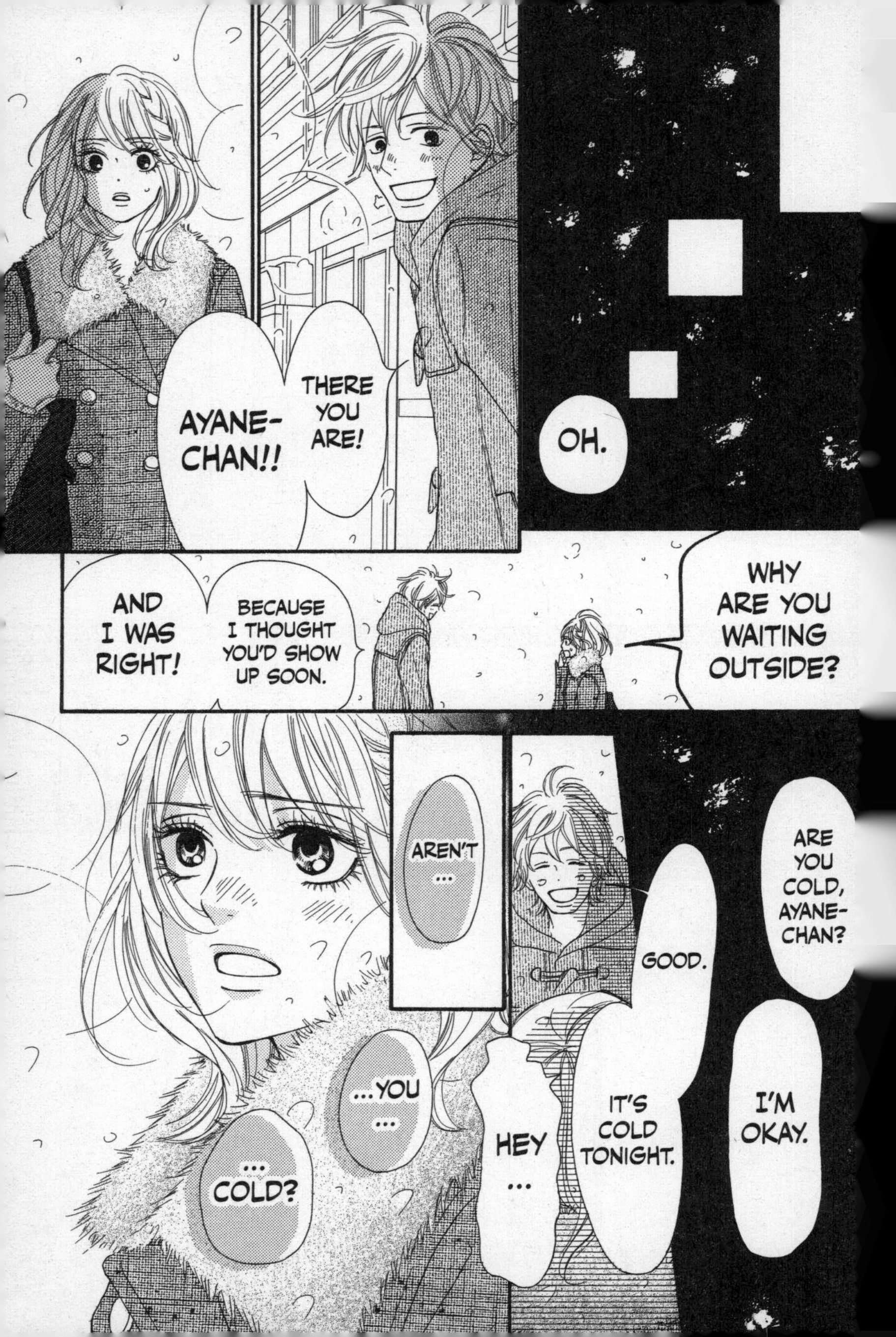
OH.
THERE YOU ARE!
AYANE-CHAN!!
WHY ARE YOU WAITING OUTSIDE?
BECAUSE I THOUGHT YOU'D SHOW UP SOON.
AND I WAS RIGHT!
ARE YOU COLD, AYANE-CHAN?
GOOD.
I'M OKAY.
IT'S COLD TONIGHT.
HEY...
AREN'T...
...YOU...
...COLD?

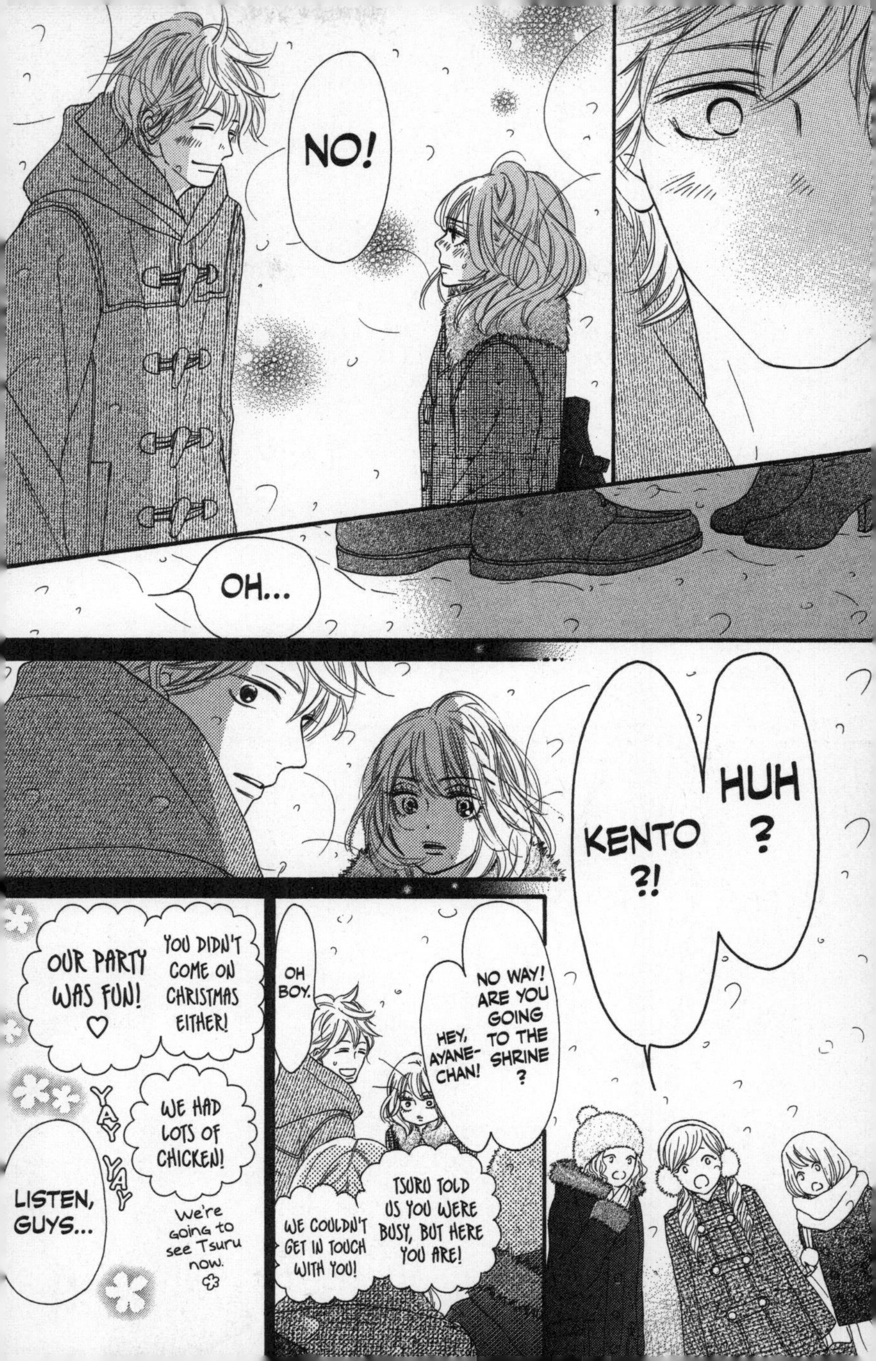
NO!
OH...
HUH? KENTO?!
HEY, AYANE-CHAN! NO WAY! ARE YOU GOING TO THE SHRINE?
TSURU TOLD US YOU WERE BUSY, BUT HERE YOU ARE!
WE COULDN'T GET IN TOUCH WITH YOU!
OH BOY.
YOU DIDN'T COME ON CHRISTMAS EITHER!
OUR PARTY WAS FUN! ♡
WE HAD LOTS OF CHICKEN!
YAY YAY
We're going to see Tsuru now.
LISTEN, GUYS...

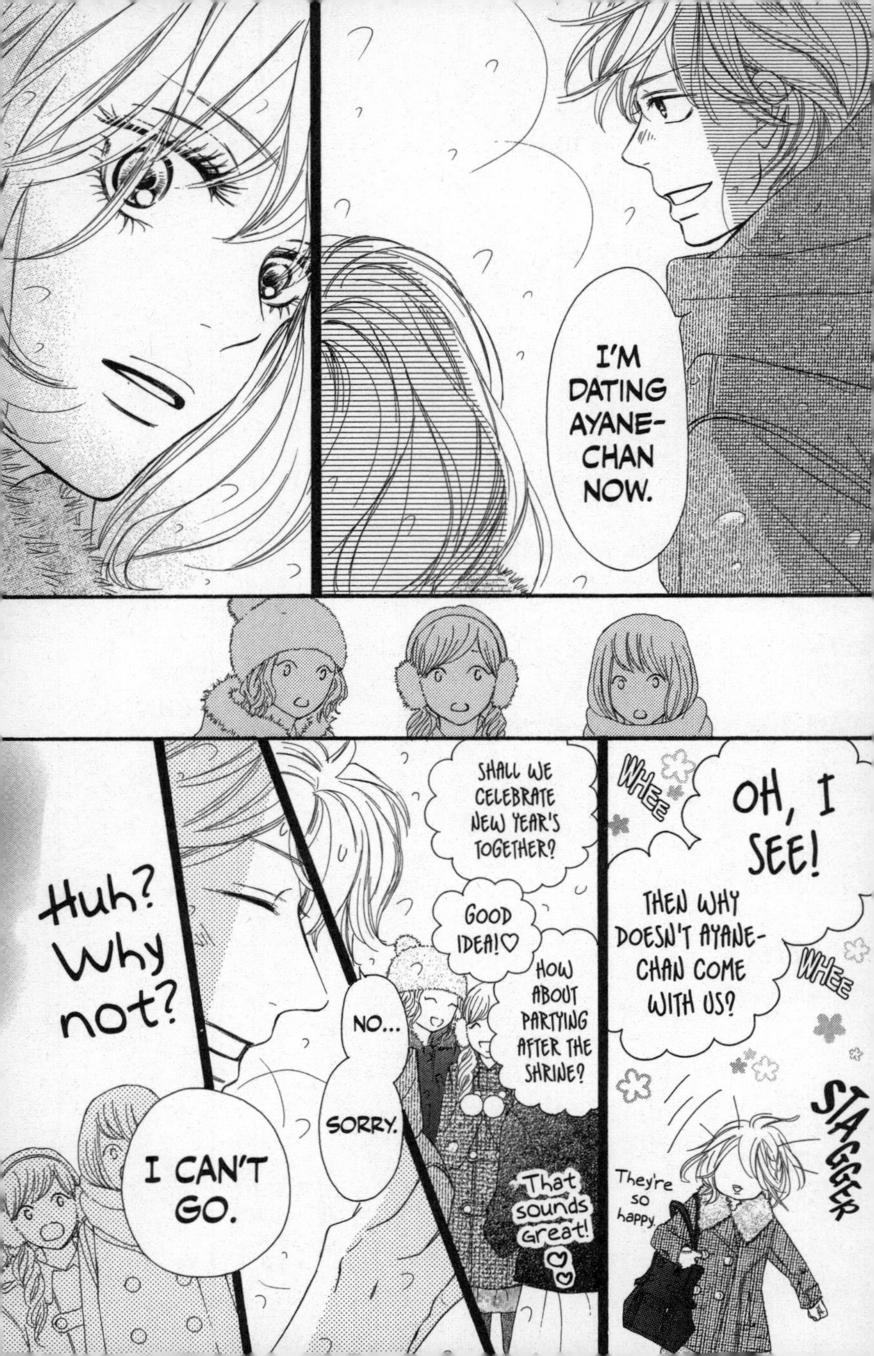
I'M DATING AYANE-CHAN NOW.
OH, I SEE!
WHEE
THEN WHY DOESN'T AYANE-CHAN COME WITH US?
WHEE
STAGGER
They're so happy.
SHALL WE CELEBRATE NEW YEAR'S TOGETHER?
GOOD IDEA!♡
HOW ABOUT PARTYING AFTER THE SHRINE?
That sounds great! ♡♡
NO...
SORRY.
I CAN'T GO.
Huh? Why not?

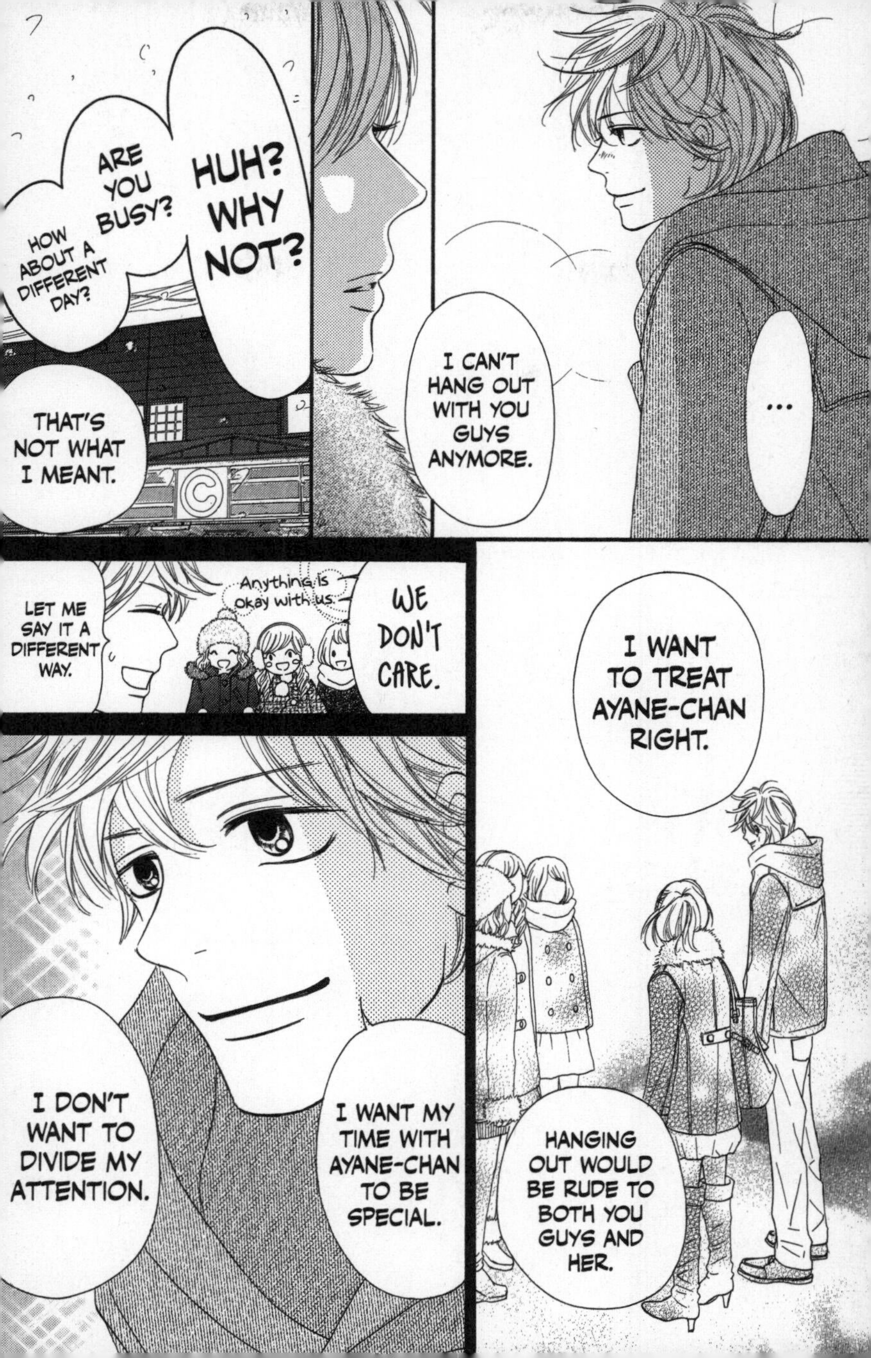
...
I CAN'T HANG OUT WITH YOU GUYS ANYMORE.
HUH? WHY NOT?
ARE YOU BUSY?
HOW ABOUT A DIFFERENT DAY?
THAT'S NOT WHAT I MEANT.
I WANT TO TREAT AYANE-CHAN RIGHT.
HANGING OUT WOULD BE RUDE TO BOTH YOU GUYS AND HER.
WE DON'T CARE.
Anything is okay with us.
LET ME SAY IT A DIFFERENT WAY.
I WANT MY TIME WITH AYANE-CHAN TO BE SPECIAL.
I DON'T WANT TO DIVIDE MY ATTENTION.

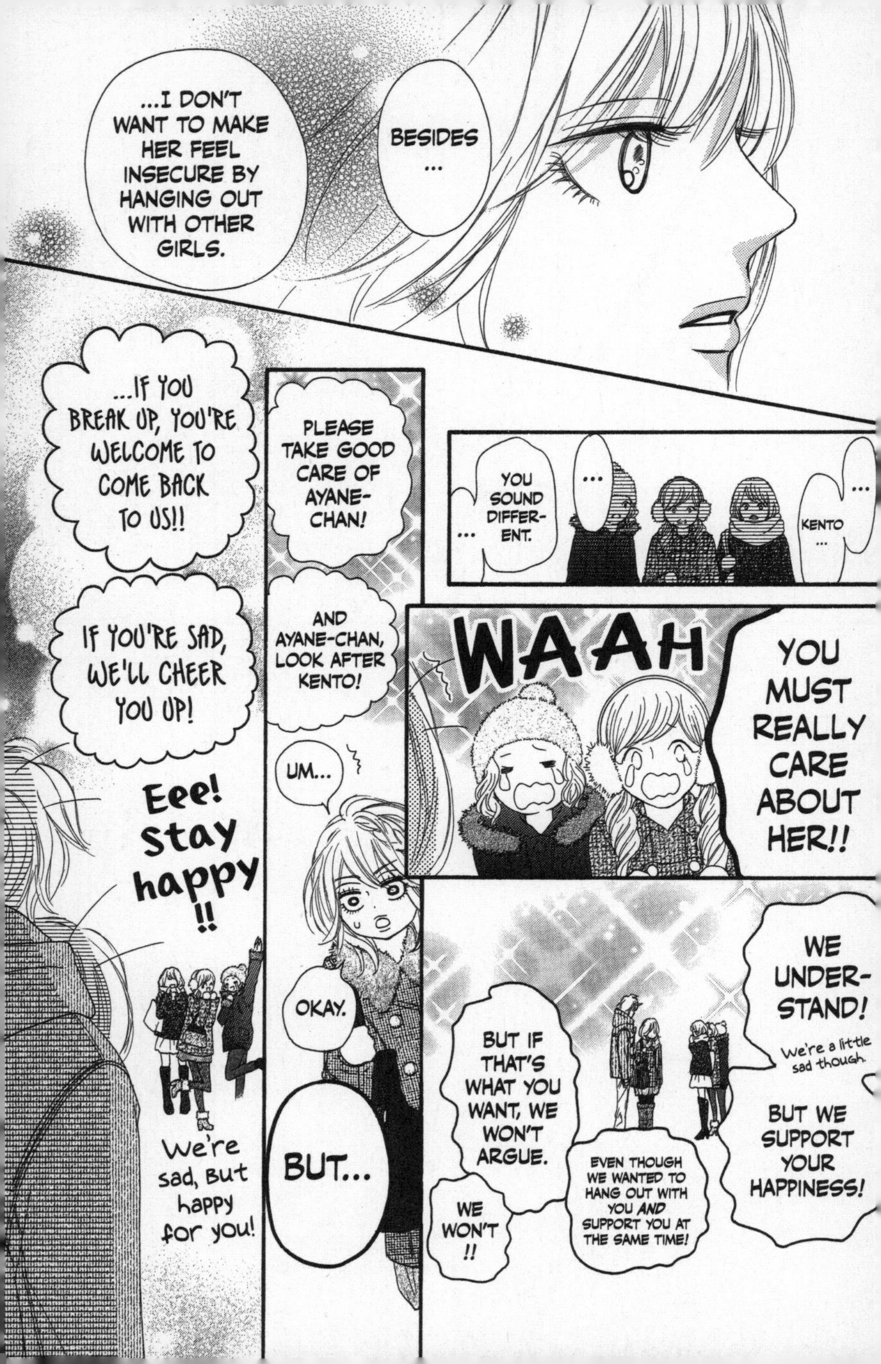
BESIDES ...
...I DON'T WANT TO MAKE HER FEEL INSECURE BY HANGING OUT WITH OTHER GIRLS.
... KENTO ...
...
YOU SOUND DIFFER- ENT. ...
YOU MUST REALLY CARE ABOUT HER!!
WAAH
WE UNDER- STAND!
We're a little sad though.
BUT WE SUPPORT YOUR HAPPINESS!
BUT IF THAT'S WHAT YOU WANT, WE WON'T ARGUE.
EVEN THOUGH WE WANTED TO HANG OUT WITH YOU AND SUPPORT YOU AT THE SAME TIME!
WE WON'T !!
PLEASE TAKE GOOD CARE OF AYANE- CHAN!
AND AYANE-CHAN, LOOK AFTER KENTO!
UM...
OKAY.
BUT...
...IF YOU BREAK UP, YOU'RE WELCOME TO COME BACK TO US!!
IF YOU'RE SAD, WE'LL CHEER YOU UP!
Eee! Stay happy !!
We're sad, but happy for you!

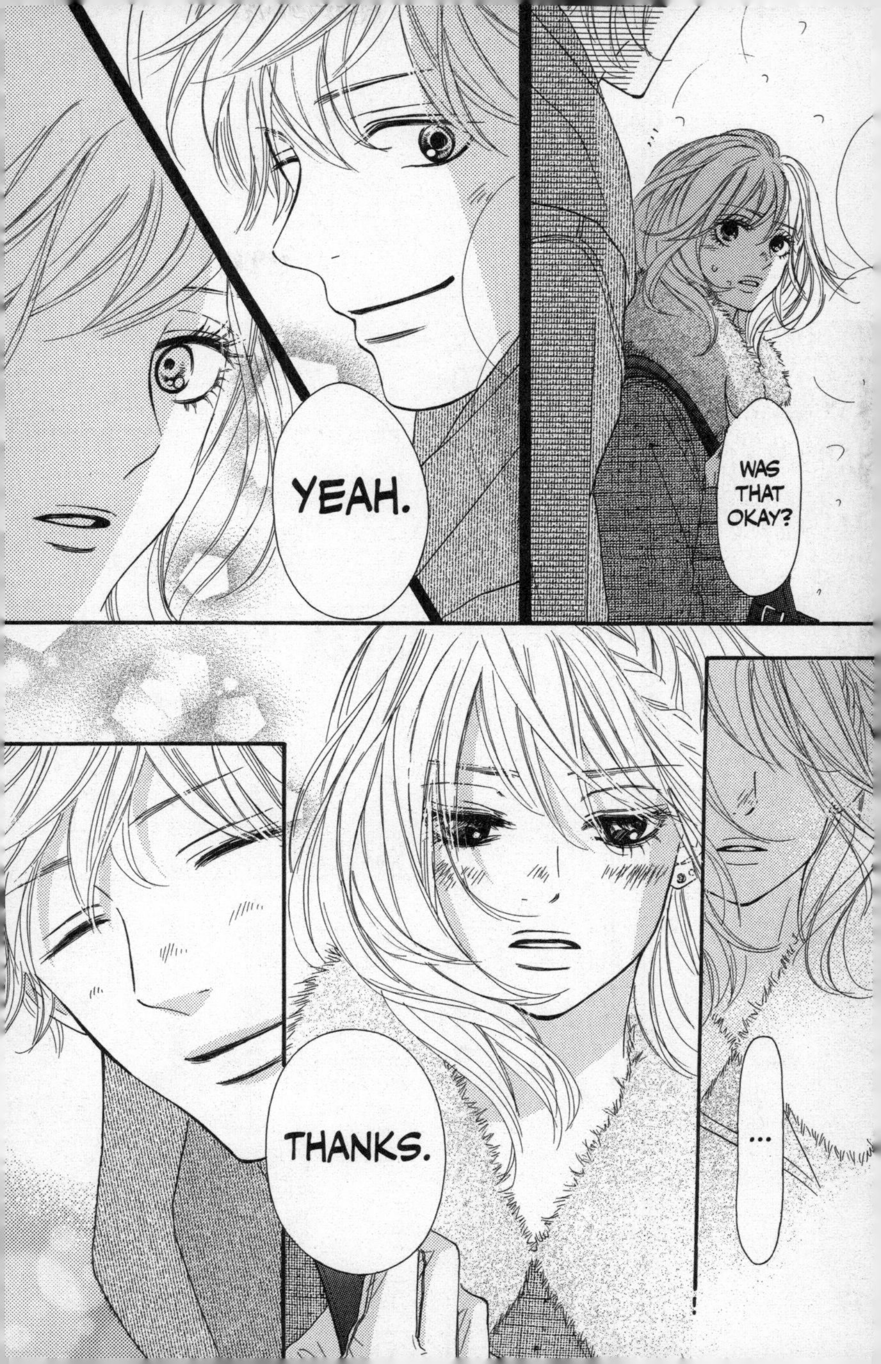
WAS THAT OKAY?
YEAH.
...
THANKS.

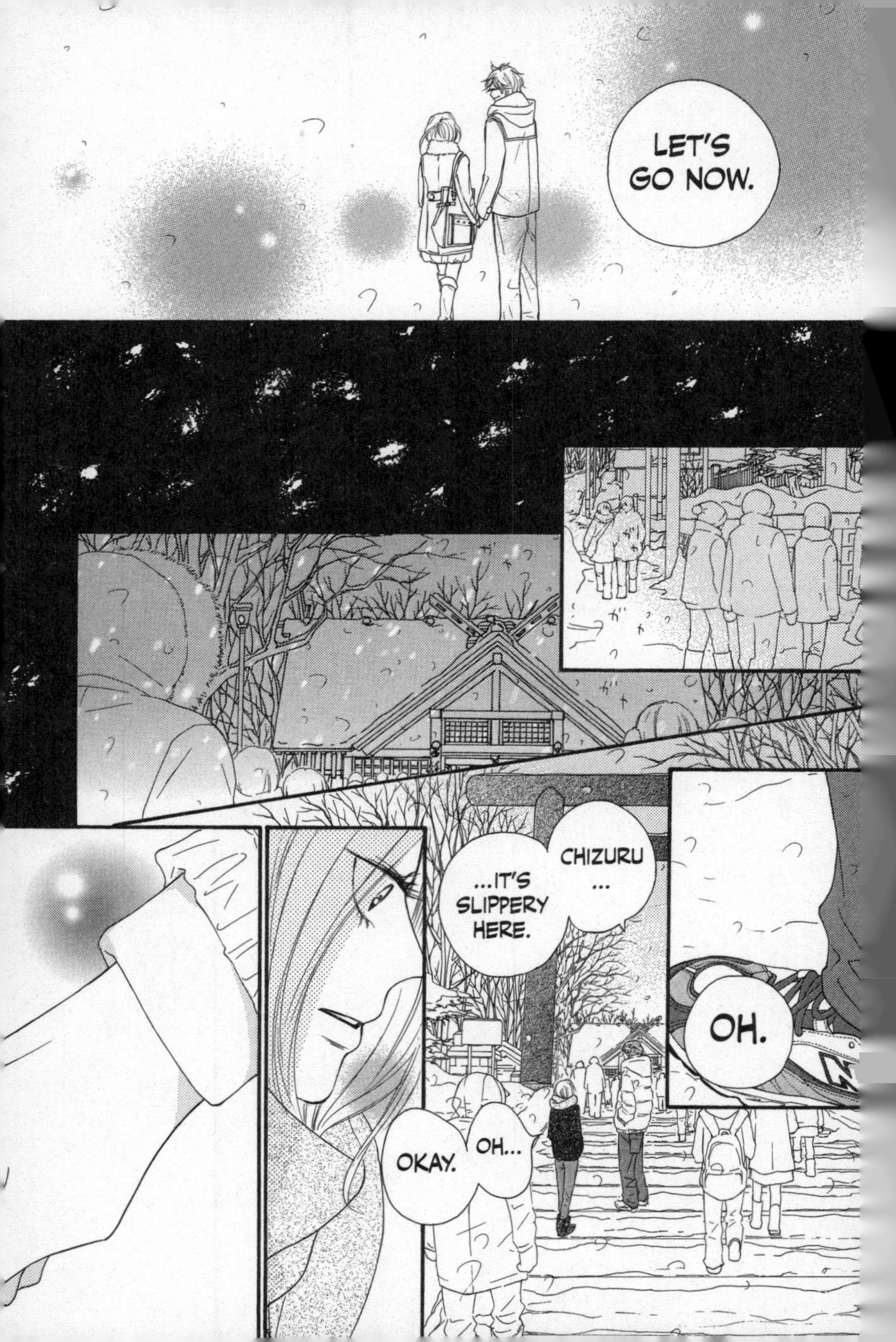
LET'S GO NOW.
OH.
CHIZURU ...
...IT'S SLIPPERY HERE.
OH...
OKAY.

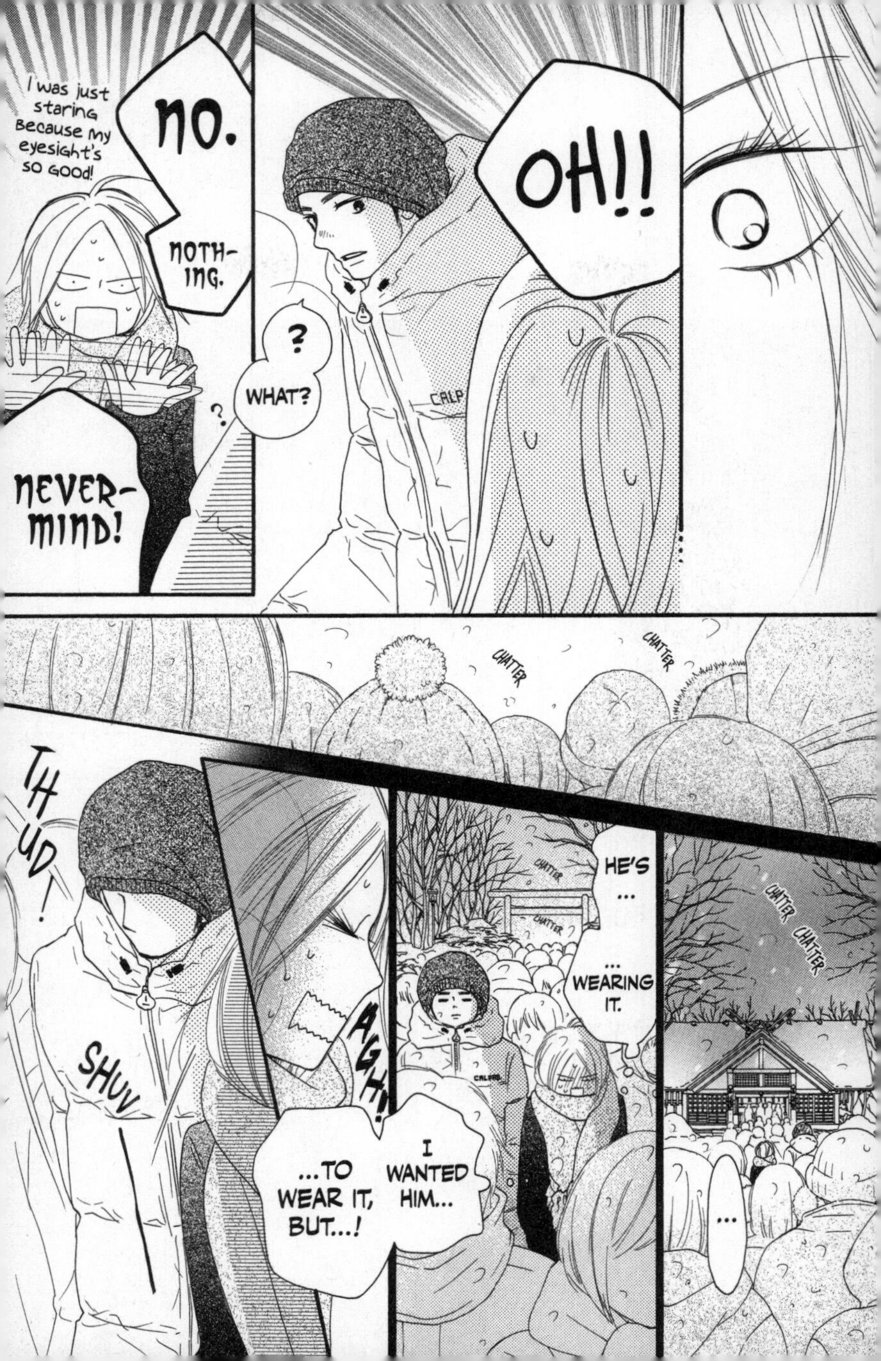
OH!!
...
?
WHAT?
no.
NOTH-ING.
I was just staring because my eyesight's so good!
?
NEVER-MIND!
CHATTER
CHATTER
CHATTER CHATTER
...
HE'S ...
... WEARING IT.
CHATTER
CHATTER
I WANTED HIM...
...TO WEAR IT, BUT...!
AGH!!
THUD!
SHUV

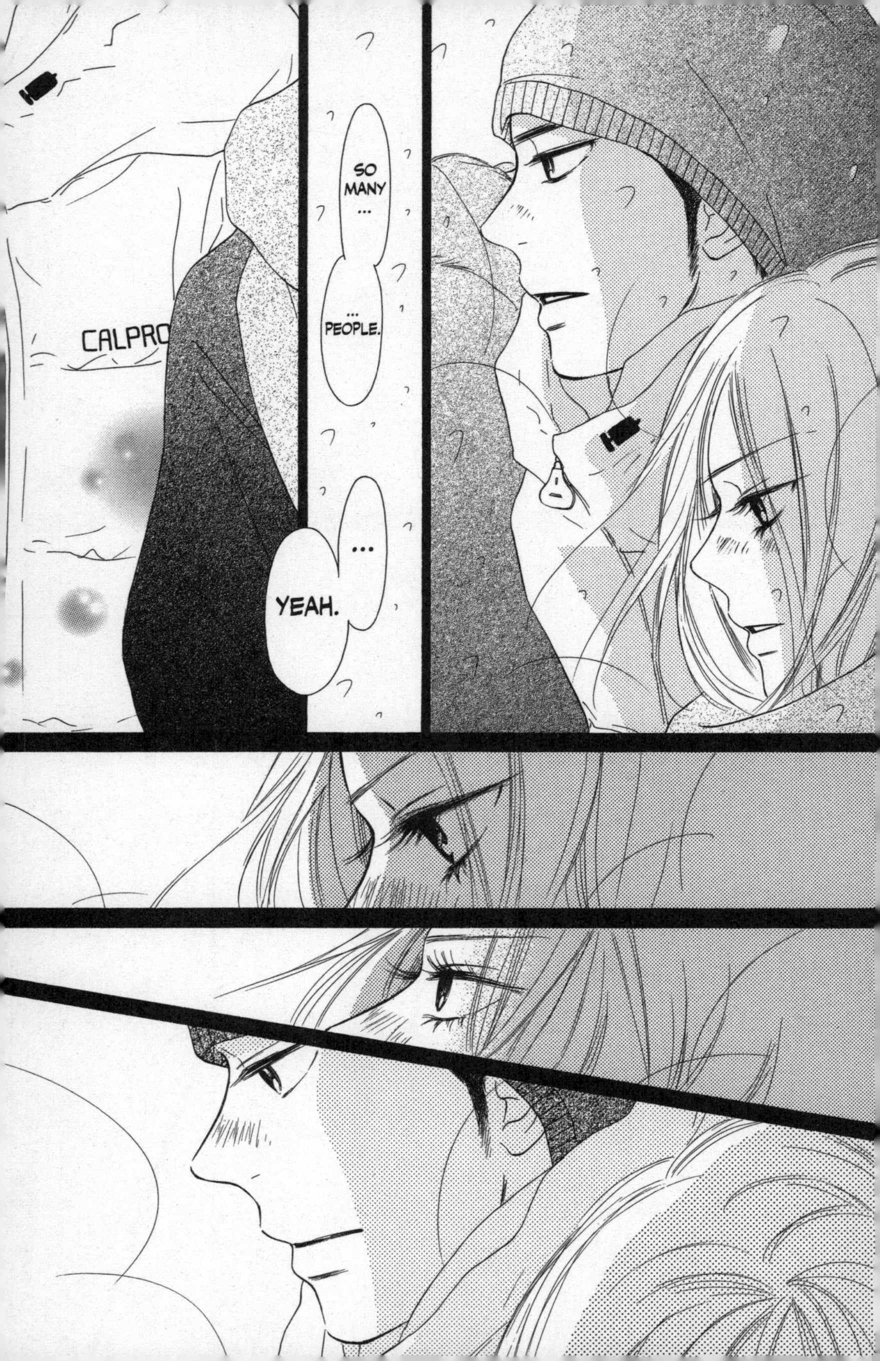
SO MANY ...
... PEOPLE.
... YEAH.
CALPRO

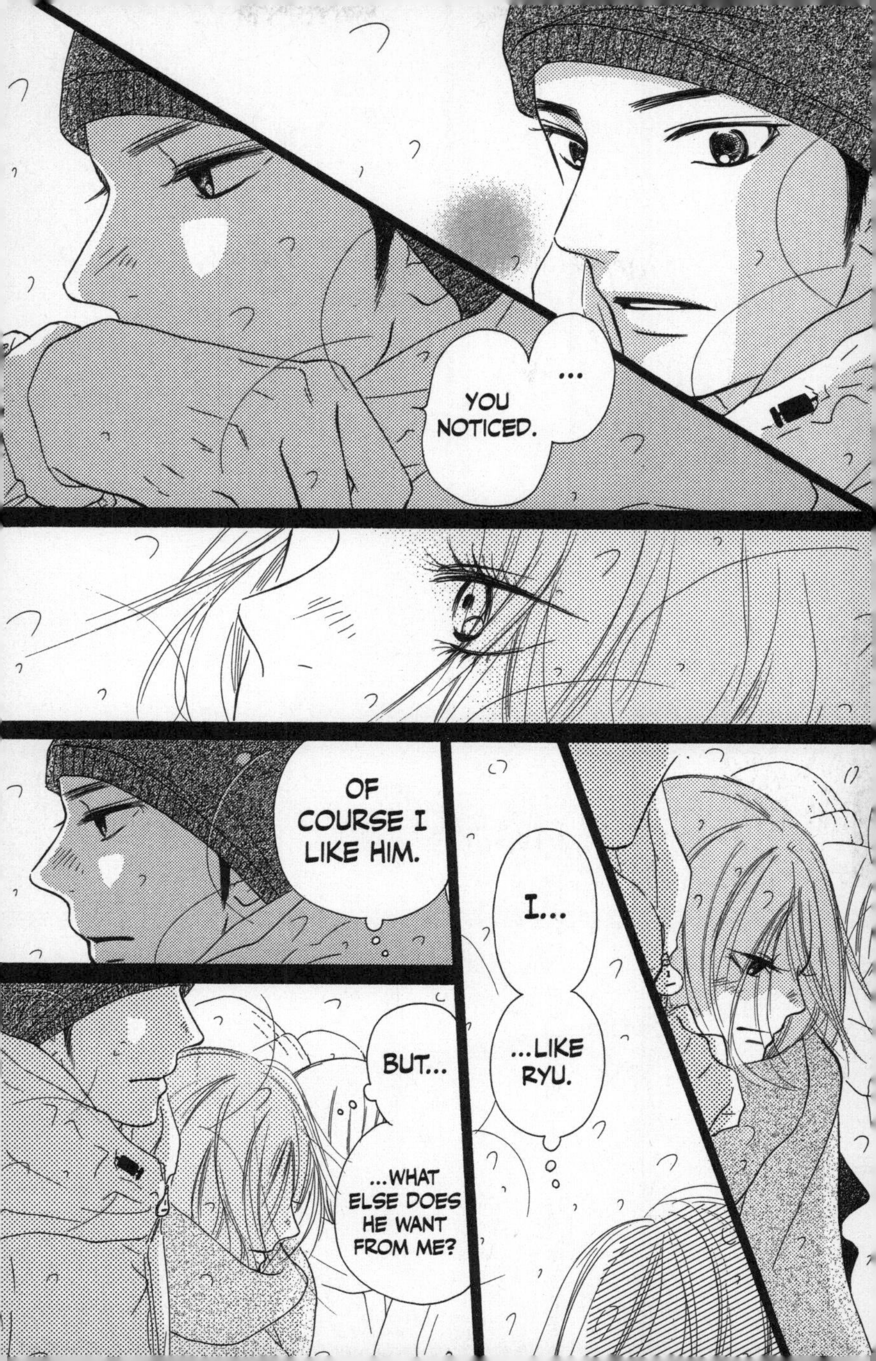
...
YOU NOTICED.
I...
...LIKE RYU.
OF COURSE I LIKE HIM.
BUT...
...WHAT ELSE DOES HE WANT FROM ME?

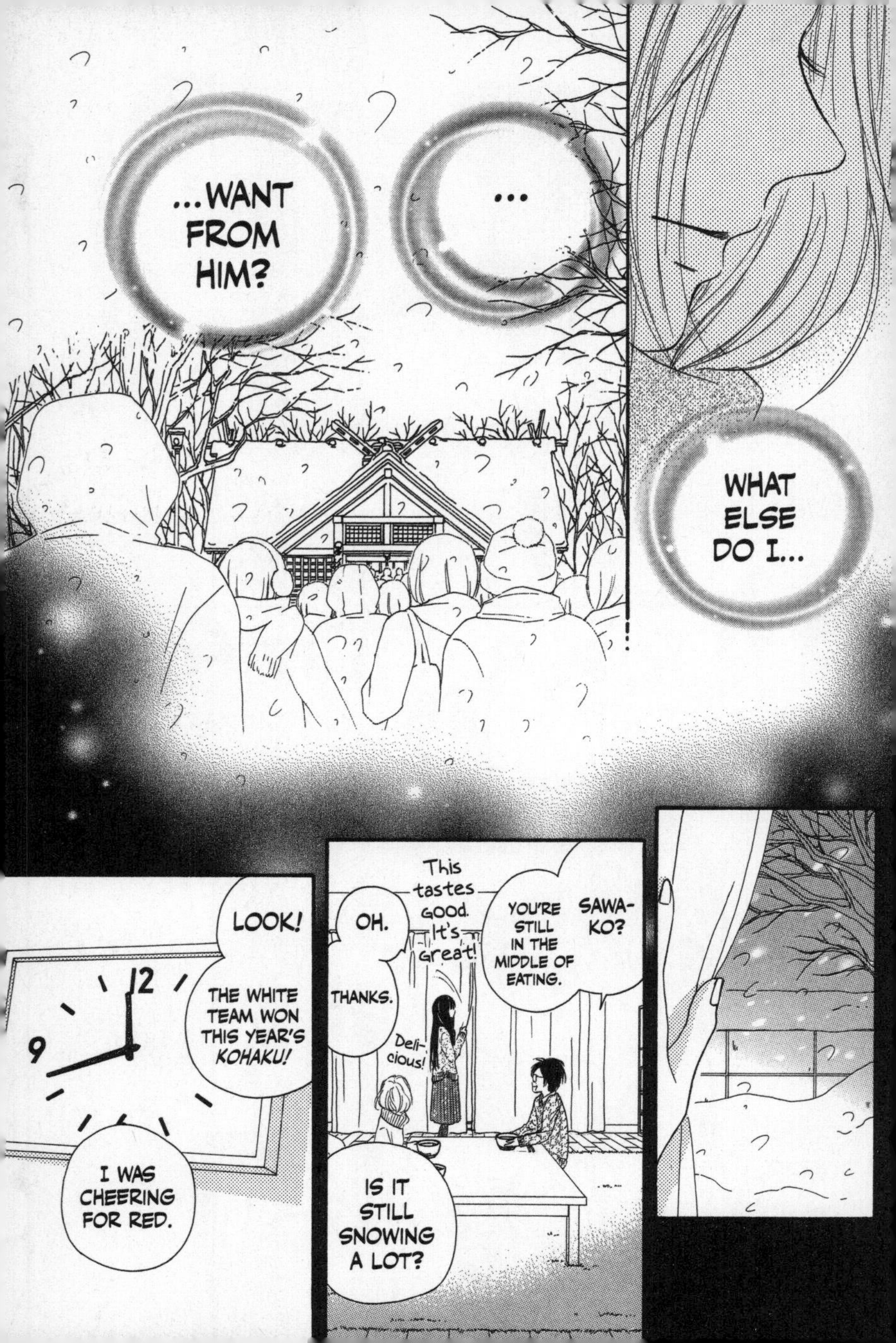
WHAT ELSE DO I...
...
...WANT FROM HIM?
SAWAKO?
YOU'RE STILL IN THE MIDDLE OF EATING.
This tastes good. It's great!
OH.
THANKS.
Delicious!
IS IT STILL SNOWING A LOT?
LOOK!
THE WHITE TEAM WON THIS YEAR'S *KOHAKU*!
I WAS CHEERING FOR RED.

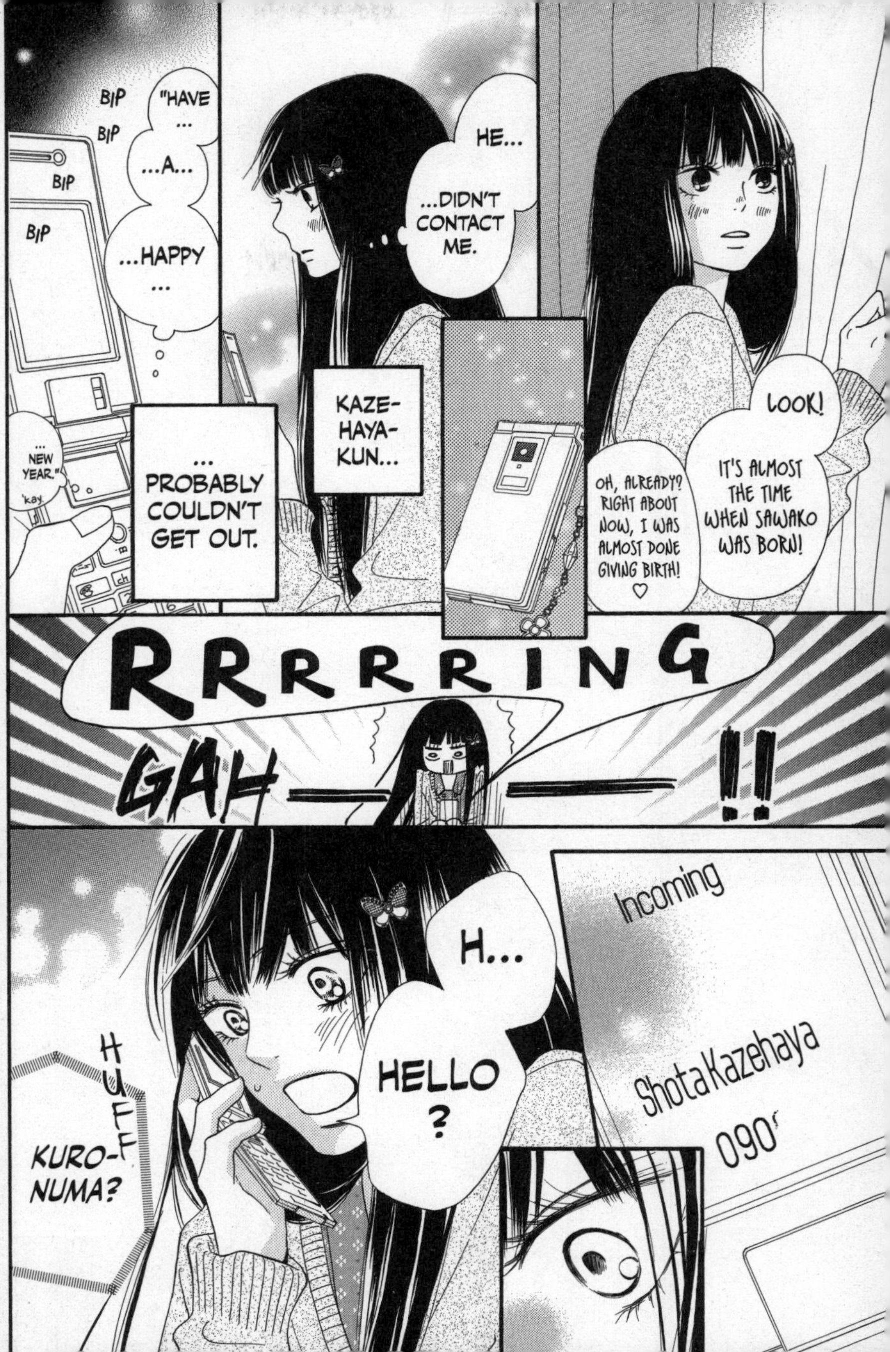
LOOK!
IT'S ALMOST THE TIME WHEN SAWAKO WAS BORN!
OH, ALREADY? RIGHT ABOUT NOW, I WAS ALMOST DONE GIVING BIRTH! ♡
HE...
...DIDN'T CONTACT ME.
KAZE-HAYA-KUN...
... PROBABLY COULDN'T GET OUT.
BIP
"HAVE ...
...A...
...HAPPY ...
BIP
BIP
BIP
... NEW YEAR."
'kay.
RRRRRING
GAH——————!!
Incoming
Shota Kazehaya
090
H...
HELLO ?
HUFF
KURO-NUMA?

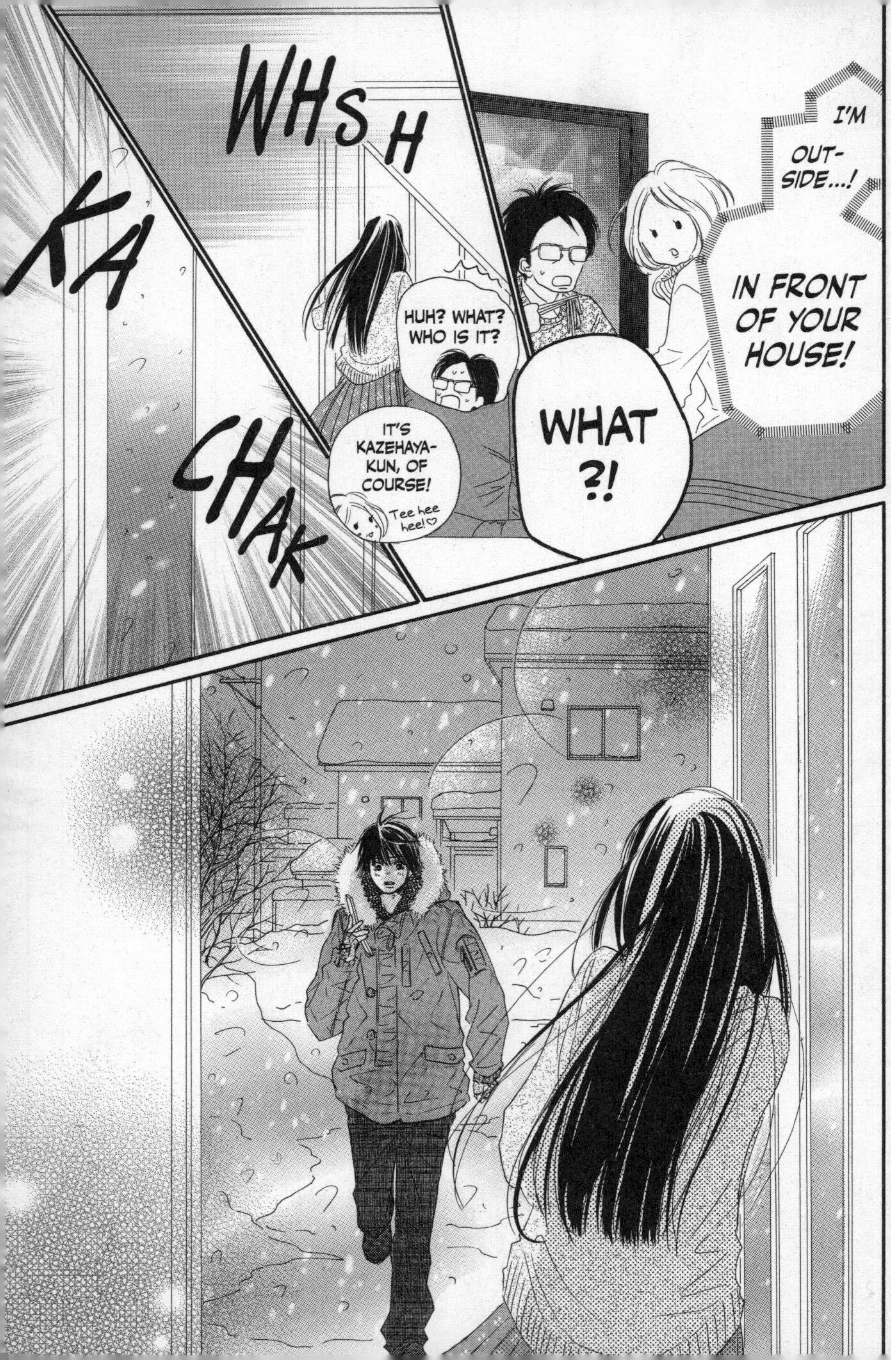
I'M OUT-SIDE...!
IN FRONT OF YOUR HOUSE!
WHAT?!
HUH? WHAT? WHO IS IT?
IT'S KAZEHAYA-KUN, OF COURSE!
Tee hee hee!♡
WHSH
KACHAK

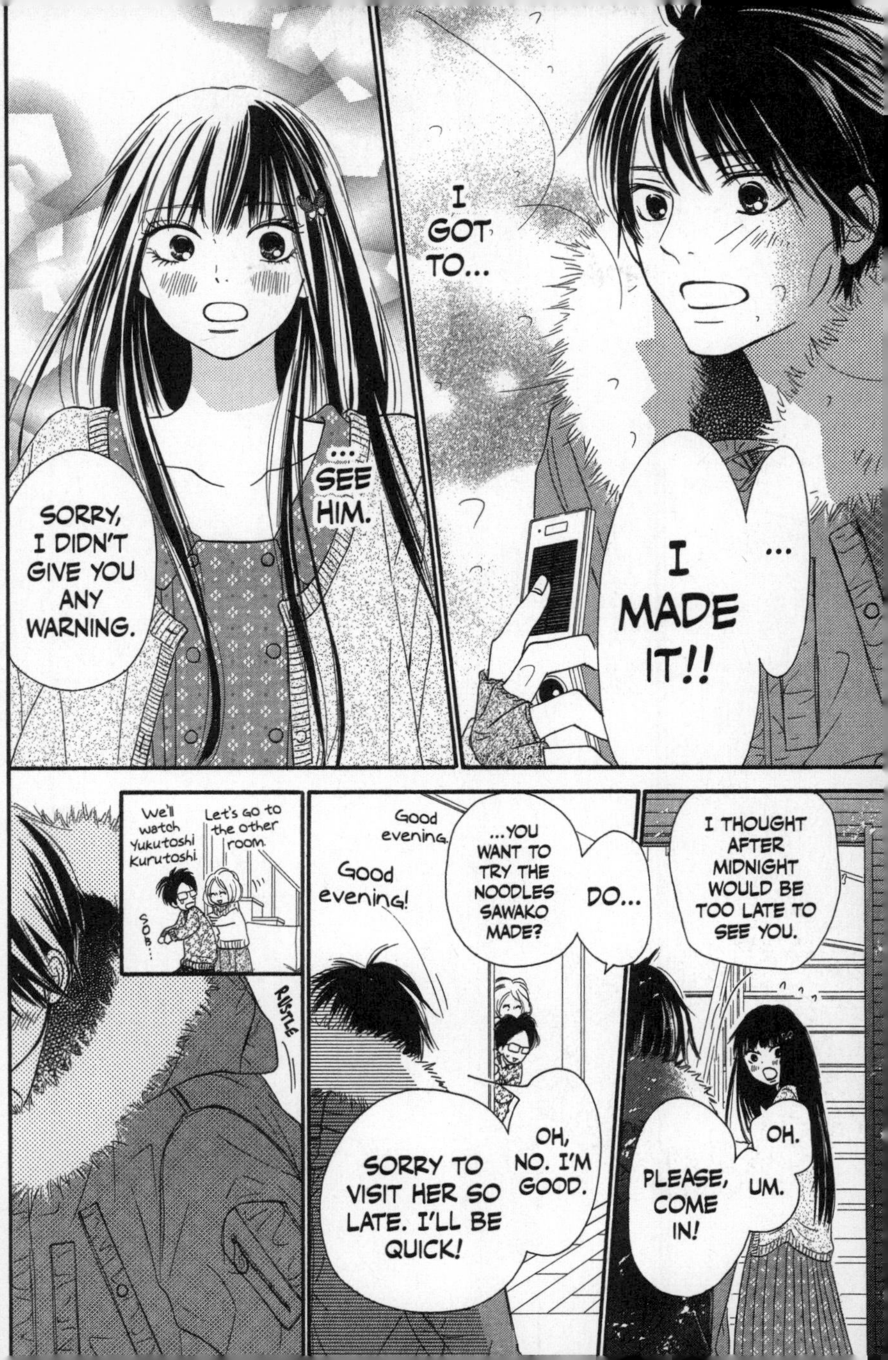
I GOT TO...
... I MADE IT!!
...SEE HIM.
SORRY, I DIDN'T GIVE YOU ANY WARNING.
I THOUGHT AFTER MIDNIGHT WOULD BE TOO LATE TO SEE YOU.
OH.
UM.
PLEASE, COME IN!
DO...
...YOU WANT TO TRY THE NOODLES SAWAKO MADE?
Good evening.
Good evening!
OH, NO. I'M GOOD.
SORRY TO VISIT HER SO LATE. I'LL BE QUICK!
Let's go to the other room.
We'll watch Yukutoshi Kurutoshi.
SOB...
RUSTLE

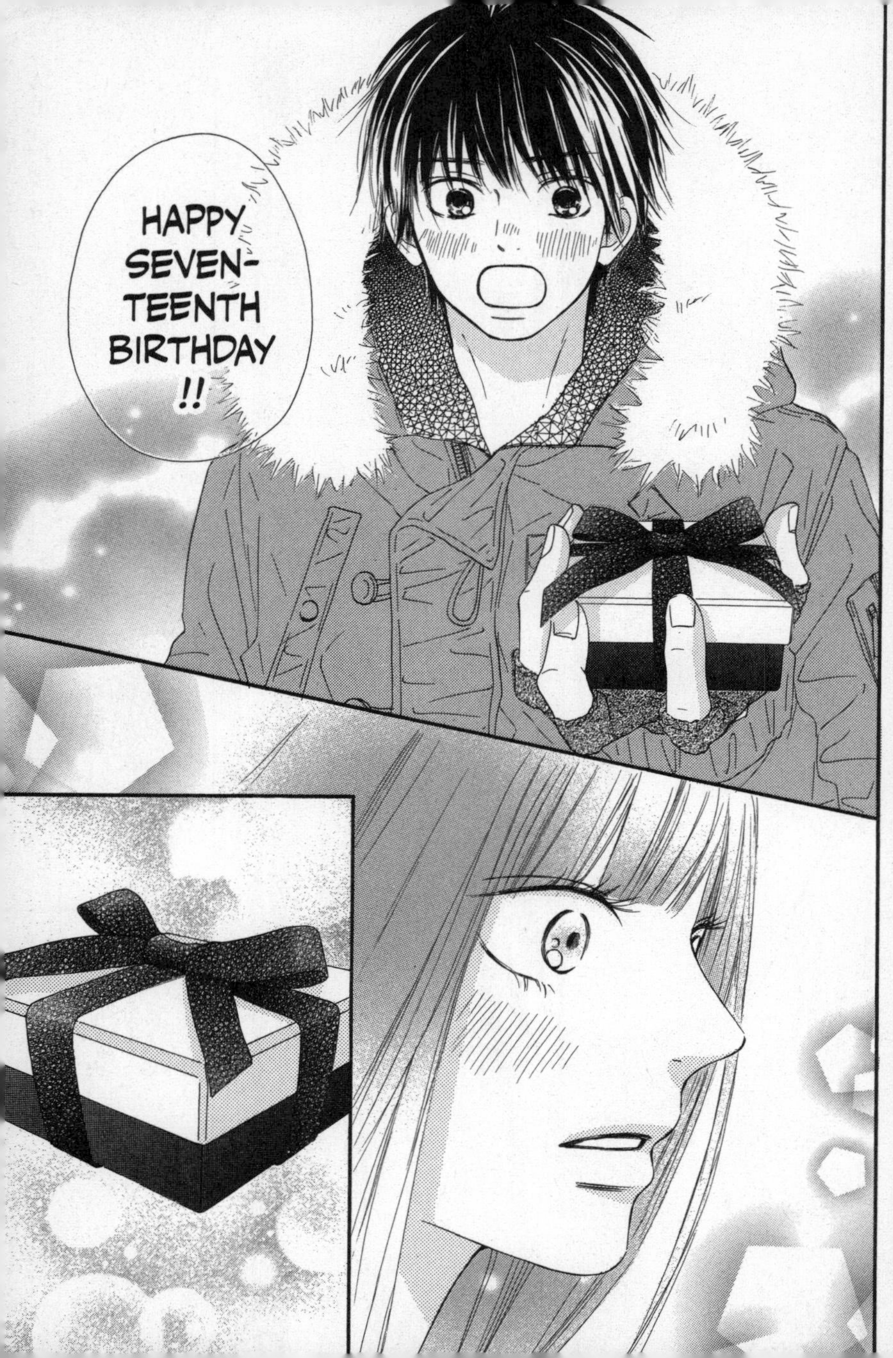
HAPPY SEVEN-TEENTH BIRTHDAY !!

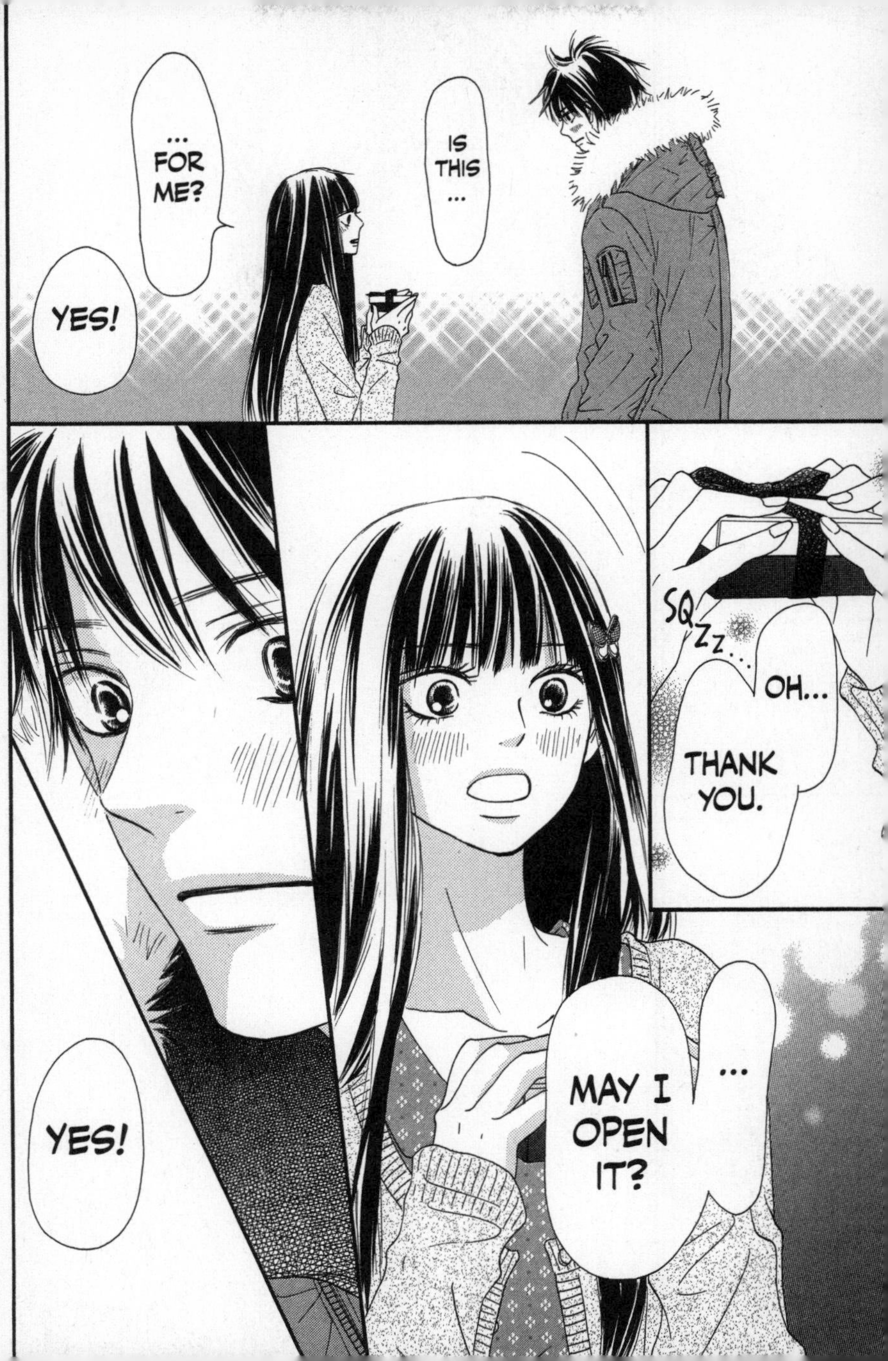
IS THIS ...
... FOR ME?
YES!
SQZZ...
OH... THANK YOU.
... MAY I OPEN IT?
YES!

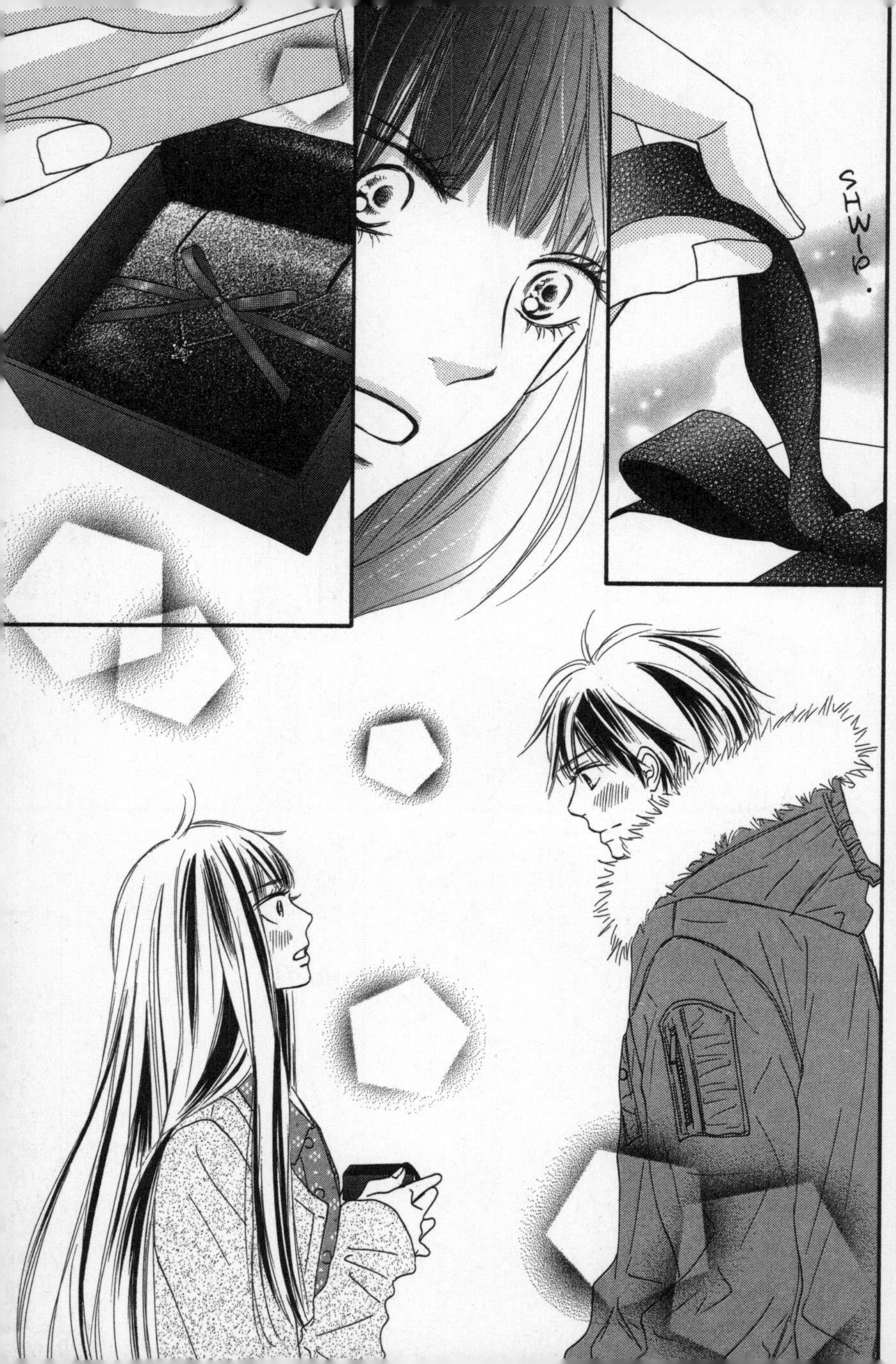
SHWIP.

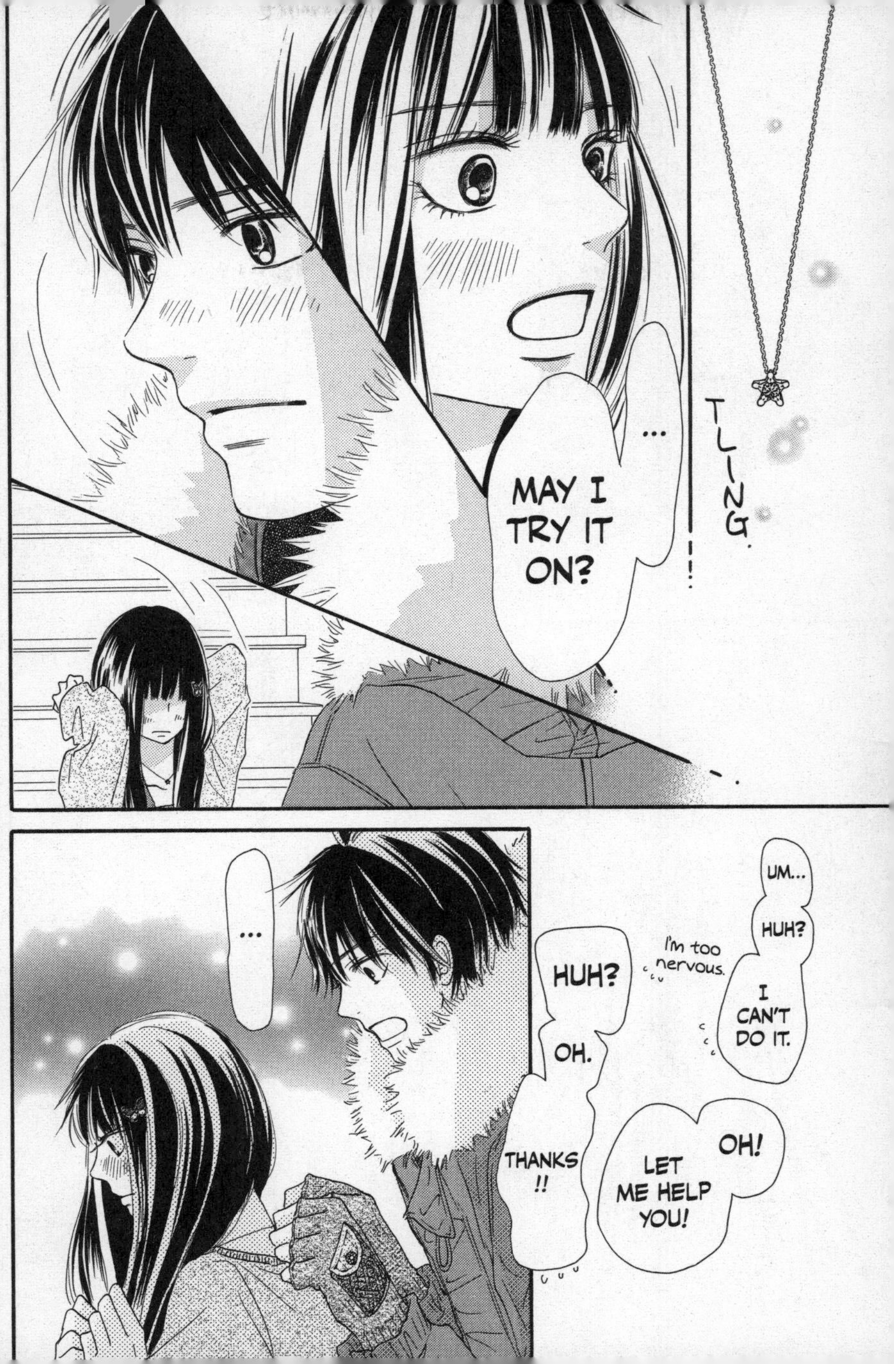
TLING.
...
MAY I TRY IT ON?
UM...
HUH?
I CAN'T DO IT.
I'm too nervous.
HUH?
OH.
OH!
LET ME HELP YOU!
THANKS!!
...

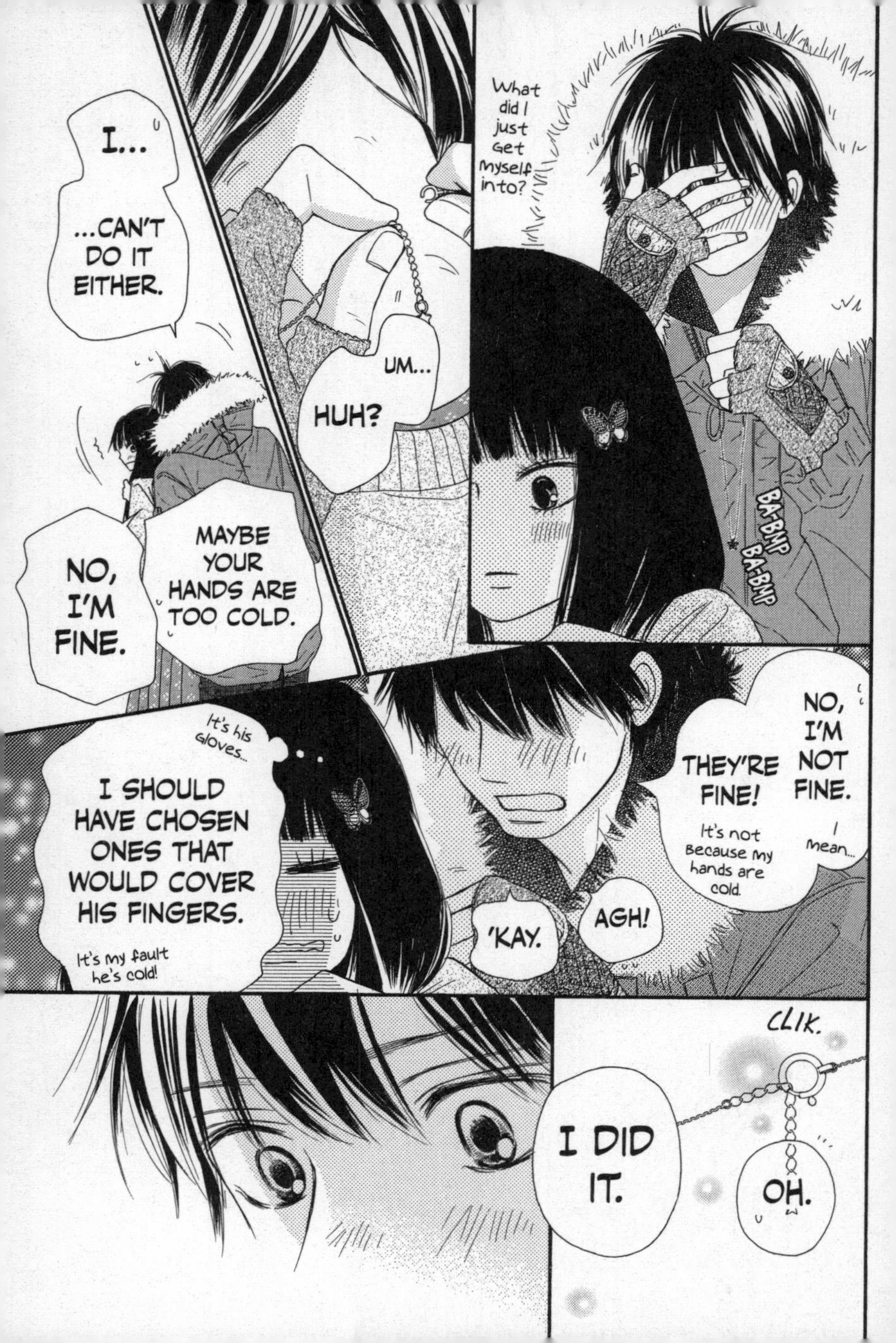
What did I just get myself into?
BA-BMP BA-BMP
UM...
HUH?
I...
...CAN'T DO IT EITHER.
MAYBE YOUR HANDS ARE TOO COLD.
NO, I'M FINE.
NO, I'M NOT FINE.
I mean...
THEY'RE FINE!
It's not because my hands are cold.
AGH!
'KAY.
It's his gloves...
I SHOULD HAVE CHOSEN ONES THAT WOULD COVER HIS FINGERS.
It's my fault he's cold!
CLIK.
OH.
I DID IT.

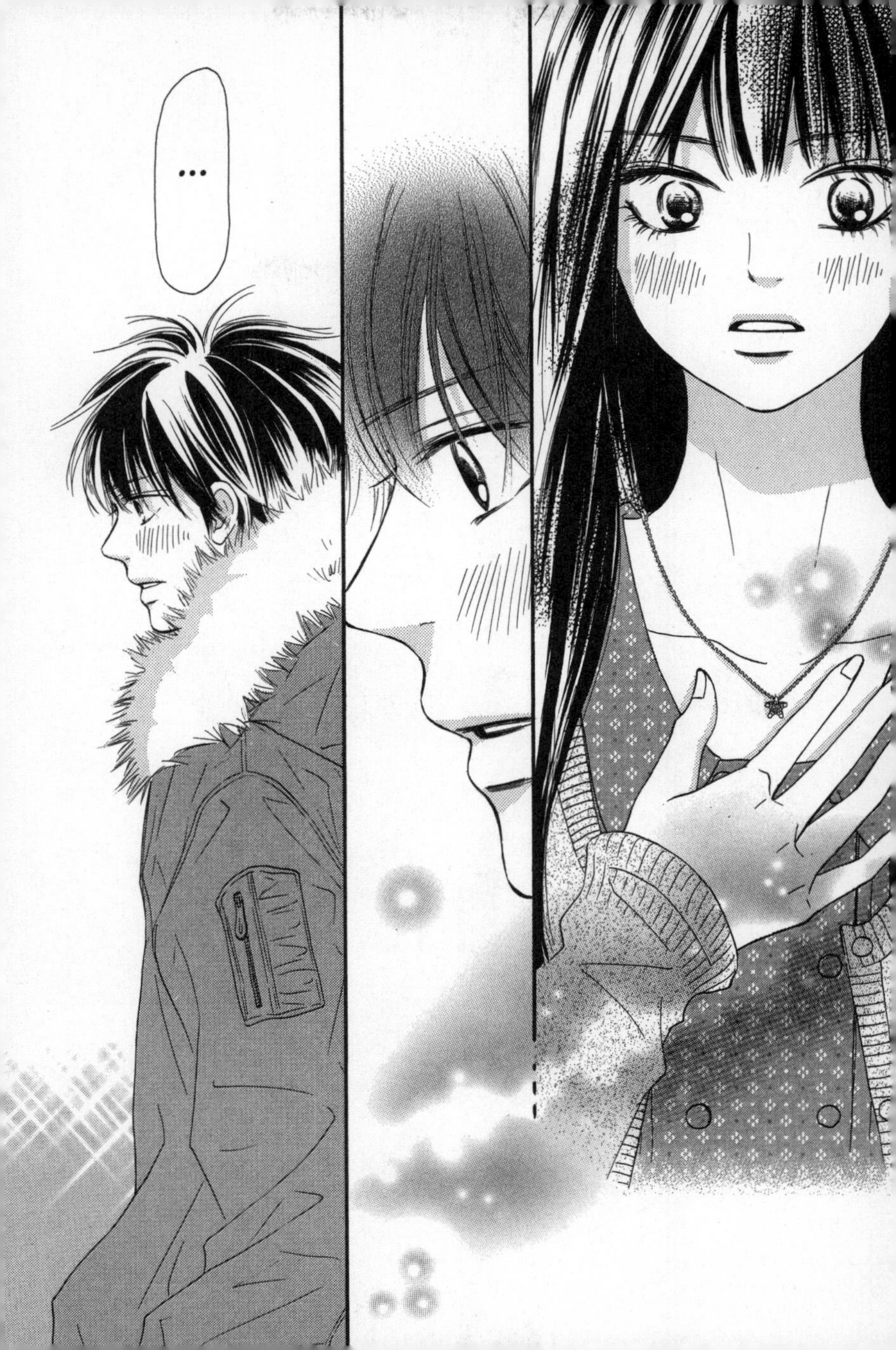
...

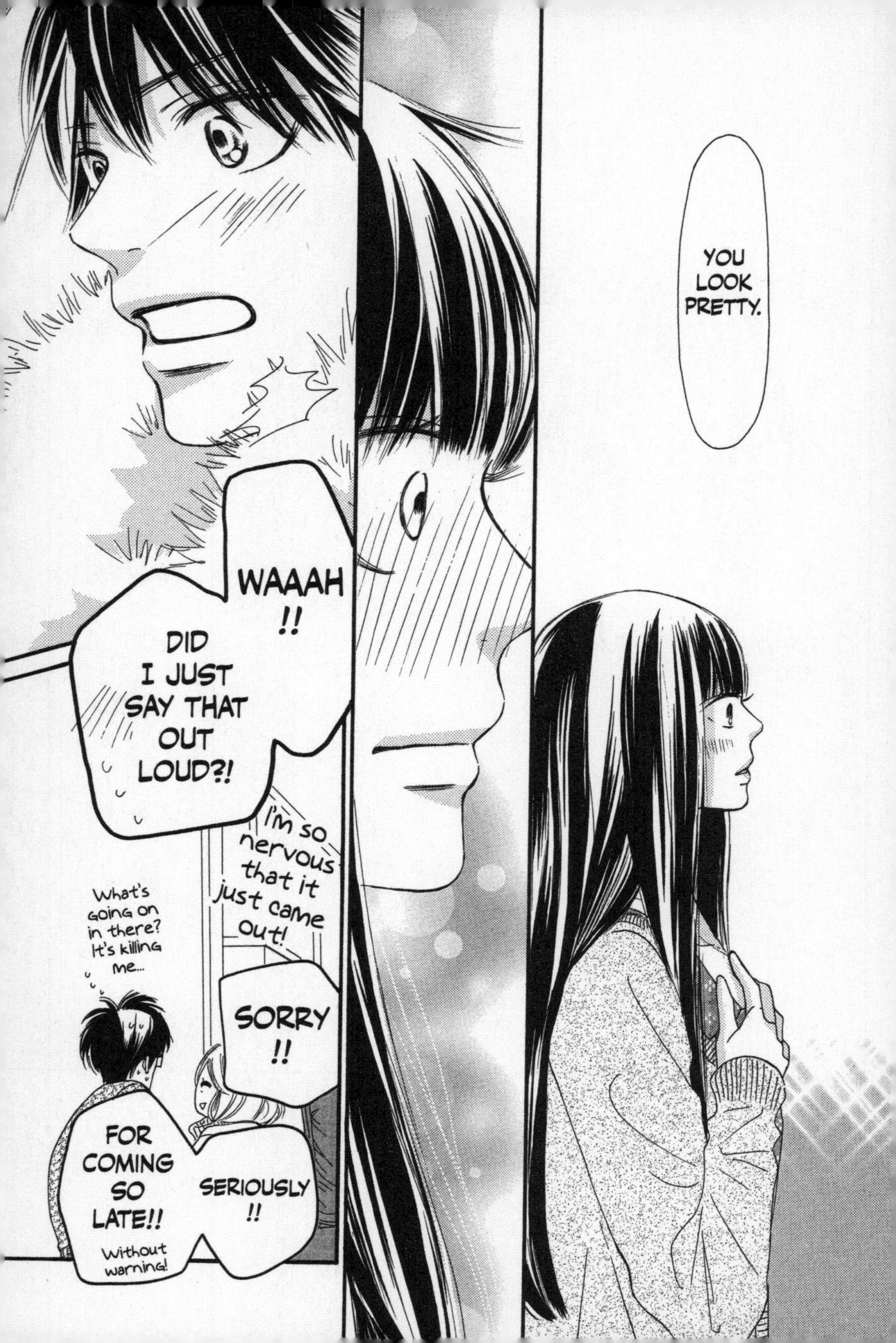
YOU LOOK PRETTY.
WAAAH!!
DID I JUST SAY THAT OUT LOUD?!
I'm so nervous that it just came out!
SORRY!!
SERIOUSLY!!
What's going on in there? It's killing me...
FOR COMING SO LATE!!
Without warning!

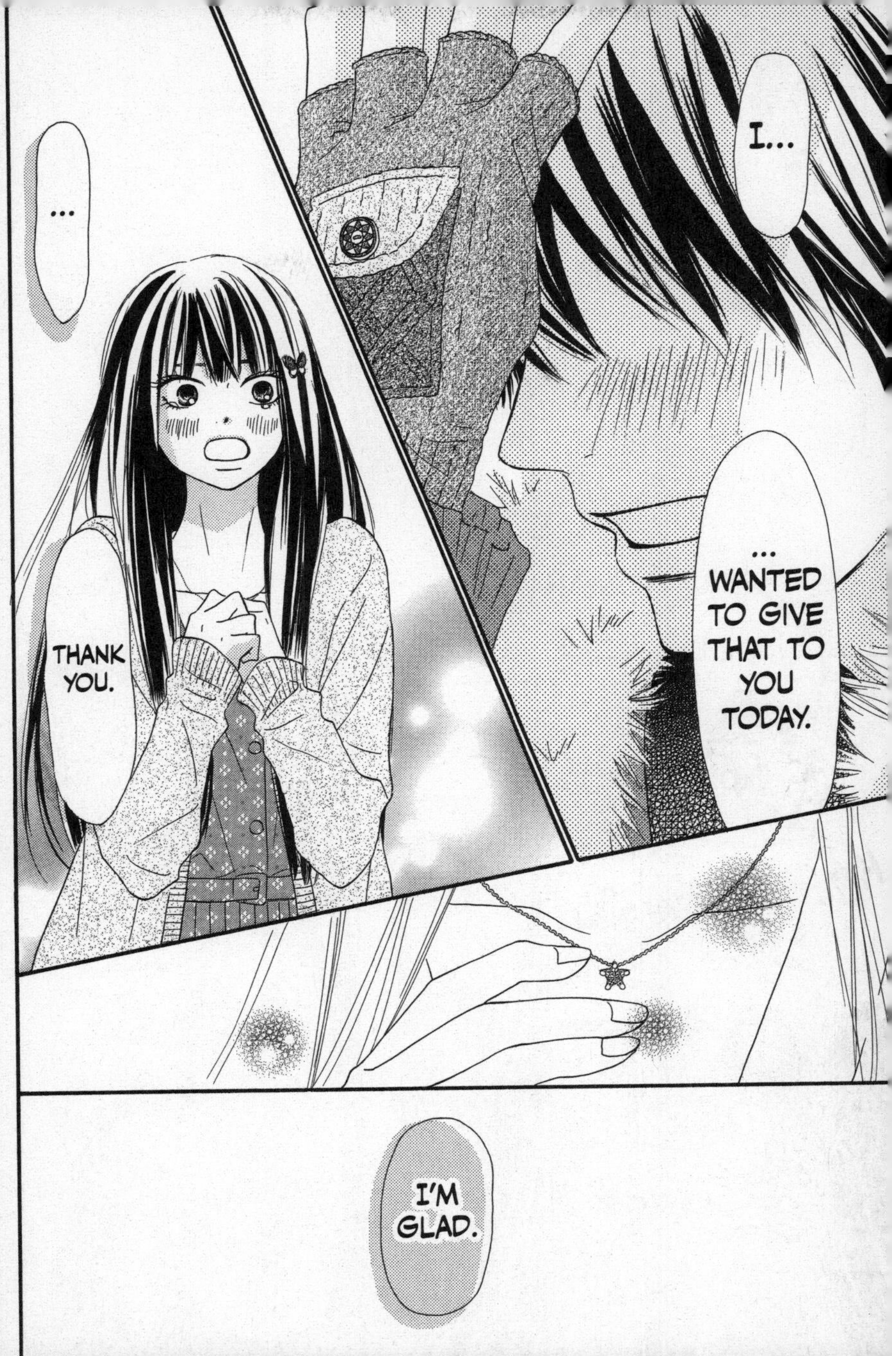
I...
... WANTED TO GIVE THAT TO YOU TODAY.
...
THANK YOU.
I'M GLAD.

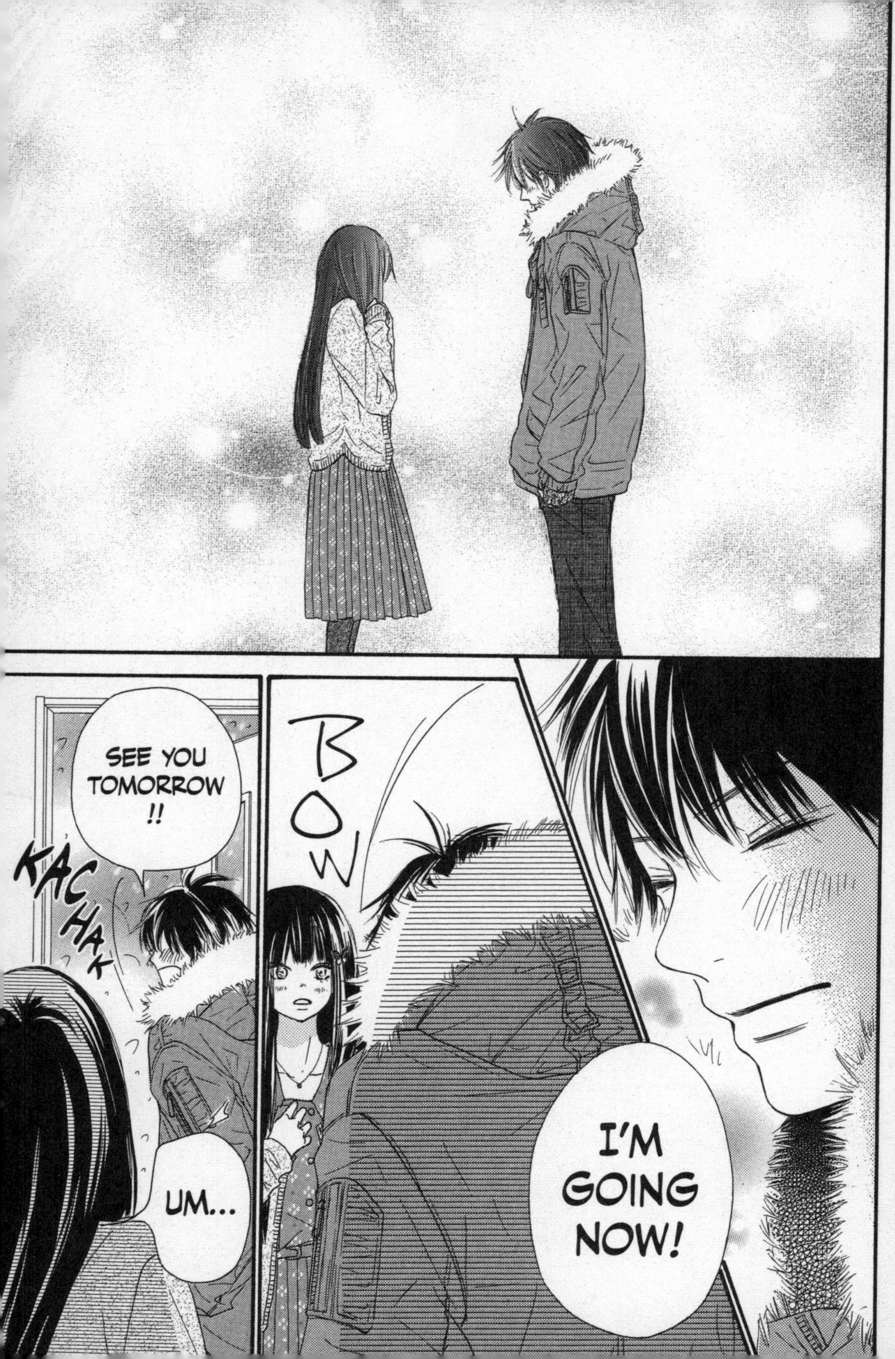
I'M GOING NOW!
BOW
SEE YOU TOMORROW !!
KACHAK
UM...

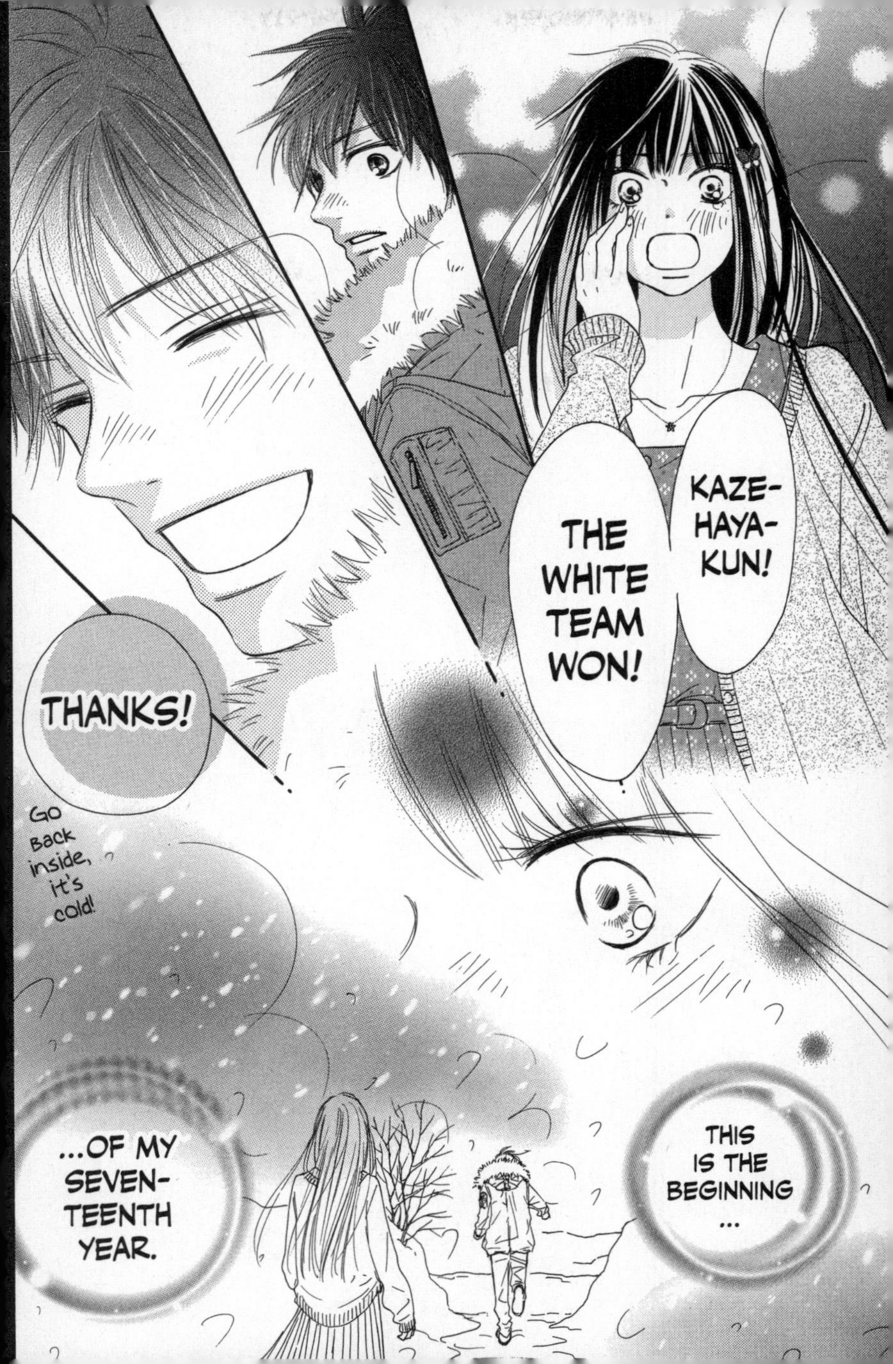
KAZE-HAYA-KUN!
THE WHITE TEAM WON!
THANKS!
Go back inside, it's cold!
THIS IS THE BEGINNING ...
...OF MY SEVENTEENTH YEAR.

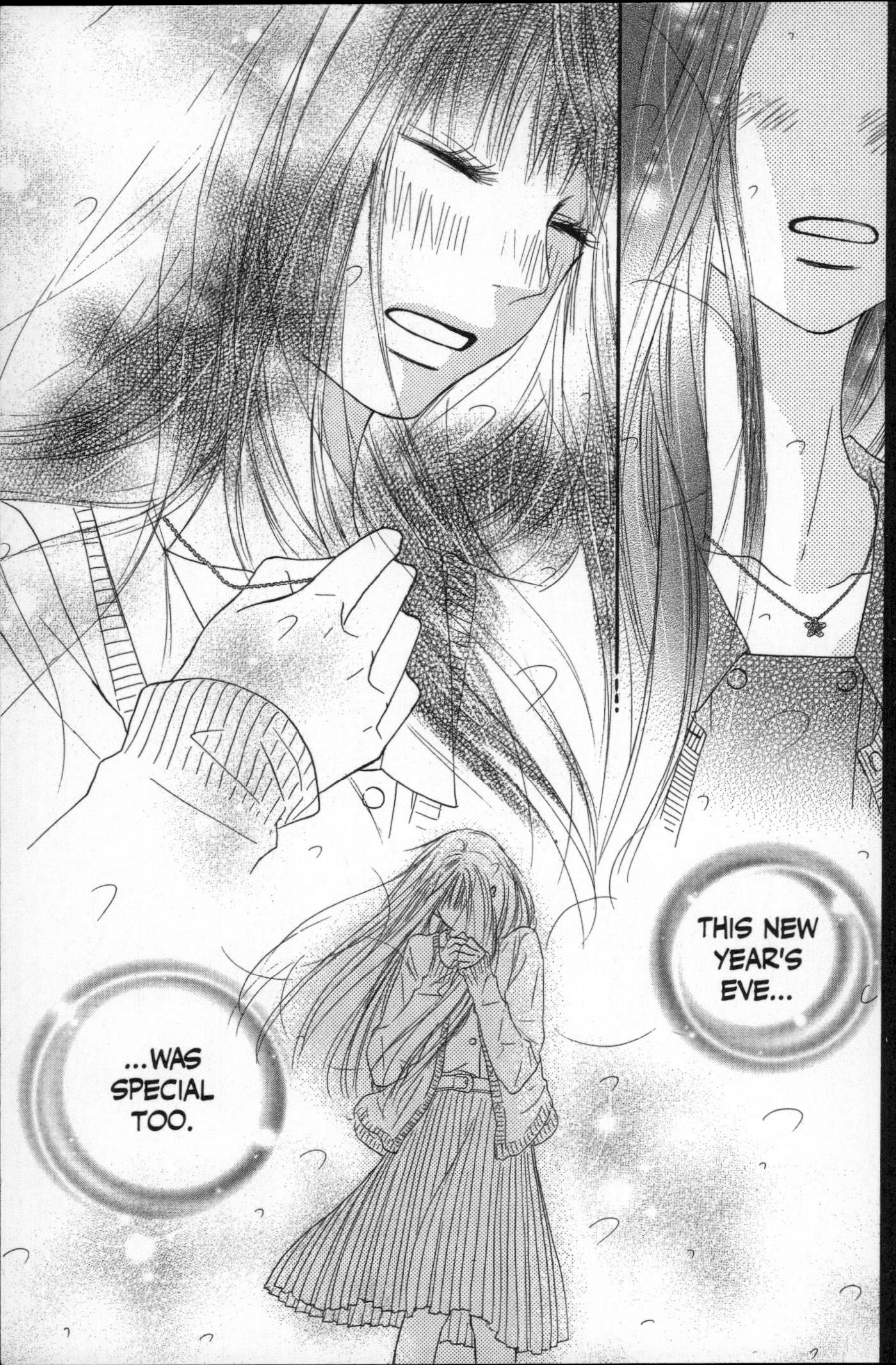
THIS NEW YEAR'S EVE...
...WAS SPECIAL TOO.

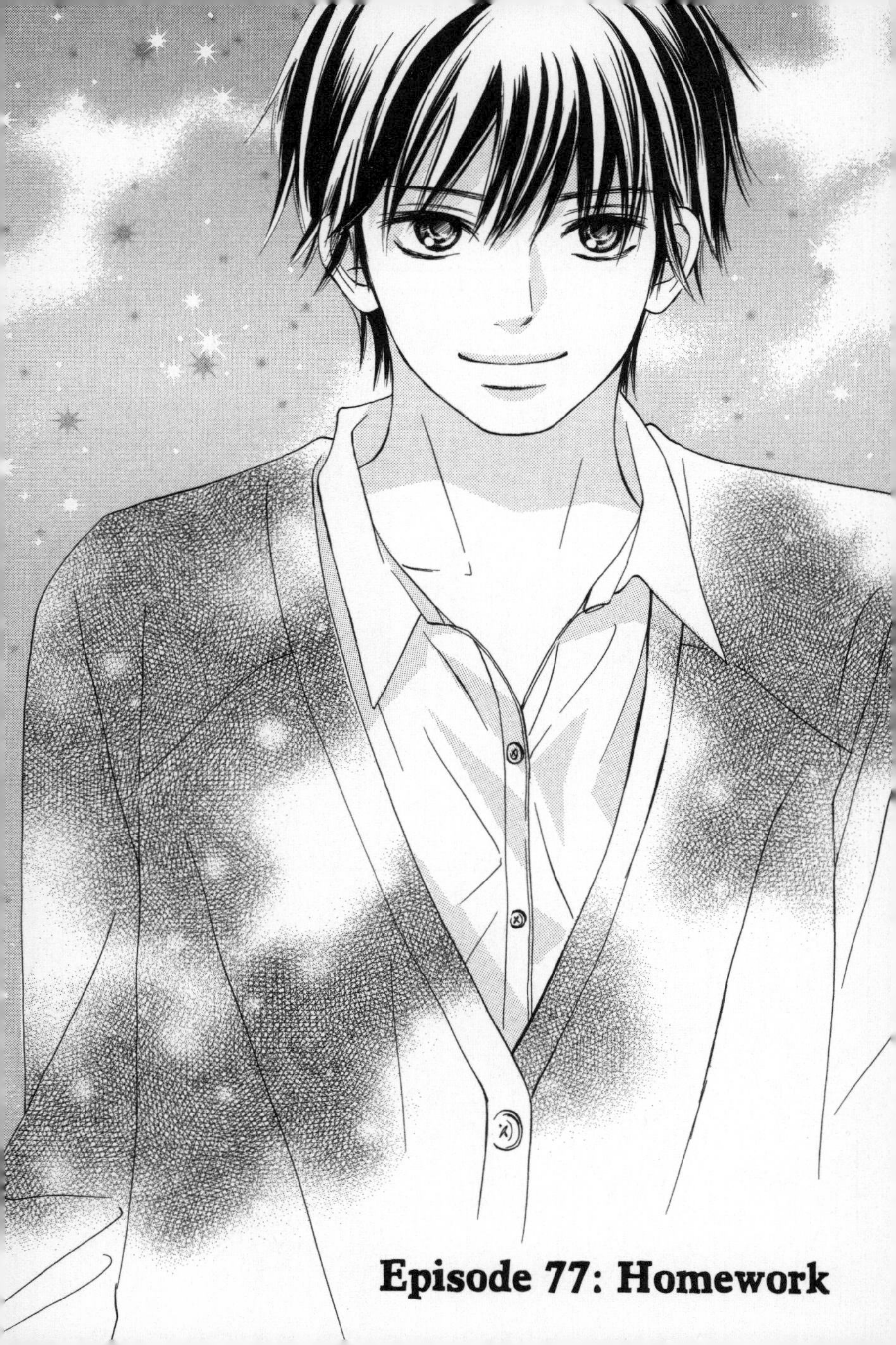

Episode 77: Homework

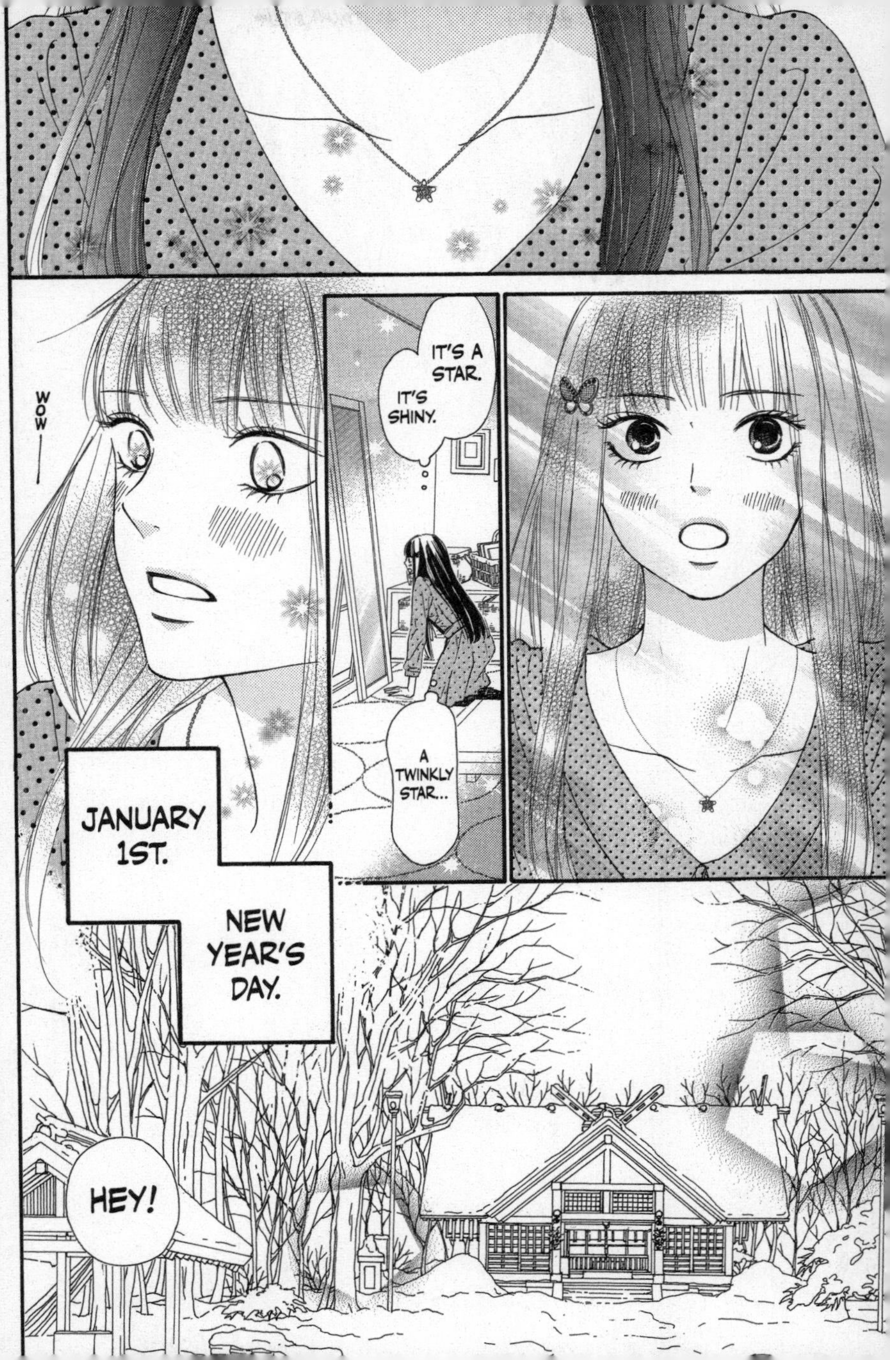
IT'S A STAR. IT'S SHINY.
A TWINKLY STAR...
WOW—
JANUARY 1ST.
NEW YEAR'S DAY.
HEY!

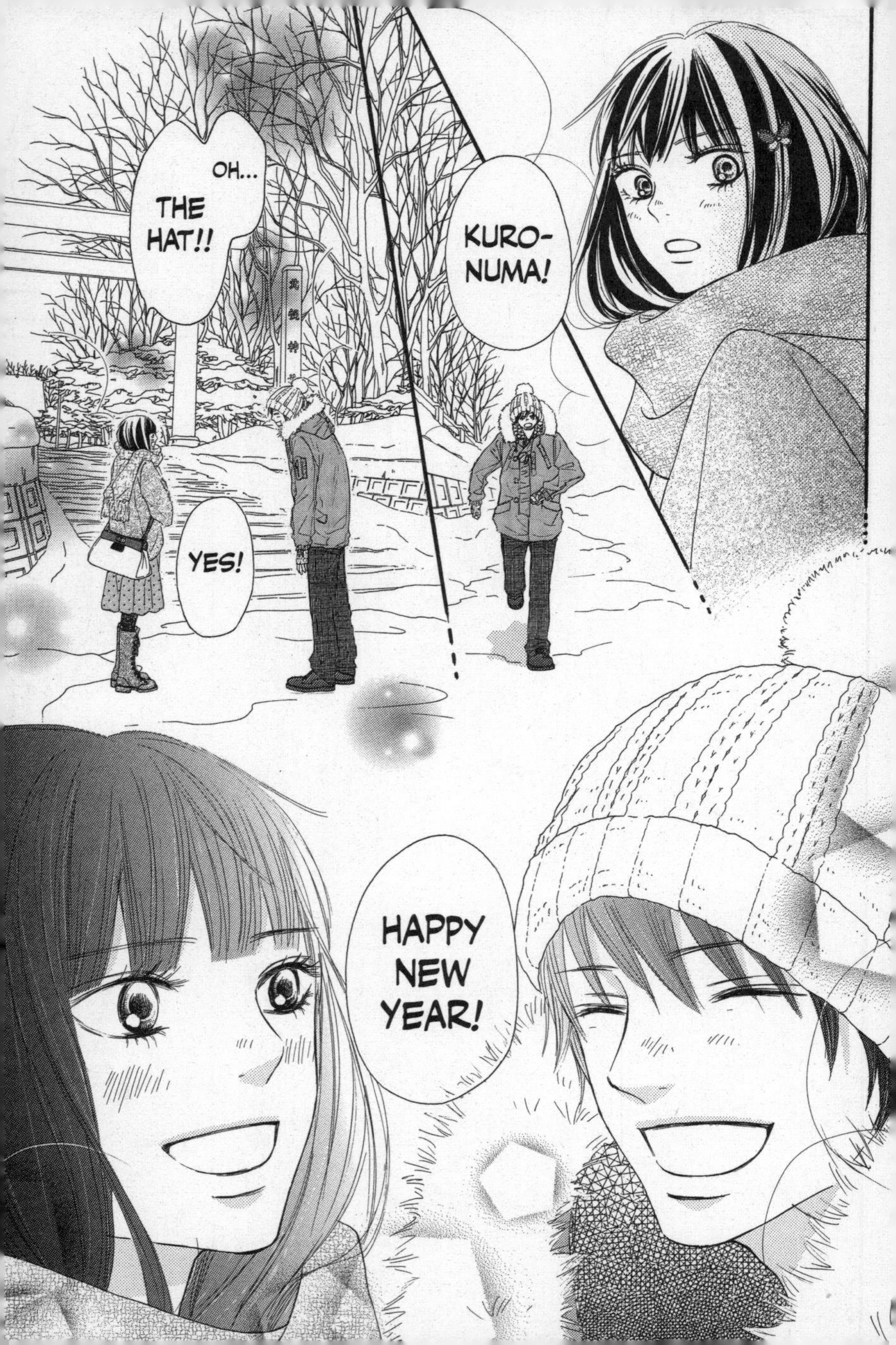
KURO-NUMA!
OH... THE HAT!!
YES!
HAPPY NEW YEAR!

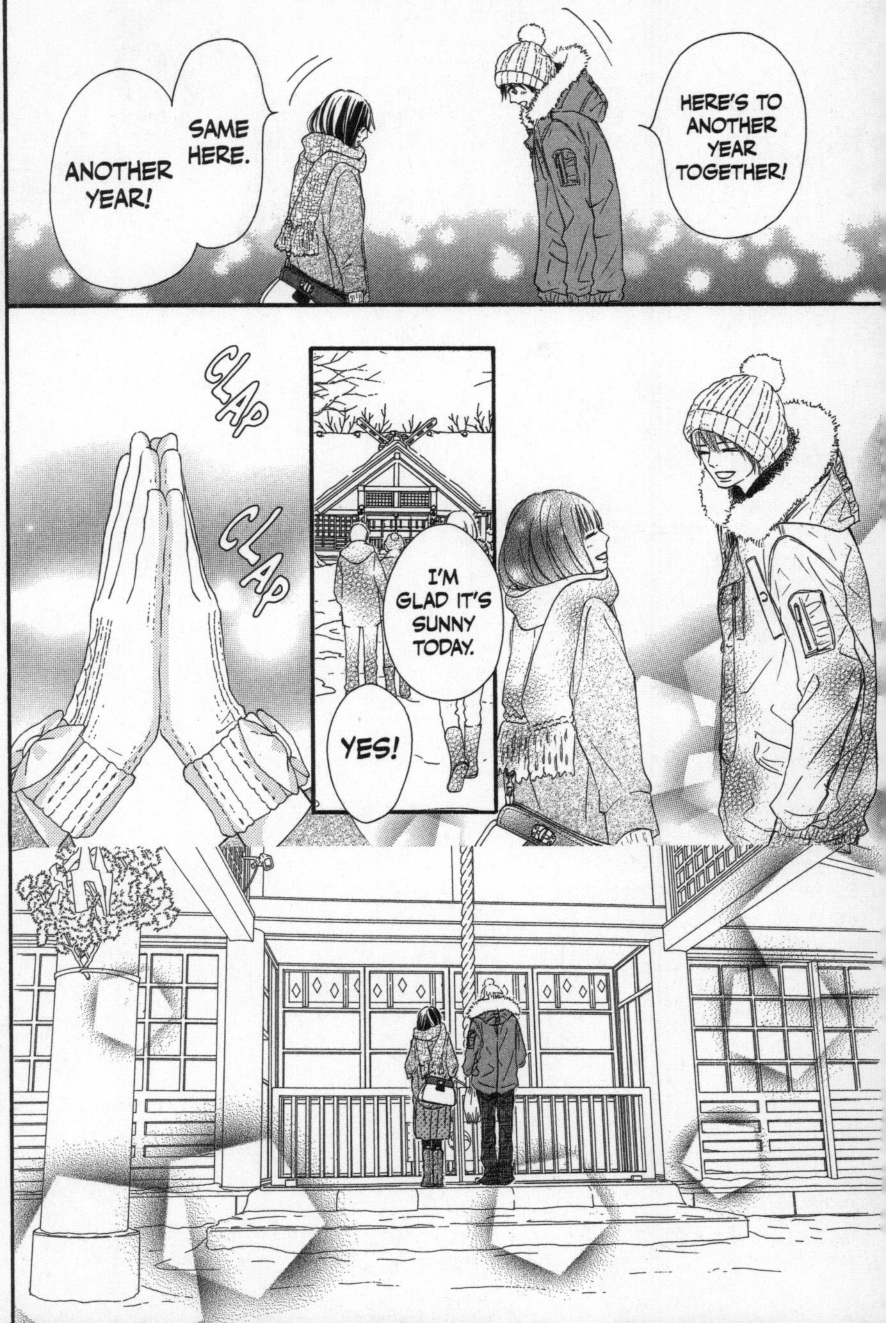
HERE'S TO ANOTHER YEAR TOGETHER!
SAME HERE.
ANOTHER YEAR!
I'M GLAD IT'S SUNNY TODAY.
YES!
CLAP
CLAP

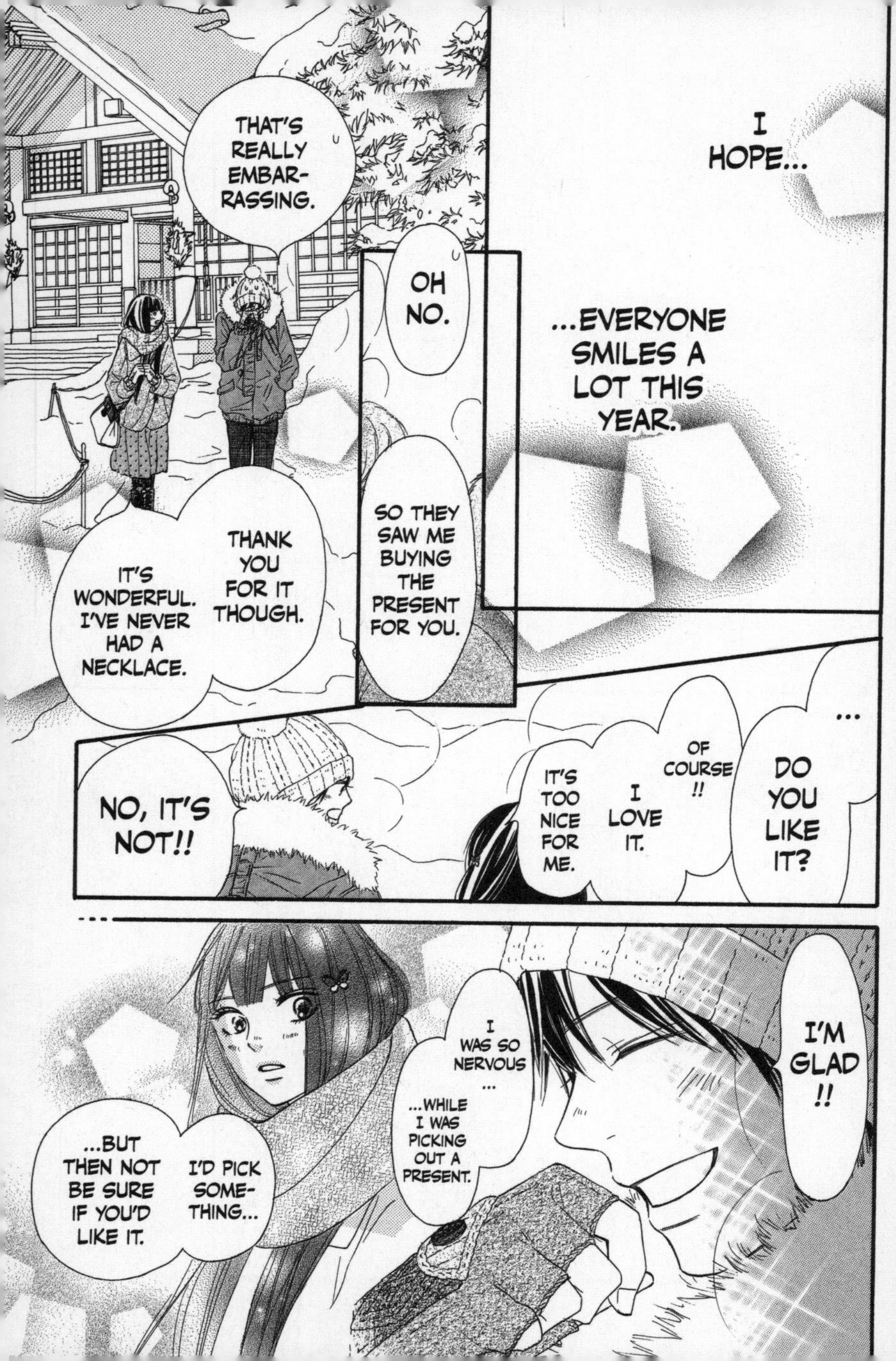
I HOPE... ...EVERYONE SMILES A LOT THIS YEAR.
OH NO.
SO THEY SAW ME BUYING THE PRESENT FOR YOU.
THAT'S REALLY EMBARRASSING.
THANK YOU FOR IT THOUGH.
IT'S WONDERFUL. I'VE NEVER HAD A NECKLACE.
...
DO YOU LIKE IT?
OF COURSE!!
I LOVE IT.
IT'S TOO NICE FOR ME.
NO, IT'S NOT!!
I'M GLAD!!
I WAS SO NERVOUS...
...WHILE I WAS PICKING OUT A PRESENT.
I'D PICK SOMETHING...
...BUT THEN NOT BE SURE IF YOU'D LIKE IT.

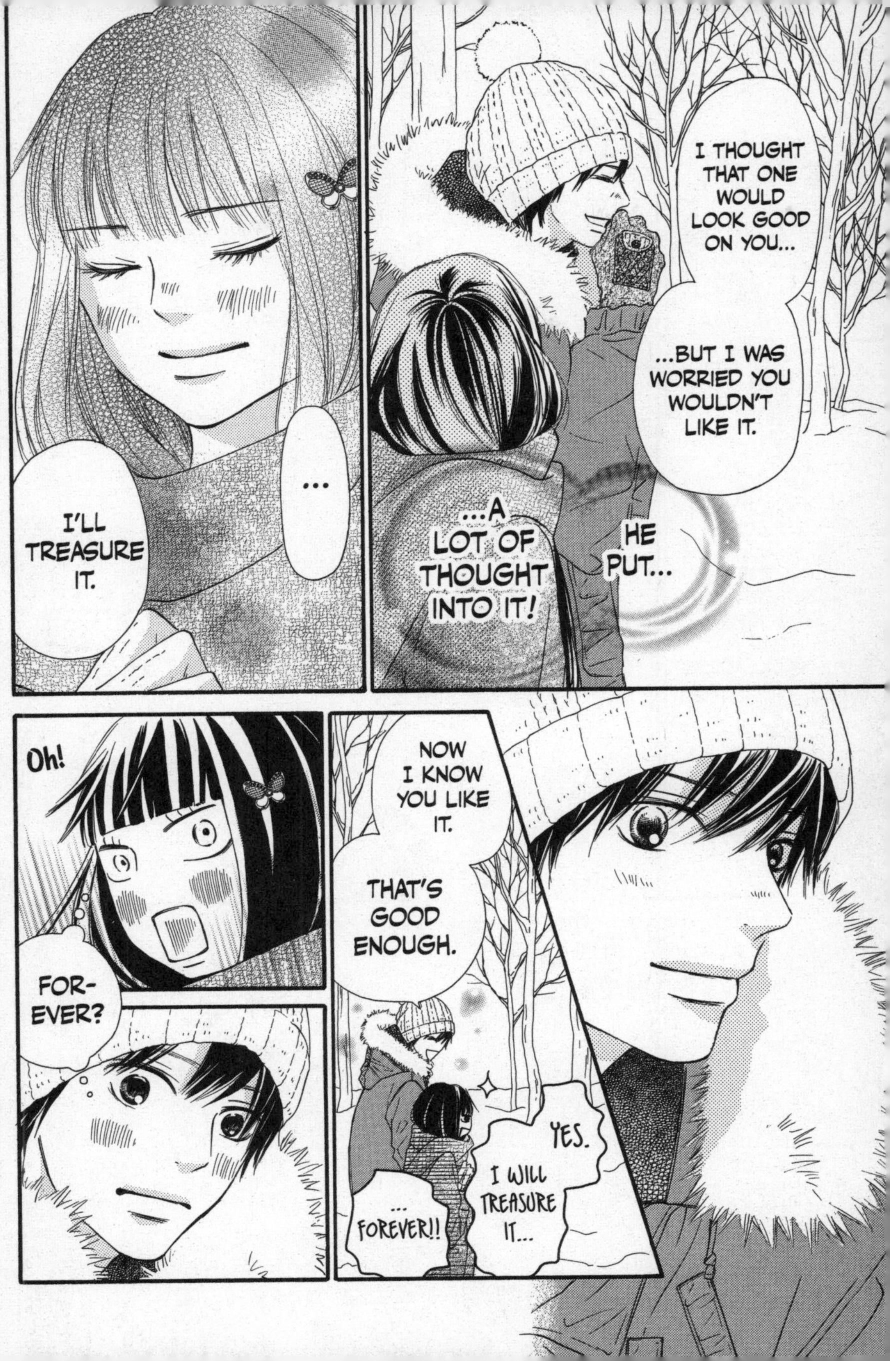

I THOUGHT THAT ONE WOULD LOOK GOOD ON YOU...
...BUT I WAS WORRIED YOU WOULDN'T LIKE IT.
HE PUT...
...A LOT OF THOUGHT INTO IT!
...
I'LL TREASURE IT.
NOW I KNOW YOU LIKE IT.
THAT'S GOOD ENOUGH.
YES.
I WILL TREASURE IT...
...FOREVER!!
Oh!
FOR-EVER?

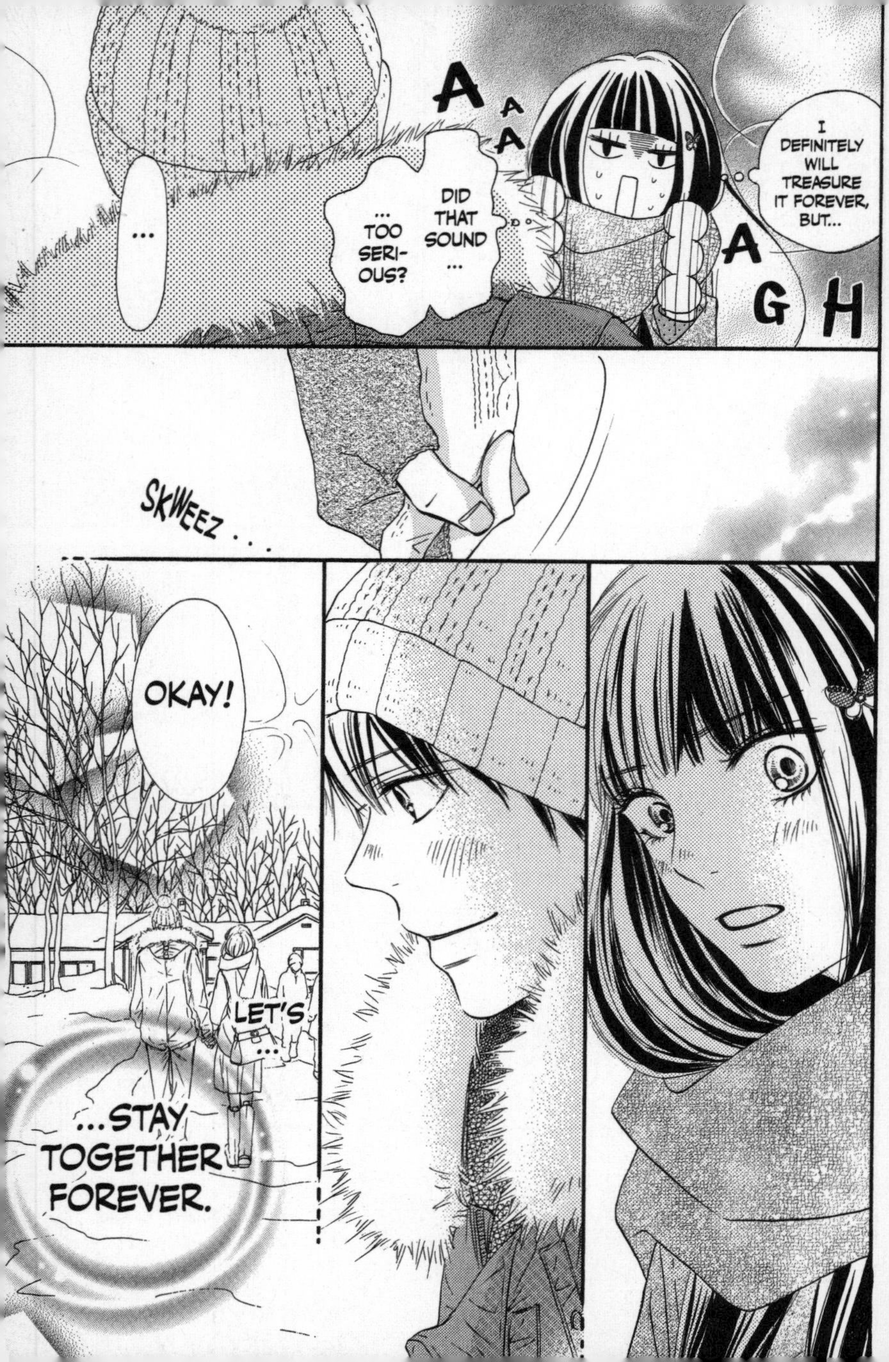

I DEFINITELY WILL TREASURE IT FOREVER, BUT...
AAAAGH
DID THAT SOUND ... ... TOO SERIOUS?
...
SKWEEZ . . .
OKAY!
LET'S ...
...STAY TOGETHER FOREVER.

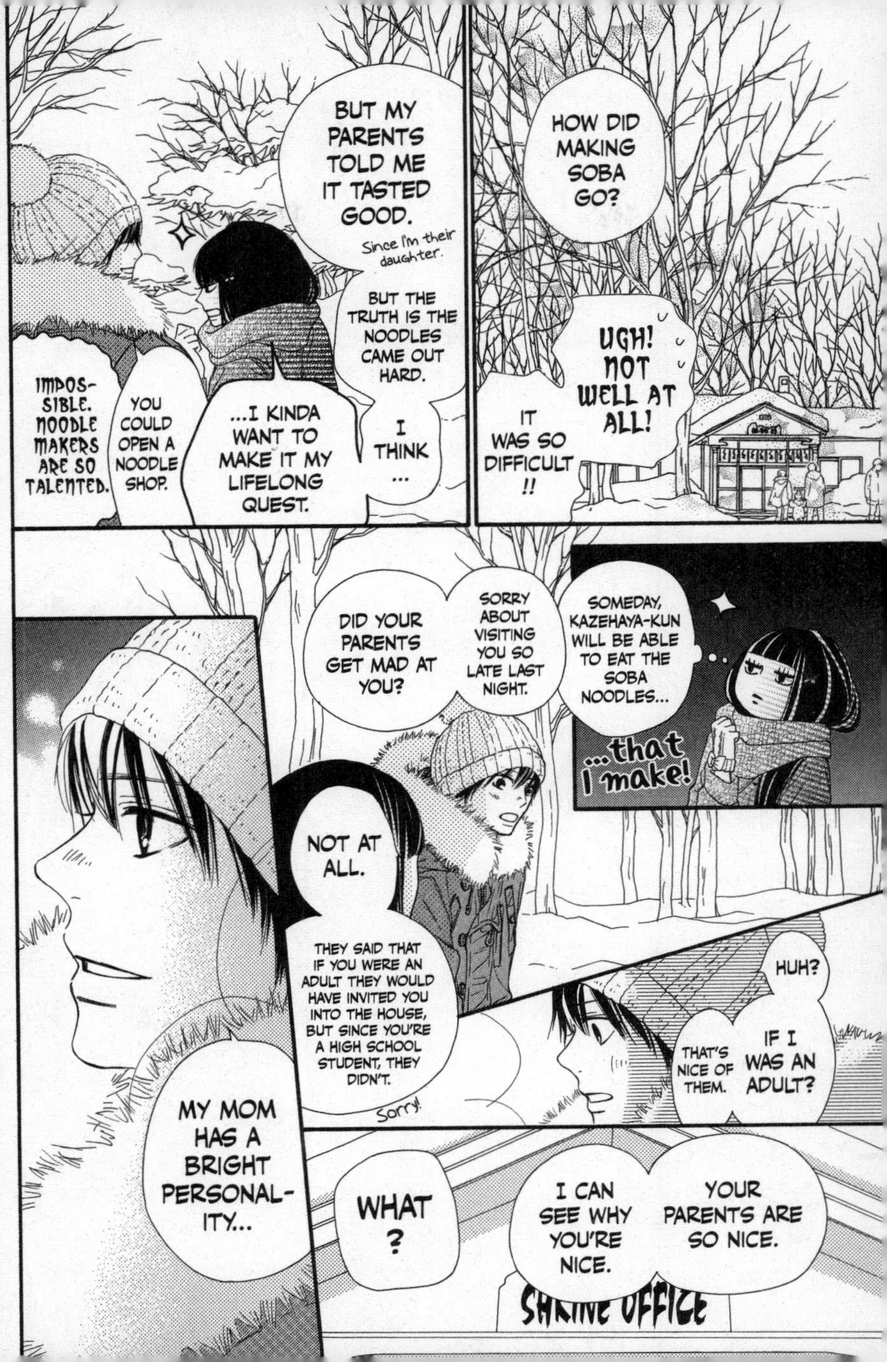

HOW DID MAKING SOBA GO?
UGH! NOT WELL AT ALL!
IT WAS SO DIFFICULT!!
BUT MY PARENTS TOLD ME IT TASTED GOOD.
Since I'm their daughter.
BUT THE TRUTH IS THE NOODLES CAME OUT HARD.
I THINK...
...I KINDA WANT TO MAKE IT MY LIFELONG QUEST.
YOU COULD OPEN A NOODLE SHOP.
IMPOSSIBLE. NOODLE MAKERS ARE SO TALENTED.
SOMEDAY, KAZEHAYA-KUN WILL BE ABLE TO EAT THE SOBA NOODLES...
...that I make!
SORRY ABOUT VISITING YOU SO LATE LAST NIGHT.
DID YOUR PARENTS GET MAD AT YOU?
NOT AT ALL.
THEY SAID THAT IF YOU WERE AN ADULT THEY WOULD HAVE INVITED YOU INTO THE HOUSE, BUT SINCE YOU'RE A HIGH SCHOOL STUDENT, THEY DIDN'T.
Sorry!
HUH?
IF I WAS AN ADULT?
THAT'S NICE OF THEM.
YOUR PARENTS ARE SO NICE.
I CAN SEE WHY YOU'RE NICE.
WHAT?
SHRINE OFFICE
MY MOM HAS A BRIGHT PERSONALITY...

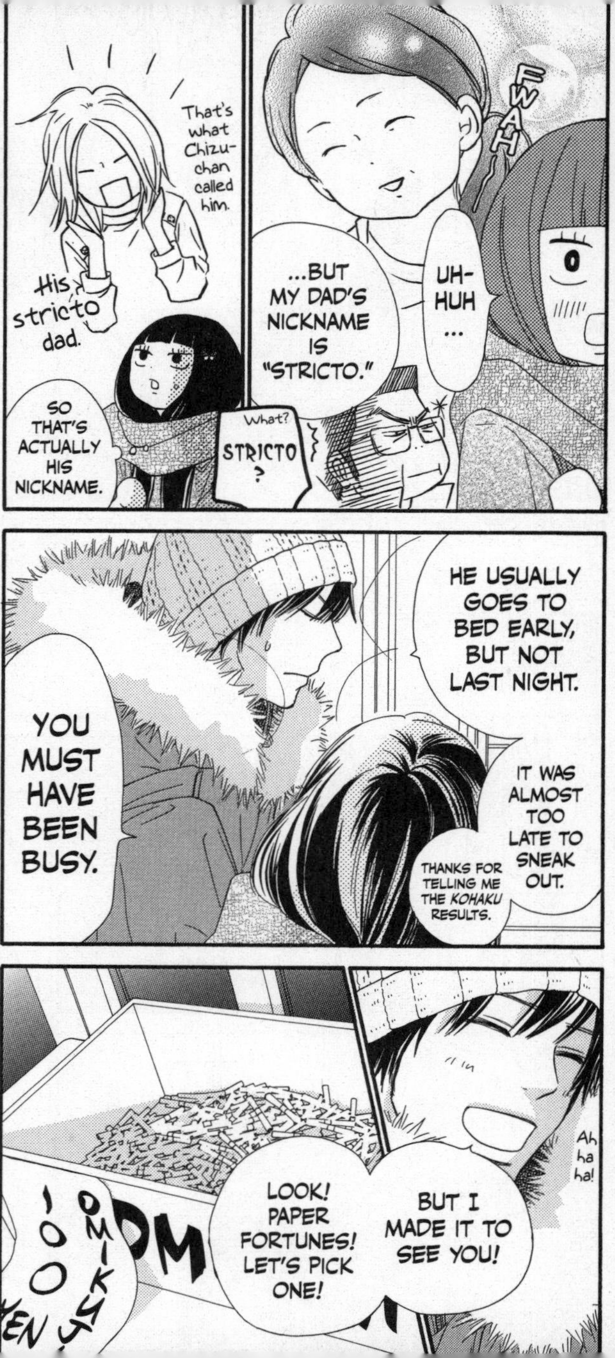
FWAH
UH-HUH...
...BUT MY DAD'S NICKNAME IS "STRICTO."
What?
STRICTO?
That's what Chizu-chan called him.
His stricto dad.
SO THAT'S ACTUALLY HIS NICKNAME.
HE USUALLY GOES TO BED EARLY, BUT NOT LAST NIGHT.
IT WAS ALMOST TOO LATE TO SNEAK OUT.
THANKS FOR TELLING ME THE *KOHAKU* RESULTS.
YOU MUST HAVE BEEN BUSY.
Ah ha ha!
BUT I MADE IT TO SEE YOU!
LOOK! PAPER FORTUNES! LET'S PICK ONE!

KARUPIN on JAPAN 2

When you're creating manga, there's a stage called "storyboards."

This means the rough sketches you draw before the pencils. Mine are terrible! Both the drawing AND the writing.

So I always worry about whether the editor can make them out. I sent storyboards to the editor via fax the other day and asked if they were readable.

I received an answer saying, "I could read them! I think I've gained the ability to read your handwriting!"

I was moved. That must have been the result of long, hard work for my editor!

Thank you so much, Editor!!!

Sorry for forcing you to acquire an unnecessary ability. But I'm so happy. Yay! Yay!

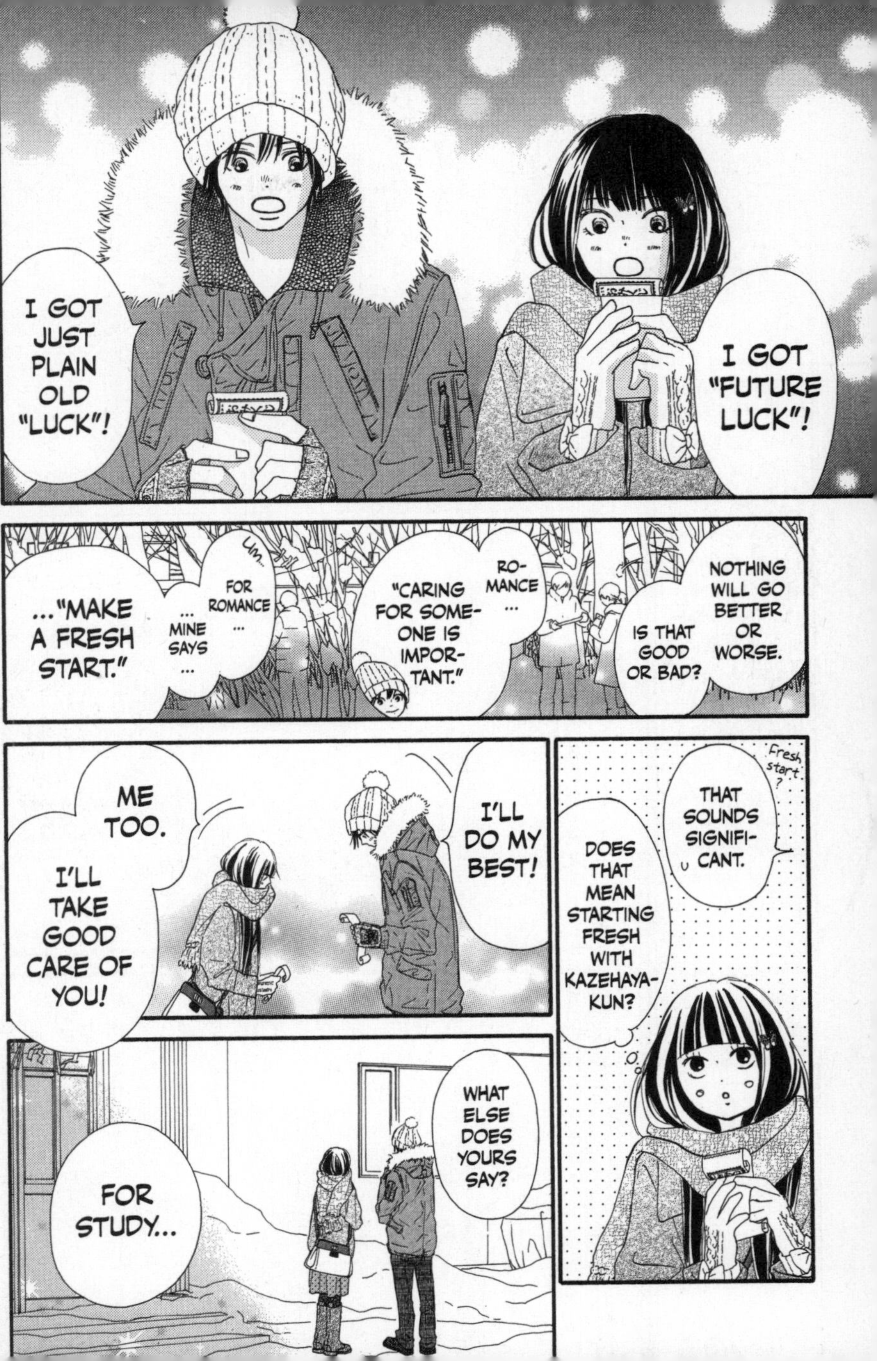
I GOT "FUTURE LUCK"!
I GOT JUST PLAIN OLD "LUCK"!
NOTHING WILL GO BETTER OR WORSE.
IS THAT GOOD OR BAD?
ROMANCE...
"CARING FOR SOMEONE IS IMPORTANT."
Um...
FOR ROMANCE...
...MINE SAYS...
..."MAKE A FRESH START."
Fresh start?
THAT SOUNDS SIGNIFICANT.
DOES THAT MEAN STARTING FRESH WITH KAZEHAYA-KUN?
I'LL DO MY BEST!
ME TOO.
I'LL TAKE GOOD CARE OF YOU!
WHAT ELSE DOES YOURS SAY?
FOR STUDY...

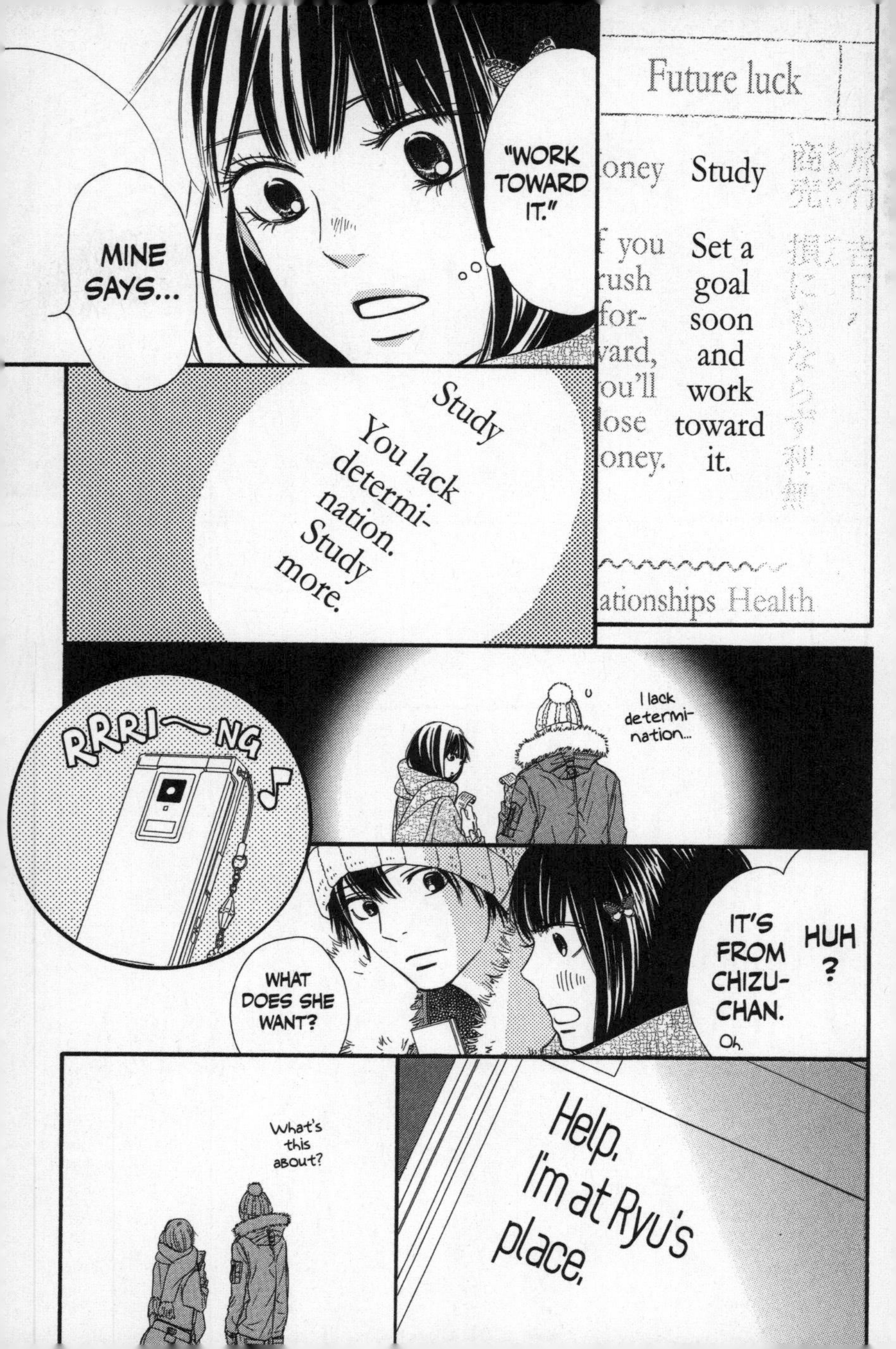

Future luck
oney
f you rush for-ward, ou'll lose oney.
Study
Set a goal soon and work toward it.
ationships Health
"WORK TOWARD IT."
MINE SAYS...
Study
You lack determi-nation. Study more.
I lack determi-nation...
RRRI~NG
HUH?
IT'S FROM CHIZU-CHAN.
Oh.
WHAT DOES SHE WANT?
Help. I'm at Ryu's place.
What's this about?

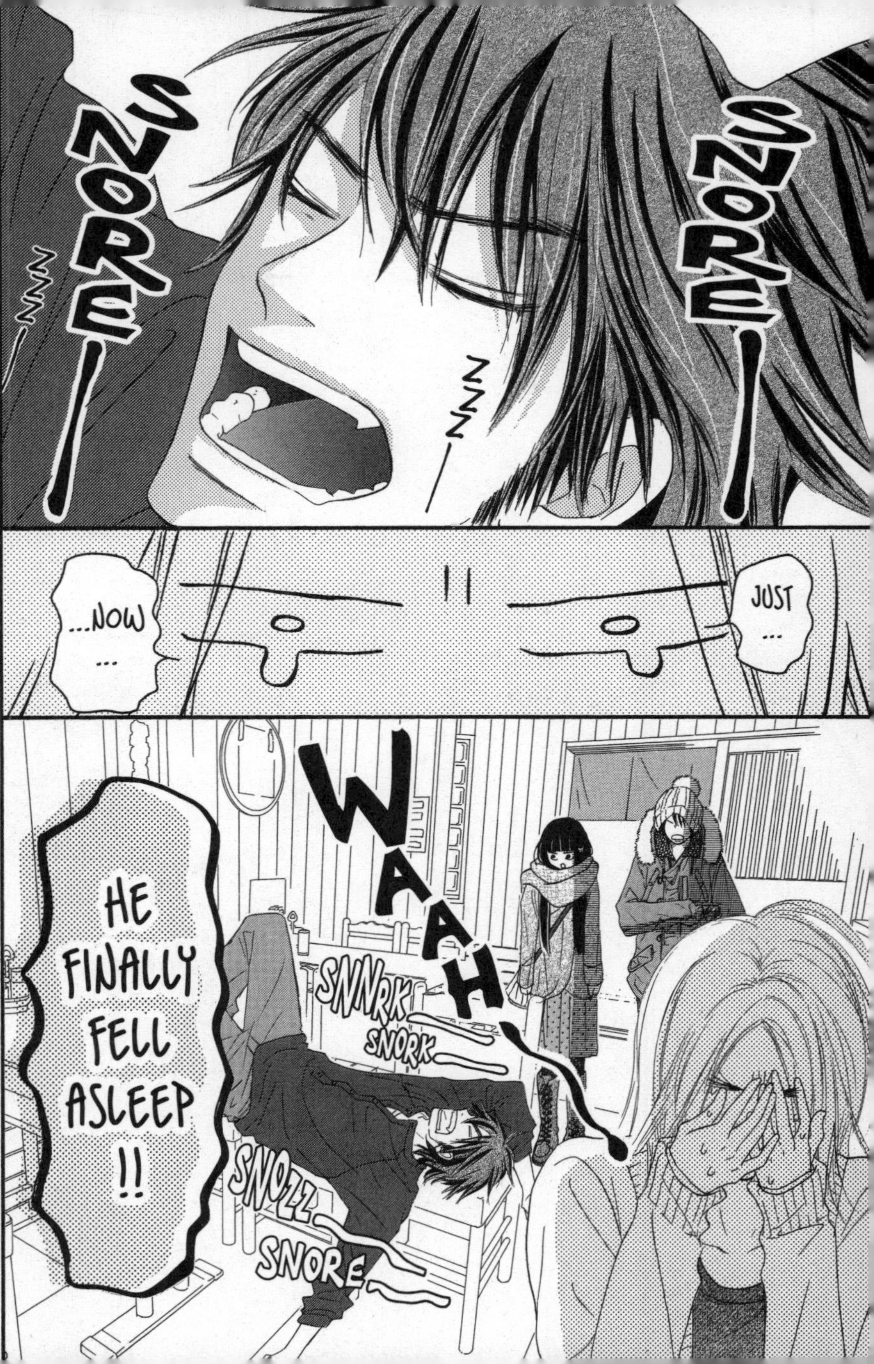
SNORE
ZZZ
SNORE
ZZZ
JUST ...
...NOW ...
WAAAH
SNNRK
SNORK
SNOZZ
SNORE
HE FINALLY FELL ASLEEP !!

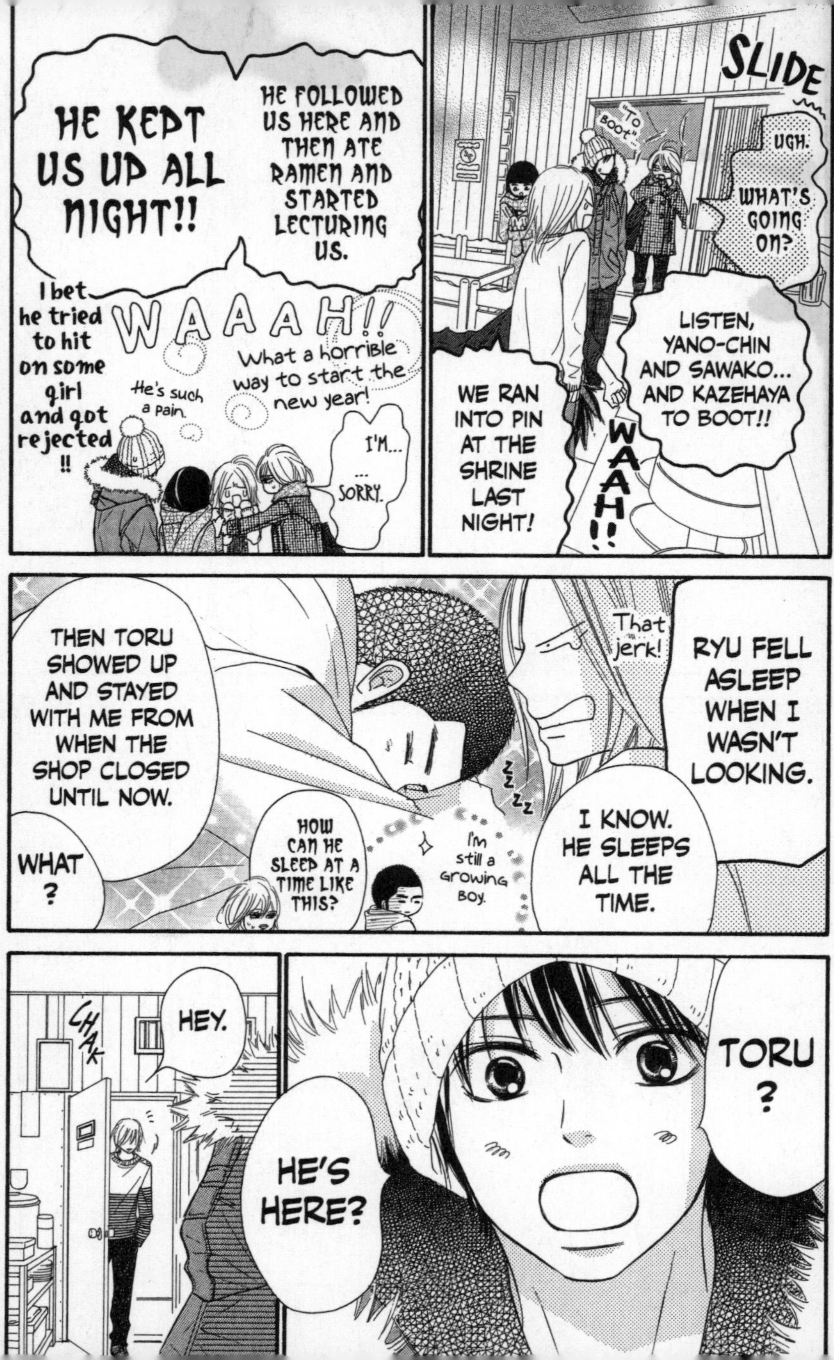
SLIDE
"To boot"...
UGH.
WHAT'S GOING ON?
LISTEN, YANO-CHIN AND SAWAKO... AND KAZEHAYA TO BOOT!!
WAAAH!!
WE RAN INTO PIN AT THE SHRINE LAST NIGHT!
HE FOLLOWED US HERE AND THEN ATE RAMEN AND STARTED LECTURING US.
HE KEPT US UP ALL NIGHT!!
WAAAH!!
I bet he tried to hit on some girl and got rejected!!
What a horrible way to start the new year!
He's such a pain.
I'M... ... SORRY.
RYU FELL ASLEEP WHEN I WASN'T LOOKING.
That jerk!
THEN TORU SHOWED UP AND STAYED WITH ME FROM WHEN THE SHOP CLOSED UNTIL NOW.
I KNOW. HE SLEEPS ALL THE TIME.
ZZZ
I'm still a growing boy.
HOW CAN HE SLEEP AT A TIME LIKE THIS?
WHAT?
TORU?
HE'S HERE?
CHAK
HEY.

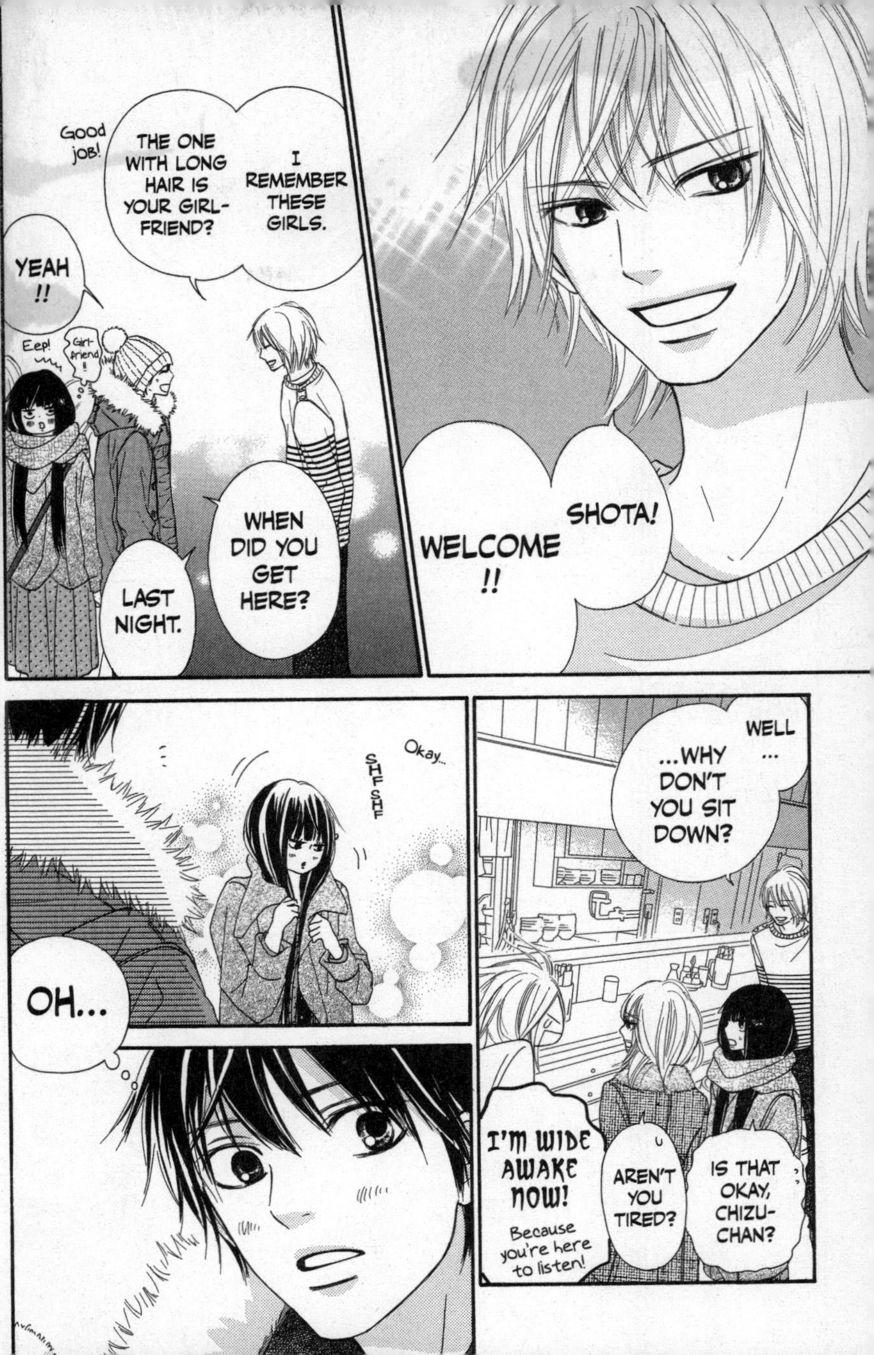
WELCOME SHOTA!!
I REMEMBER THESE GIRLS.
THE ONE WITH LONG HAIR IS YOUR GIRL-FRIEND?
Good job!
YEAH!!
Girl-friend!!
Eep!
WHEN DID YOU GET HERE?
LAST NIGHT.
WELL...
...WHY DON'T YOU SIT DOWN?
IS THAT OKAY, CHIZU-CHAN?
AREN'T YOU TIRED?
I'M WIDE AWAKE NOW!
Because you're here to listen!
Okay...
SHF SHF
OH...

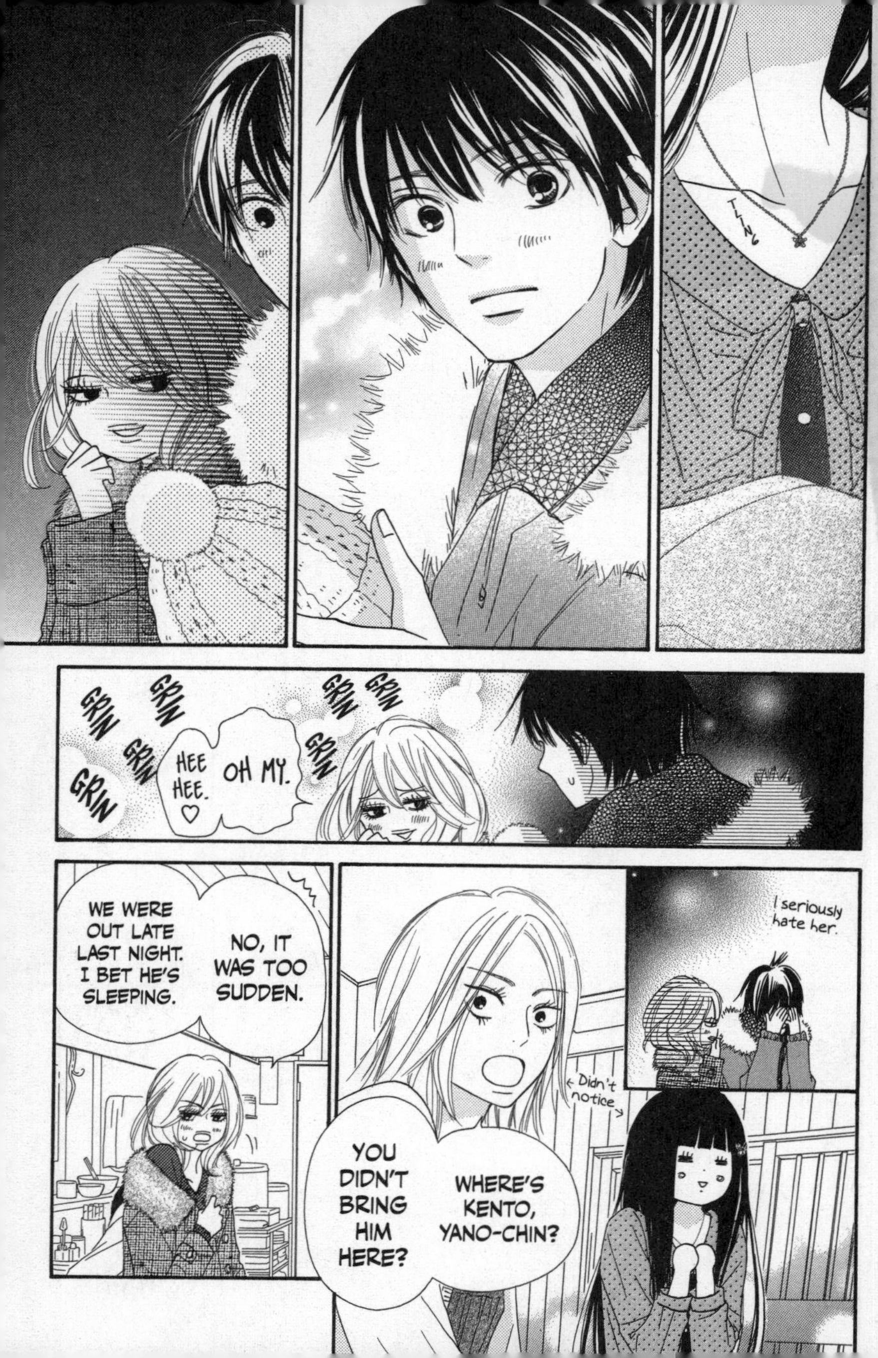
TWING
GRIN GRIN
GRIN
OH MY.
HEE HEE. ♡
GRIN GRIN GRIN
I seriously hate her.
WHERE'S KENTO, YANO-CHIN?
YOU DIDN'T BRING HIM HERE?
← Didn't notice →
NO, IT WAS TOO SUDDEN.
WE WERE OUT LATE LAST NIGHT. I BET HE'S SLEEPING.

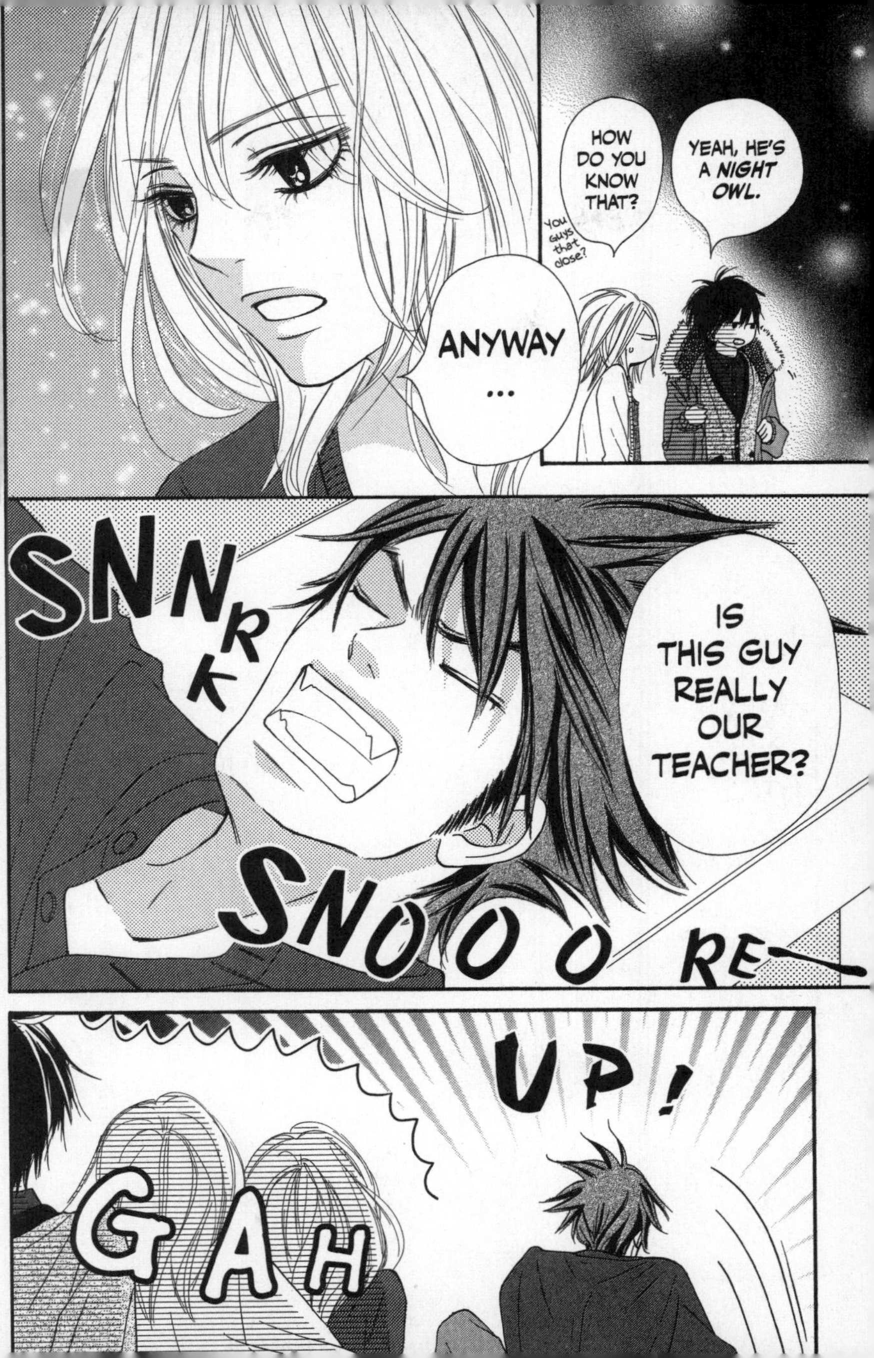
YEAH, HE'S A NIGHT OWL.
HOW DO YOU KNOW THAT?
You guys that close?
ANYWAY ...
IS THIS GUY REALLY OUR TEACHER?
SNNRK
SNOOORE—
UP!
GAH

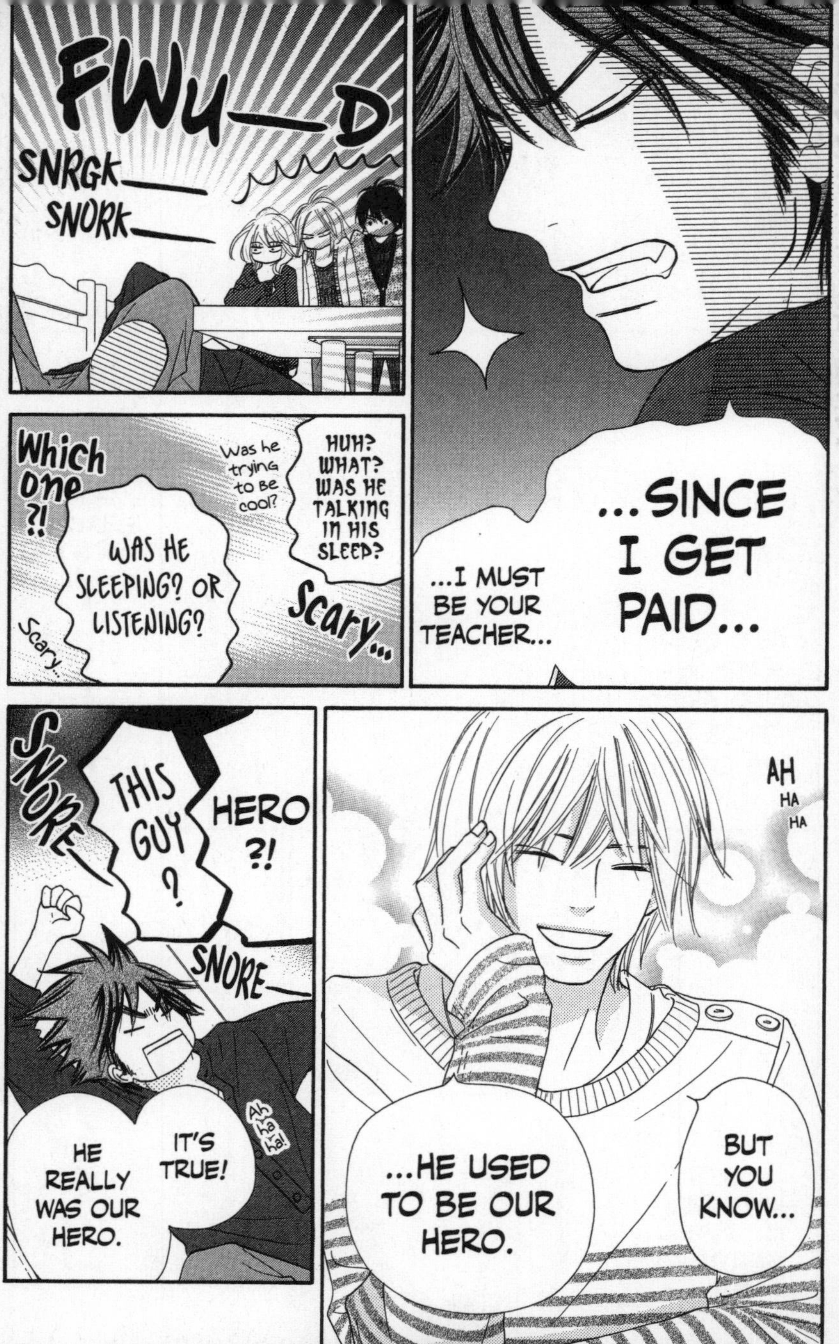
...SINCE I GET PAID...
...I MUST BE YOUR TEACHER...
FWU—D
SNRGK—
SNORK—
HUH? WHAT? WAS HE TALKING IN HIS SLEEP?
Was he trying to be cool?
Which one ?!
WAS HE SLEEPING? OR LISTENING?
Scary...
Scary...
AH HA HA
BUT YOU KNOW...
...HE USED TO BE OUR HERO.
HERO ?!
THIS GUY ?
SNORE—
SNORE—
Ah ha ha!
IT'S TRUE!
HE REALLY WAS OUR HERO.

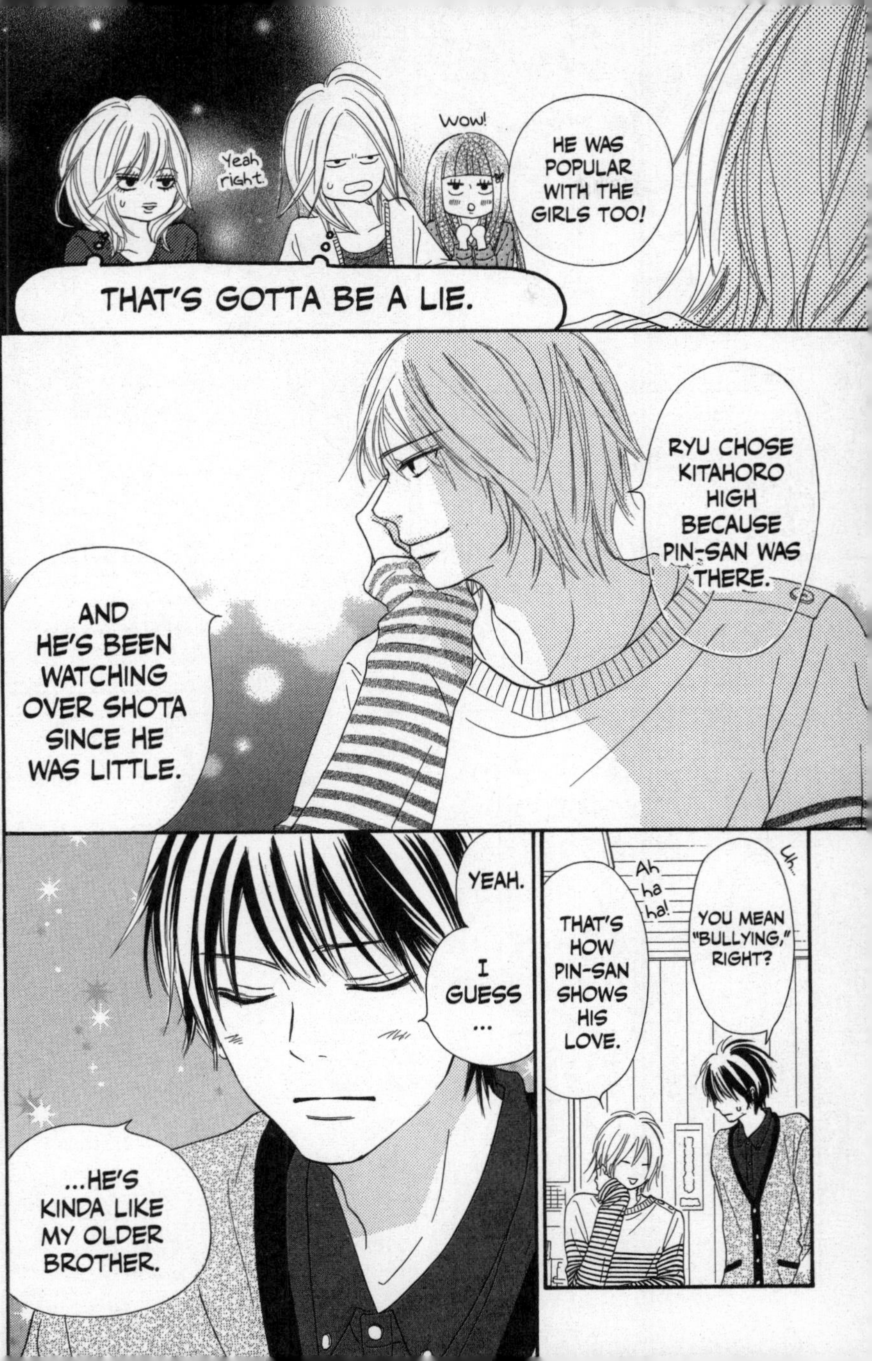
HE WAS POPULAR WITH THE GIRLS TOO!
Wow!
Yeah right.
THAT'S GOTTA BE A LIE.
RYU CHOSE KITAHORO HIGH BECAUSE PIN-SAN WAS THERE.
AND HE'S BEEN WATCHING OVER SHOTA SINCE HE WAS LITTLE.
Uh...
YOU MEAN "BULLYING," RIGHT?
Ah ha ha!
THAT'S HOW PIN-SAN SHOWS HIS LOVE.
YEAH.
I GUESS...
...HE'S KINDA LIKE MY OLDER BROTHER.

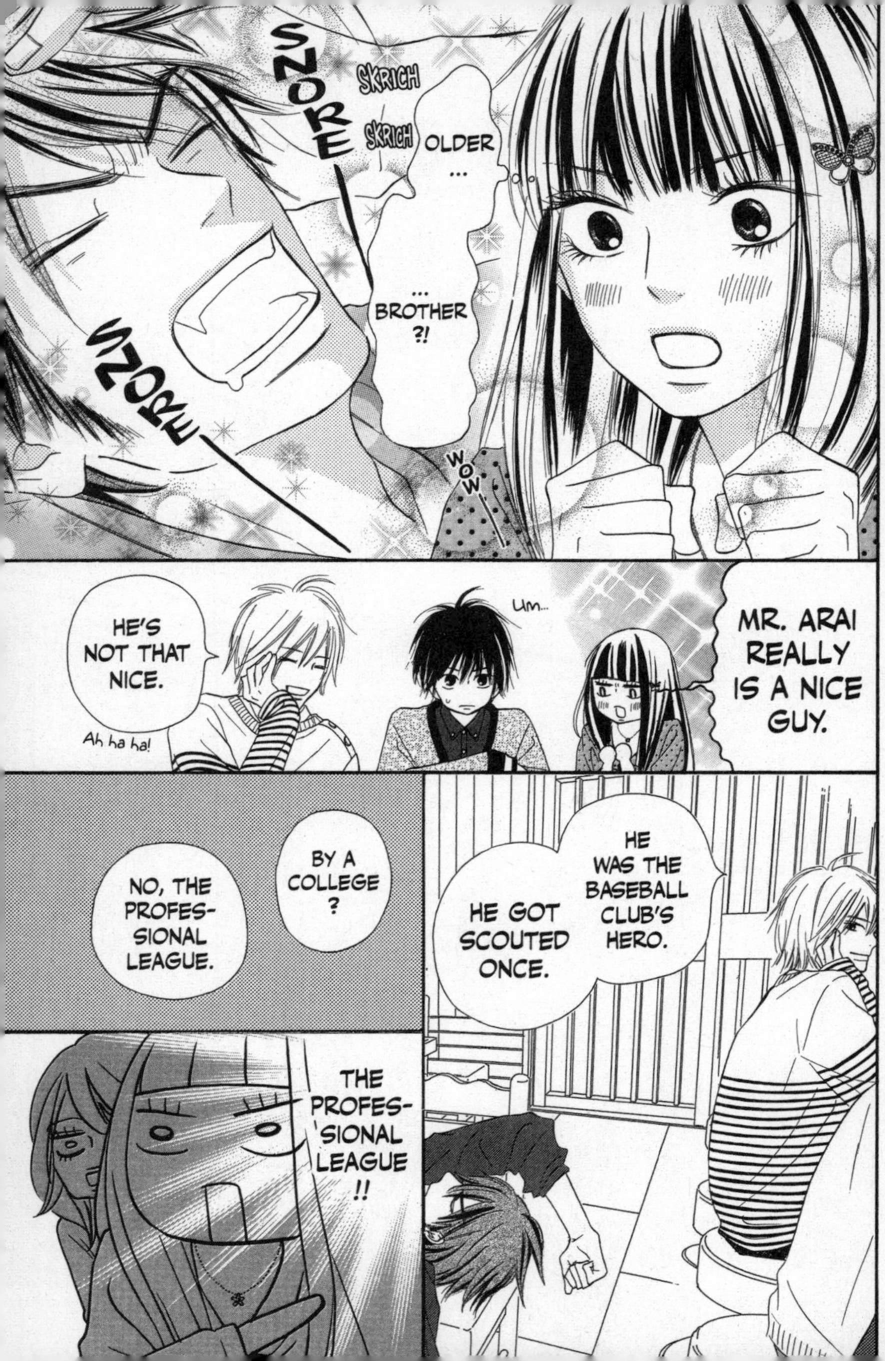
OLDER ...
... BROTHER ?!
SKRICH
SKRICH
SNORE
WOW
SNORE
MR. ARAI REALLY IS A NICE GUY.
Um...
HE'S NOT THAT NICE.
Ah ha ha!
HE WAS THE BASEBALL CLUB'S HERO.
HE GOT SCOUTED ONCE.
BY A COLLEGE?
NO, THE PROFESSIONAL LEAGUE.
THE PROFESSIONAL LEAGUE!!

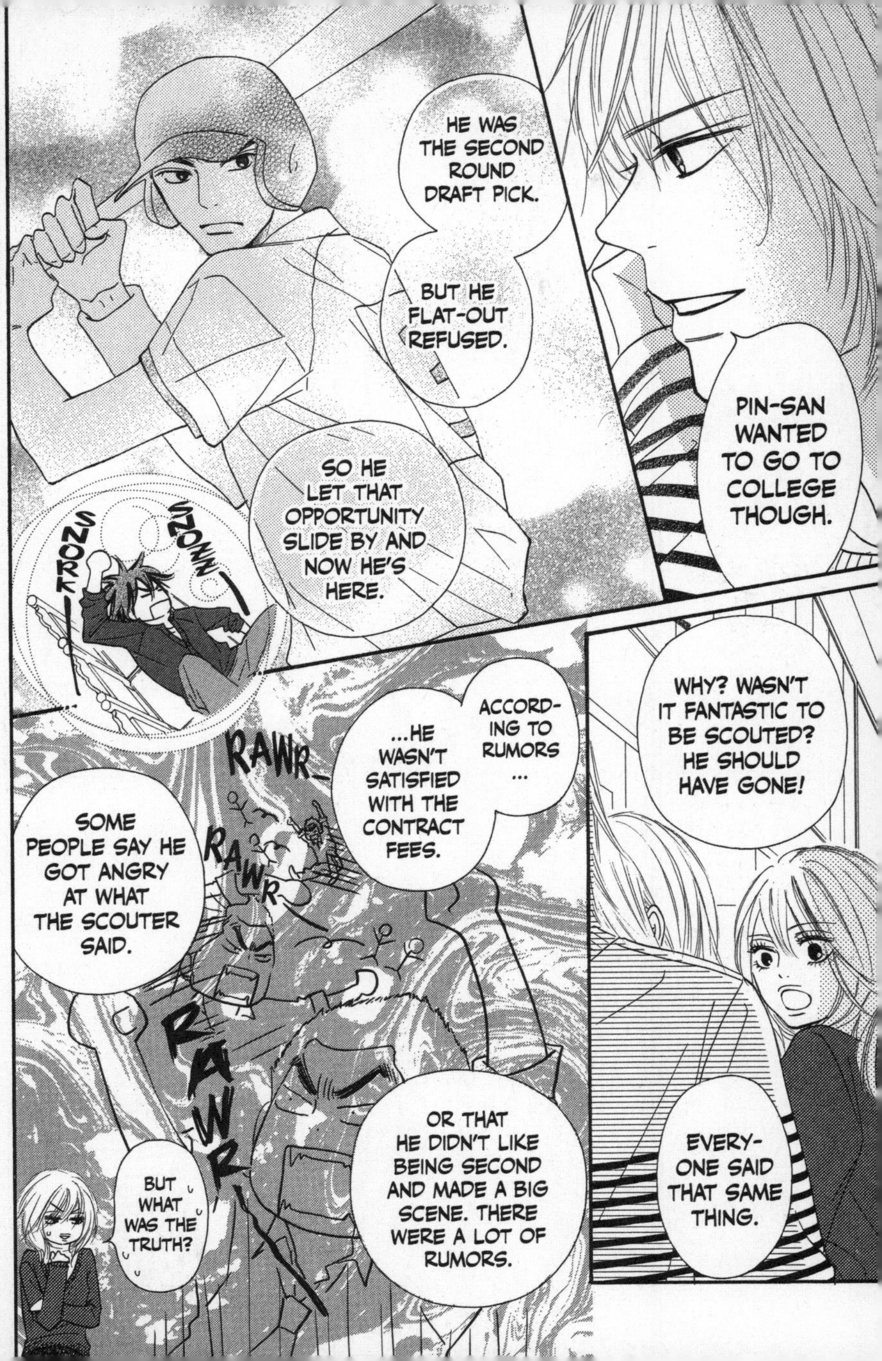
PIN-SAN WANTED TO GO TO COLLEGE THOUGH.
HE WAS THE SECOND ROUND DRAFT PICK.
BUT HE FLAT-OUT REFUSED.
SO HE LET THAT OPPORTUNITY SLIDE BY AND NOW HE'S HERE.
SNORK—
SNOZZ—
WHY? WASN'T IT FANTASTIC TO BE SCOUTED? HE SHOULD HAVE GONE!
EVERY-ONE SAID THAT SAME THING.
ACCORD-ING TO RUMORS ...
...HE WASN'T SATISFIED WITH THE CONTRACT FEES.
RAWR—
RAWR
SOME PEOPLE SAY HE GOT ANGRY AT WHAT THE SCOUTER SAID.
RAWR
OR THAT HE DIDN'T LIKE BEING SECOND AND MADE A BIG SCENE. THERE WERE A LOT OF RUMORS.
BUT WHAT WAS THE TRUTH?

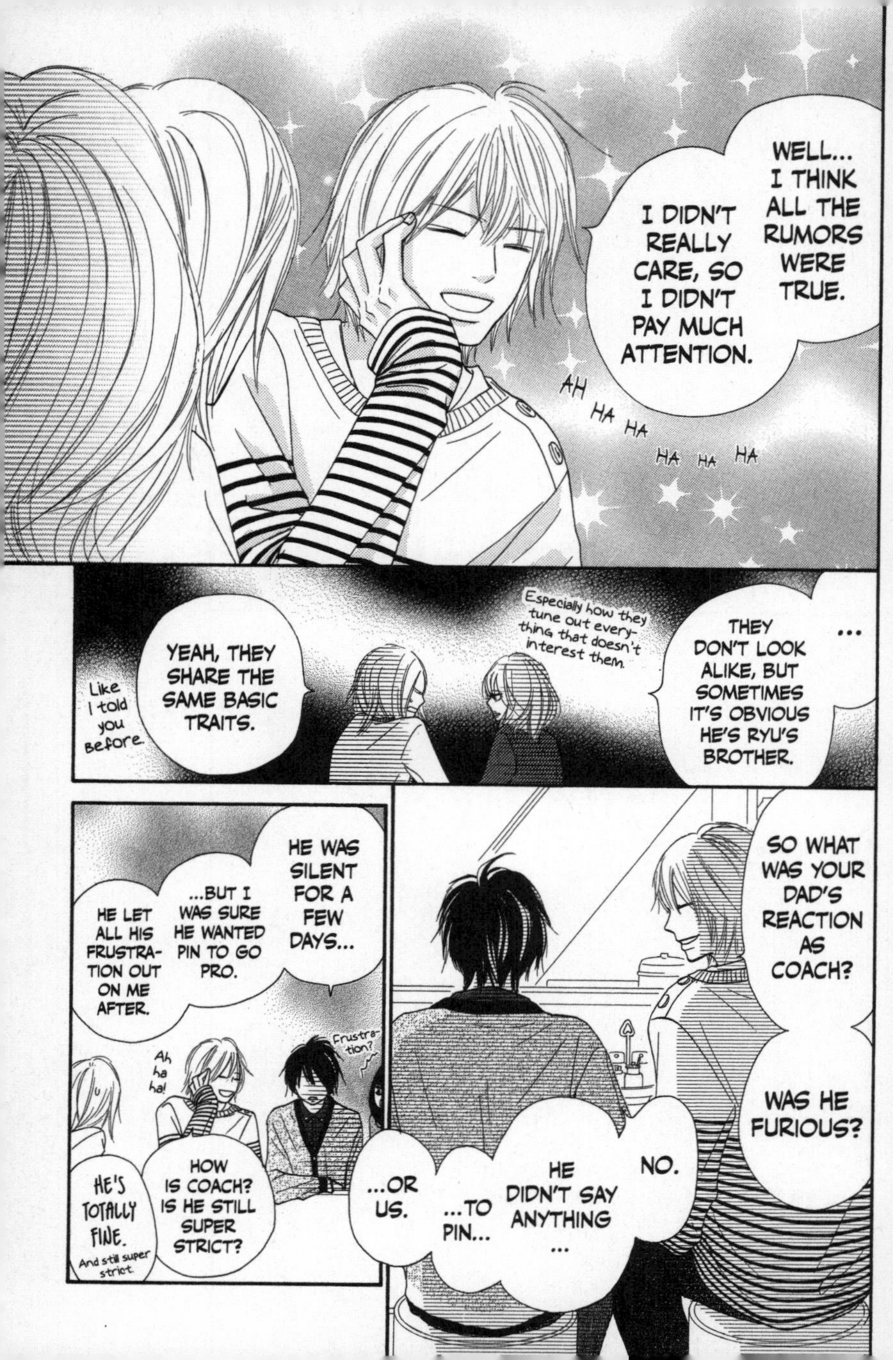
WELL... I THINK ALL THE RUMORS WERE TRUE.
I DIDN'T REALLY CARE, SO I DIDN'T PAY MUCH ATTENTION.
AH HA HA HA HA HA
...
THEY DON'T LOOK ALIKE, BUT SOMETIMES IT'S OBVIOUS HE'S RYU'S BROTHER.
Especially how they tune out every-thing that doesn't interest them.
YEAH, THEY SHARE THE SAME BASIC TRAITS.
Like I told you before.
SO WHAT WAS YOUR DAD'S REACTION AS COACH?
WAS HE FURIOUS?
NO.
HE DIDN'T SAY ANYTHING ...
...TO PIN...
...OR US.
HE WAS SILENT FOR A FEW DAYS...
...BUT I WAS SURE HE WANTED PIN TO GO PRO.
HE LET ALL HIS FRUSTRA-TION OUT ON ME AFTER.
Frustra-tion?
Ah ha ha!
HOW IS COACH? IS HE STILL SUPER STRICT?
HE'S TOTALLY FINE.
And still super strict.

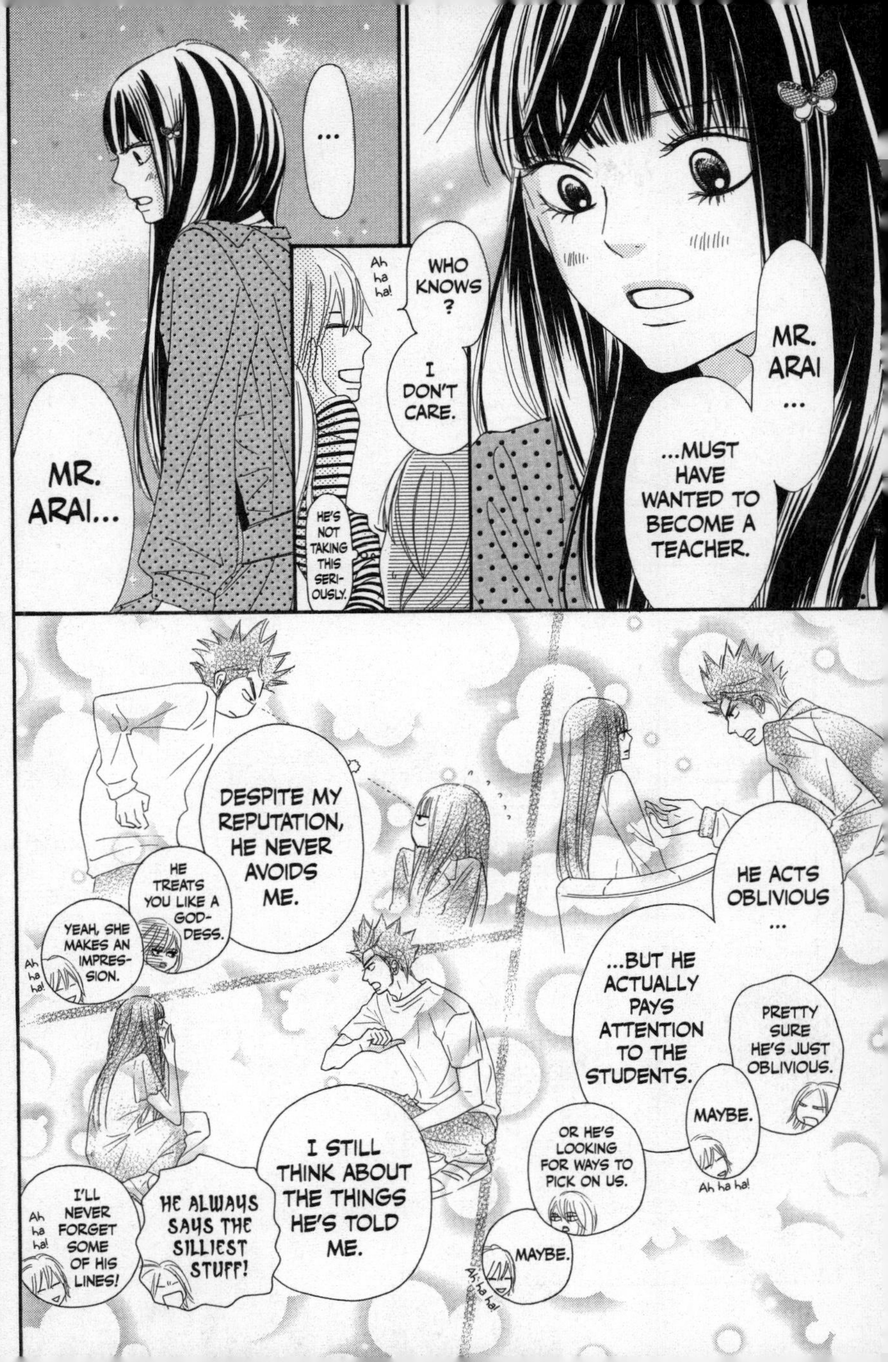
MR. ARAI ...
...MUST HAVE WANTED TO BECOME A TEACHER.
WHO KNOWS?
Ah ha ha!
I DON'T CARE.
HE'S NOT TAKING THIS SERI-OUSLY.
...
MR. ARAI...
HE ACTS OBLIVIOUS ...
...BUT HE ACTUALLY PAYS ATTENTION TO THE STUDENTS.
PRETTY SURE HE'S JUST OBLIVIOUS.
MAYBE.
Ah ha ha!
OR HE'S LOOKING FOR WAYS TO PICK ON US.
MAYBE.
Ah ha ha!
DESPITE MY REPUTATION, HE NEVER AVOIDS ME.
HE TREATS YOU LIKE A GOD-DESS.
YEAH, SHE MAKES AN IMPRES-SION.
Ah ha ha!
I STILL THINK ABOUT THE THINGS HE'S TOLD ME.
HE ALWAYS SAYS THE SILLIEST STUFF!
I'LL NEVER FORGET SOME OF HIS LINES!
Ah ha ha!

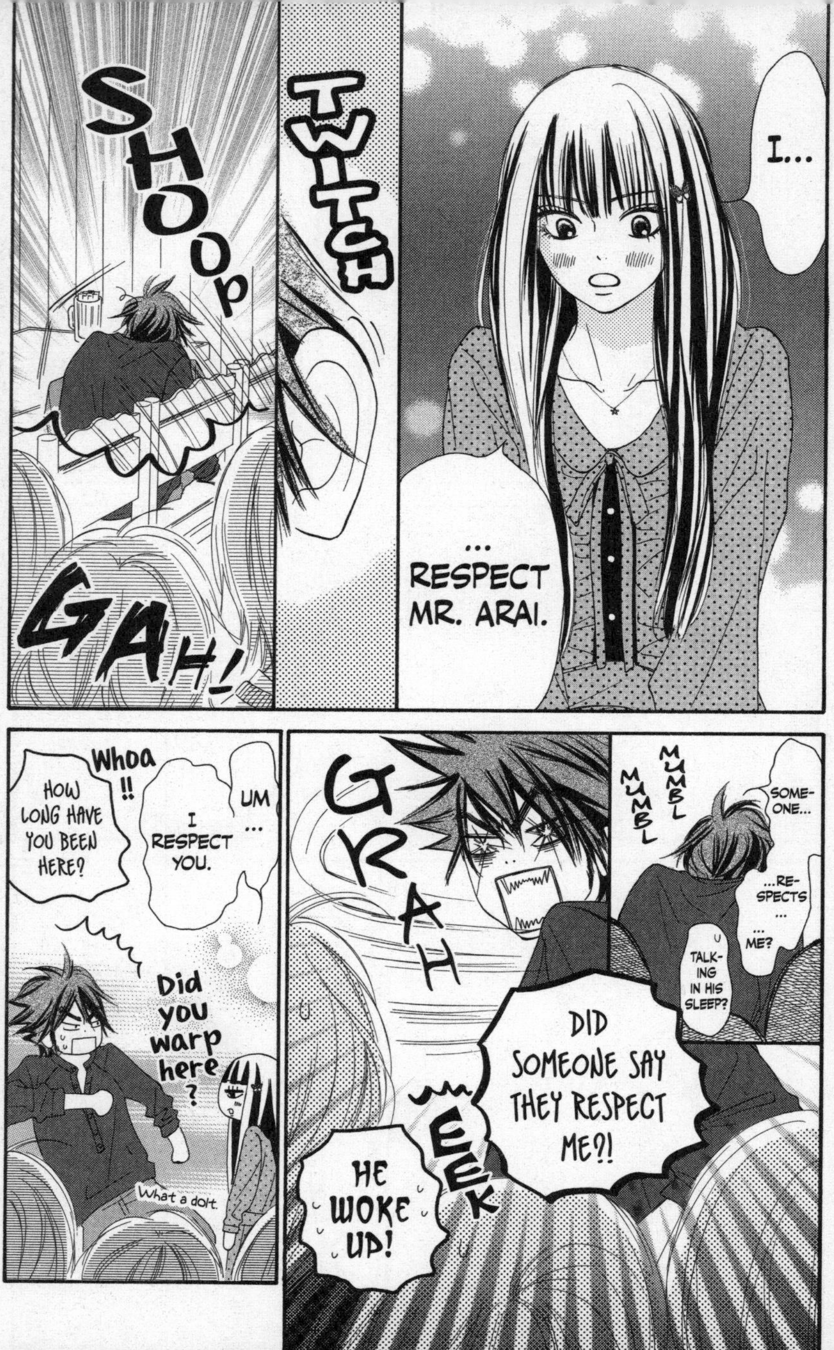
I...
...RESPECT MR. ARAI.
TWITCH
SHOOOp
GAH!
MUMBL MUMBL
SOME-ONE...
...RE-SPECTS... ...ME?
TALK-ING IN HIS SLEEP?
GRAH
DID SOMEONE SAY THEY RESPECT ME?!
EEEK
HE WOKE UP!
UM...
I RESPECT YOU.
Whoa!!
HOW LONG HAVE YOU BEEN HERE?
Did you warp here?
What a dolt.

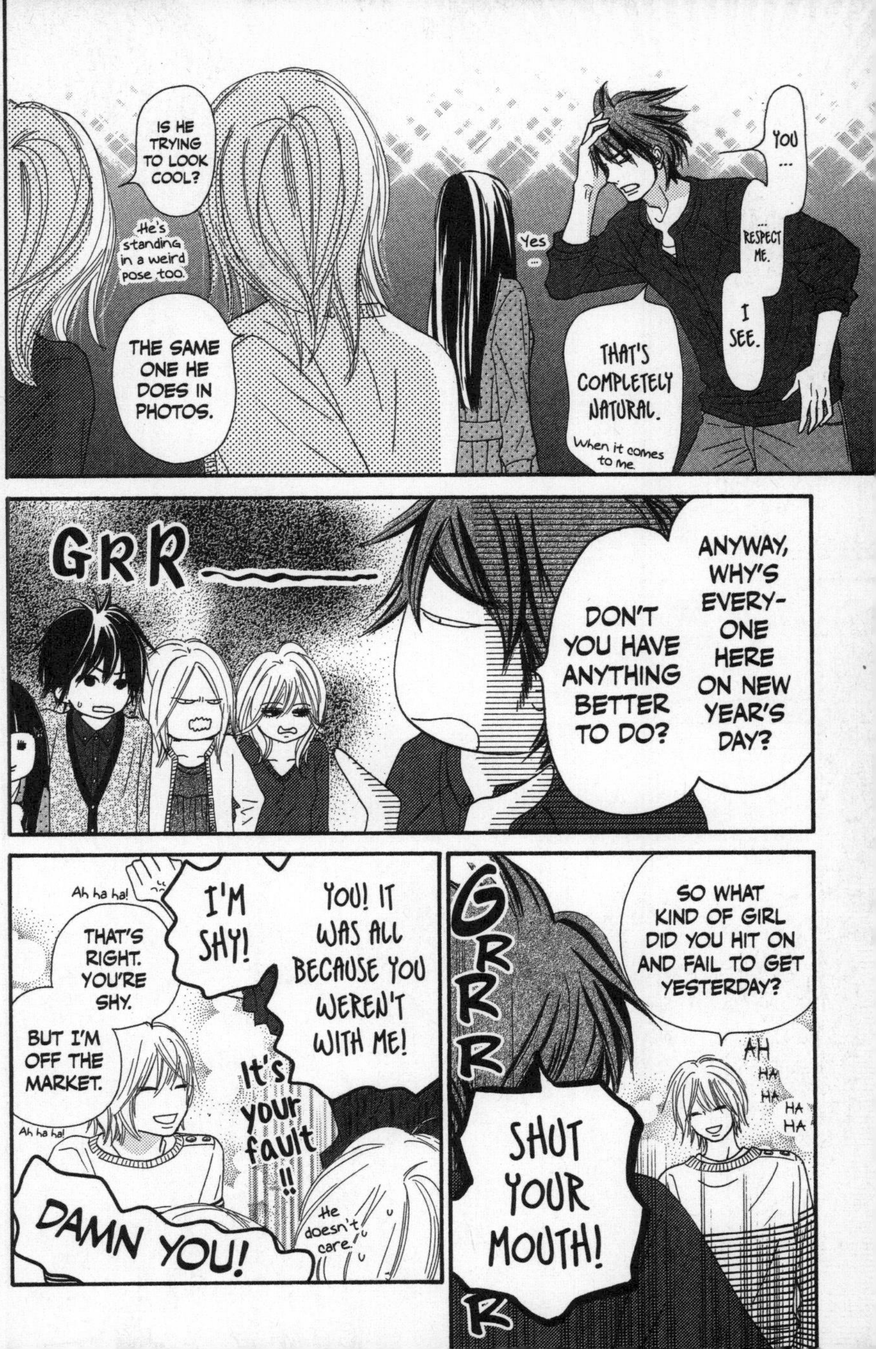
YOU ...
... RESPECT ME.
I SEE.
THAT'S COMPLETELY NATURAL.
When it comes to me.
Yes ...
IS HE TRYING TO LOOK COOL?
He's standing in a weird pose too.
THE SAME ONE HE DOES IN PHOTOS.
ANYWAY, WHY'S EVERYONE HERE ON NEW YEAR'S DAY?
DON'T YOU HAVE ANYTHING BETTER TO DO?
GRR
SO WHAT KIND OF GIRL DID YOU HIT ON AND FAIL TO GET YESTERDAY?
AH HA HA HA HA
GRRRR
SHUT YOUR MOUTH!
YOU! IT WAS ALL BECAUSE YOU WEREN'T WITH ME!
I'M SHY!
Ah ha ha!
THAT'S RIGHT. YOU'RE SHY.
BUT I'M OFF THE MARKET.
Ah ha ha!
It's your fault!!
He doesn't care.
DAMN YOU!

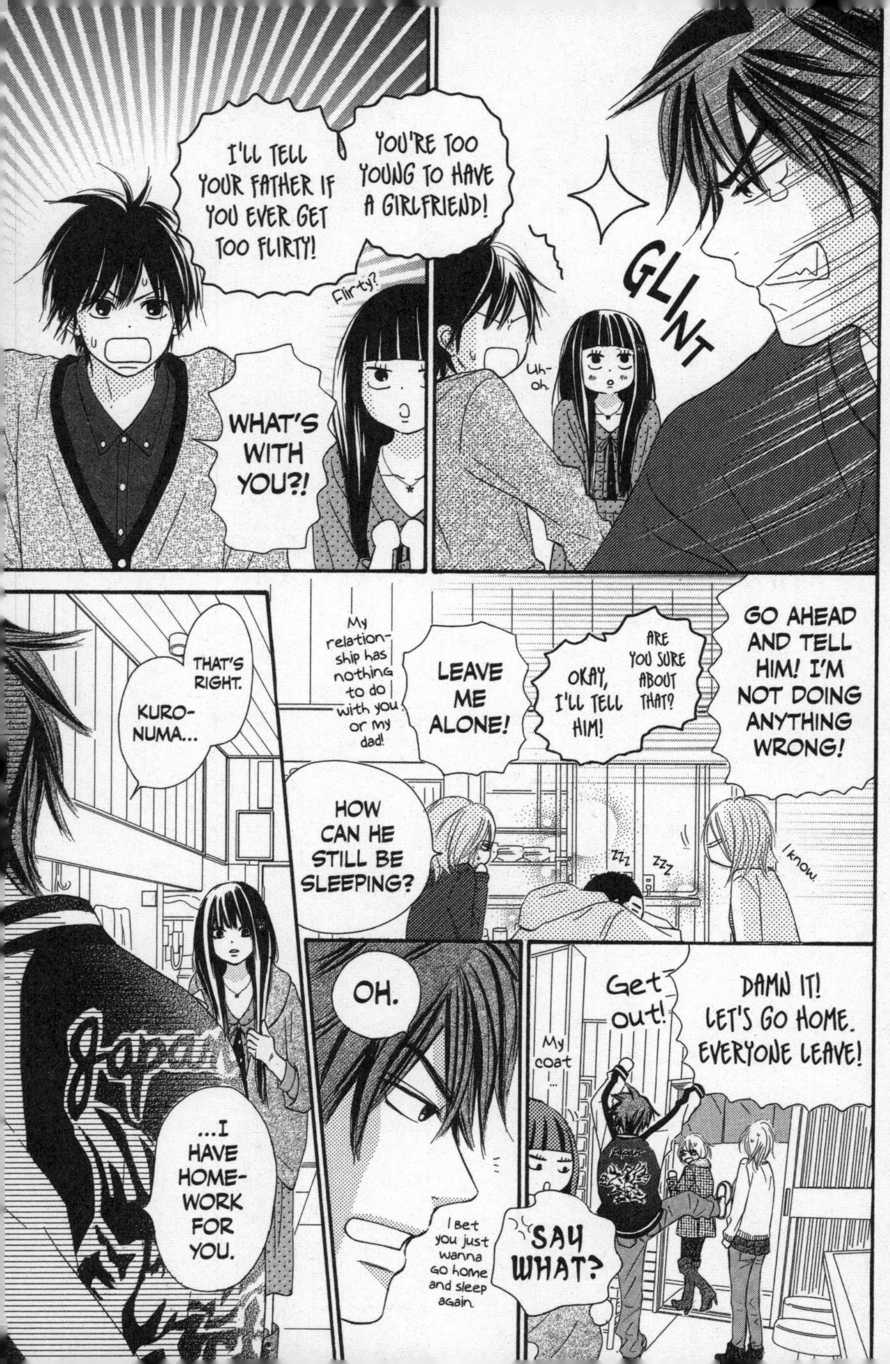

GLINT
Uh-oh.
YOU'RE TOO YOUNG TO HAVE A GIRLFRIEND!
I'LL TELL YOUR FATHER IF YOU EVER GET TOO FLIRTY!
Flirty?
WHAT'S WITH YOU?!
GO AHEAD AND TELL HIM! I'M NOT DOING ANYTHING WRONG!
ARE YOU SURE ABOUT THAT?
OKAY, I'LL TELL HIM!
LEAVE ME ALONE!
My relationship has nothing to do with you or my dad!
I know.
ZZZ
ZZZ
HOW CAN HE STILL BE SLEEPING?
DAMN IT! LET'S GO HOME. EVERYONE LEAVE!
Get out!
My coat!...
SAY WHAT?
I bet you just wanna go home and sleep again.
OH.
THAT'S RIGHT.
KURONUMA...
...I HAVE HOMEWORK FOR YOU.

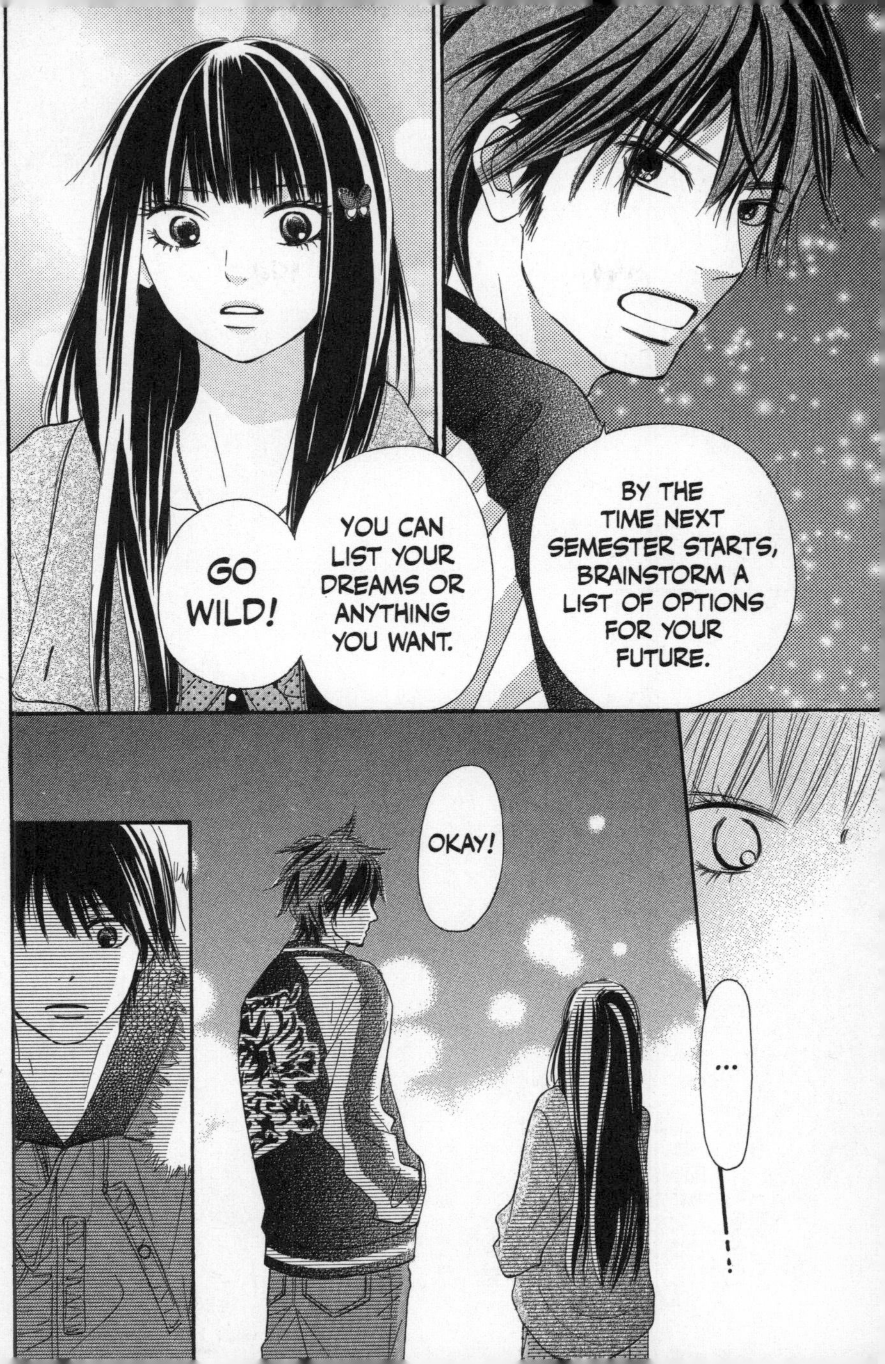
BY THE TIME NEXT SEMESTER STARTS, BRAINSTORM A LIST OF OPTIONS FOR YOUR FUTURE.
YOU CAN LIST YOUR DREAMS OR ANYTHING YOU WANT.
GO WILD!
OKAY!
...

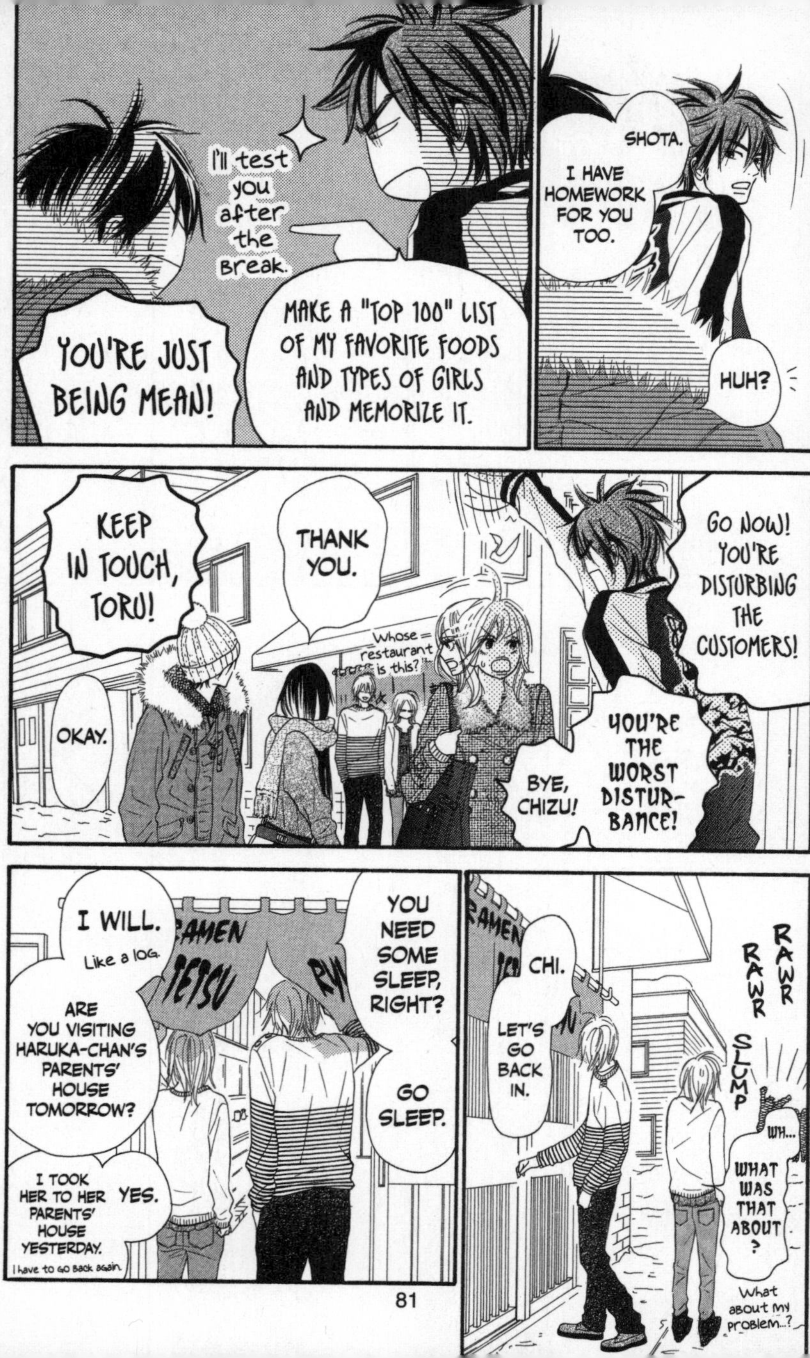
SHOTA.
I HAVE HOMEWORK FOR YOU TOO.
HUH?
I'll test you after the break.
MAKE A "TOP 100" LIST OF MY FAVORITE FOODS AND TYPES OF GIRLS AND MEMORIZE IT.
YOU'RE JUST BEING MEAN!
GO NOW! YOU'RE DISTURBING THE CUSTOMERS!
YOU'RE THE WORST DISTURBANCE!
BYE, CHIZU!
Whose restaurant is this?
THANK YOU.
KEEP IN TOUCH, TORU!
OKAY.
RAWR RAWR
SLUMP
CHI.
LET'S GO BACK IN.
WH...
WHAT WAS THAT ABOUT?
What about my problem...?
RAMEN TETSU
YOU NEED SOME SLEEP, RIGHT?
I WILL.
Like a log.
ARE YOU VISITING HARUKA-CHAN'S PARENTS' HOUSE TOMORROW?
GO SLEEP.
YES.
I TOOK HER TO HER PARENTS' HOUSE YESTERDAY.
I have to go back again.

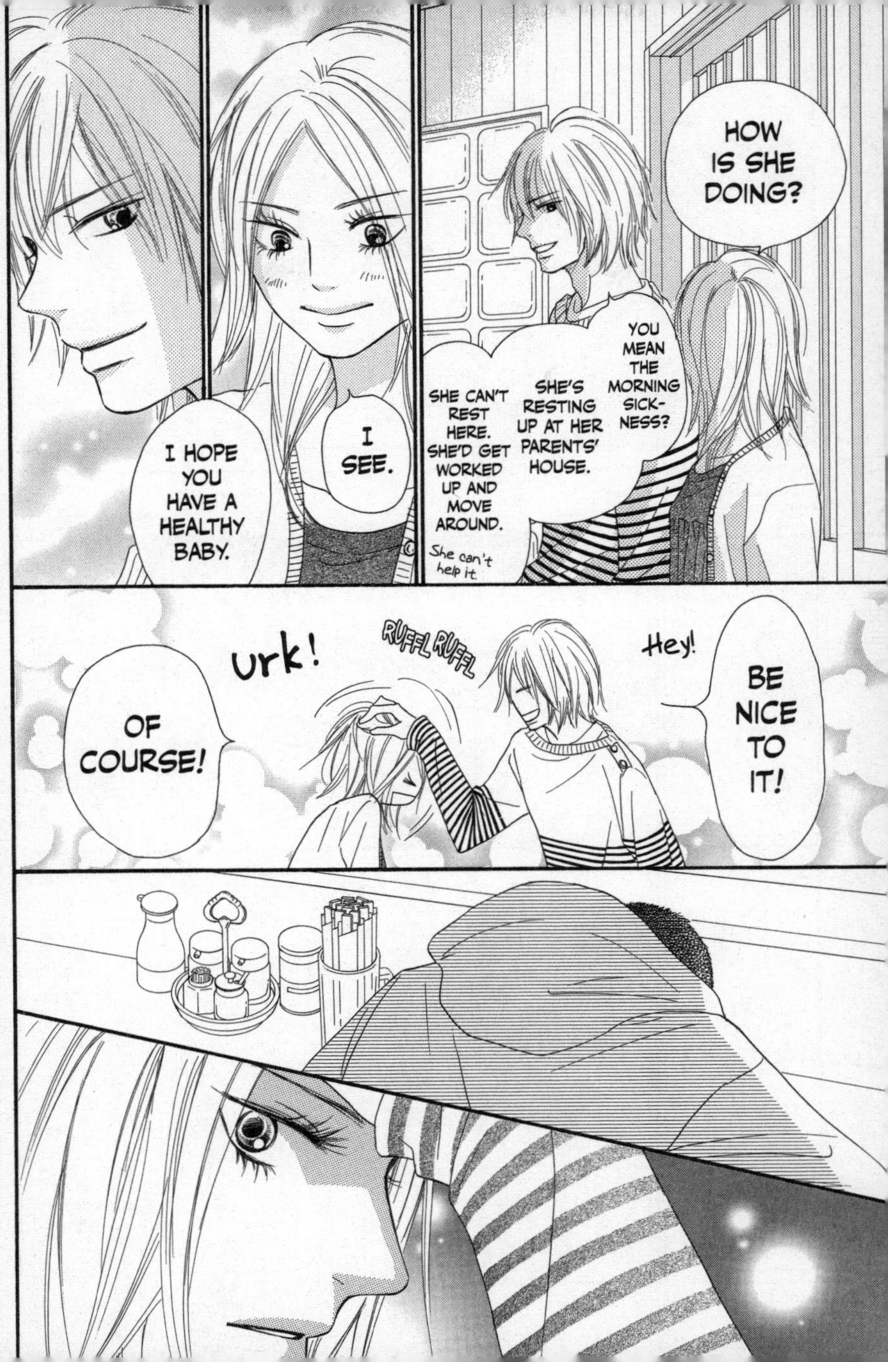
HOW IS SHE DOING?
YOU MEAN THE MORNING SICK-NESS?
SHE'S RESTING UP AT HER PARENTS' HOUSE.
SHE CAN'T REST HERE. SHE'D GET WORKED UP AND MOVE AROUND.
She can't help it.
I SEE.
I HOPE YOU HAVE A HEALTHY BABY.
BE NICE TO IT!
Hey!
RUFFL RUFFL
Urk!
OF COURSE!

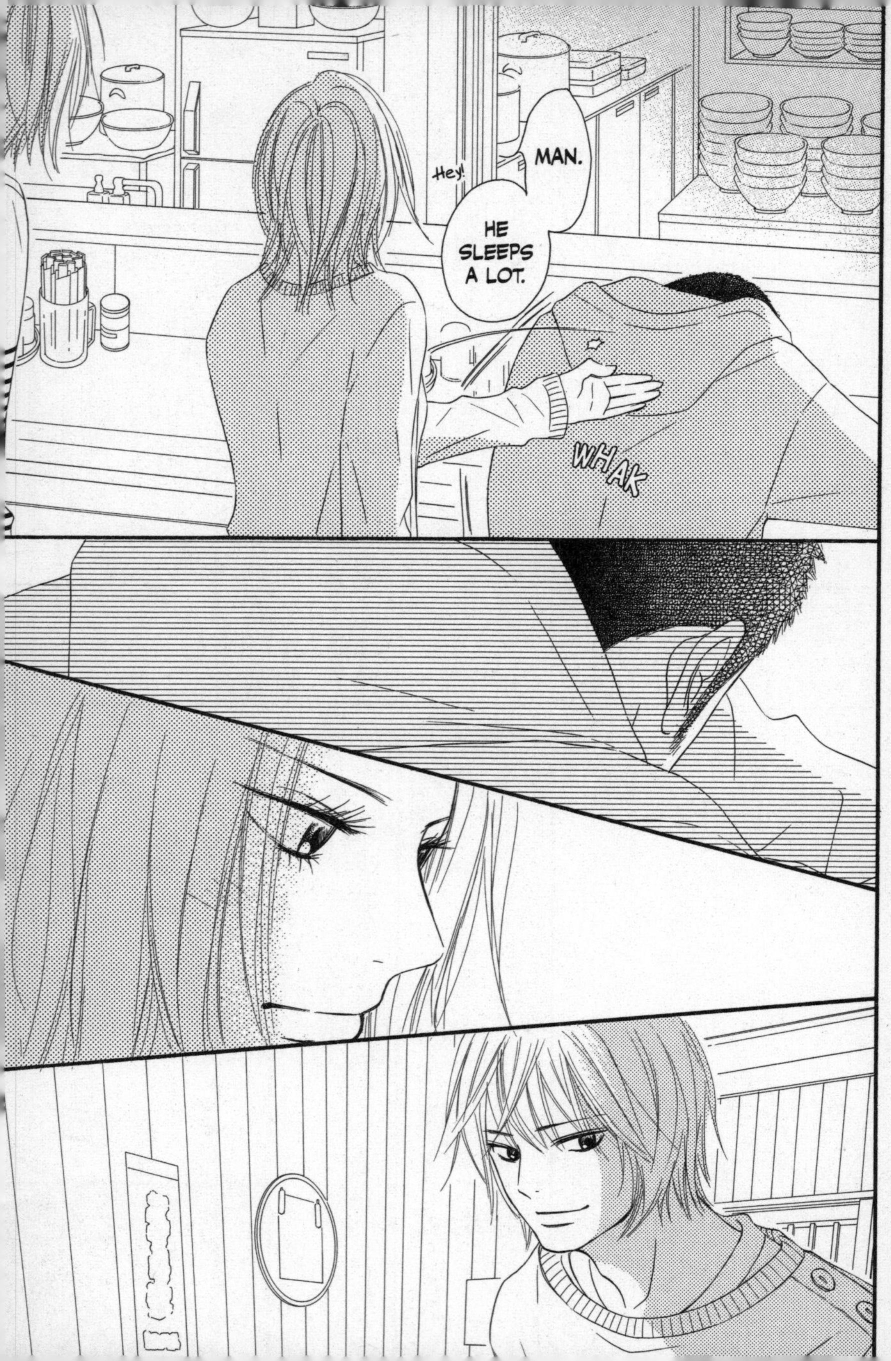
MAN.
HE SLEEPS A LOT.
Hey!
WHAK

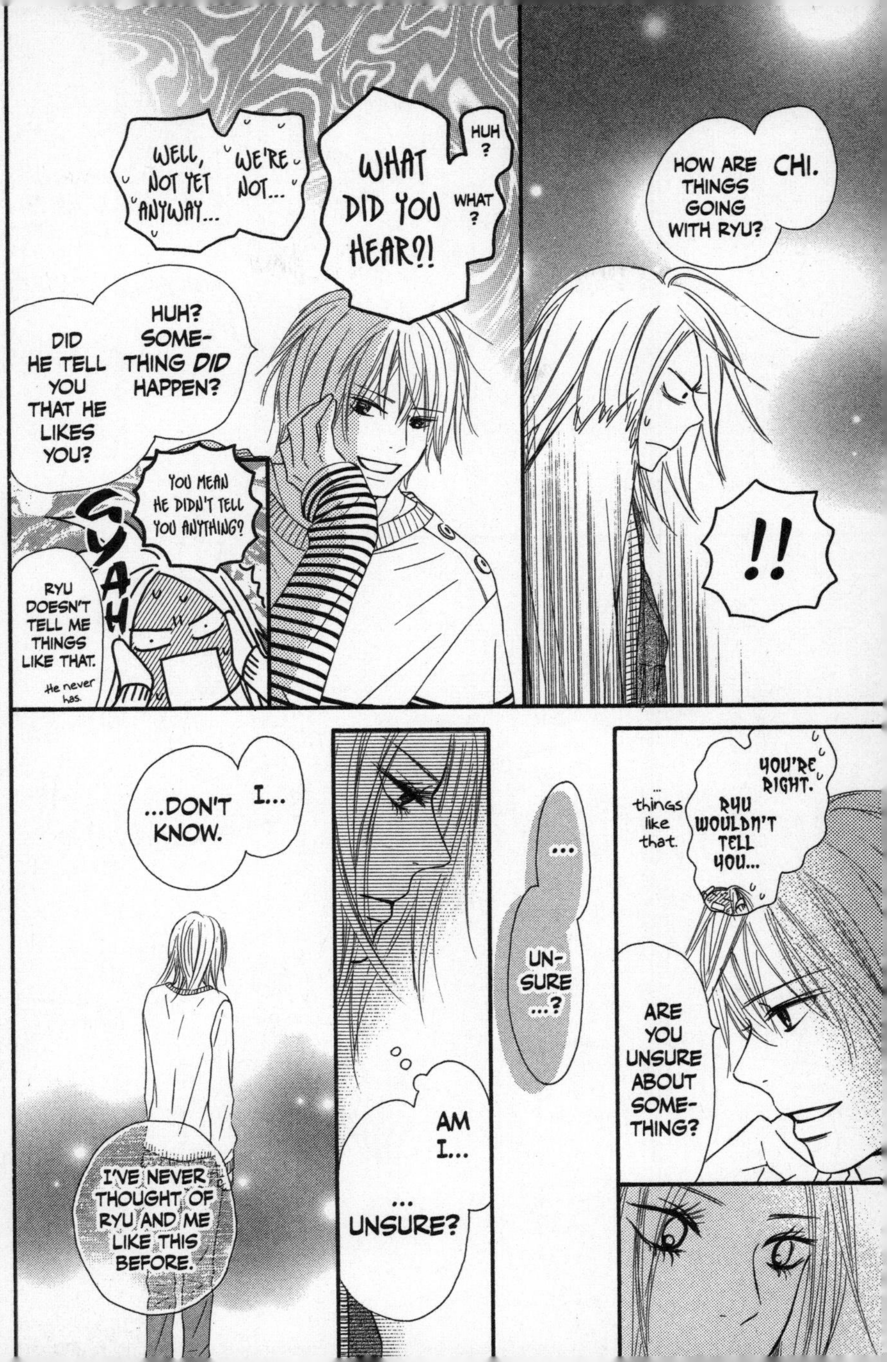
CHI.
HOW ARE THINGS GOING WITH RYU?
!!
HUH? WHAT?
WHAT DID YOU HEAR?!
WE'RE NOT...
WELL, NOT YET ANYWAY...
HUH? SOMETHING *DID* HAPPEN?
DID HE TELL YOU THAT HE LIKES YOU?
YOU MEAN HE DIDN'T TELL YOU ANYTHING?
SYAH
RYU DOESN'T TELL ME THINGS LIKE THAT.
He never has.
YOU'RE RIGHT. RYU WOULDN'T TELL YOU...
... things like that.
ARE YOU UNSURE ABOUT SOMETHING?
...
UN-SURE ...?
AM I...
... UNSURE?
I...
...DON'T KNOW.
I'VE NEVER THOUGHT OF RYU AND ME LIKE THIS BEFORE.

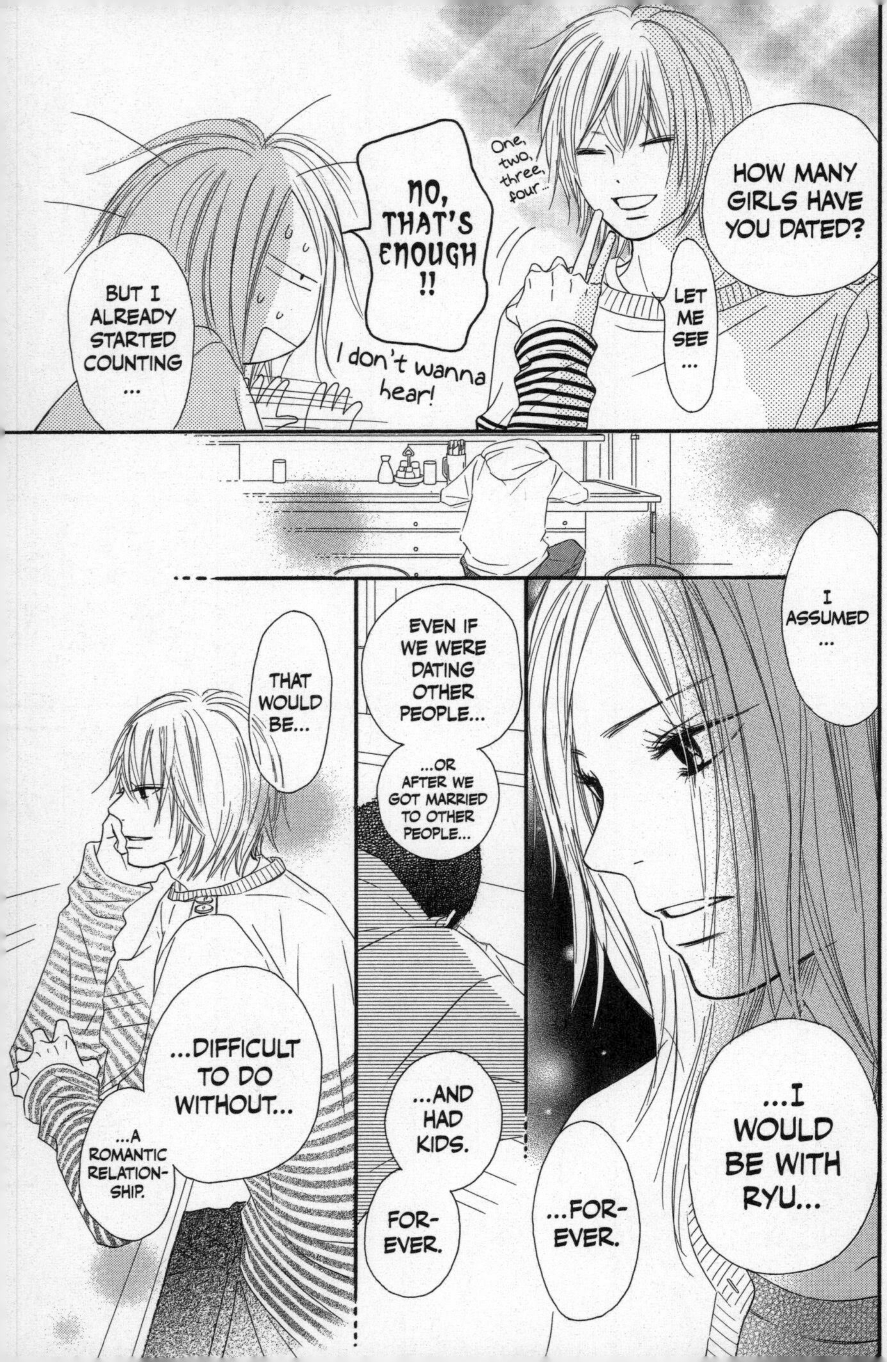
HOW MANY GIRLS HAVE YOU DATED?
LET ME SEE ...
One, two, three, four...
NO, THAT'S ENOUGH !!
I don't wanna hear!
BUT I ALREADY STARTED COUNTING ...
I ASSUMED ...
...I WOULD BE WITH RYU...
...FOR-EVER.
EVEN IF WE WERE DATING OTHER PEOPLE...
...OR AFTER WE GOT MARRIED TO OTHER PEOPLE...
...AND HAD KIDS.
FOR-EVER.
THAT WOULD BE...
...DIFFICULT TO DO WITHOUT...
...A ROMANTIC RELATION-SHIP.

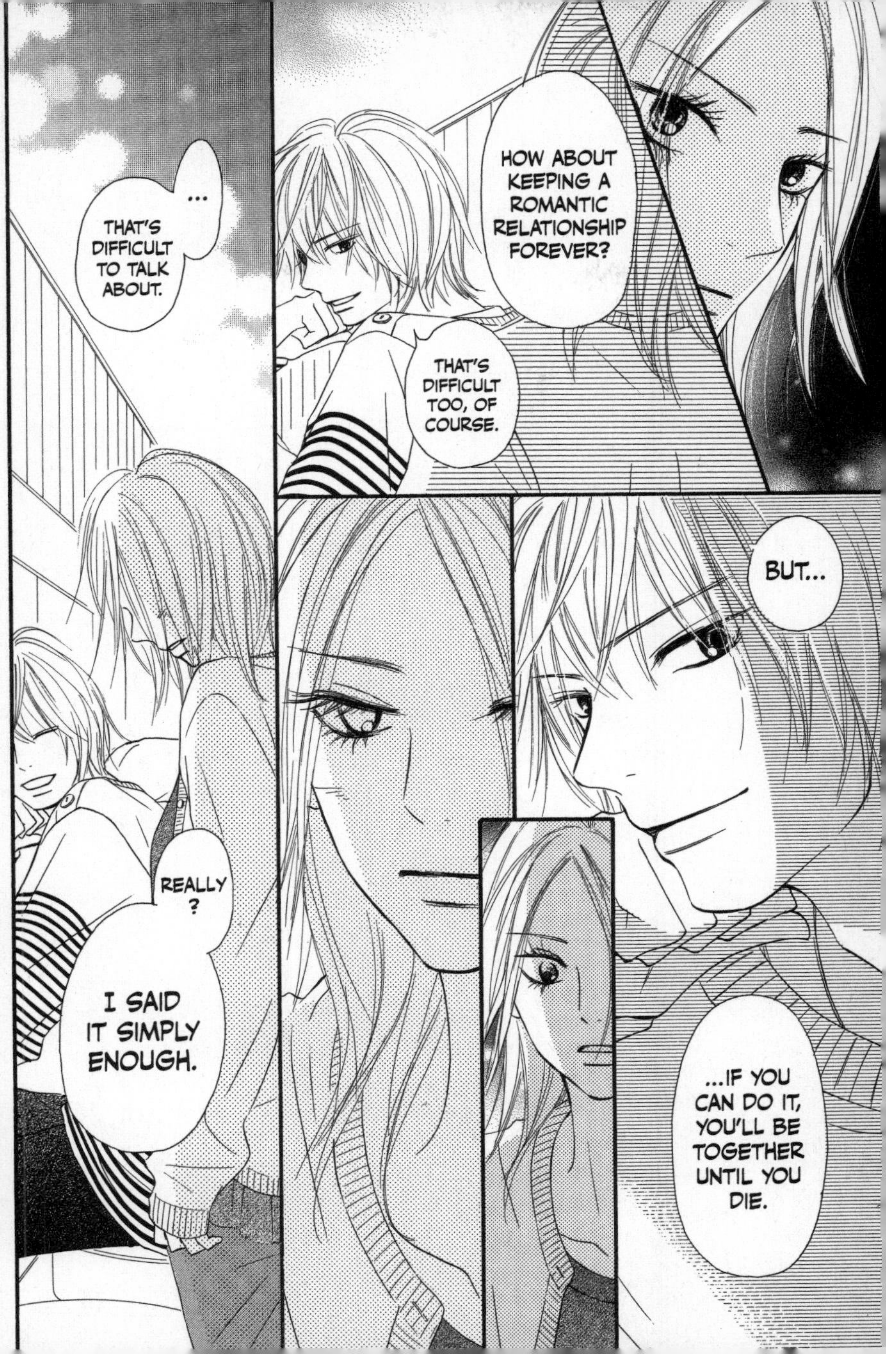
HOW ABOUT KEEPING A ROMANTIC RELATIONSHIP FOREVER?
THAT'S DIFFICULT TOO, OF COURSE.
BUT...
...IF YOU CAN DO IT, YOU'LL BE TOGETHER UNTIL YOU DIE.
...
THAT'S DIFFICULT TO TALK ABOUT.
REALLY?
I SAID IT SIMPLY ENOUGH.

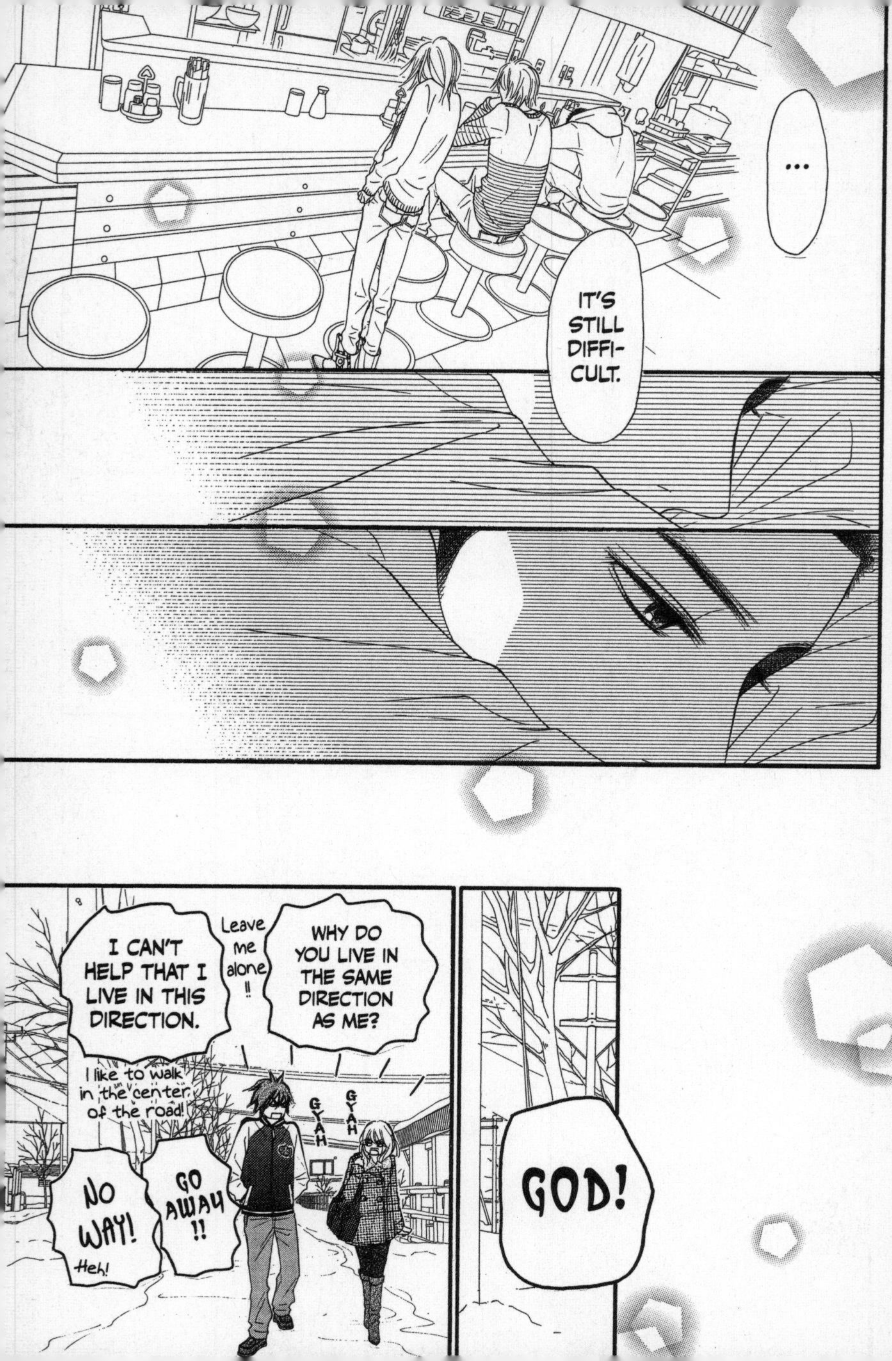
...
IT'S STILL DIFFICULT.
GOD!
WHY DO YOU LIVE IN THE SAME DIRECTION AS ME?
Leave me alone!!
I CAN'T HELP THAT I LIVE IN THIS DIRECTION.
GYAH GYAH
I like to walk in the center of the road!
GO AWAY!!
NO WAY!
Heh!

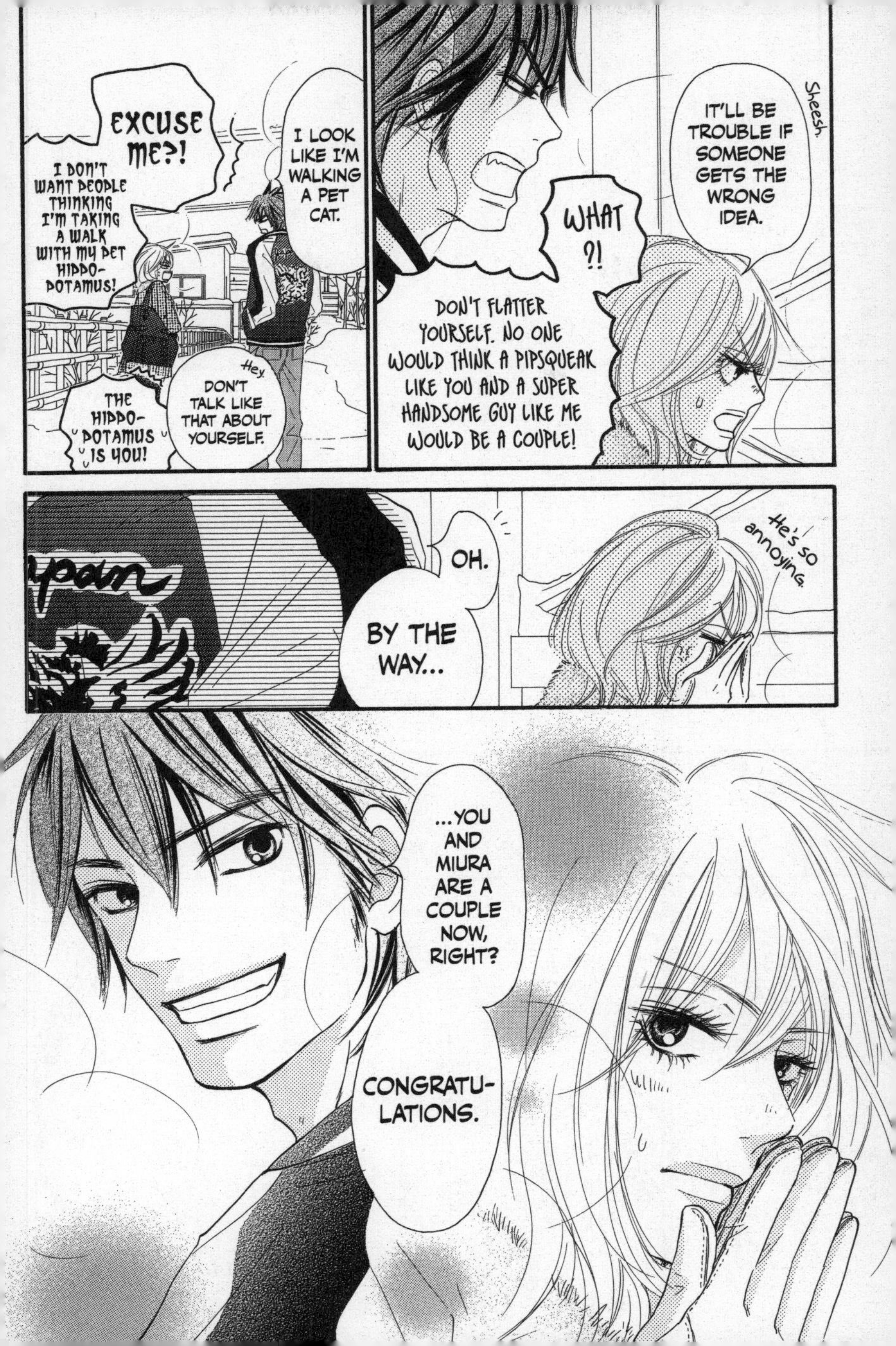
Sheesh.
IT'LL BE TROUBLE IF SOMEONE GETS THE WRONG IDEA.
WHAT?!
DON'T FLATTER YOURSELF. NO ONE WOULD THINK A PIPSQUEAK LIKE YOU AND A SUPER HANDSOME GUY LIKE ME WOULD BE A COUPLE!
I LOOK LIKE I'M WALKING A PET CAT.
EXCUSE ME?!
I DON'T WANT PEOPLE THINKING I'M TAKING A WALK WITH MY PET HIPPO-POTAMUS!
Hey.
DON'T TALK LIKE THAT ABOUT YOURSELF.
THE HIPPO-POTAMUS IS YOU!
He's so annoying.
OH.
BY THE WAY...
...YOU AND MIURA ARE A COUPLE NOW, RIGHT?
CONGRATU-LATIONS.

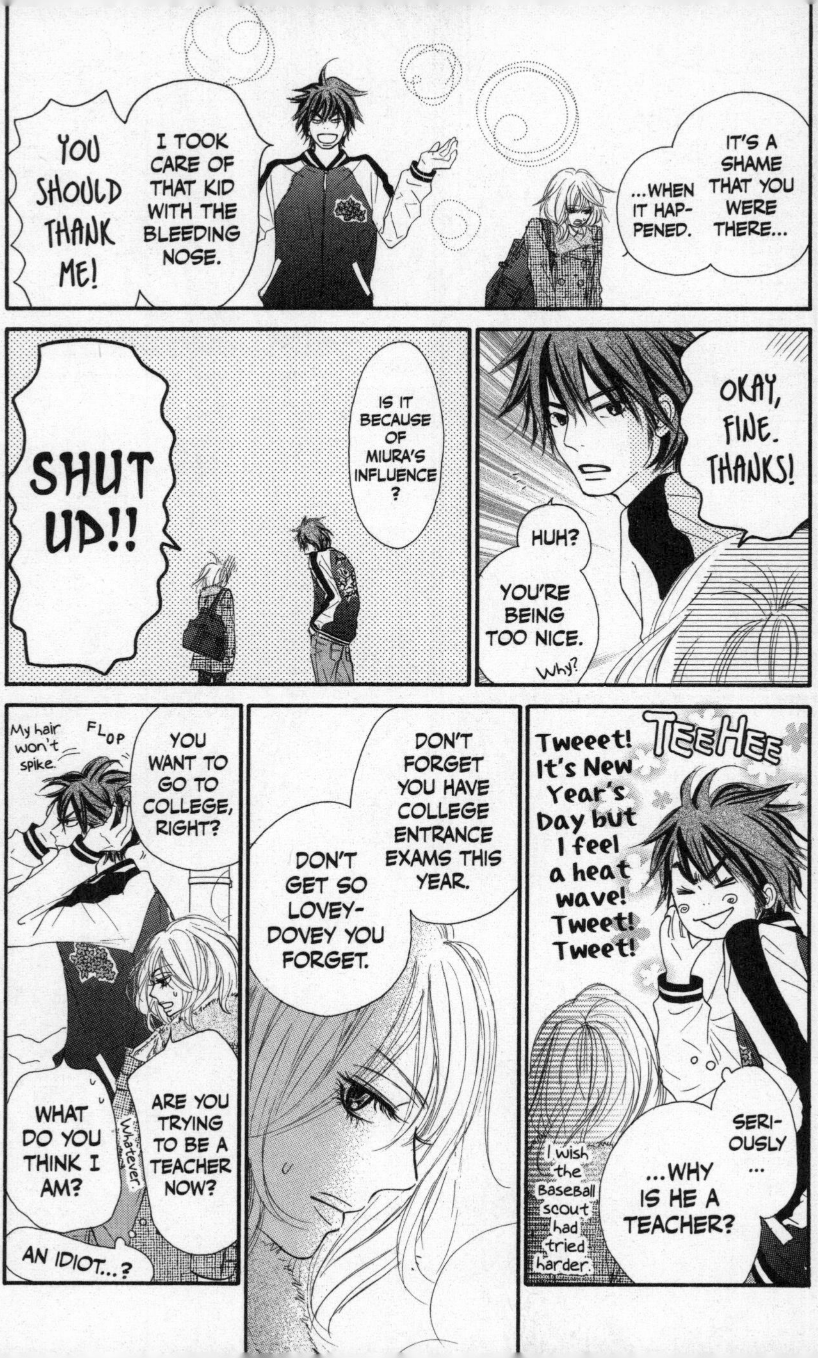
IT'S A SHAME THAT YOU WERE THERE...
...WHEN IT HAPPENED.
I TOOK CARE OF THAT KID WITH THE BLEEDING NOSE.
YOU SHOULD THANK ME!
OKAY, FINE. THANKS!
HUH?
YOU'RE BEING TOO NICE.
Why?
IS IT BECAUSE OF MIURA'S INFLUENCE?
SHUT UP!!
TEEHEE
Tweeet! It's New Year's Day but I feel a heat wave! Tweet! Tweet!
SERIOUSLY...
...WHY IS HE A TEACHER?
I wish the Baseball scout had tried harder.
DON'T FORGET YOU HAVE COLLEGE ENTRANCE EXAMS THIS YEAR.
DON'T GET SO LOVEY-DOVEY YOU FORGET.
YOU WANT TO GO TO COLLEGE, RIGHT?
FLOP
My hair won't spike.
ARE YOU TRYING TO BE A TEACHER NOW?
Whatever.
WHAT DO YOU THINK I AM?
AN IDIOT...?

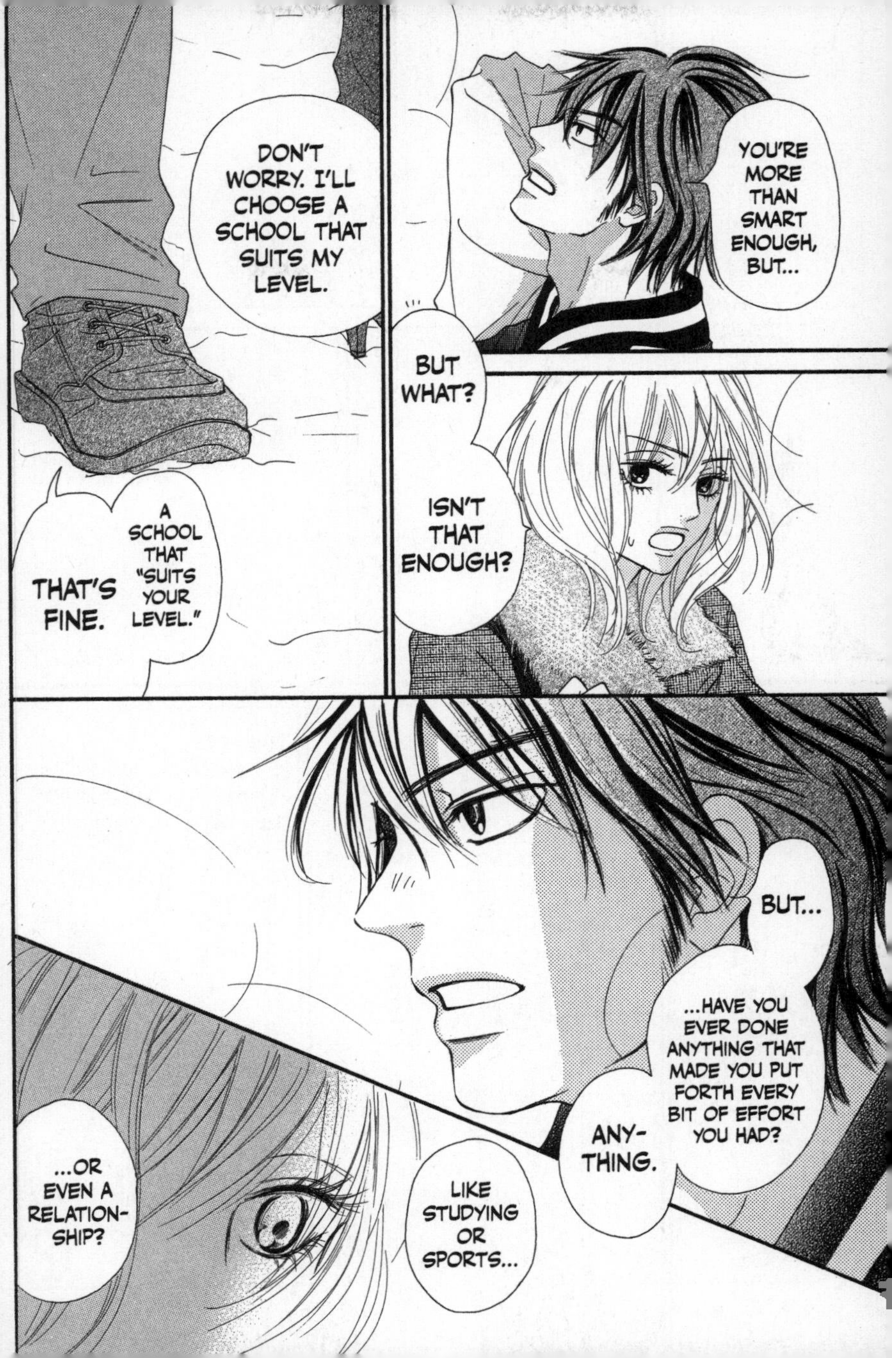
DON'T WORRY. I'LL CHOOSE A SCHOOL THAT SUITS MY LEVEL.
YOU'RE MORE THAN SMART ENOUGH, BUT...
BUT WHAT?
ISN'T THAT ENOUGH?
A SCHOOL THAT "SUITS YOUR LEVEL."
THAT'S FINE.
BUT...
...HAVE YOU EVER DONE ANYTHING THAT MADE YOU PUT FORTH EVERY BIT OF EFFORT YOU HAD?
ANY-THING.
LIKE STUDYING OR SPORTS...
...OR EVEN A RELATIONSHIP?

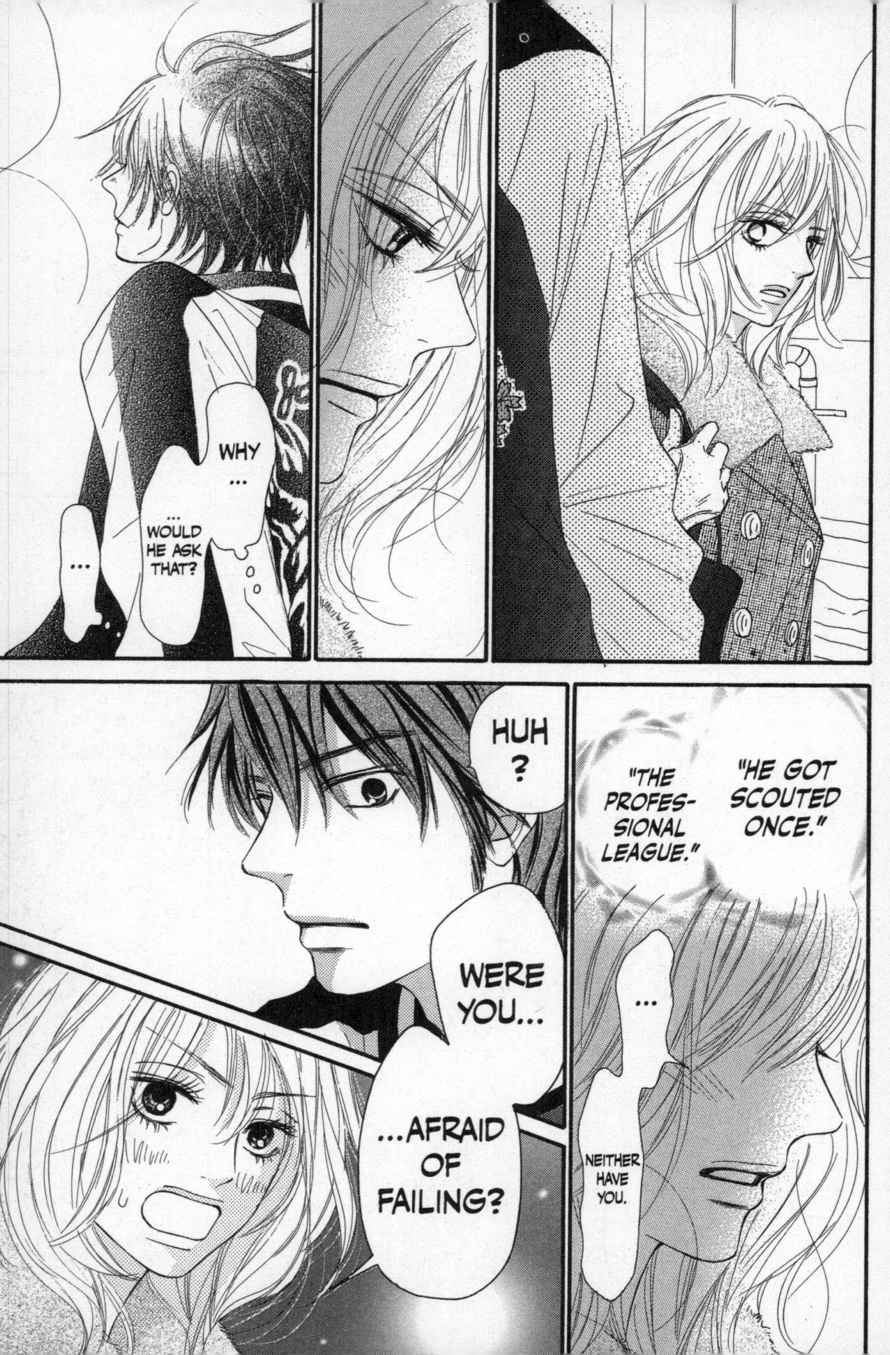
WHY ...
... WOULD HE ASK THAT?
...
"HE GOT SCOUTED ONCE."
"THE PROFES-SIONAL LEAGUE."
...
NEITHER HAVE YOU.
HUH ?
WERE YOU...
...AFRAID OF FAILING?

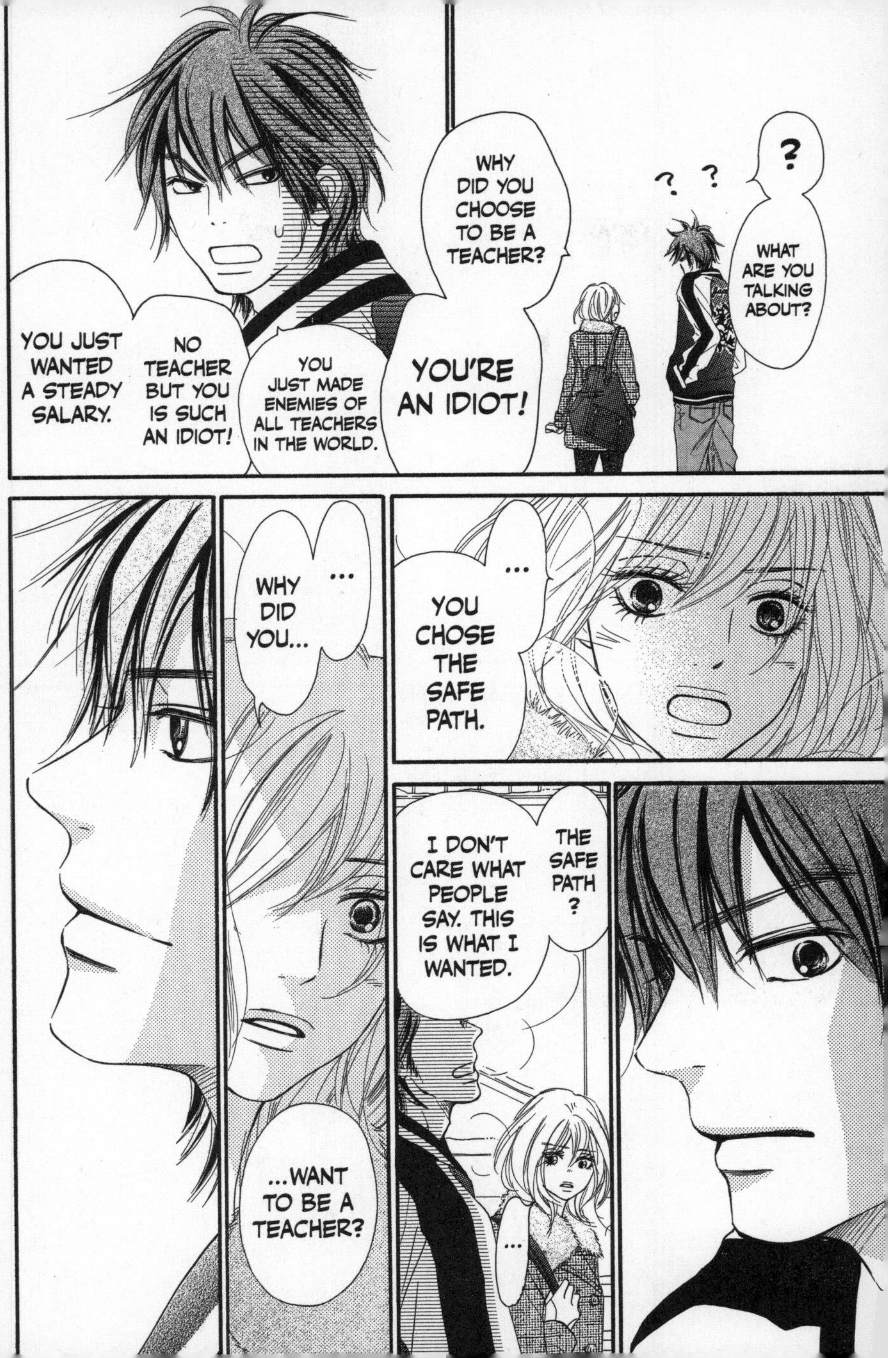
?
WHAT ARE YOU TALKING ABOUT?
? ?
WHY DID YOU CHOOSE TO BE A TEACHER?
YOU'RE AN IDIOT!
YOU JUST MADE ENEMIES OF ALL TEACHERS IN THE WORLD.
NO TEACHER BUT YOU IS SUCH AN IDIOT!
YOU JUST WANTED A STEADY SALARY.
...
YOU CHOSE THE SAFE PATH.
THE SAFE PATH?
I DON'T CARE WHAT PEOPLE SAY. THIS IS WHAT I WANTED.
...
...
WHY DID YOU...
...WANT TO BE A TEACHER?

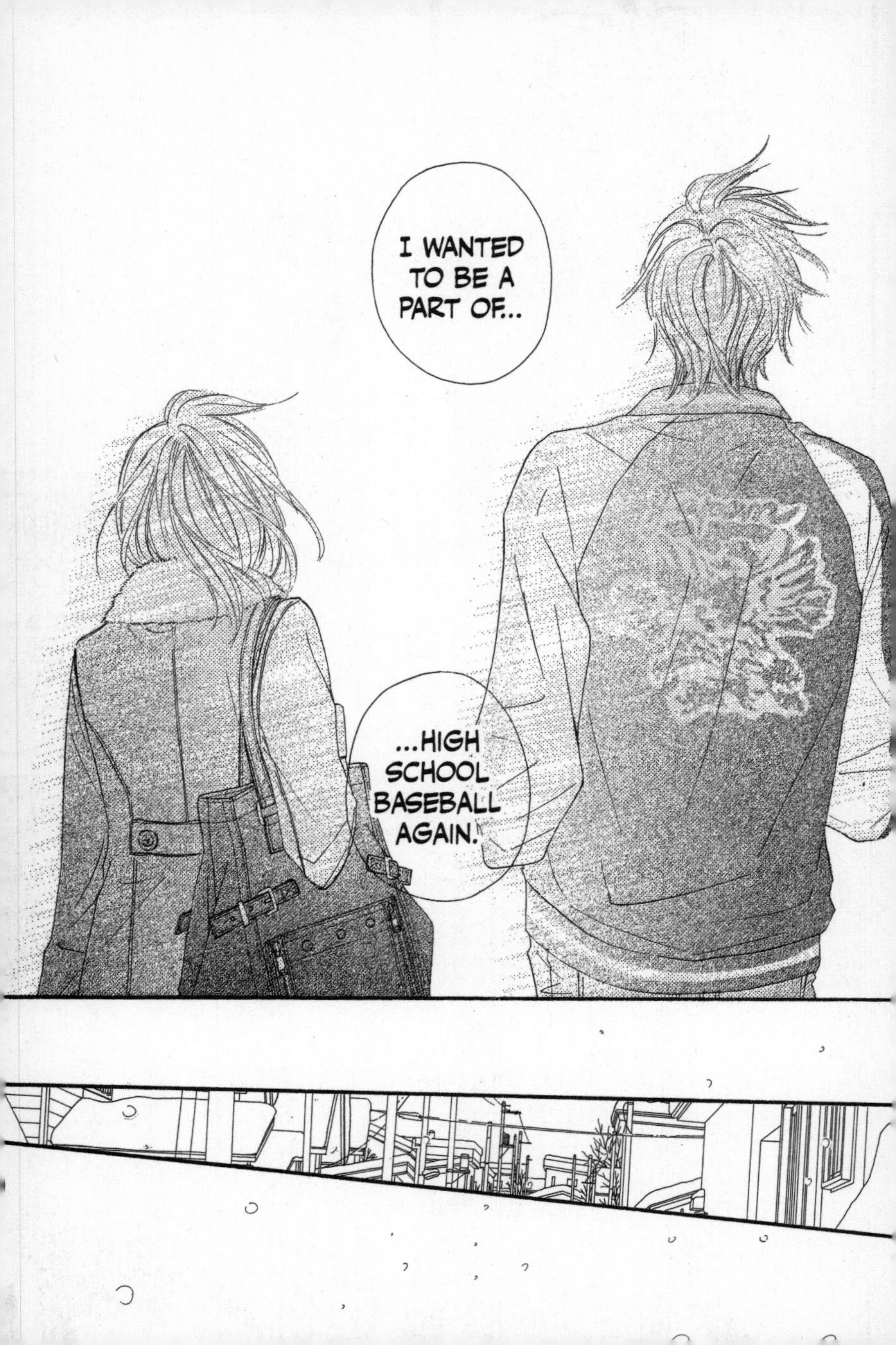
I WANTED TO BE A PART OF...
...HIGH SCHOOL BASEBALL AGAIN.

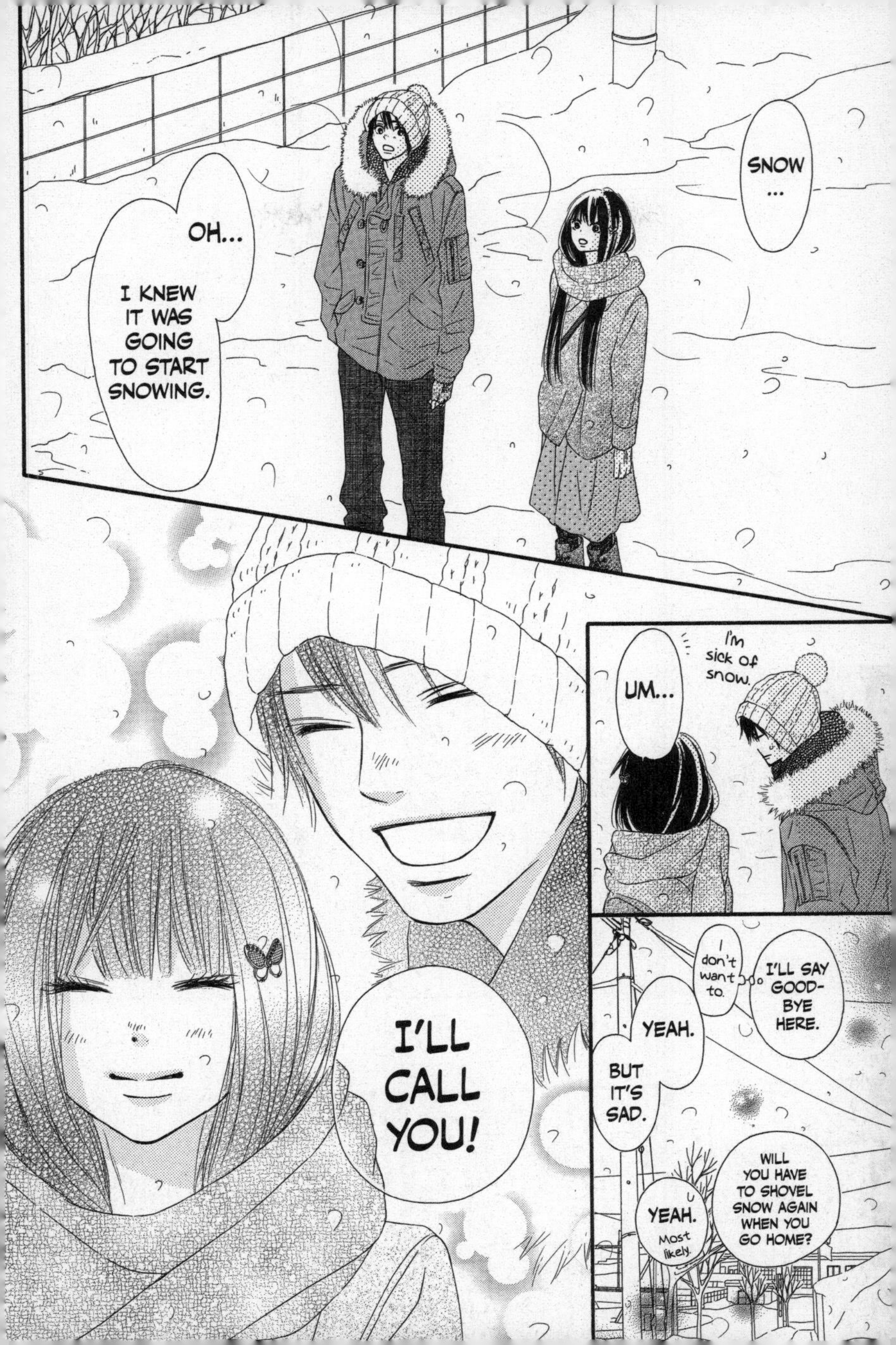
SNOW ...
OH...
I KNEW IT WAS GOING TO START SNOWING.
I'm sick of snow.
UM...
I'LL SAY GOOD-BYE HERE.
I don't want to.
YEAH.
BUT IT'S SAD.
WILL YOU HAVE TO SHOVEL SNOW AGAIN WHEN YOU GO HOME?
YEAH.
Most likely.
I'LL CALL YOU!

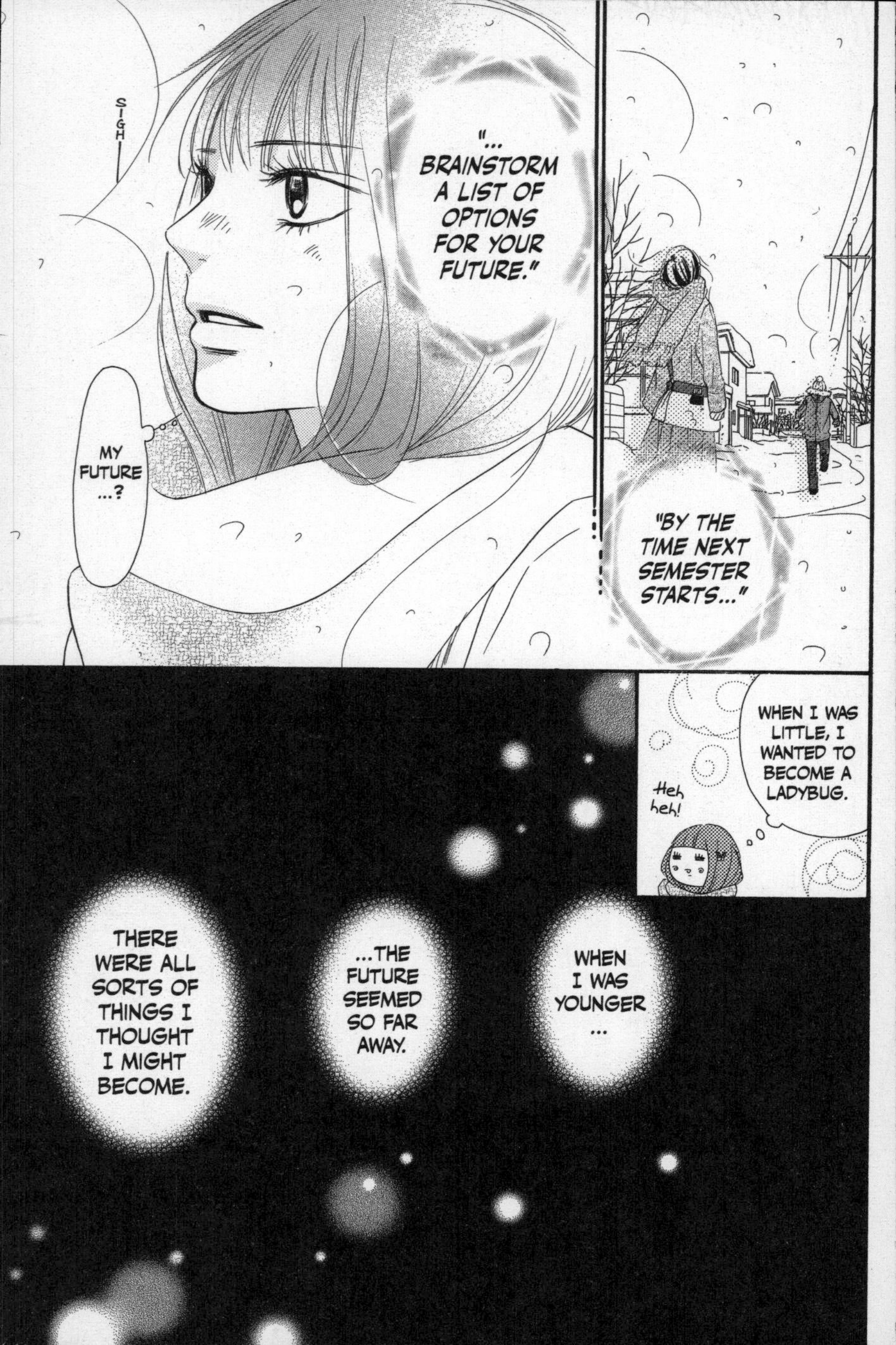
"BY THE TIME NEXT SEMESTER STARTS..."
"... BRAINSTORM A LIST OF OPTIONS FOR YOUR FUTURE."
SIGH
MY FUTURE ...?
WHEN I WAS LITTLE, I WANTED TO BECOME A LADYBUG.
Heh heh!
WHEN I WAS YOUNGER ...
...THE FUTURE SEEMED SO FAR AWAY.
THERE WERE ALL SORTS OF THINGS I THOUGHT I MIGHT BECOME.

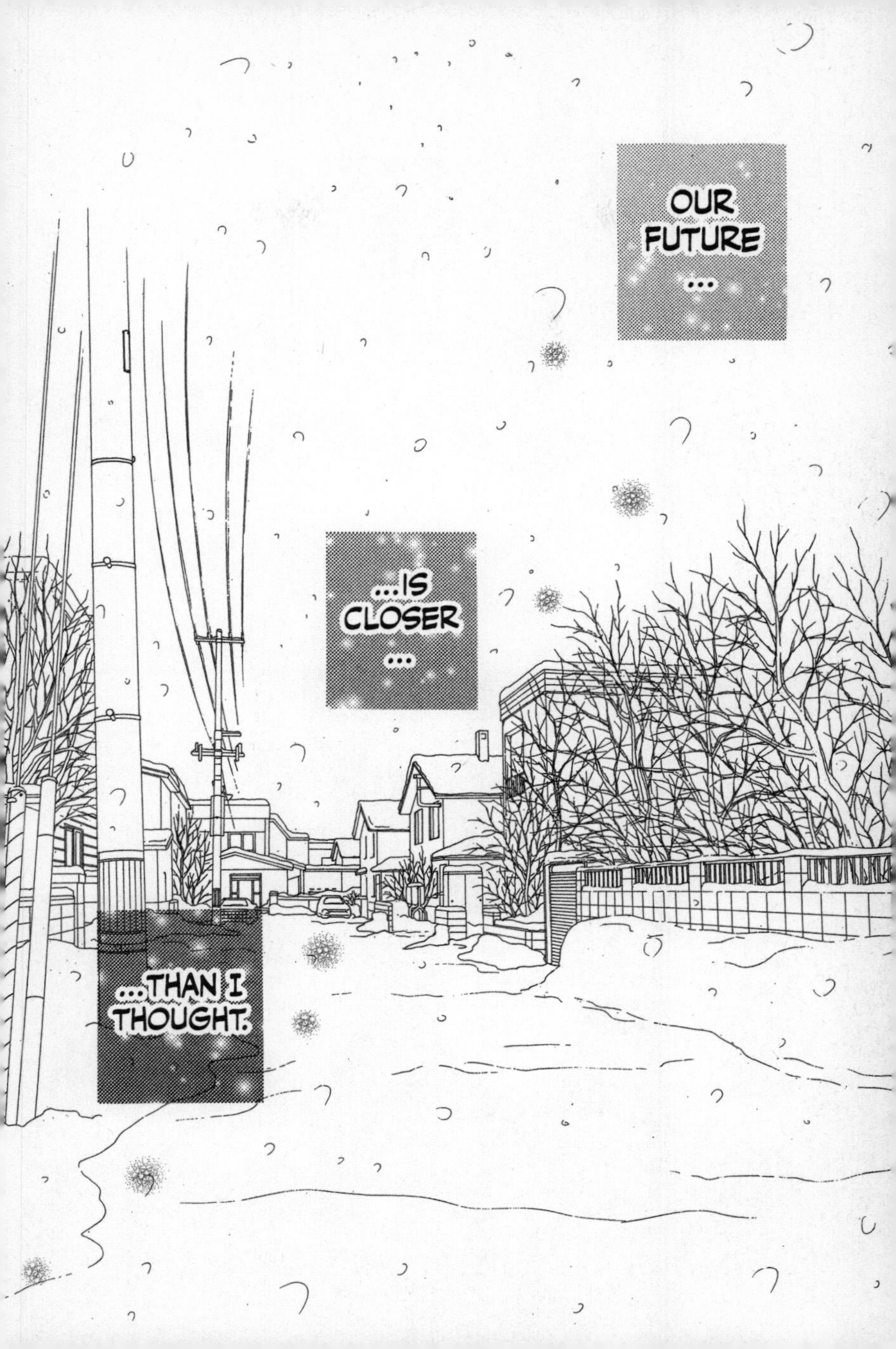
OUR FUTURE ...
...IS CLOSER ...
...THAN I THOUGHT.

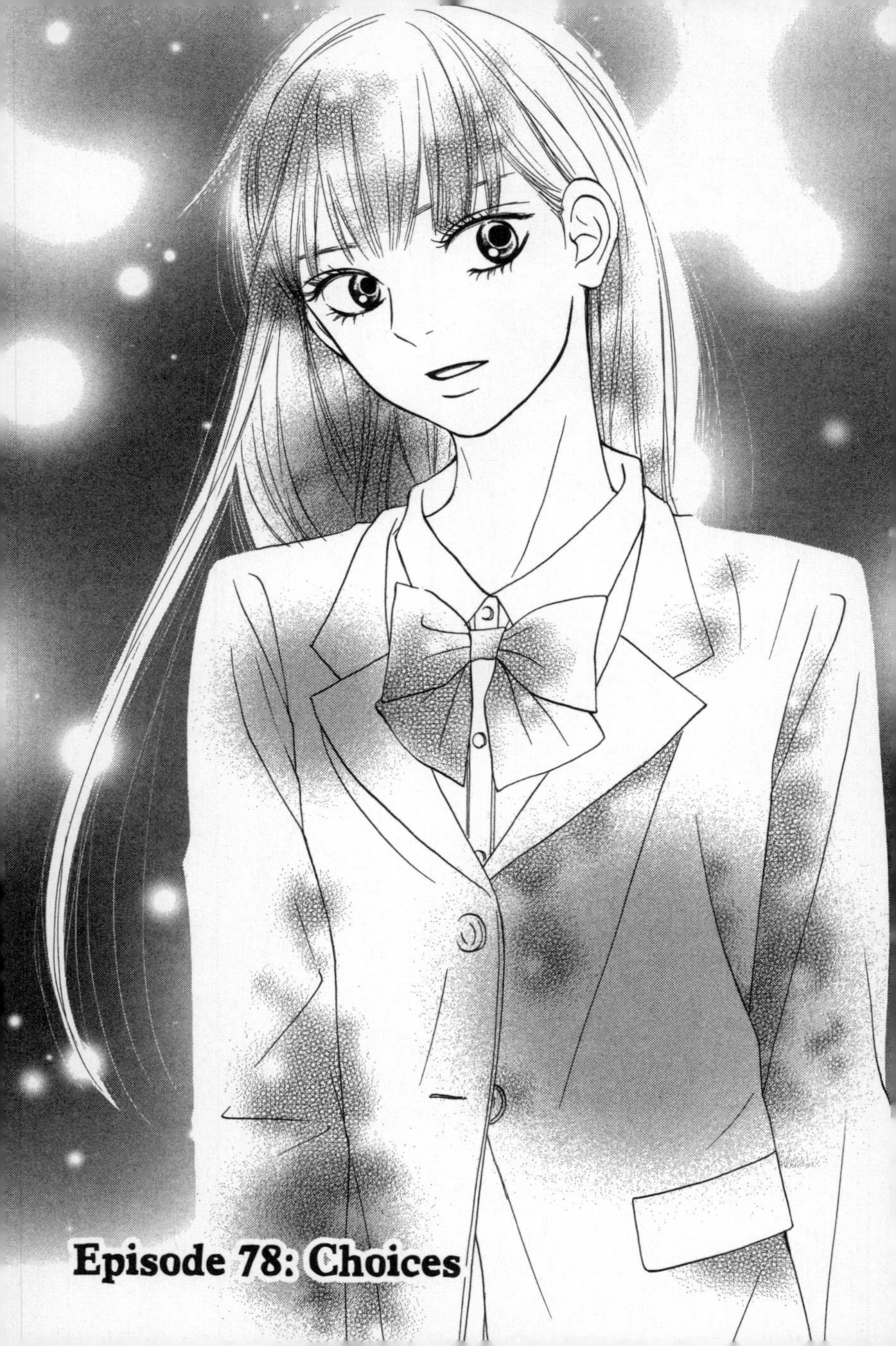
Episode 78: Choices

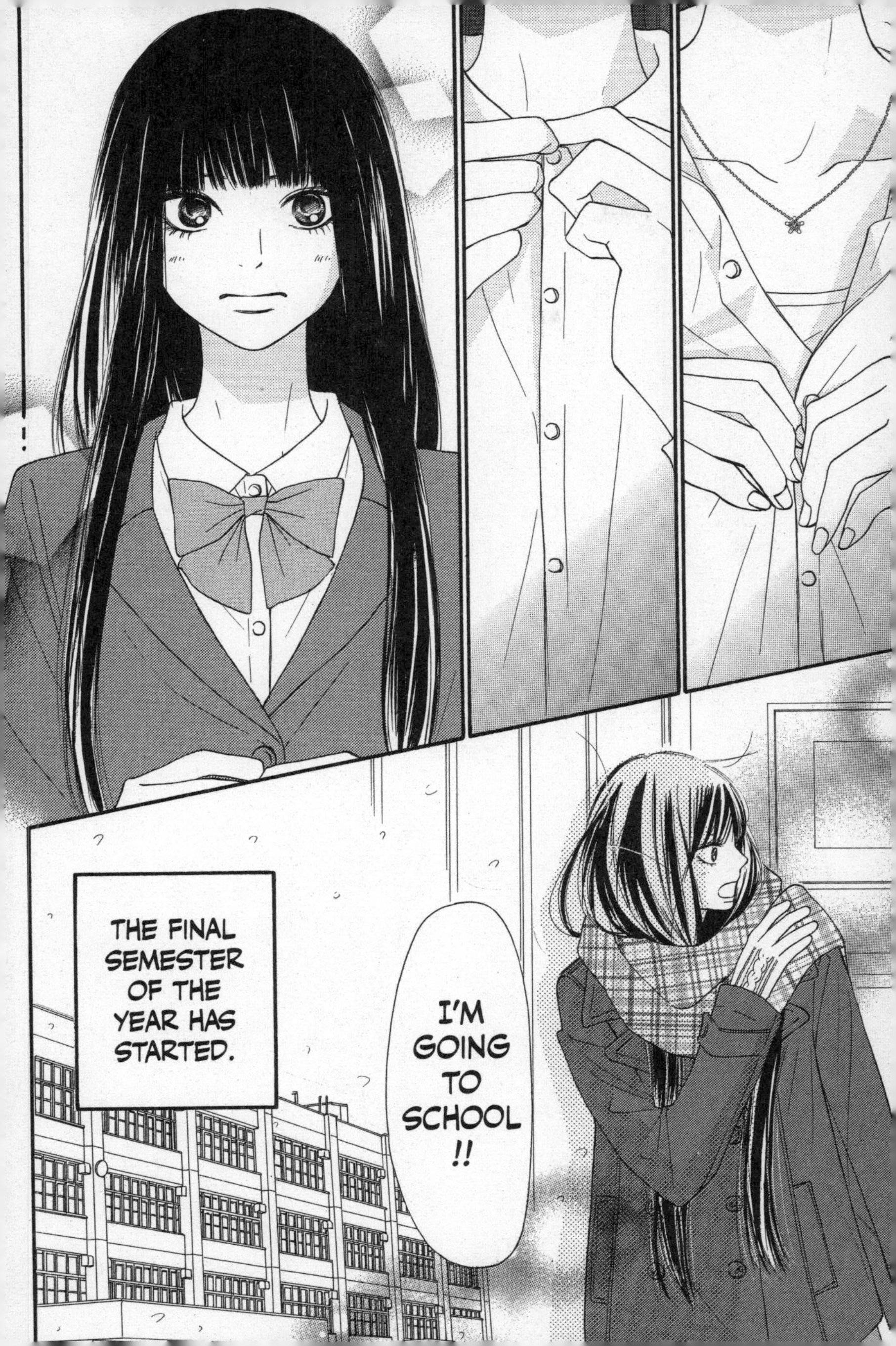
I'M GOING TO SCHOOL !!
THE FINAL SEMESTER OF THE YEAR HAS STARTED.

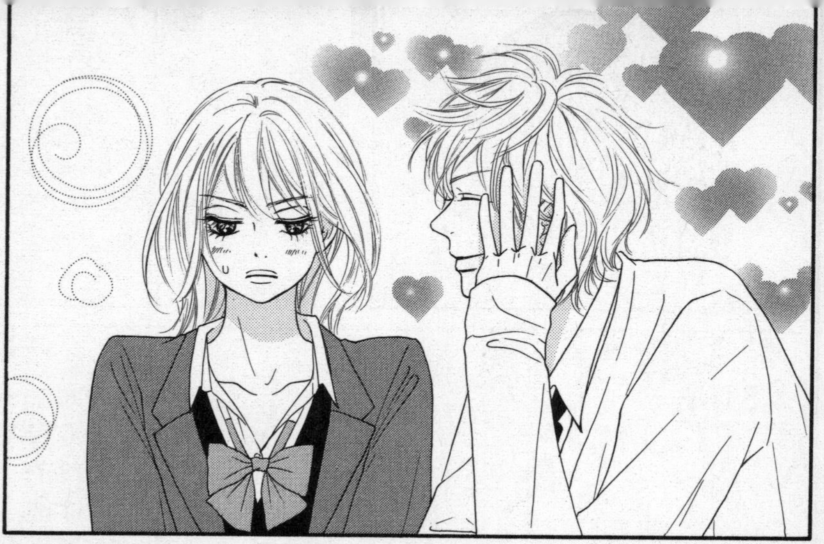

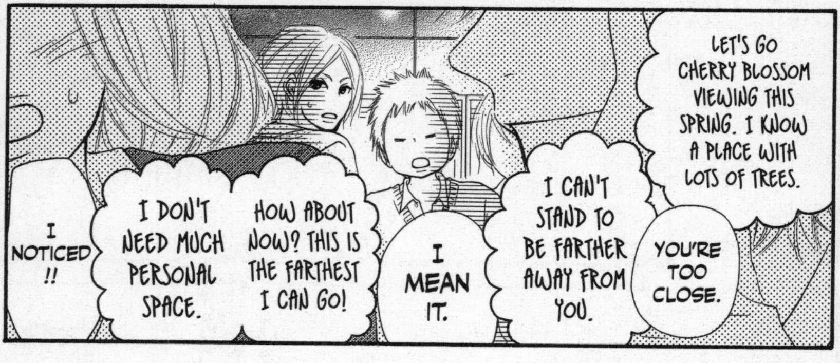
LET'S GO CHERRY BLOSSOM VIEWING THIS SPRING. I KNOW A PLACE WITH LOTS OF TREES.
YOU'RE TOO CLOSE.
I CAN'T STAND TO BE FARTHER AWAY FROM YOU.
I MEAN IT.
HOW ABOUT NOW? THIS IS THE FARTHEST I CAN GO!
I DON'T NEED MUCH PERSONAL SPACE.
I NOTICED !!

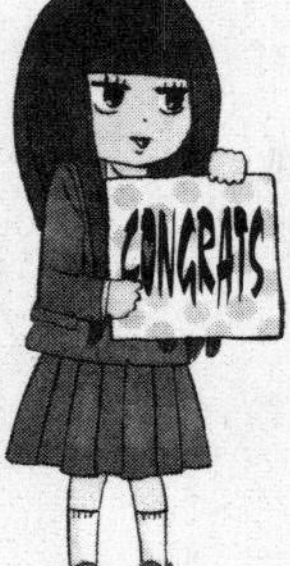
CONGRATS

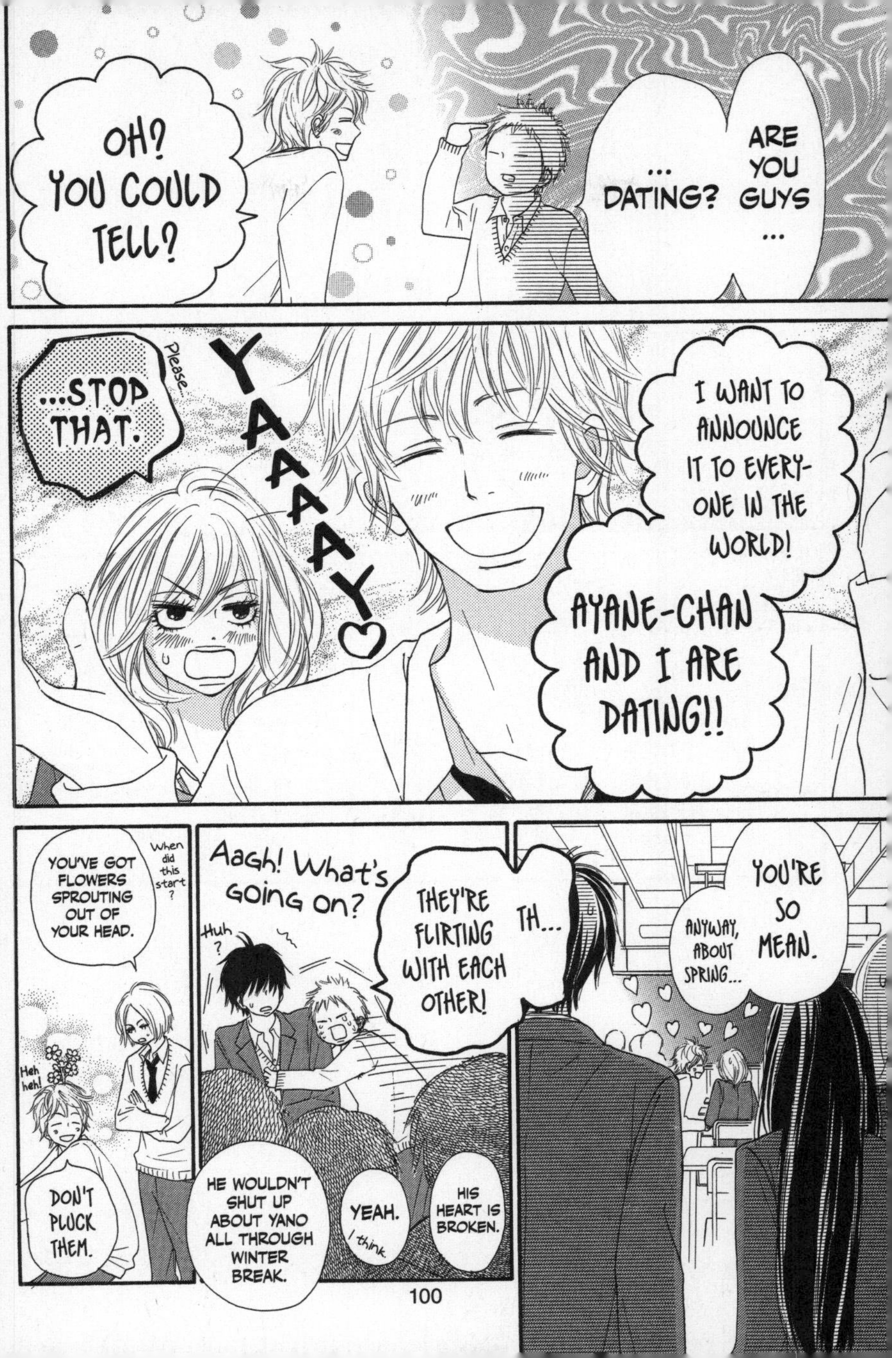
ARE YOU GUYS ...
... DATING?
OH? YOU COULD TELL?
I WANT TO ANNOUNCE IT TO EVERY-ONE IN THE WORLD!
AYANE-CHAN AND I ARE DATING!!
YAAAAY♡
Please...
...STOP THAT.
YOU'RE SO MEAN.
ANYWAY, ABOUT SPRING...
TH...
THEY'RE FLIRTING WITH EACH OTHER!
Aagh! What's going on?
Huh?
HIS HEART IS BROKEN.
YEAH.
I think.
HE WOULDN'T SHUT UP ABOUT YANO ALL THROUGH WINTER BREAK.
When did this start?
YOU'VE GOT FLOWERS SPROUTING OUT OF YOUR HEAD.
Heh heh!
DON'T PLUCK THEM.

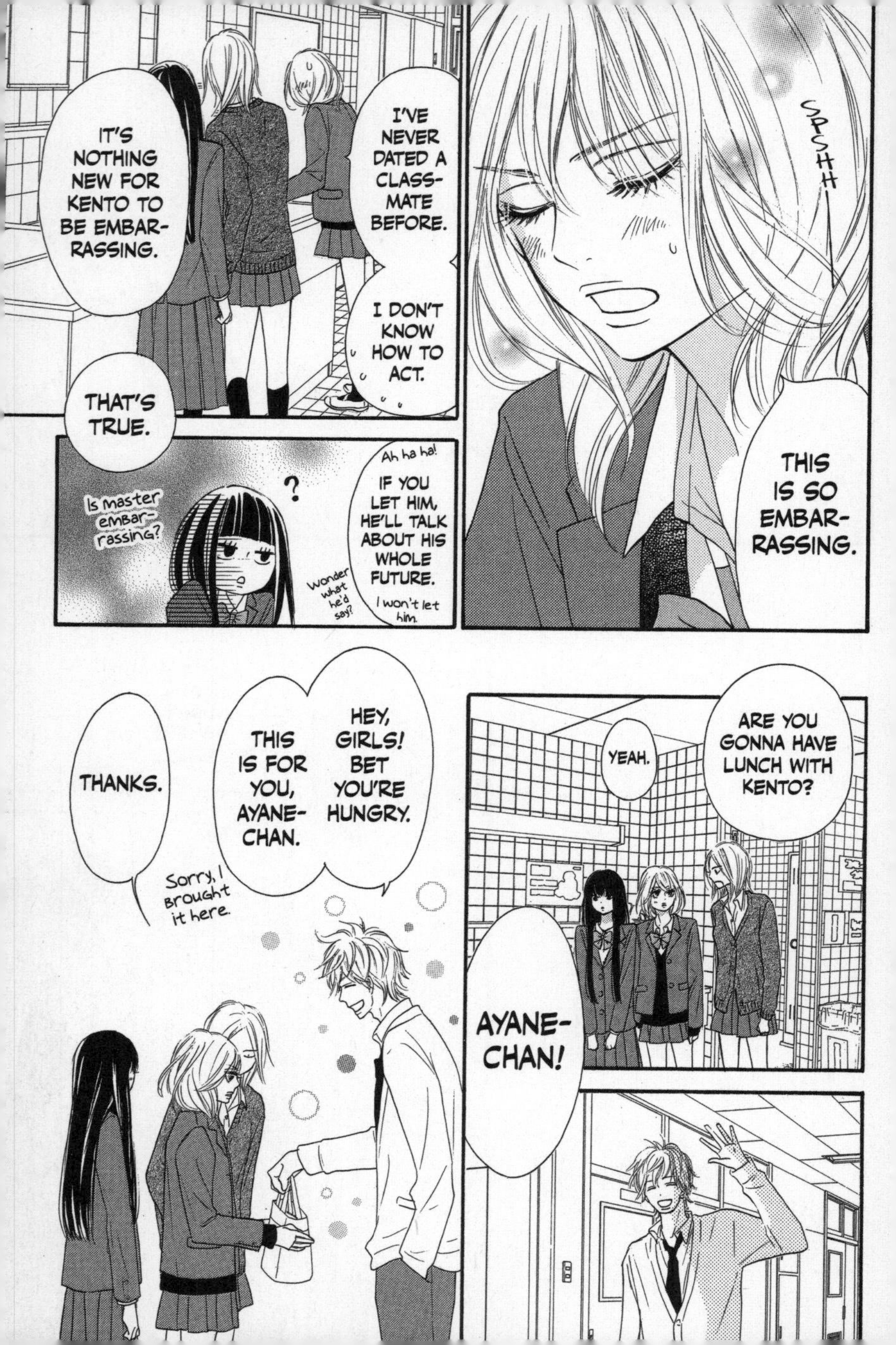
SPSHH
THIS IS SO EMBARRASSING.
I'VE NEVER DATED A CLASSMATE BEFORE.
I DON'T KNOW HOW TO ACT.
IT'S NOTHING NEW FOR KENTO TO BE EMBARRASSING.
THAT'S TRUE.
Ah ha ha!
IF YOU LET HIM, HE'LL TALK ABOUT HIS WHOLE FUTURE.
I won't let him.
Wonder what he'd say?
?
Is master embarrassing?
ARE YOU GONNA HAVE LUNCH WITH KENTO?
YEAH.
AYANE-CHAN!
HEY, GIRLS! BET YOU'RE HUNGRY.
THIS IS FOR YOU, AYANE-CHAN.
THANKS.
Sorry, I brought it here.

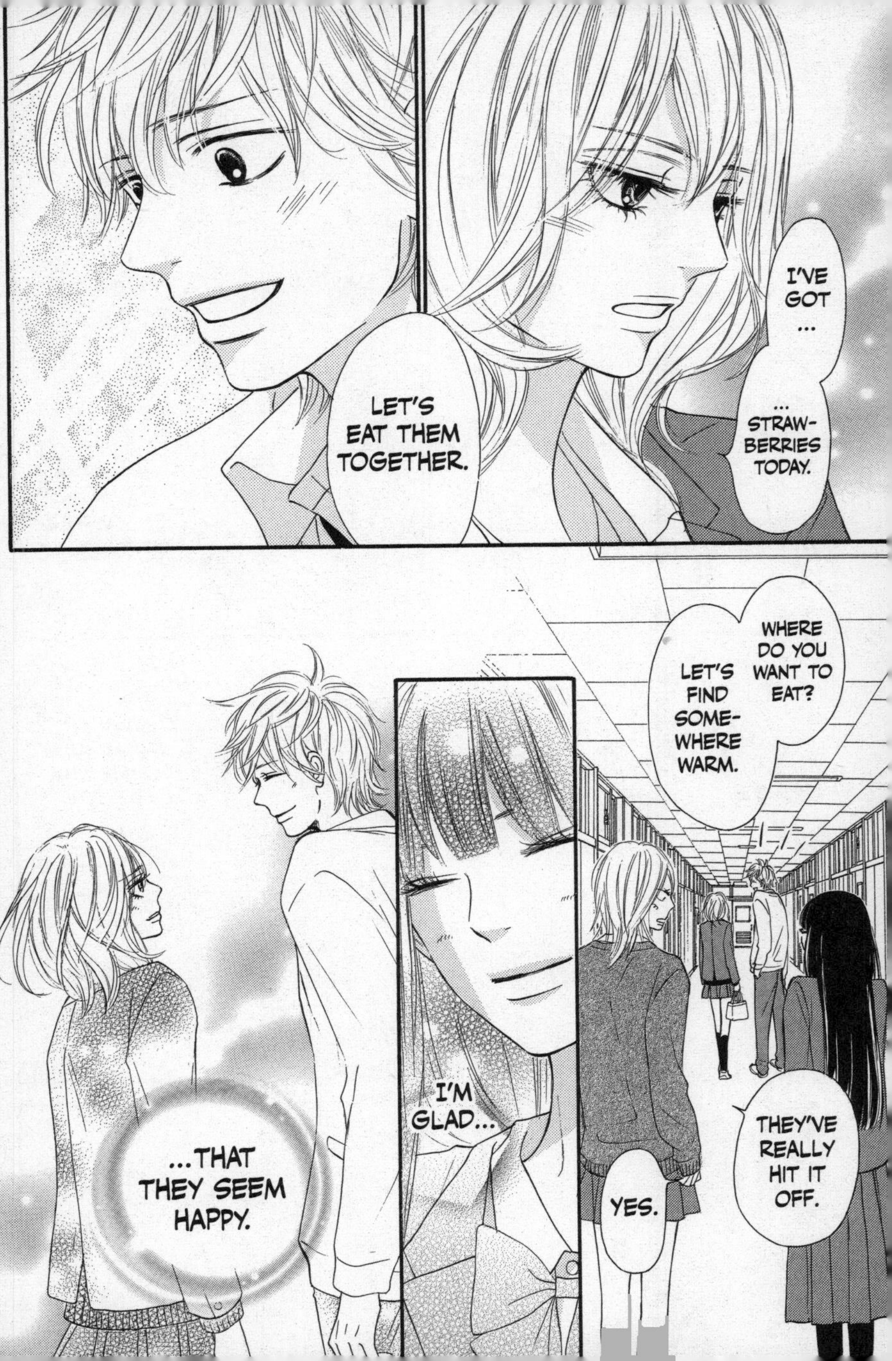
I'VE GOT ...
... STRAWBERRIES TODAY.
LET'S EAT THEM TOGETHER.
WHERE DO YOU WANT TO EAT?
LET'S FIND SOMEWHERE WARM.
THEY'VE REALLY HIT IT OFF.
YES.
I'M GLAD...
...THAT THEY SEEM HAPPY.

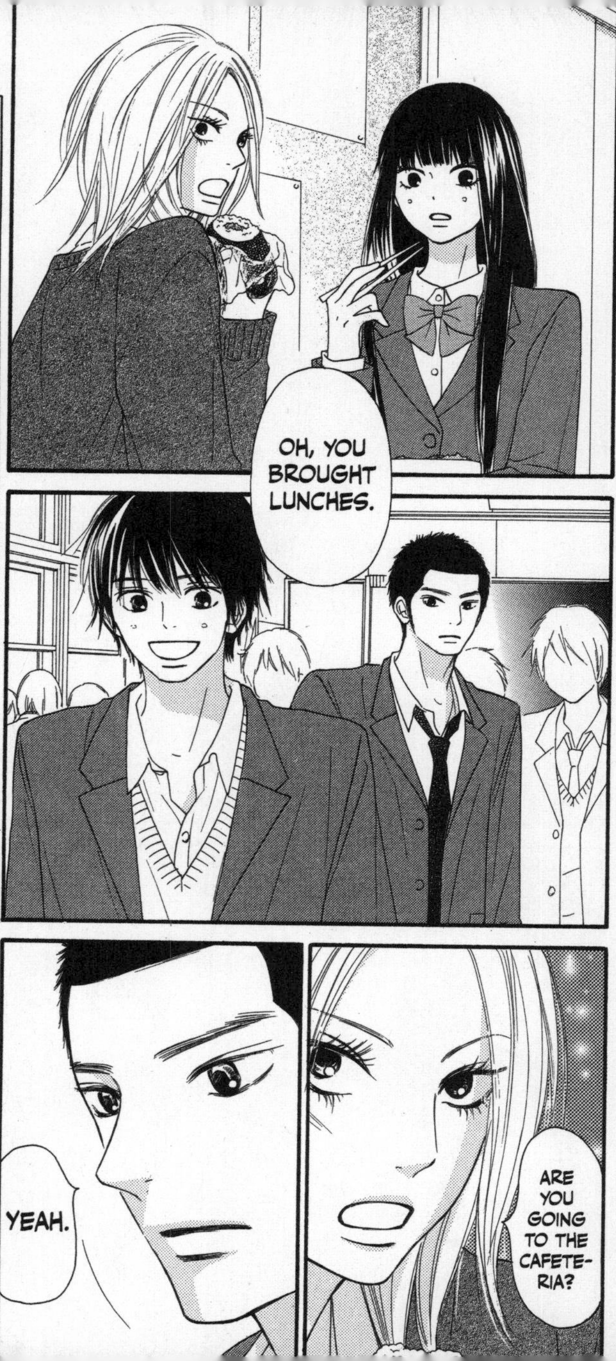
OH, YOU BROUGHT LUNCHES.
ARE YOU GOING TO THE CAFETERIA?
YEAH.

KARUPIN on JAPAN 3

So this is Vol.19. Phew! It's been a long series.

There must be readers who have been reading the whole time, readers who have stopped reading, and readers who have started reading recently.

I grew up reading so many different manga.

I have favorite manga, manga that I only remember the titles of, manga that I still like, and manga whose existence I have completely forgotten! But it's all good!

There's a ton of manga out there and mine are among them! Whether people like them, or whether they are important, or whether people know about them, all I can say is that it's a happy feeling they exist.

Obviously, the best thing would be if people liked them. I wish I had a better way to say this, but it makes me really happy to be a manga author.

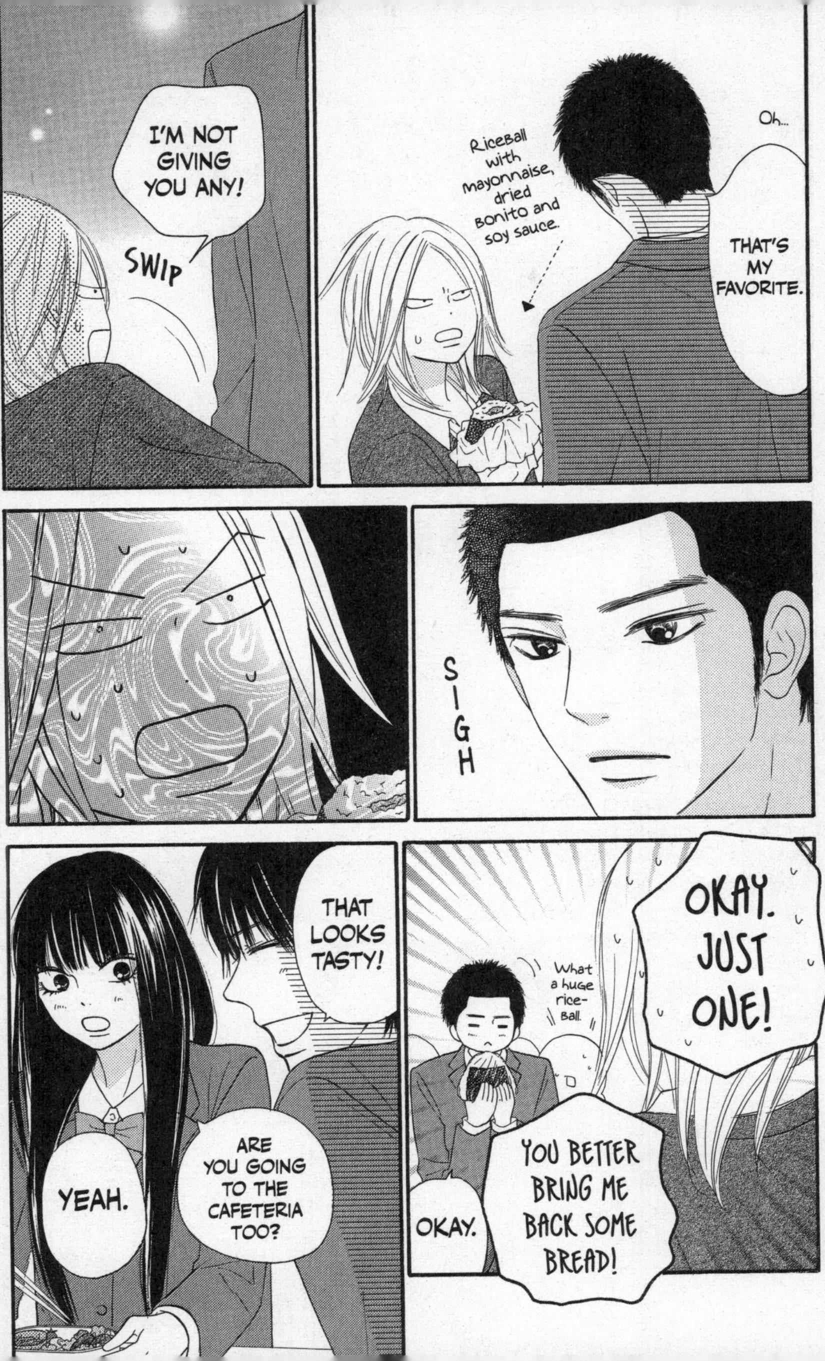

Oh...
THAT'S MY FAVORITE.
Riceball with mayonnaise, dried bonito and soy sauce.
I'M NOT GIVING YOU ANY!
SWIP
SIGH
OKAY. JUST ONE!
What a huge rice-ball.
YOU BETTER BRING ME BACK SOME BREAD!
OKAY.
THAT LOOKS TASTY!
ARE YOU GOING TO THE CAFETERIA TOO?
YEAH.

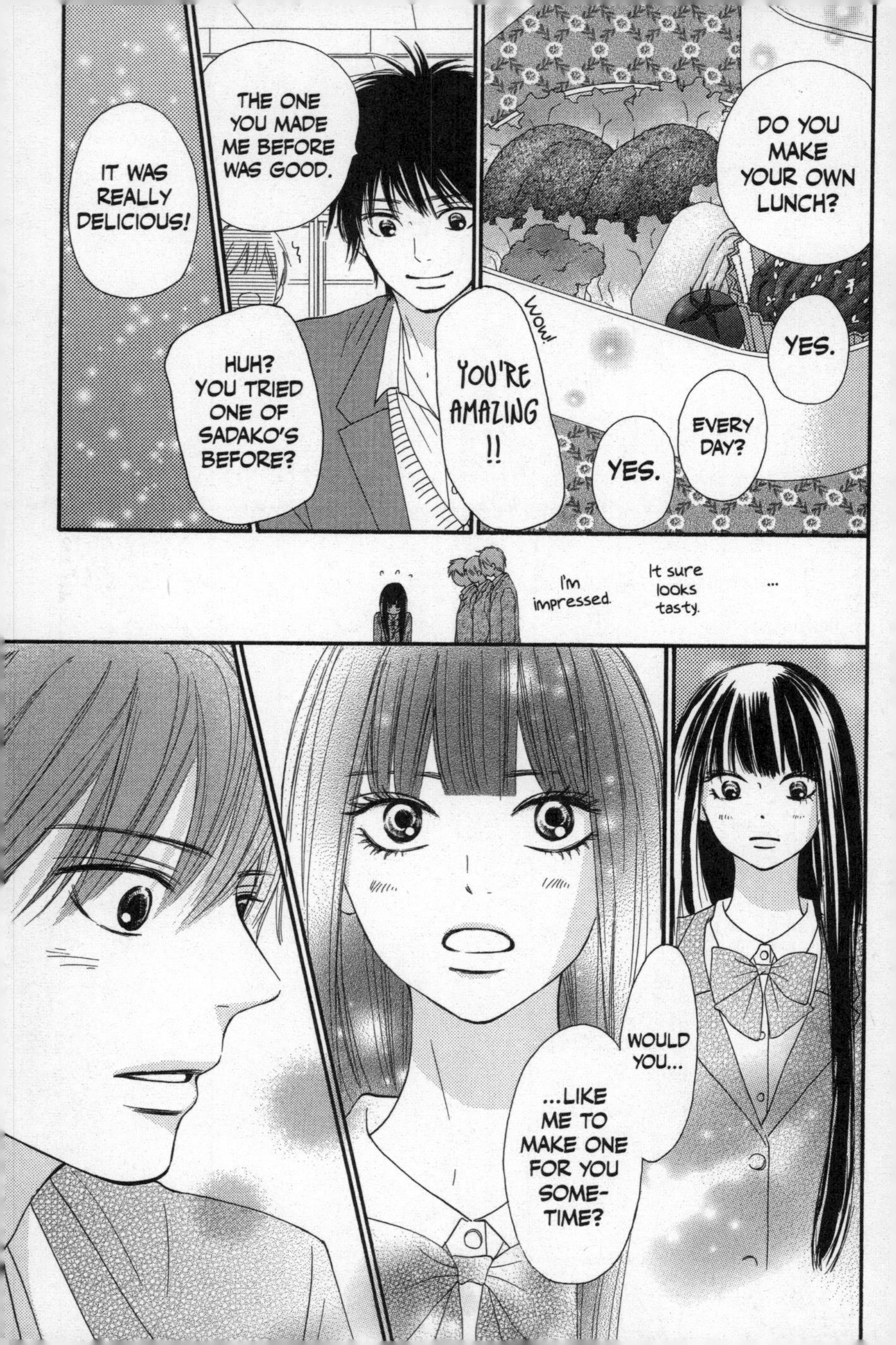

DO YOU MAKE YOUR OWN LUNCH?
YES.
EVERY DAY?
YES.
WOW!
YOU'RE AMAZING !!
THE ONE YOU MADE ME BEFORE WAS GOOD.
IT WAS REALLY DELICIOUS!
HUH? YOU TRIED ONE OF SADAKO'S BEFORE?
...
It sure looks tasty.
I'm impressed.
WOULD YOU...
...LIKE ME TO MAKE ONE FOR YOU SOME-TIME?

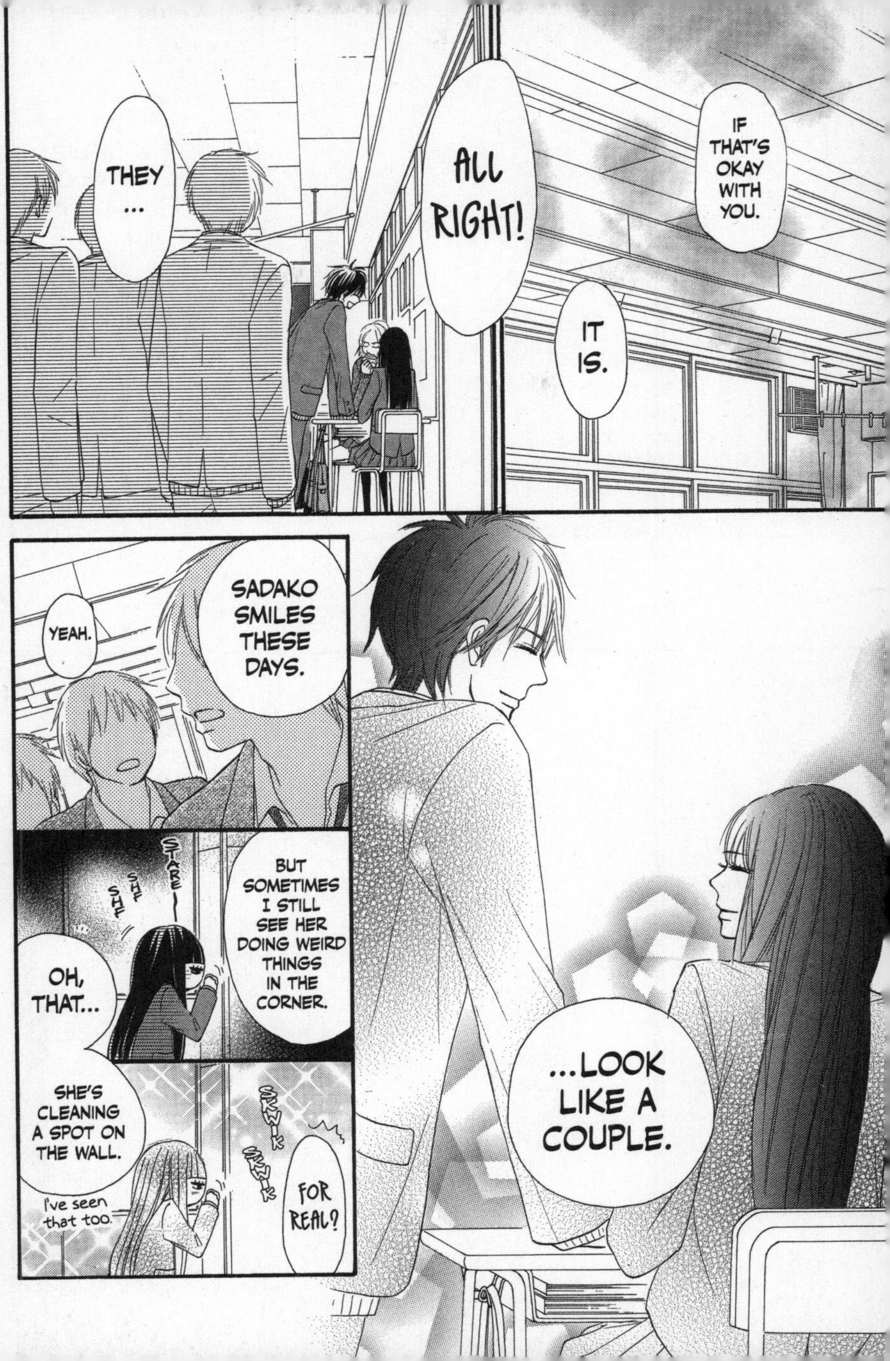
IF THAT'S OKAY WITH YOU.
IT IS.
ALL RIGHT!
THEY ...
...LOOK LIKE A COUPLE.
SADAKO SMILES THESE DAYS.
YEAH.
BUT SOMETIMES I STILL SEE HER DOING WEIRD THINGS IN THE CORNER.
STARE
SHF SHF
OH, THAT...
FOR REAL?
SKWIK SKWIK
SHE'S CLEANING A SPOT ON THE WALL.
I've seen that too.

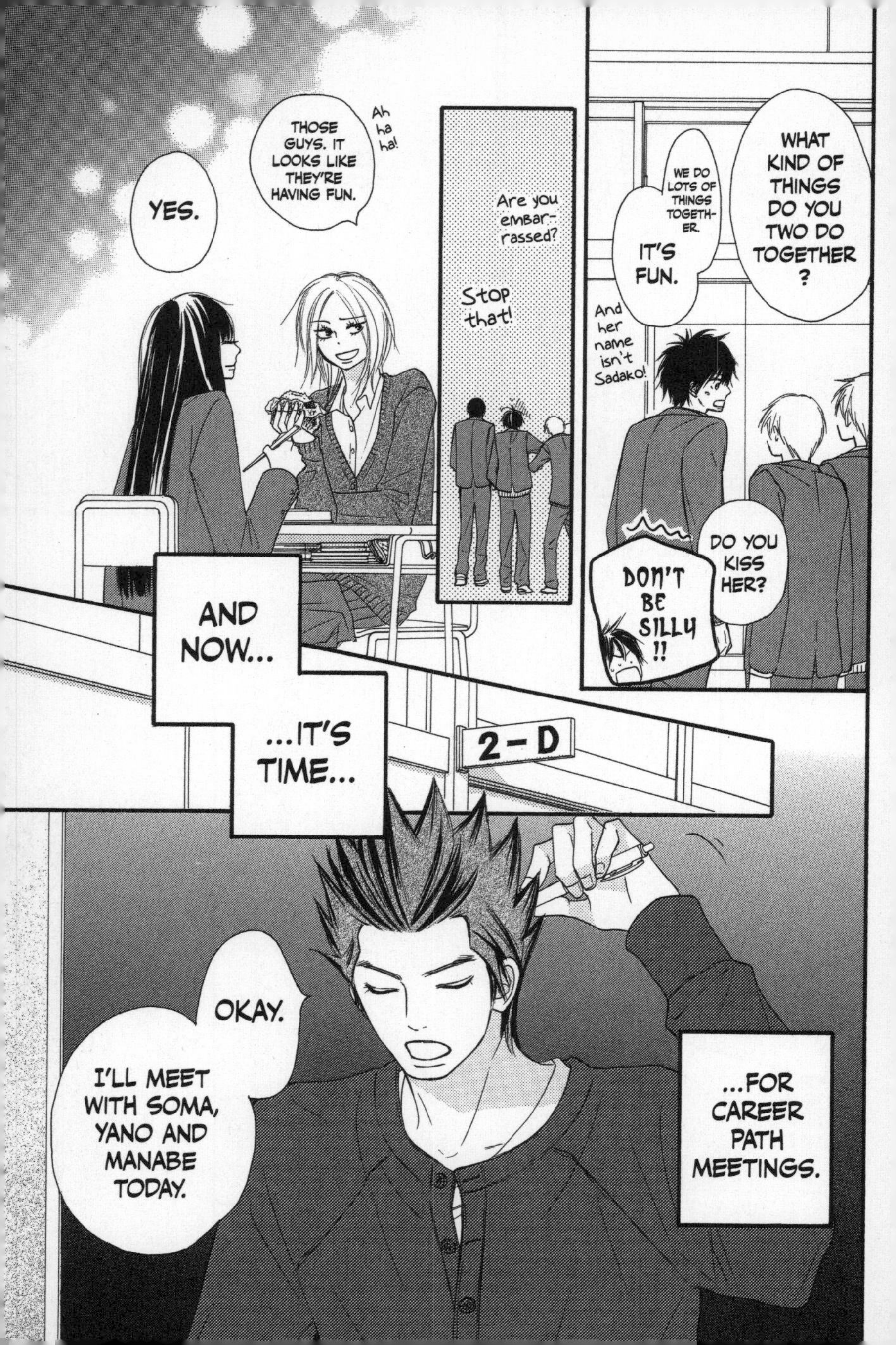

WHAT KIND OF THINGS DO YOU TWO DO TOGETHER?
WE DO LOTS OF THINGS TOGETHER.
IT'S FUN.
And her name isn't Sadako!
DO YOU KISS HER?
DON'T BE SILLY!!
Are you embarrassed?
Stop that!
Ah ha ha!
THOSE GUYS. IT LOOKS LIKE THEY'RE HAVING FUN.
YES.
AND NOW...
...IT'S TIME...
2-D
...FOR CAREER PATH MEETINGS.
OKAY.
I'LL MEET WITH SOMA, YANO AND MANABE TODAY.

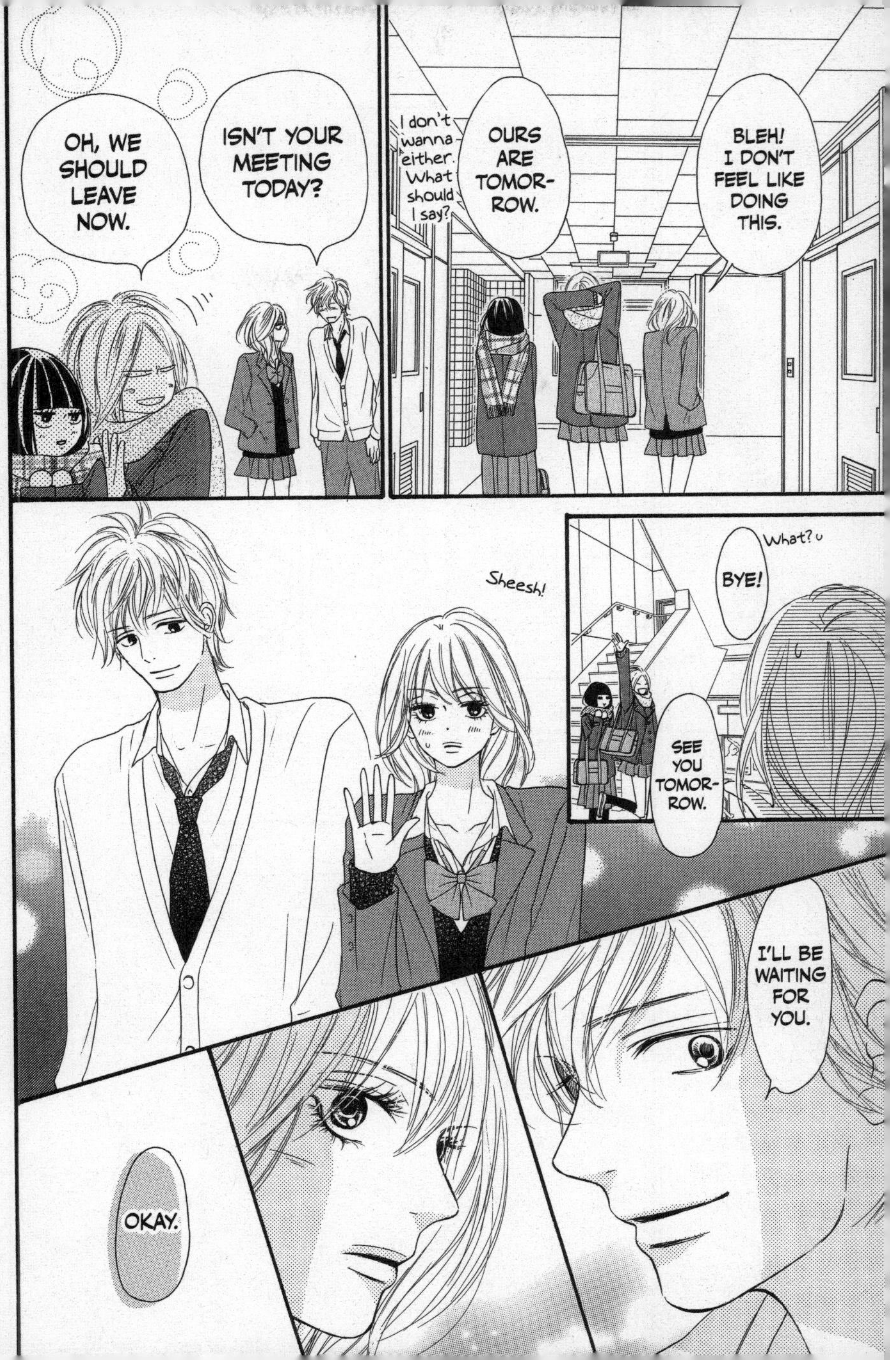
BLEH! I DON'T FEEL LIKE DOING THIS.
OURS ARE TOMOR-ROW.
I don't wanna either. What should I say?
ISN'T YOUR MEETING TODAY?
OH, WE SHOULD LEAVE NOW.
What?
BYE!
SEE YOU TOMOR-ROW.
Sheesh!
I'LL BE WAITING FOR YOU.
OKAY.

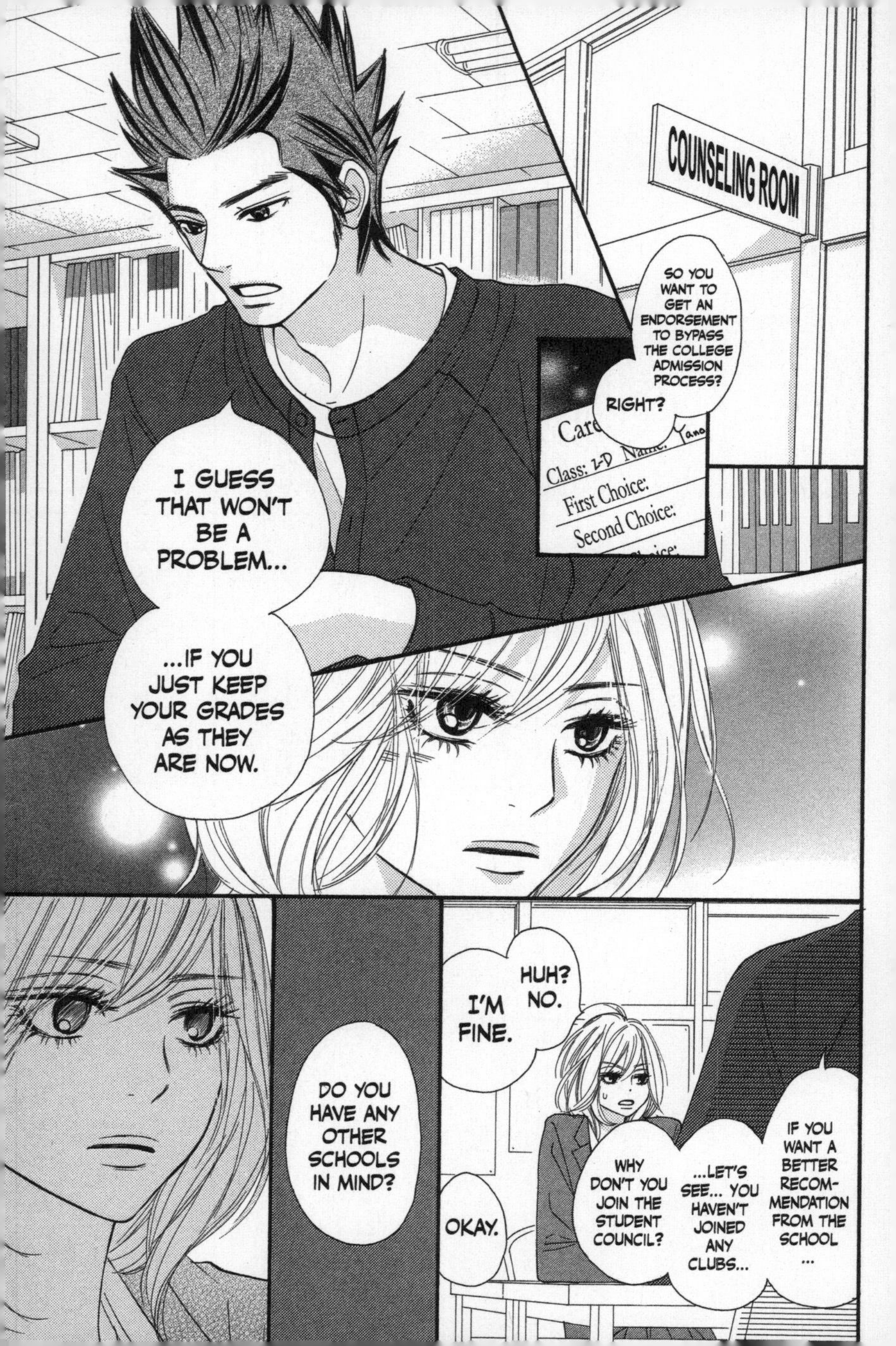
COUNSELING ROOM
SO YOU WANT TO GET AN ENDORSEMENT TO BYPASS THE COLLEGE ADMISSION PROCESS?
RIGHT?
Yano
Class: 2-D Name:
First Choice:
Second Choice:
I GUESS THAT WON'T BE A PROBLEM...
...IF YOU JUST KEEP YOUR GRADES AS THEY ARE NOW.
IF YOU WANT A BETTER RECOM-MENDATION FROM THE SCHOOL ...
...LET'S SEE... YOU HAVEN'T JOINED ANY CLUBS...
WHY DON'T YOU JOIN THE STUDENT COUNCIL?
HUH? NO.
I'M FINE.
OKAY.
DO YOU HAVE ANY OTHER SCHOOLS IN MIND?

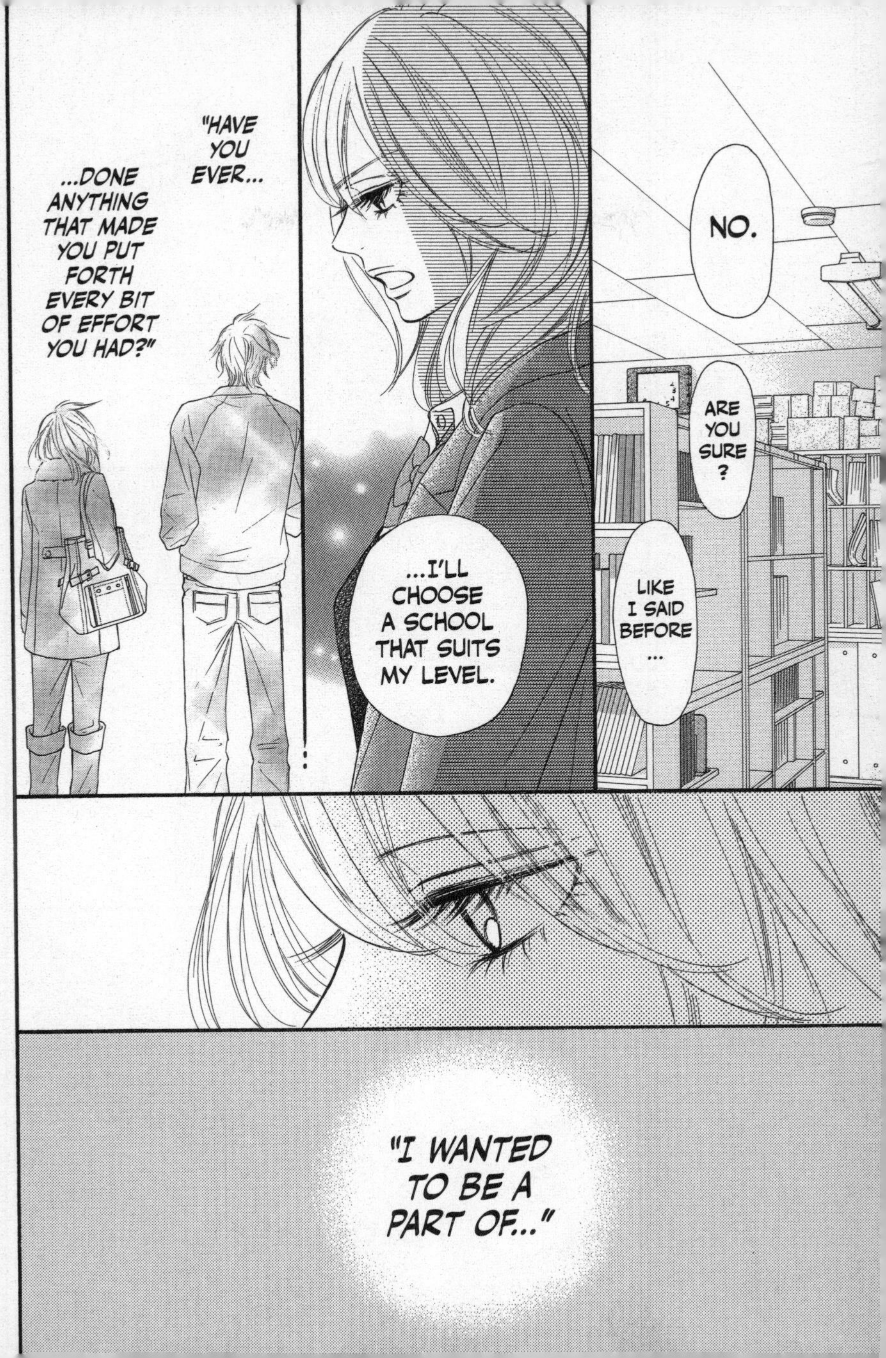
NO.
ARE YOU SURE?
LIKE I SAID BEFORE...
...I'LL CHOOSE A SCHOOL THAT SUITS MY LEVEL.
"HAVE YOU EVER...
...DONE ANYTHING THAT MADE YOU PUT FORTH EVERY BIT OF EFFORT YOU HAD?"
"I WANTED TO BE A PART OF..."

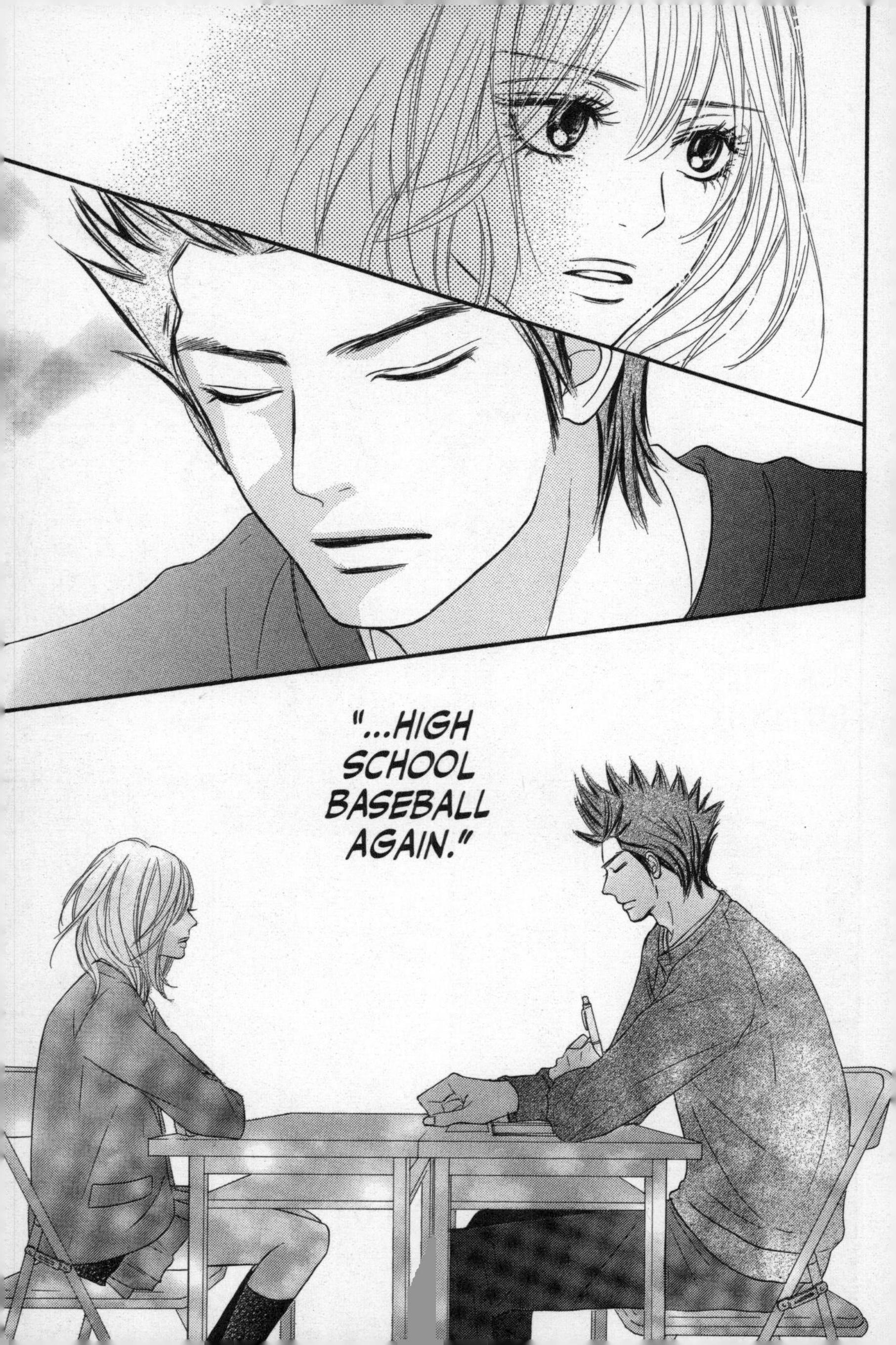
"...HIGH SCHOOL BASEBALL AGAIN."

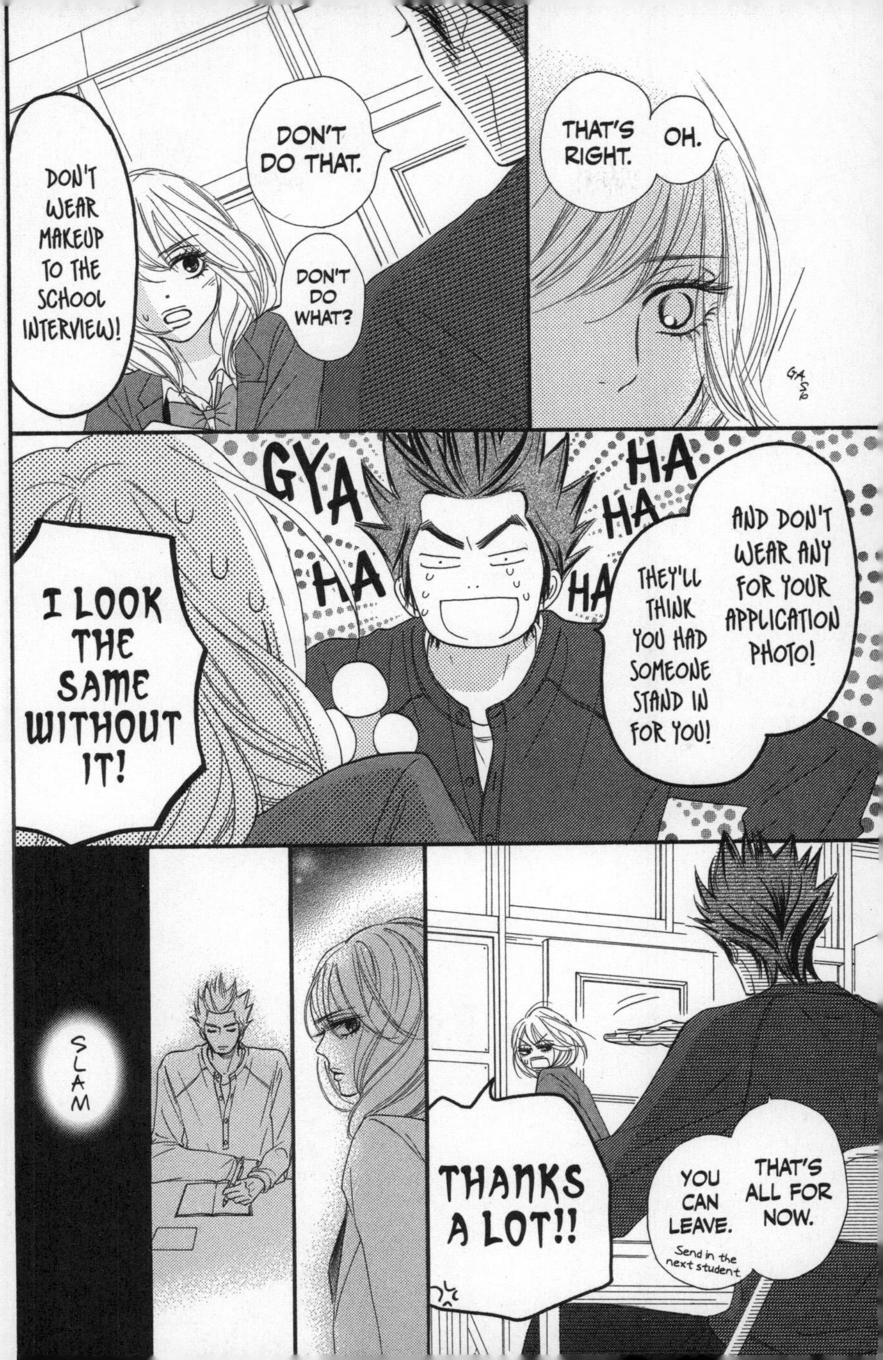
OH.
THAT'S RIGHT.
DON'T DO THAT.
DON'T DO WHAT?
DON'T WEAR MAKEUP TO THE SCHOOL INTERVIEW!
AND DON'T WEAR ANY FOR YOUR APPLICATION PHOTO!
THEY'LL THINK YOU HAD SOMEONE STAND IN FOR YOU!
GYA HA HA HA HA
I LOOK THE SAME WITHOUT IT!
THAT'S ALL FOR NOW.
YOU CAN LEAVE.
Send in the next student.
THANKS A LOT!!
SLAM

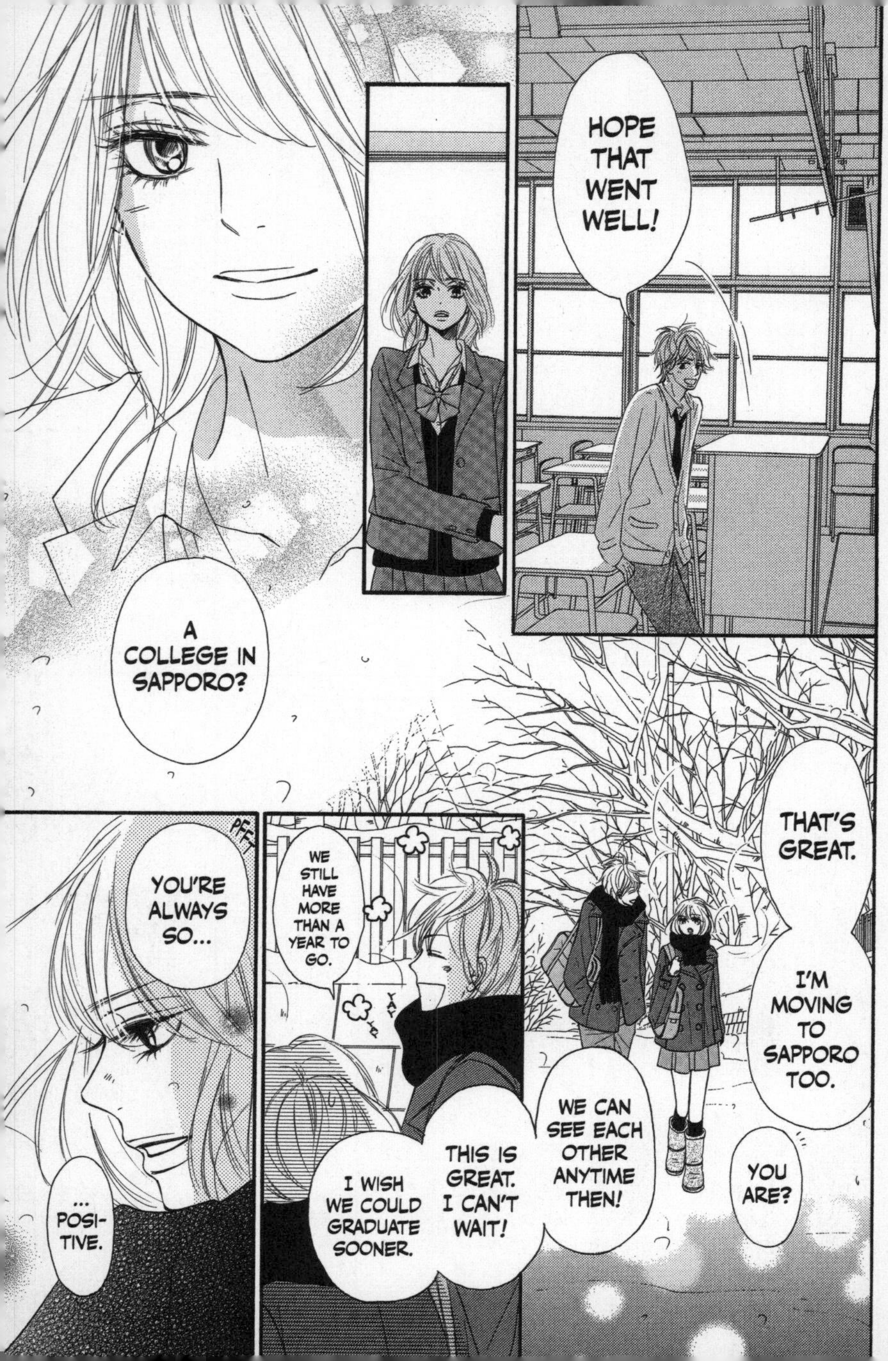
HOPE THAT WENT WELL!
A COLLEGE IN SAPPORO?
THAT'S GREAT.
I'M MOVING TO SAPPORO TOO.
YOU ARE?
WE CAN SEE EACH OTHER ANYTIME THEN!
THIS IS GREAT. I CAN'T WAIT!
I WISH WE COULD GRADUATE SOONER.
WE STILL HAVE MORE THAN A YEAR TO GO.
YAY
PFFT
YOU'RE ALWAYS SO...
...POSI-TIVE.

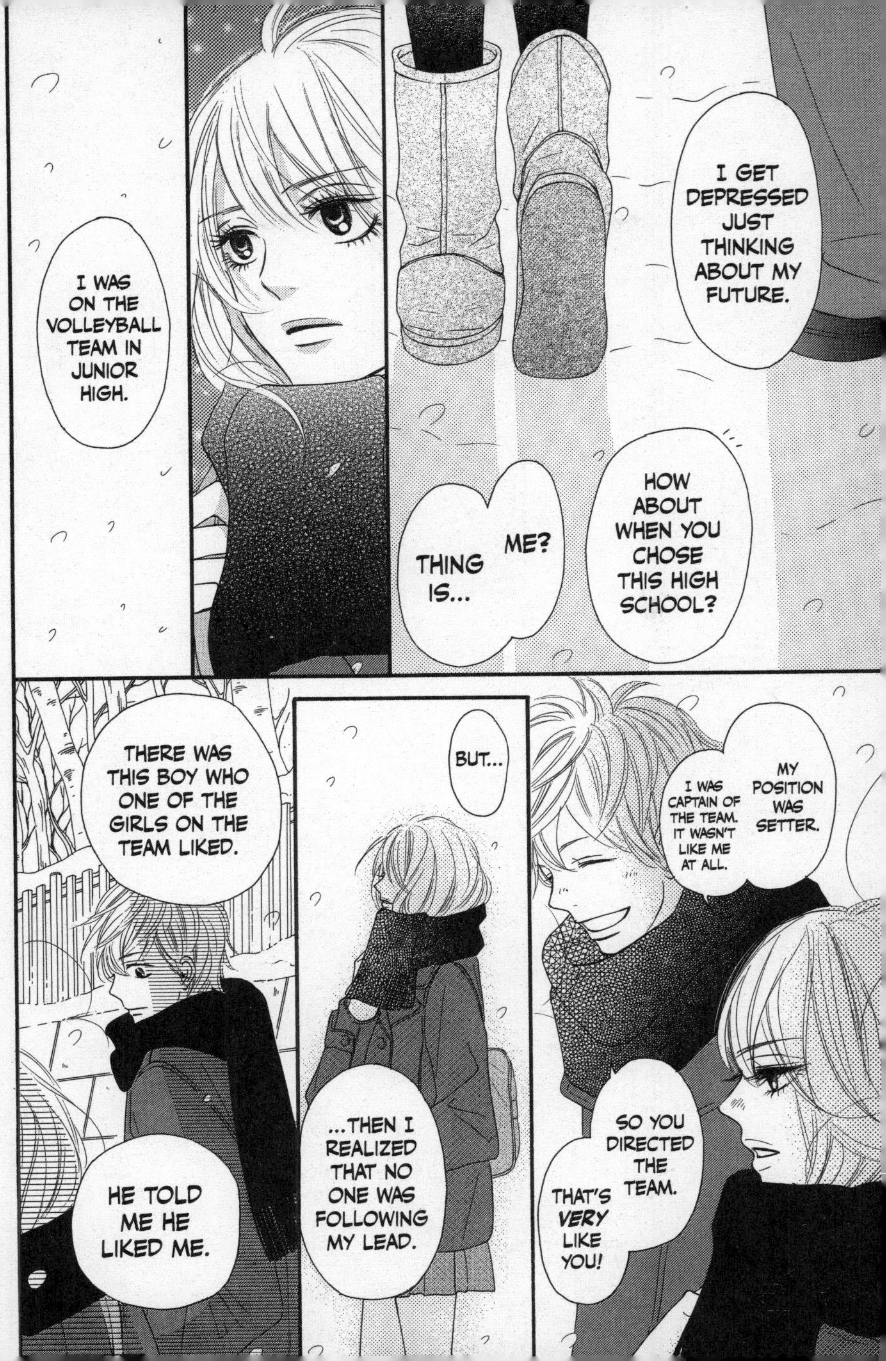
I GET DEPRESSED JUST THINKING ABOUT MY FUTURE.
HOW ABOUT WHEN YOU CHOSE THIS HIGH SCHOOL?
ME?
THING IS...
I WAS ON THE VOLLEYBALL TEAM IN JUNIOR HIGH.
MY POSITION WAS SETTER.
I WAS CAPTAIN OF THE TEAM. IT WASN'T LIKE ME AT ALL.
SO YOU DIRECTED THE TEAM.
THAT'S *VERY* LIKE YOU!
BUT...
...THEN I REALIZED THAT NO ONE WAS FOLLOWING MY LEAD.
THERE WAS THIS BOY WHO ONE OF THE GIRLS ON THE TEAM LIKED.
HE TOLD ME HE LIKED ME.

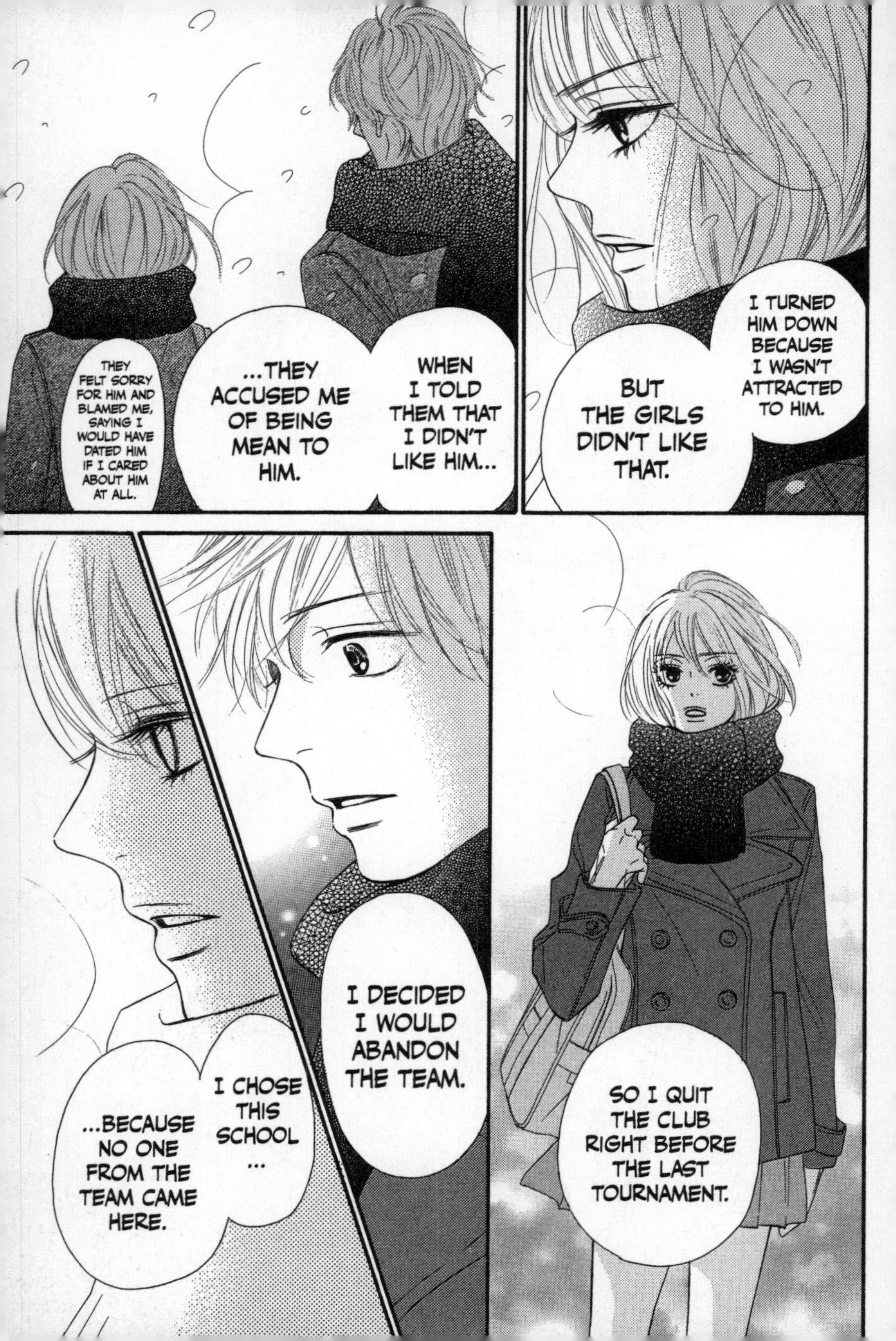
I TURNED HIM DOWN BECAUSE I WASN'T ATTRACTED TO HIM.
BUT THE GIRLS DIDN'T LIKE THAT.
WHEN I TOLD THEM THAT I DIDN'T LIKE HIM...
...THEY ACCUSED ME OF BEING MEAN TO HIM.
THEY FELT SORRY FOR HIM AND BLAMED ME, SAYING I WOULD HAVE DATED HIM IF I CARED ABOUT HIM AT ALL.
SO I QUIT THE CLUB RIGHT BEFORE THE LAST TOURNAMENT.
I DECIDED I WOULD ABANDON THE TEAM.
I CHOSE THIS SCHOOL ...
...BECAUSE NO ONE FROM THE TEAM CAME HERE.

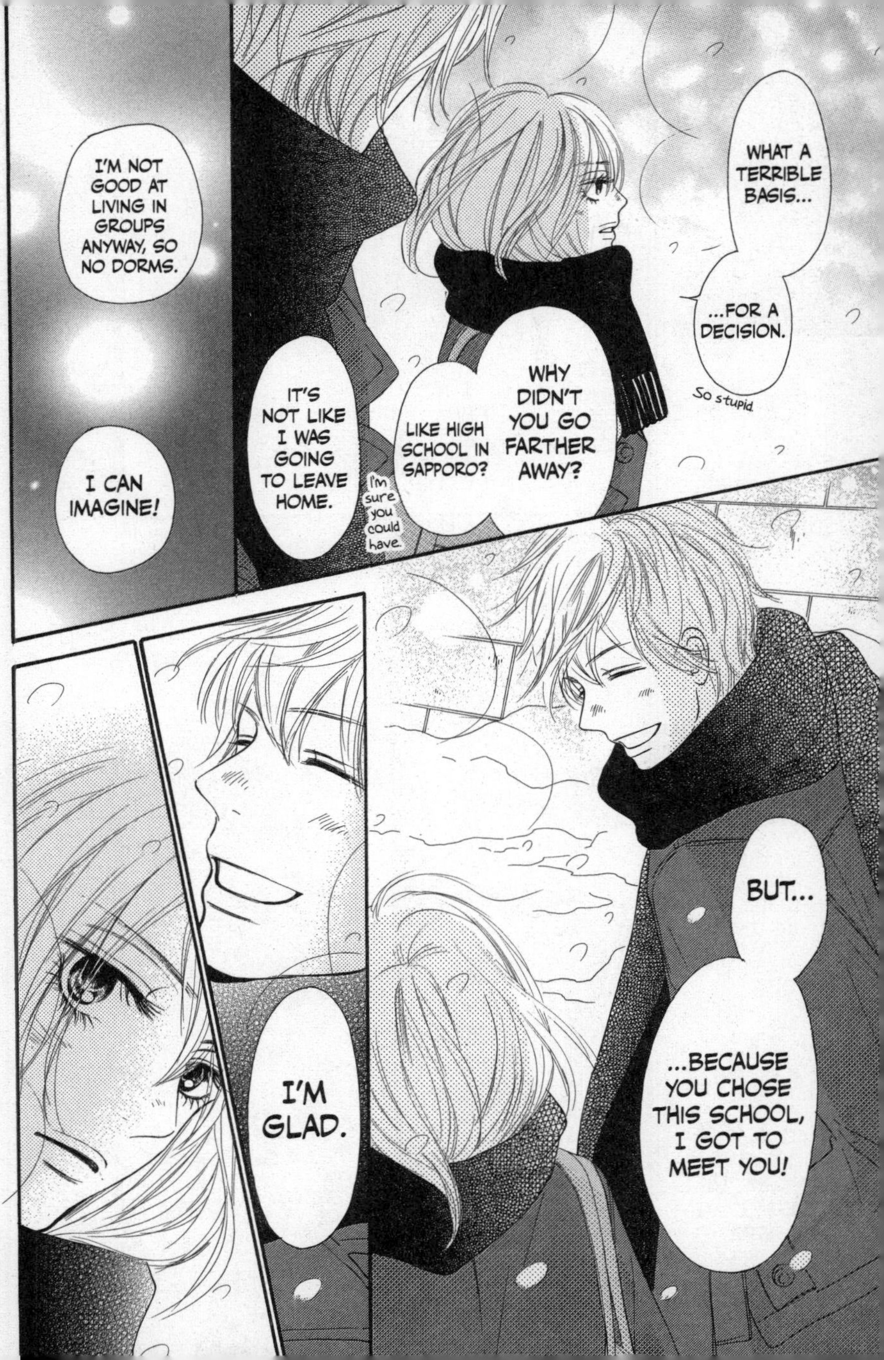
WHAT A TERRIBLE BASIS...
...FOR A DECISION.
So stupid.
WHY DIDN'T YOU GO FARTHER AWAY?
LIKE HIGH SCHOOL IN SAPPORO?
I'm sure you could have.
IT'S NOT LIKE I WAS GOING TO LEAVE HOME.
I'M NOT GOOD AT LIVING IN GROUPS ANYWAY, SO NO DORMS.
I CAN IMAGINE!
BUT...
...BECAUSE YOU CHOSE THIS SCHOOL, I GOT TO MEET YOU!
I'M GLAD.

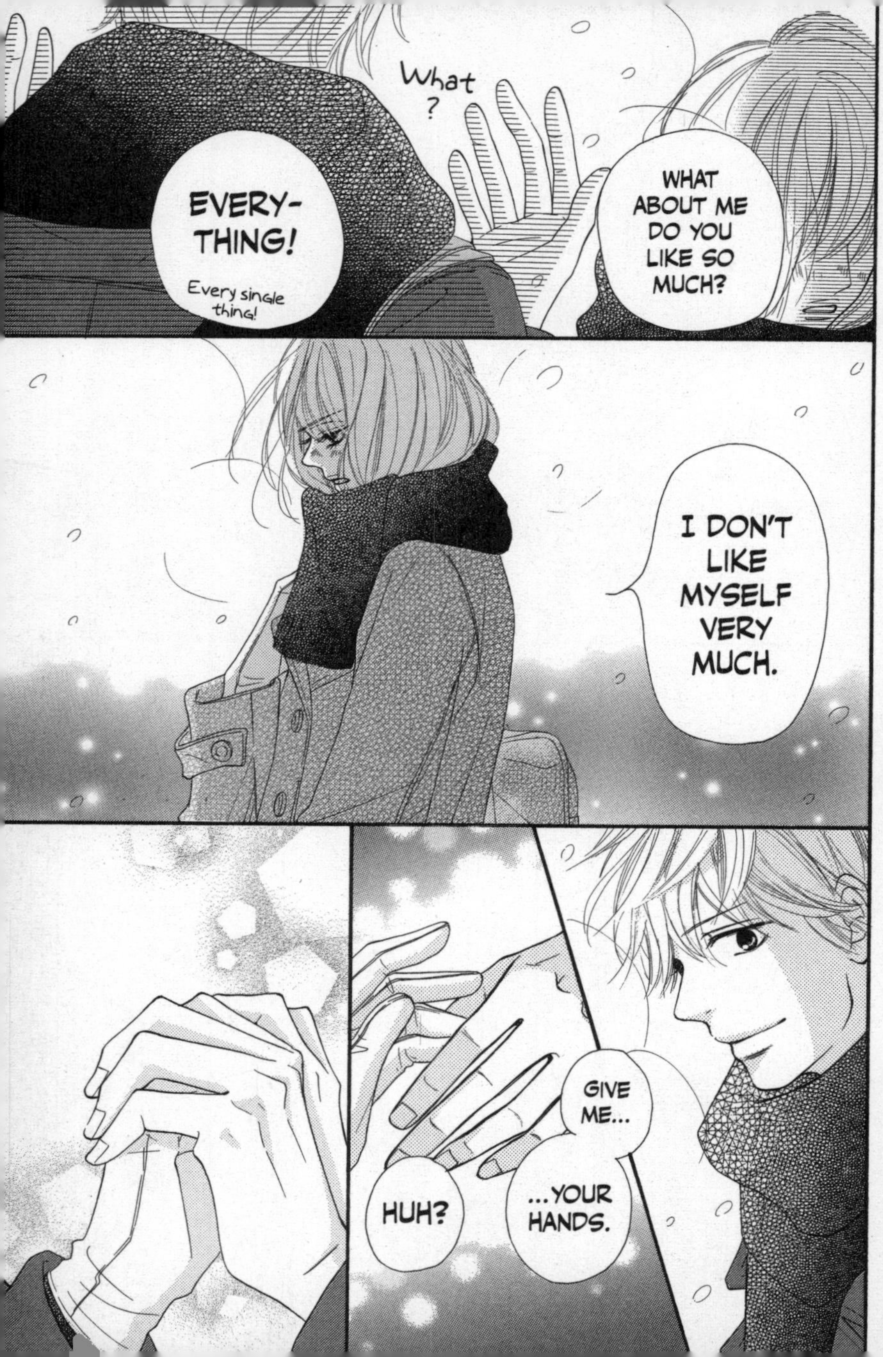
WHAT ABOUT ME DO YOU LIKE SO MUCH?
What ?
EVERY-THING!
Every single thing!
I DON'T LIKE MYSELF VERY MUCH.
GIVE ME...
...YOUR HANDS.
HUH?

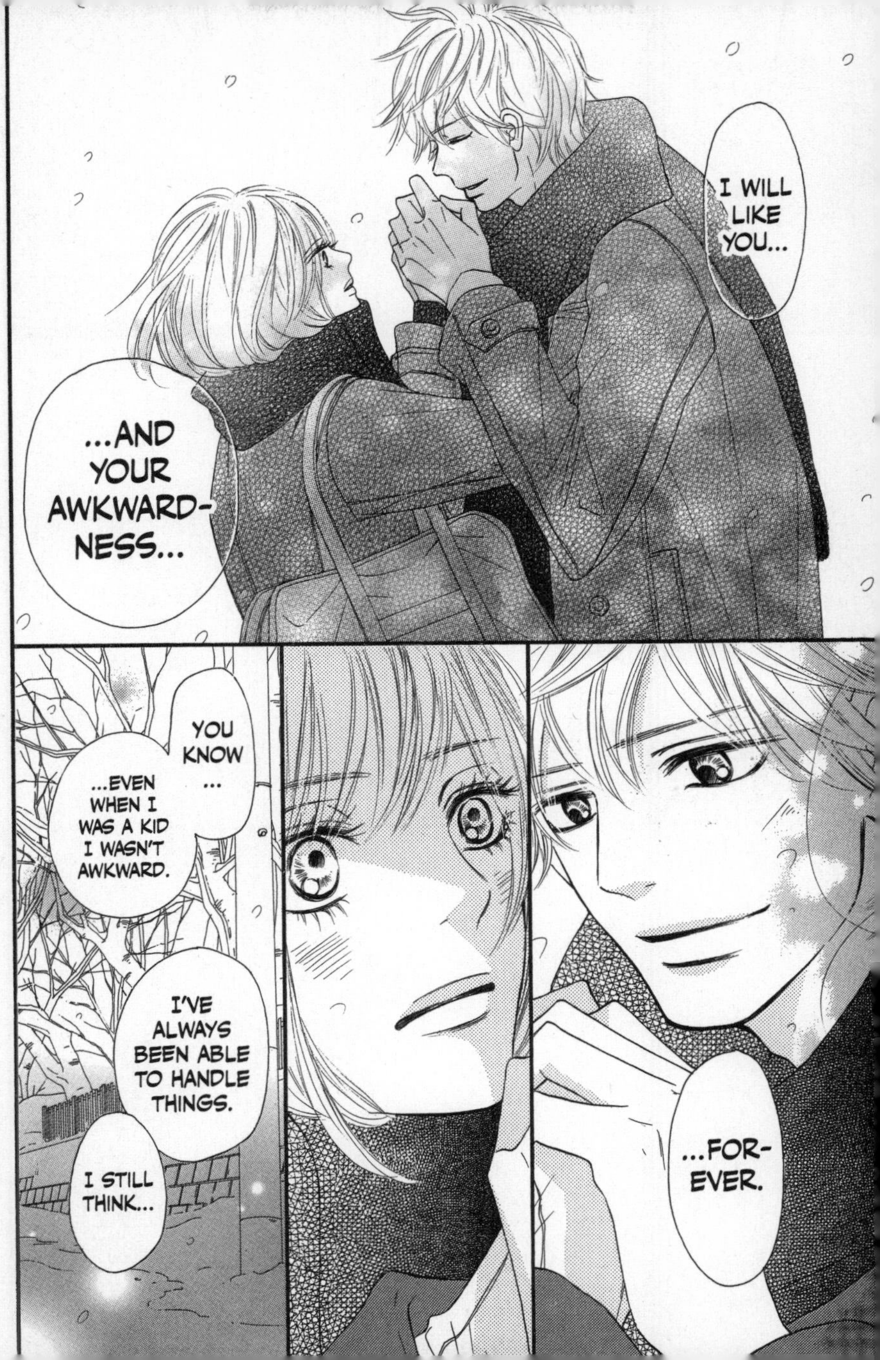
I WILL LIKE YOU...
...AND YOUR AWKWARD-NESS...
...FOR-EVER.
YOU KNOW ...
...EVEN WHEN I WAS A KID I WASN'T AWKWARD.
I'VE ALWAYS BEEN ABLE TO HANDLE THINGS.
I STILL THINK...

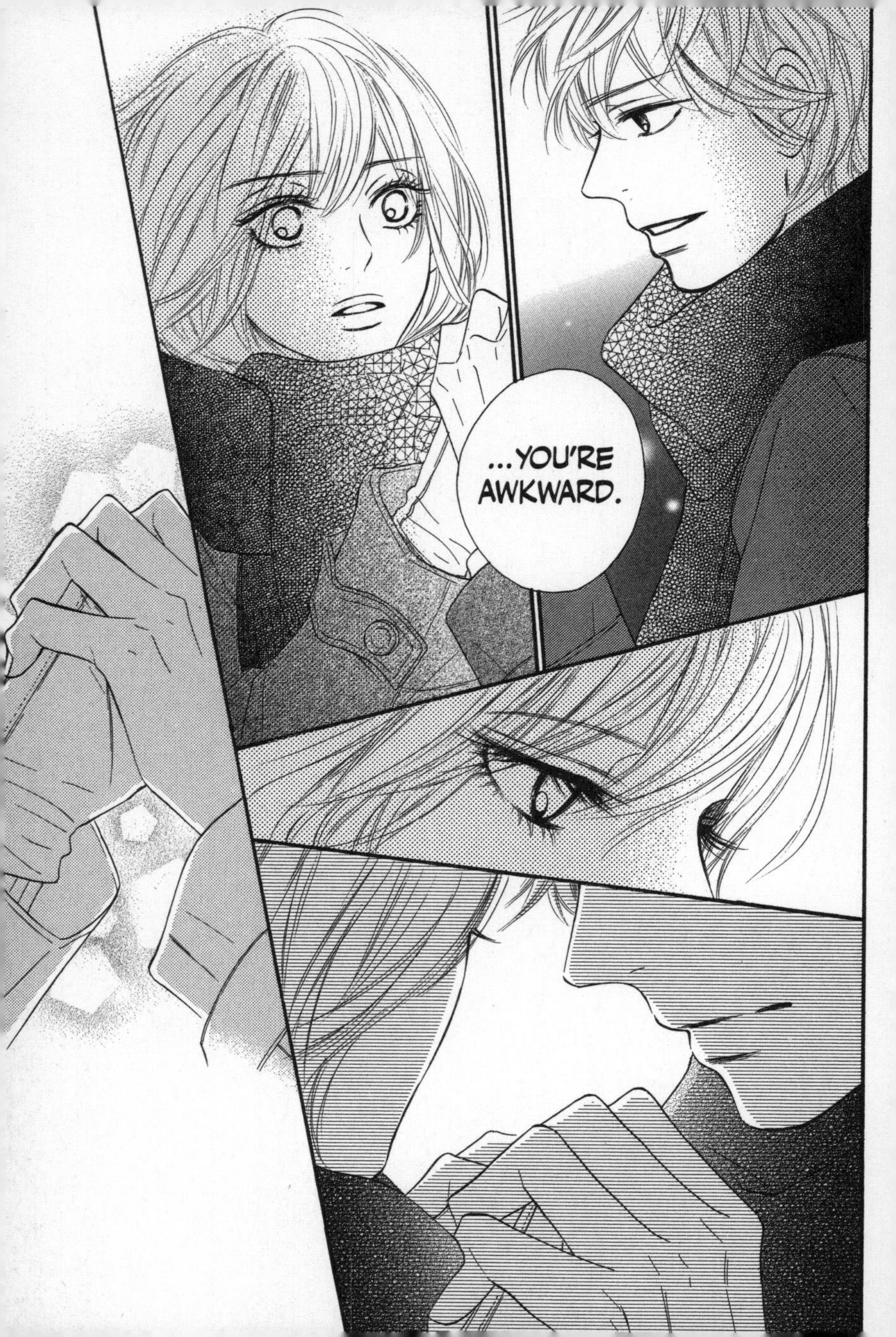
...YOU'RE AWKWARD.

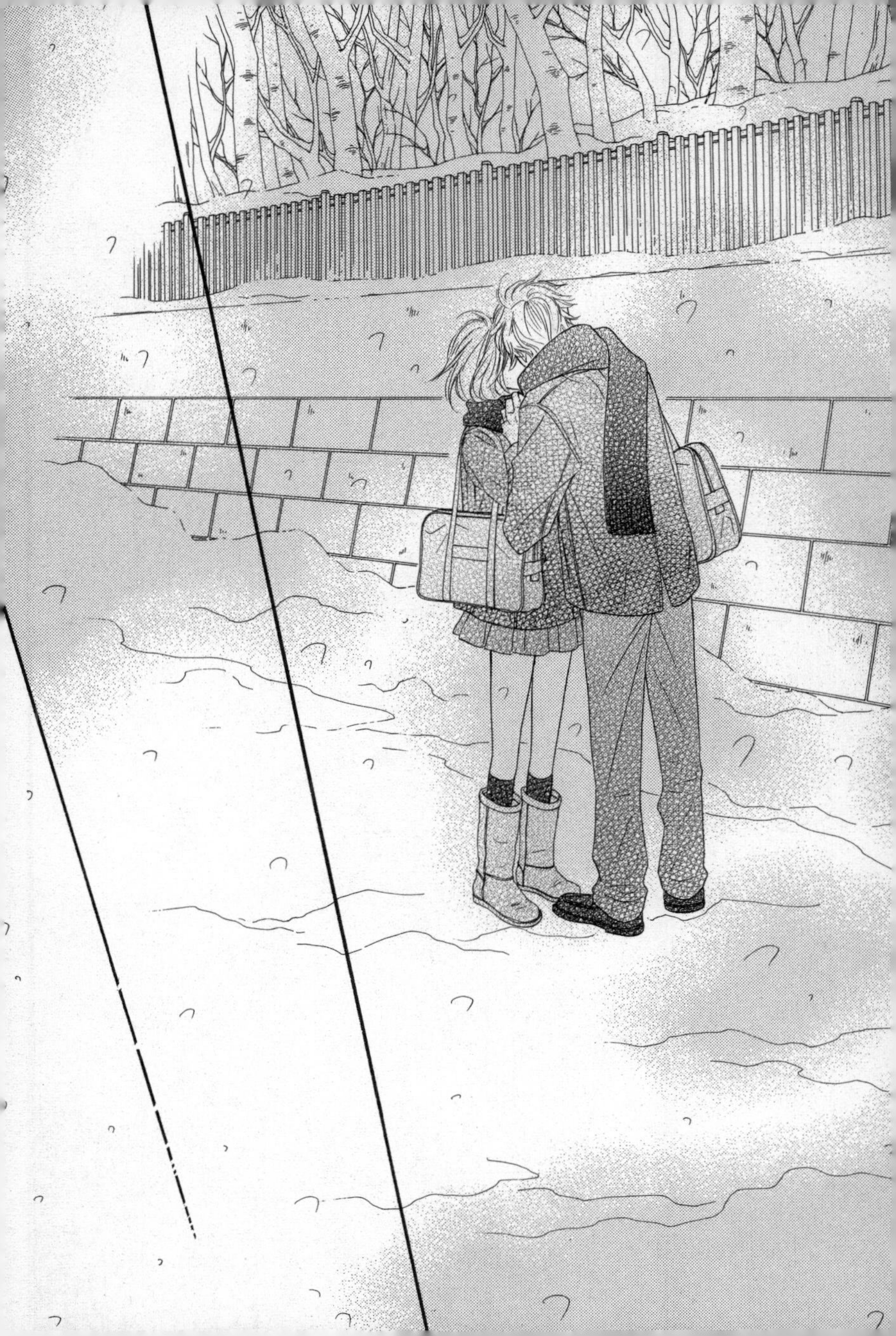

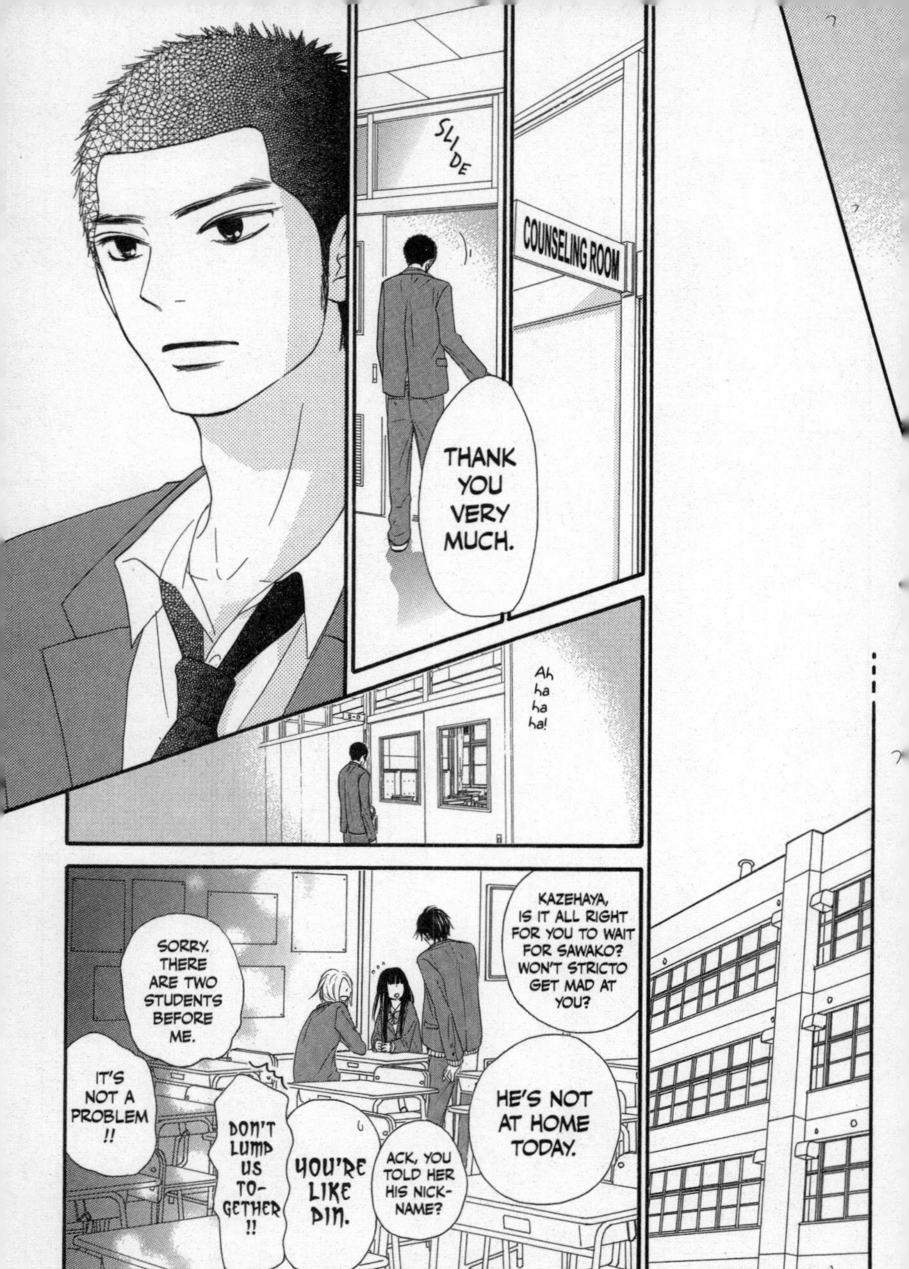
SLIDE
COUNSELING ROOM
THANK YOU VERY MUCH.
Ah ha ha ha!
KAZEHAYA, IS IT ALL RIGHT FOR YOU TO WAIT FOR SAWAKO? WON'T STRICTO GET MAD AT YOU?
HE'S NOT AT HOME TODAY.
SORRY. THERE ARE TWO STUDENTS BEFORE ME.
ACK, YOU TOLD HER HIS NICK-NAME?
YOU'RE LIKE PIN.
DON'T LUMP US TO-GETHER!!
IT'S NOT A PROBLEM!!

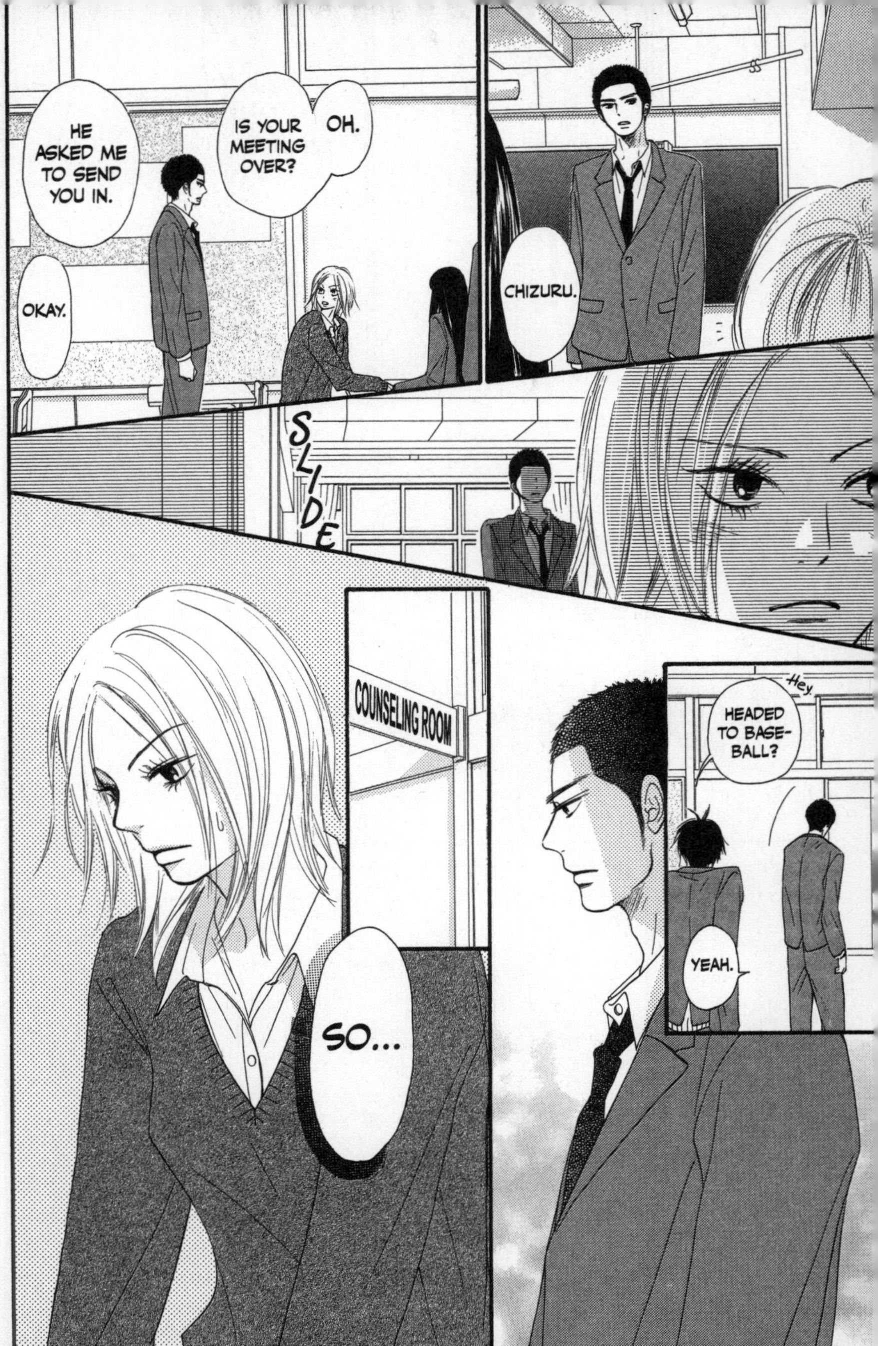
CHIZURU.
OH.
IS YOUR MEETING OVER?
HE ASKED ME TO SEND YOU IN.
OKAY.
SLIDE
Hey.
HEADED TO BASE-BALL?
YEAH.
COUNSELING ROOM
SO...

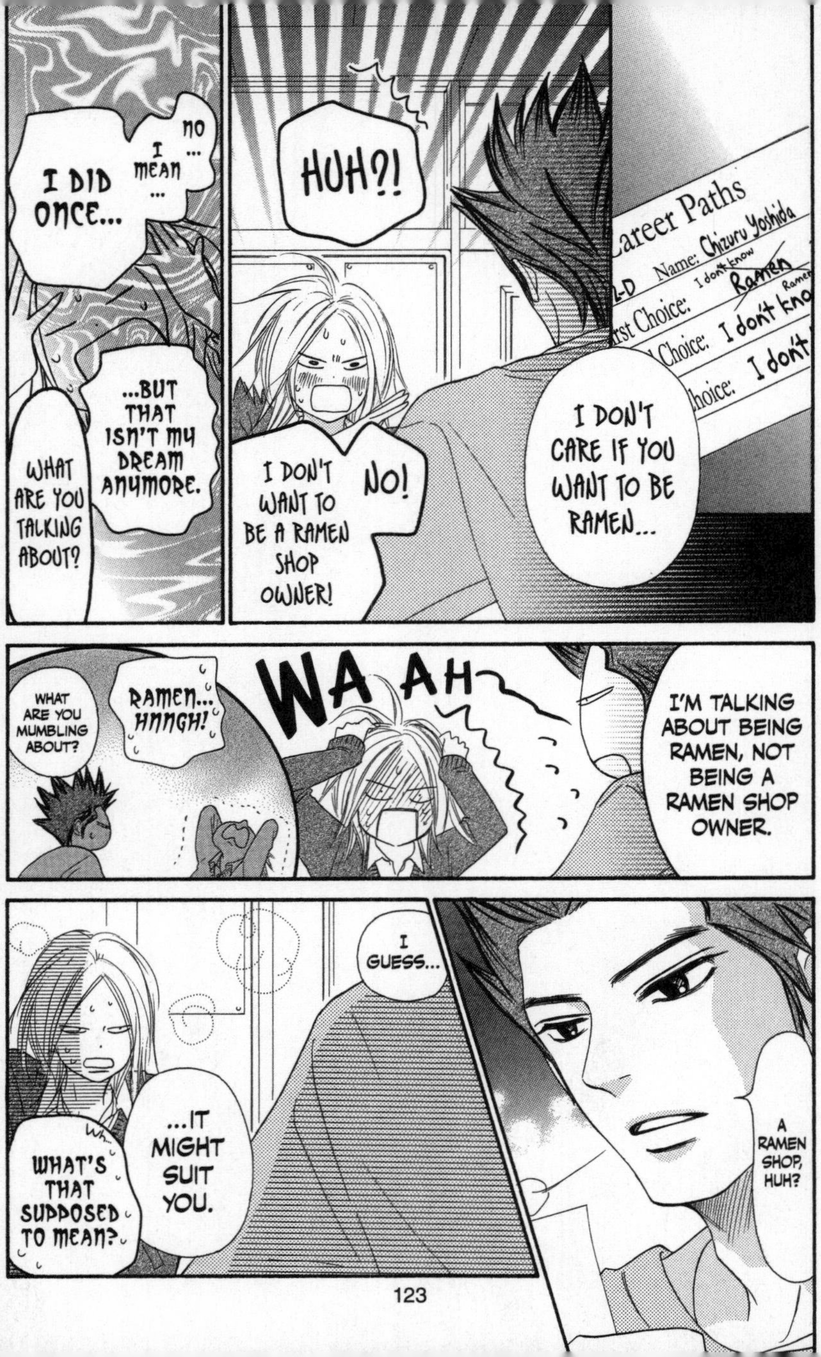
areer Paths
-D Name: Chizuru Yoshida
rst Choice: I don't know Ramen
Choice: Ramen I don't kno
hoice: I don't
I DON'T CARE IF YOU WANT TO BE RAMEN...
HUH?!
NO!
I DON'T WANT TO BE A RAMEN SHOP OWNER!
I DID ONCE... I MEAN ... NO ...
...BUT THAT ISN'T MY DREAM ANYMORE.
WHAT ARE YOU TALKING ABOUT?
I'M TALKING ABOUT BEING RAMEN, NOT BEING A RAMEN SHOP OWNER.
WA AH
RAMEN... HNNGH!
WHAT ARE YOU MUMBLING ABOUT?
A RAMEN SHOP, HUH?
I GUESS...
...IT MIGHT SUIT YOU.
Wh...
WHAT'S THAT SUPPOSED TO MEAN?

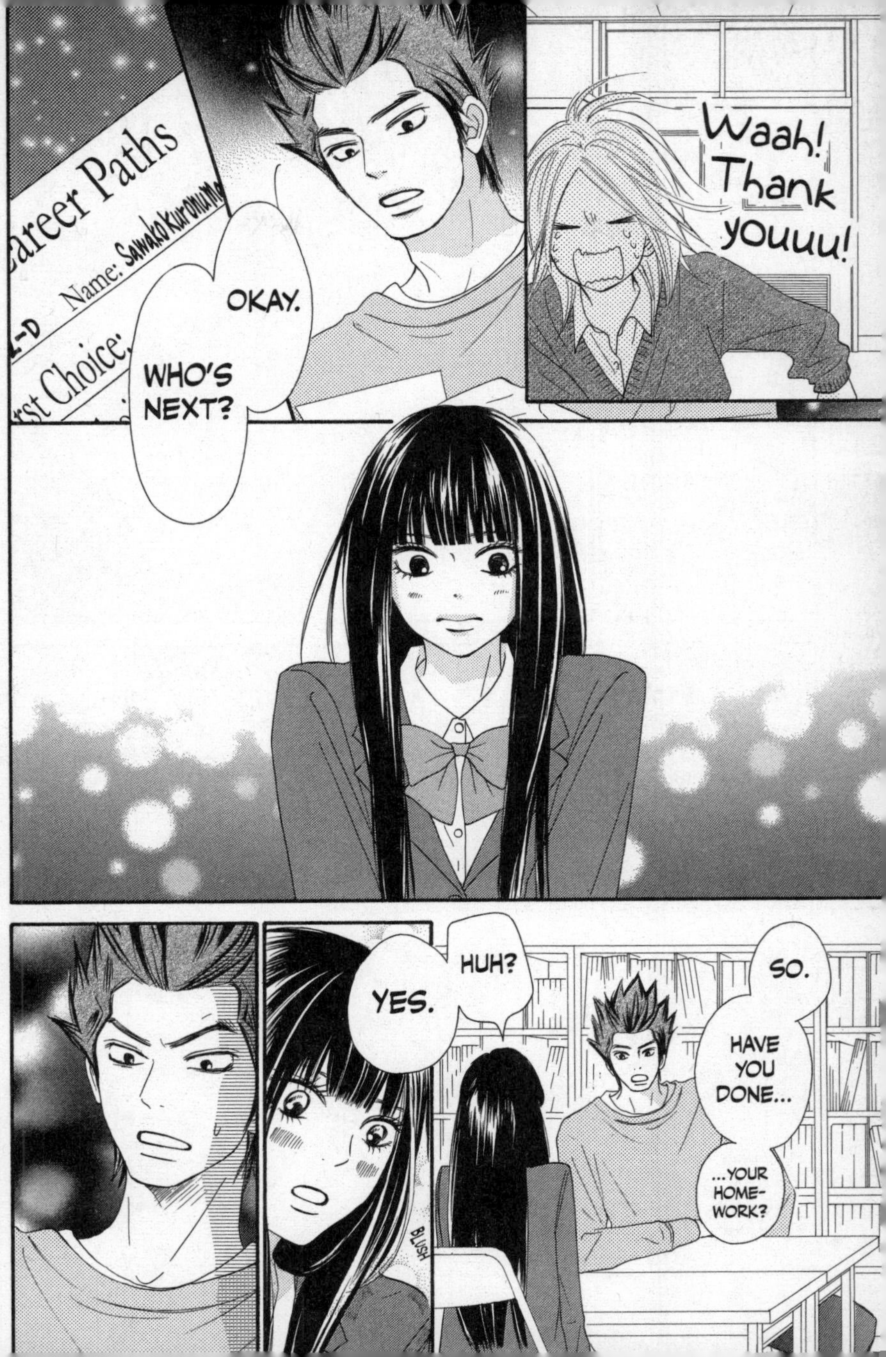
Waah! Thank youuu!
areer Paths
Name: Sawako Kuronum
rst Choice:
OKAY.
WHO'S NEXT?
SO.
HAVE YOU DONE...
...YOUR HOMEWORK?
HUH?
YES.
BLUSH

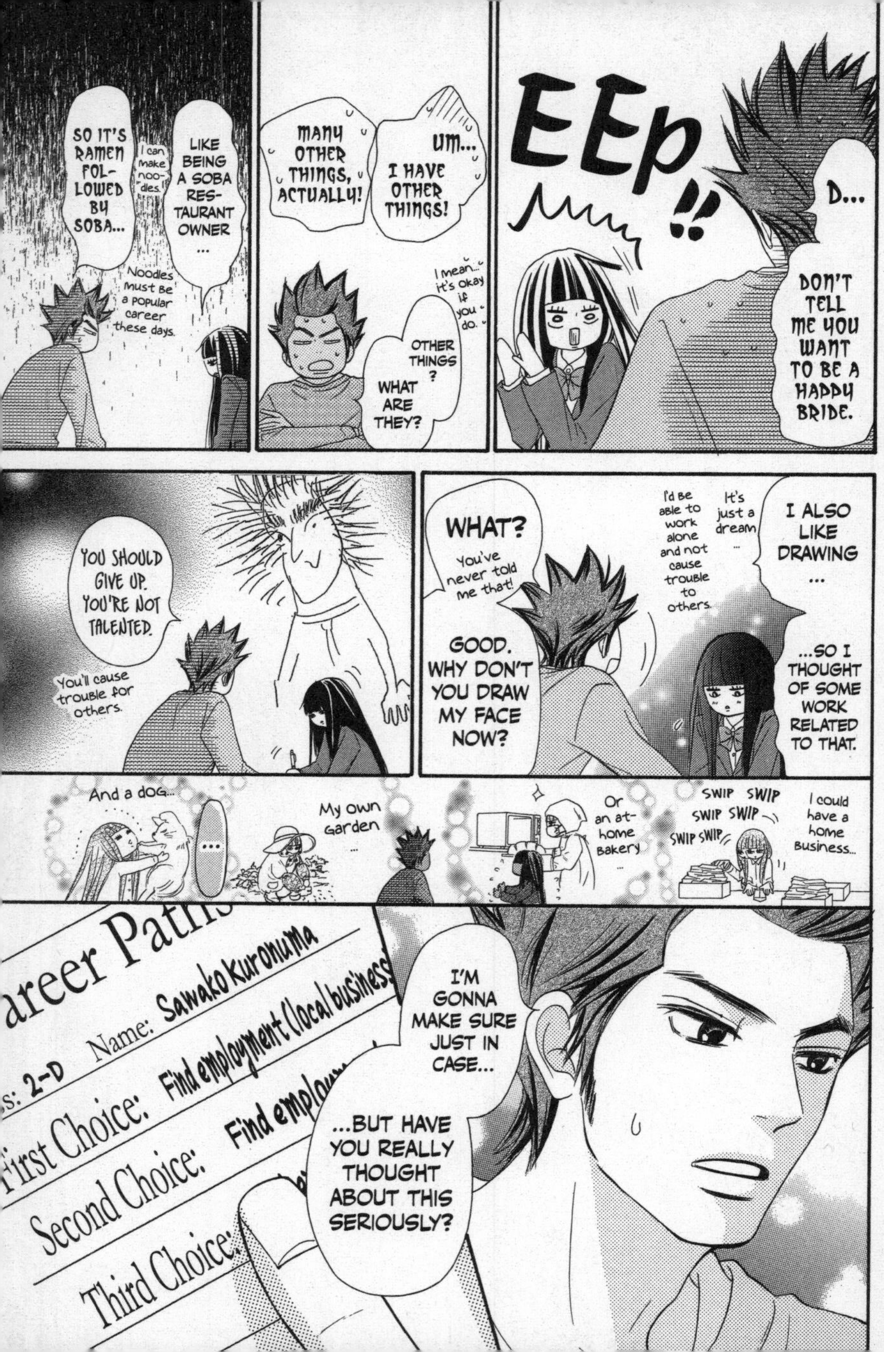
D...
DON'T TELL ME YOU WANT TO BE A HAPPY BRIDE.
EEp!!
UM... I HAVE OTHER THINGS!
MANY OTHER THINGS, ACTUALLY!
I mean... it's okay if you do.
OTHER THINGS? WHAT ARE THEY?
LIKE BEING A SOBA RES-TAURANT OWNER...
I can make noo-dles.
SO IT'S RAMEN FOL-LOWED BY SOBA...
Noodles must be a popular career these days.
I ALSO LIKE DRAWING...
It's just a dream...
I'd be able to work alone and not cause trouble to others.
WHAT?
You've never told me that!
...SO I THOUGHT OF SOME WORK RELATED TO THAT.
GOOD. WHY DON'T YOU DRAW MY FACE NOW?
YOU SHOULD GIVE UP. YOU'RE NOT TALENTED.
You'll cause trouble for others.
I could have a home business...
SWIP SWIP SWIP SWIP SWIP SWIP
Or an at-home bakery...
My own garden...
...
And a dog...
I'M GONNA MAKE SURE JUST IN CASE...
...BUT HAVE YOU REALLY THOUGHT ABOUT THIS SERIOUSLY?
areer Paths
Name: Sawako Kuronuma
2-D
First Choice: Find employment (local business
Second Choice:
Third Choice:

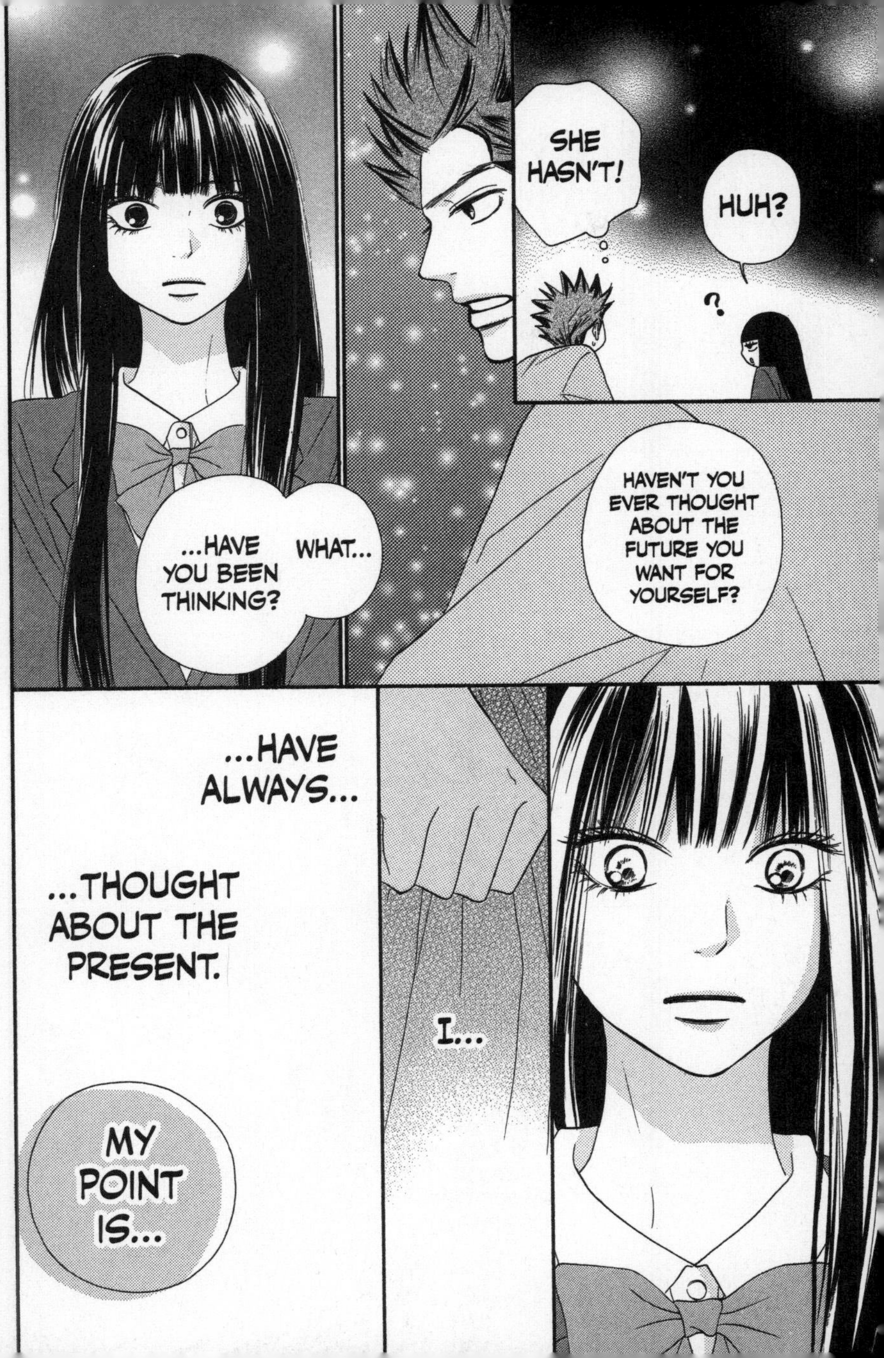
HUH?
SHE HASN'T!
HAVEN'T YOU EVER THOUGHT ABOUT THE FUTURE YOU WANT FOR YOURSELF?
WHAT...
...HAVE YOU BEEN THINKING?
I...
...HAVE ALWAYS...
...THOUGHT ABOUT THE PRESENT.
MY POINT IS...

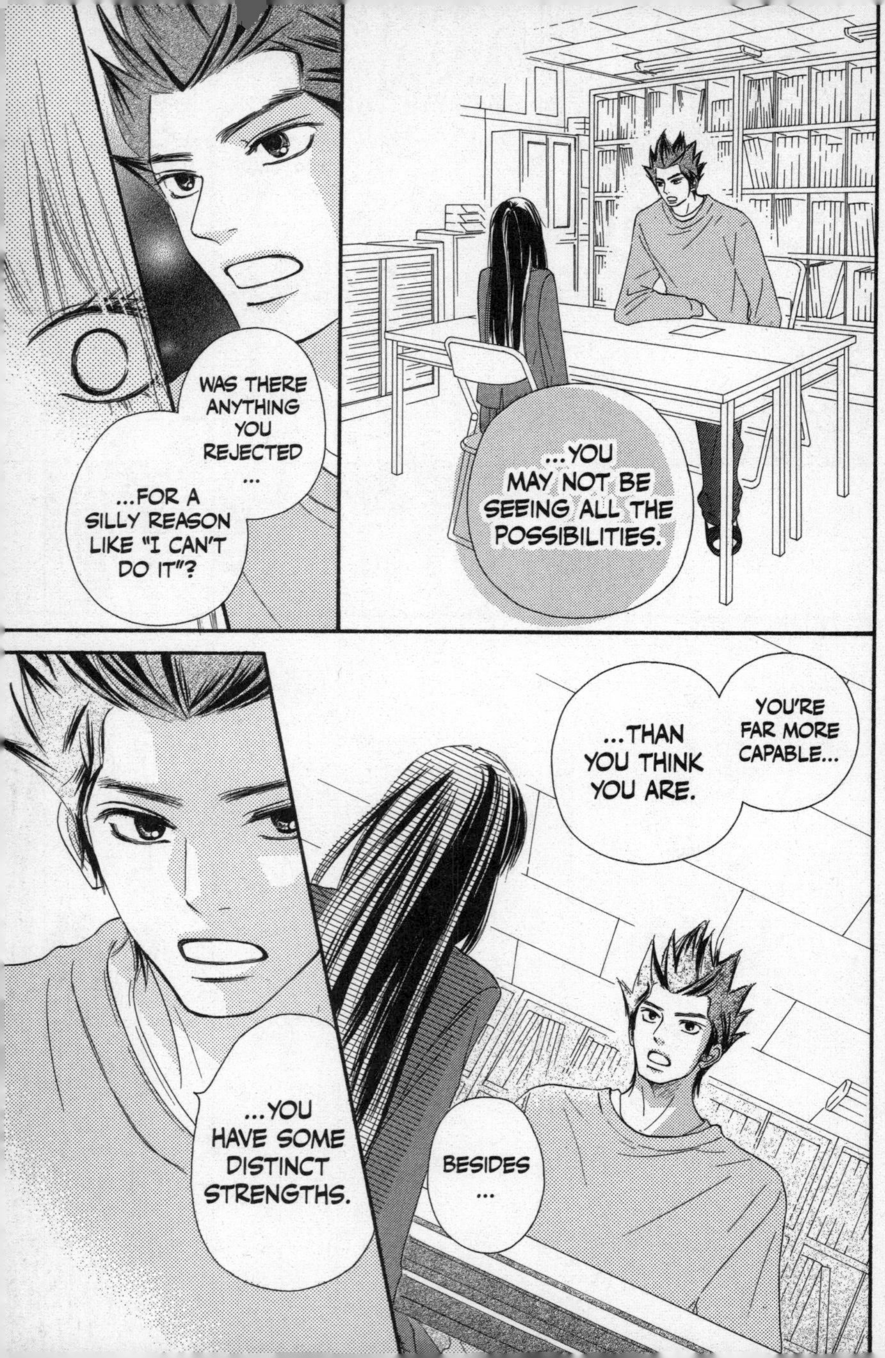
...YOU MAY NOT BE SEEING ALL THE POSSIBILITIES.
WAS THERE ANYTHING YOU REJECTED ...
...FOR A SILLY REASON LIKE "I CAN'T DO IT"?
YOU'RE FAR MORE CAPABLE...
...THAN YOU THINK YOU ARE.
BESIDES ...
...YOU HAVE SOME DISTINCT STRENGTHS.

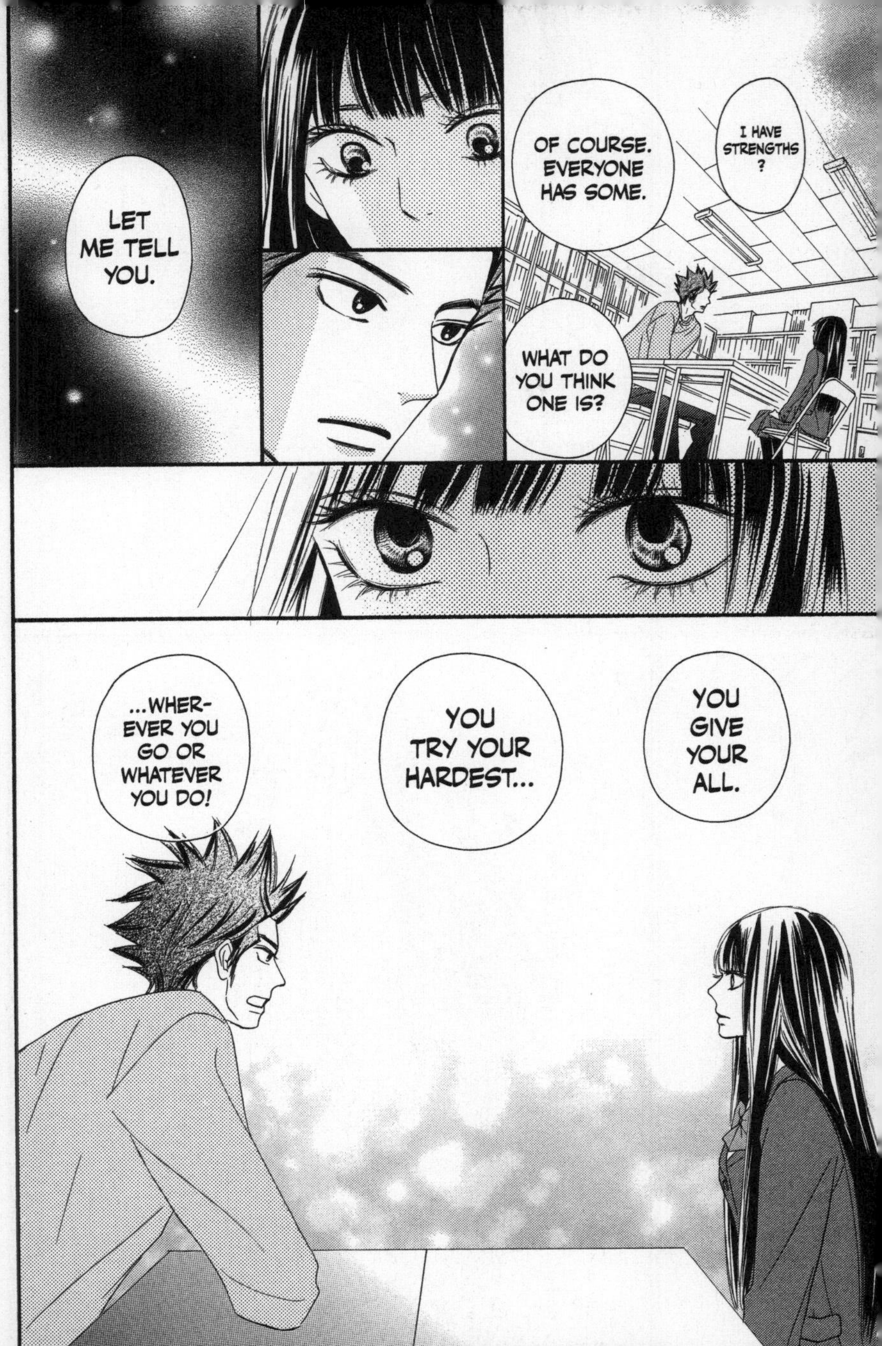
I HAVE STRENGTHS?
OF COURSE. EVERYONE HAS SOME.
WHAT DO YOU THINK ONE IS?
LET ME TELL YOU.
YOU GIVE YOUR ALL.
YOU TRY YOUR HARDEST...
...WHER-EVER YOU GO OR WHATEVER YOU DO!

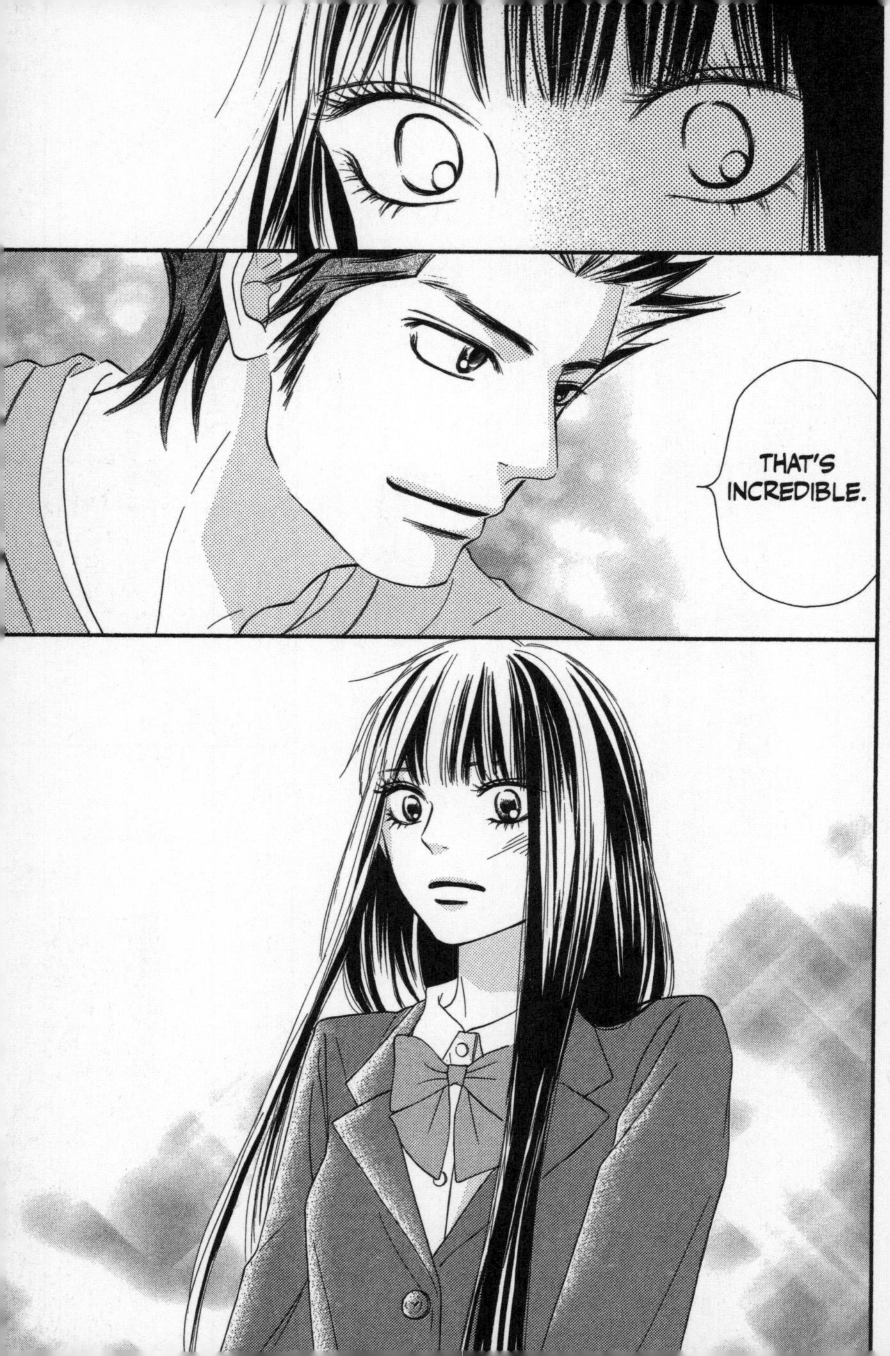
THAT'S INCREDIBLE.

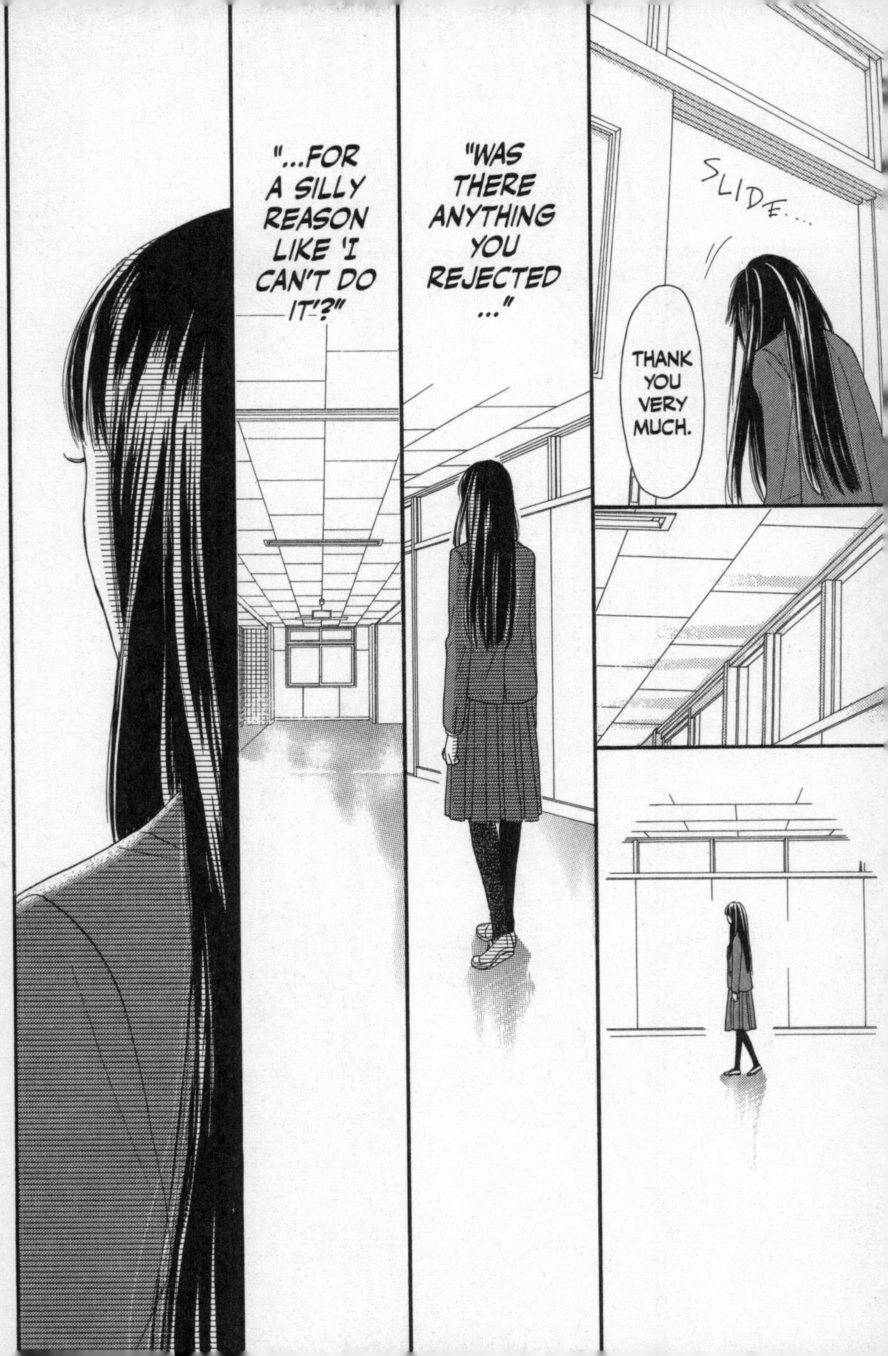
SLIDE....
THANK YOU VERY MUCH.
"WAS THERE ANYTHING YOU REJECTED ..."
"...FOR A SILLY REASON LIKE 'I CAN'T DO IT'?"

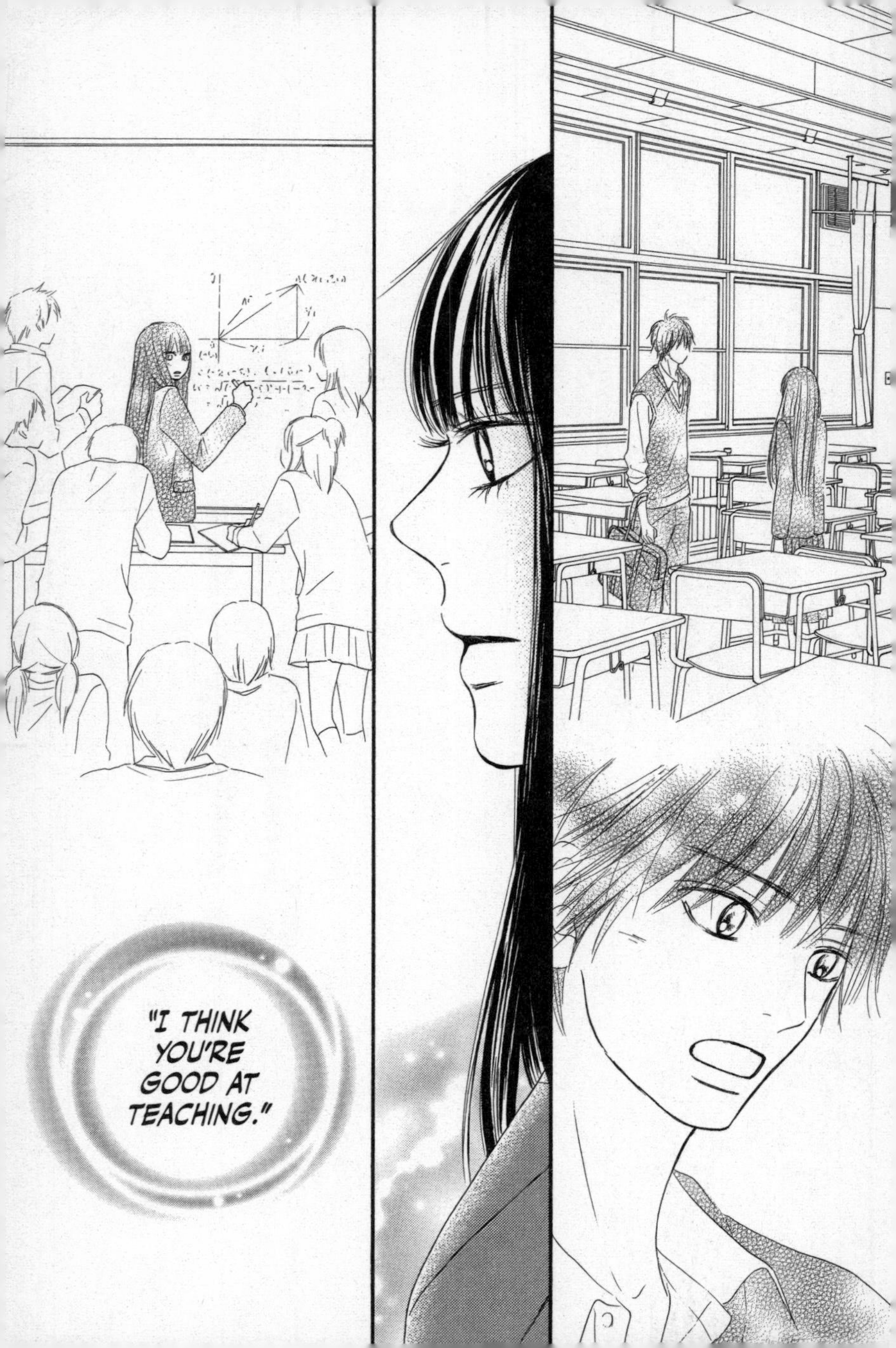
"I THINK YOU'RE GOOD AT TEACHING."

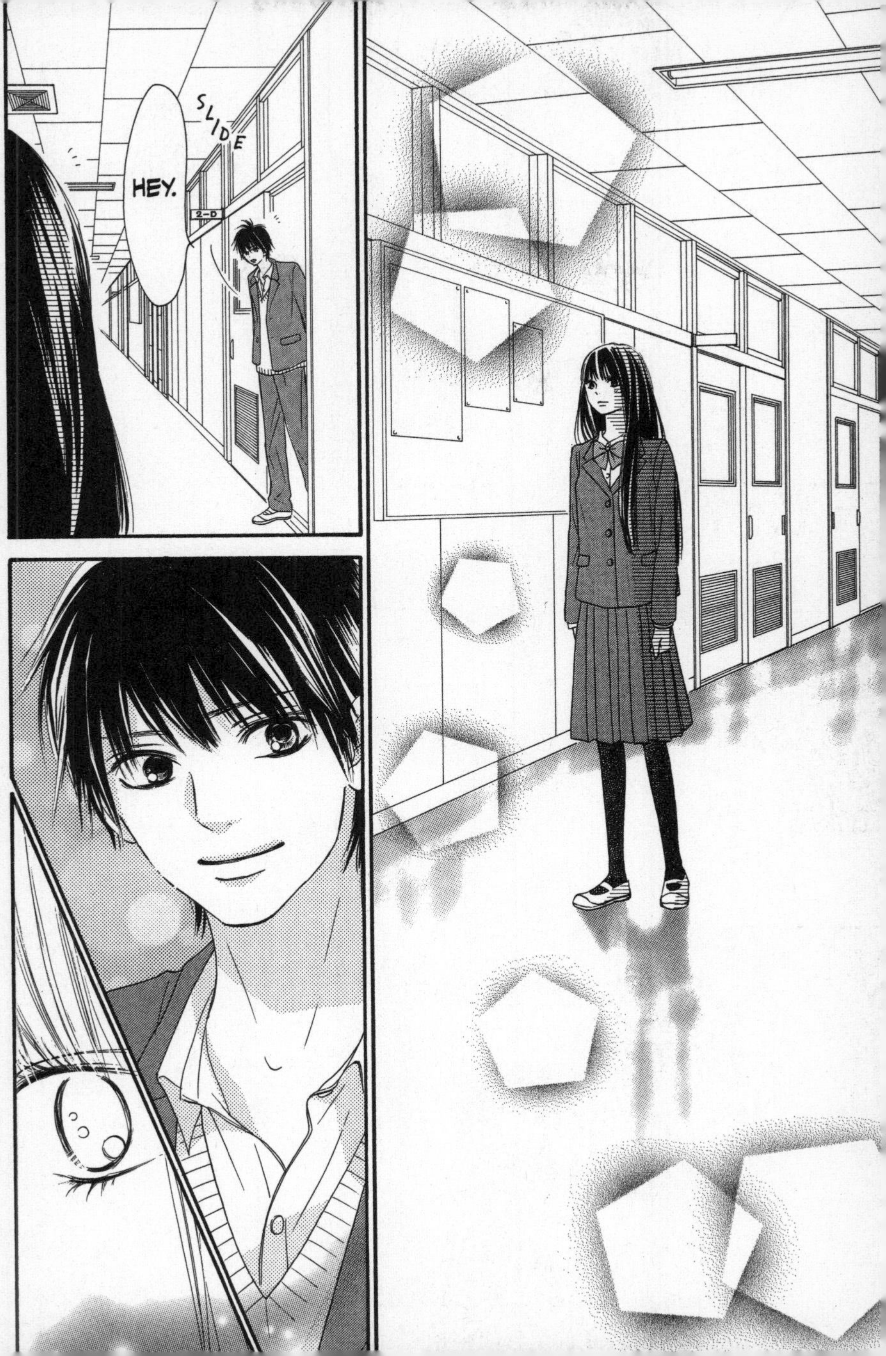
SLIDE
HEY.

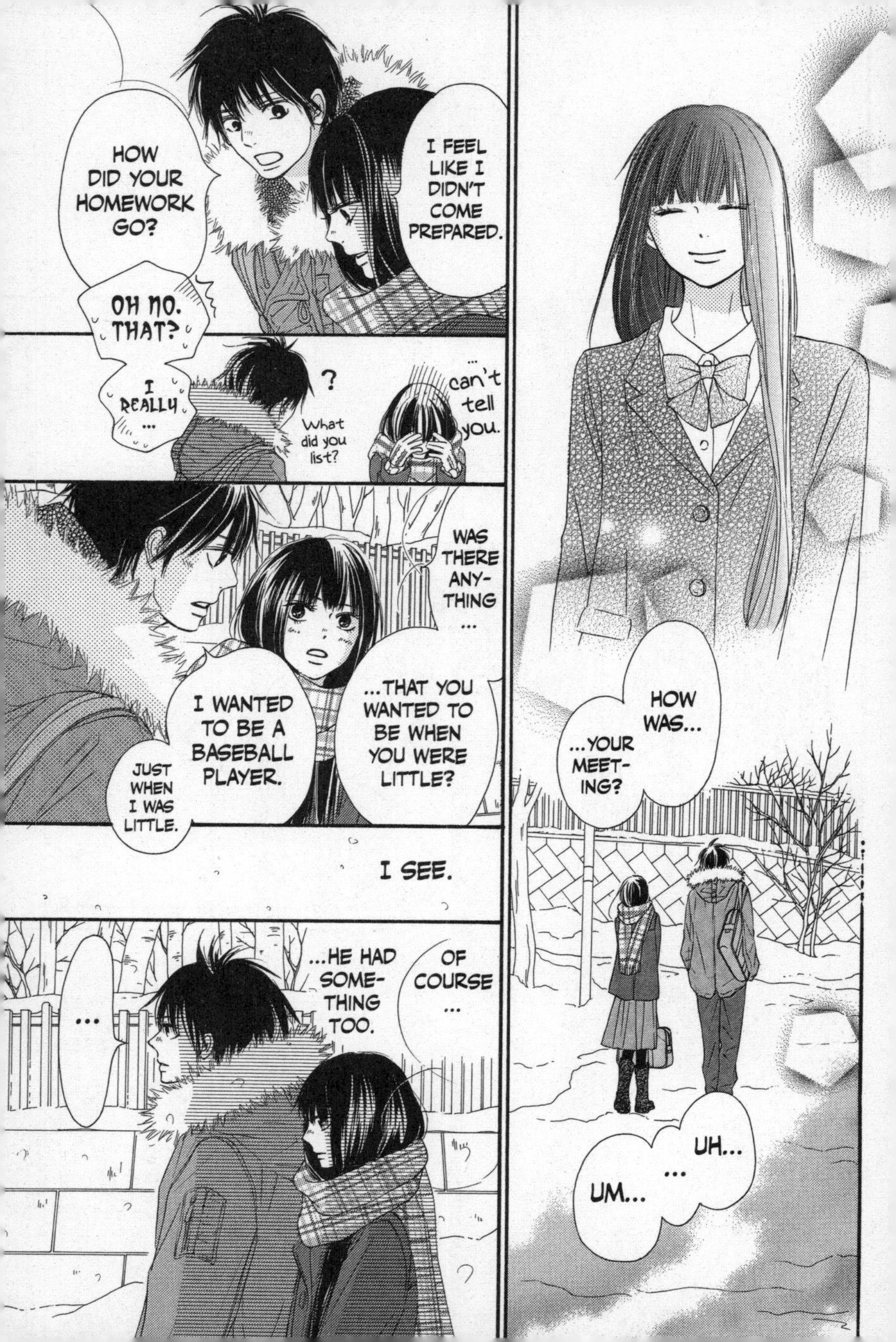
HOW WAS...
...YOUR MEETING?
UH...
...
UM...
I FEEL LIKE I DIDN'T COME PREPARED.
HOW DID YOUR HOMEWORK GO?
OH NO. THAT?
...can't tell you.
?
What did you list?
I REALLY ...
WAS THERE ANYTHING ...
...THAT YOU WANTED TO BE WHEN YOU WERE LITTLE?
I WANTED TO BE A BASEBALL PLAYER.
JUST WHEN I WAS LITTLE.
I SEE.
OF COURSE ...
...HE HAD SOMETHING TOO.
...

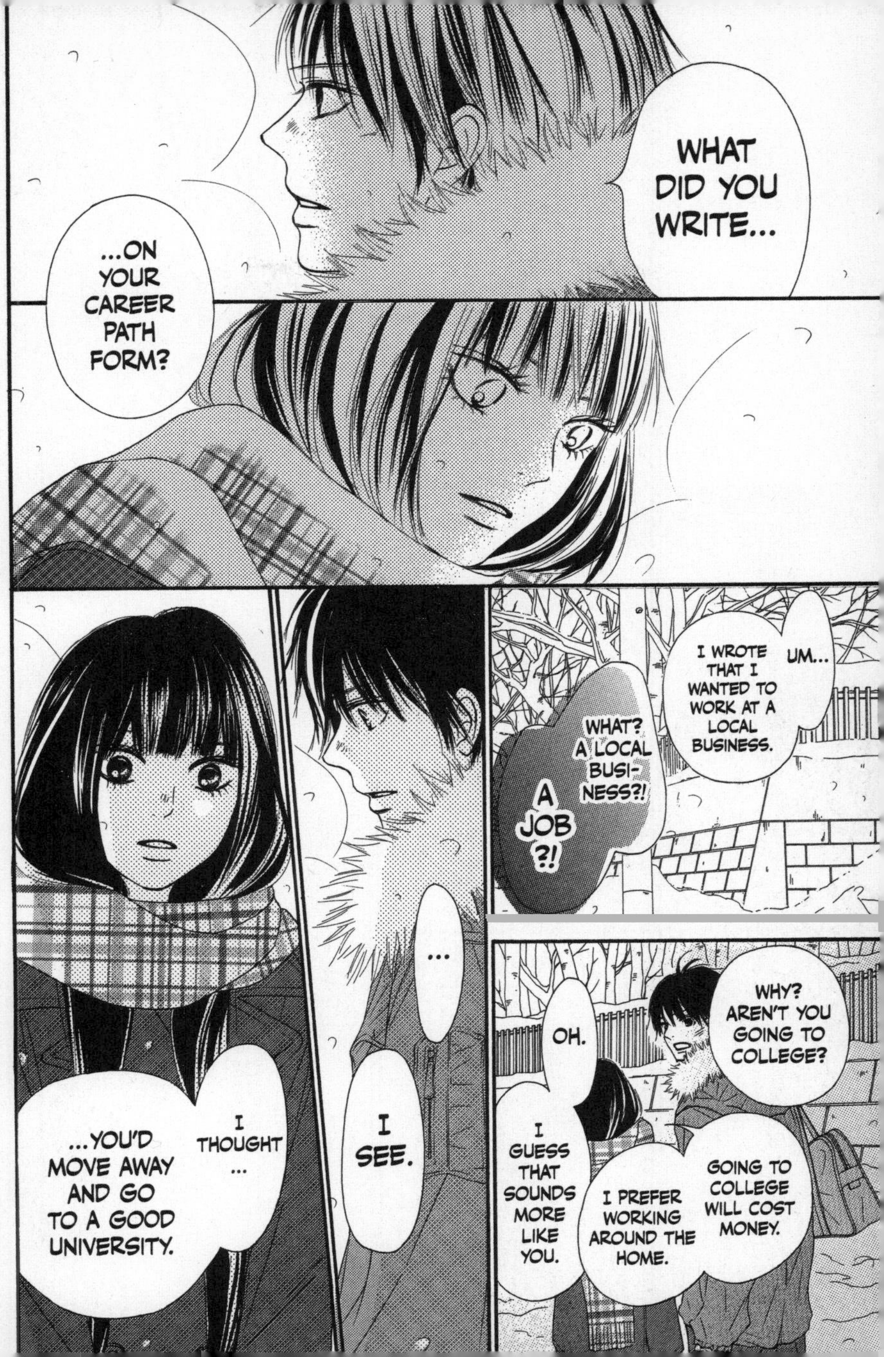

WHAT DID YOU WRITE...
...ON YOUR CAREER PATH FORM?
UM...
I WROTE THAT I WANTED TO WORK AT A LOCAL BUSINESS.
WHAT? A LOCAL BUSI- NESS?!
A JOB ?!
WHY? AREN'T YOU GOING TO COLLEGE?
OH.
GOING TO COLLEGE WILL COST MONEY.
I PREFER WORKING AROUND THE HOME.
I GUESS THAT SOUNDS MORE LIKE YOU.
...
I SEE.
I THOUGHT ...
...YOU'D MOVE AWAY AND GO TO A GOOD UNIVERSITY.

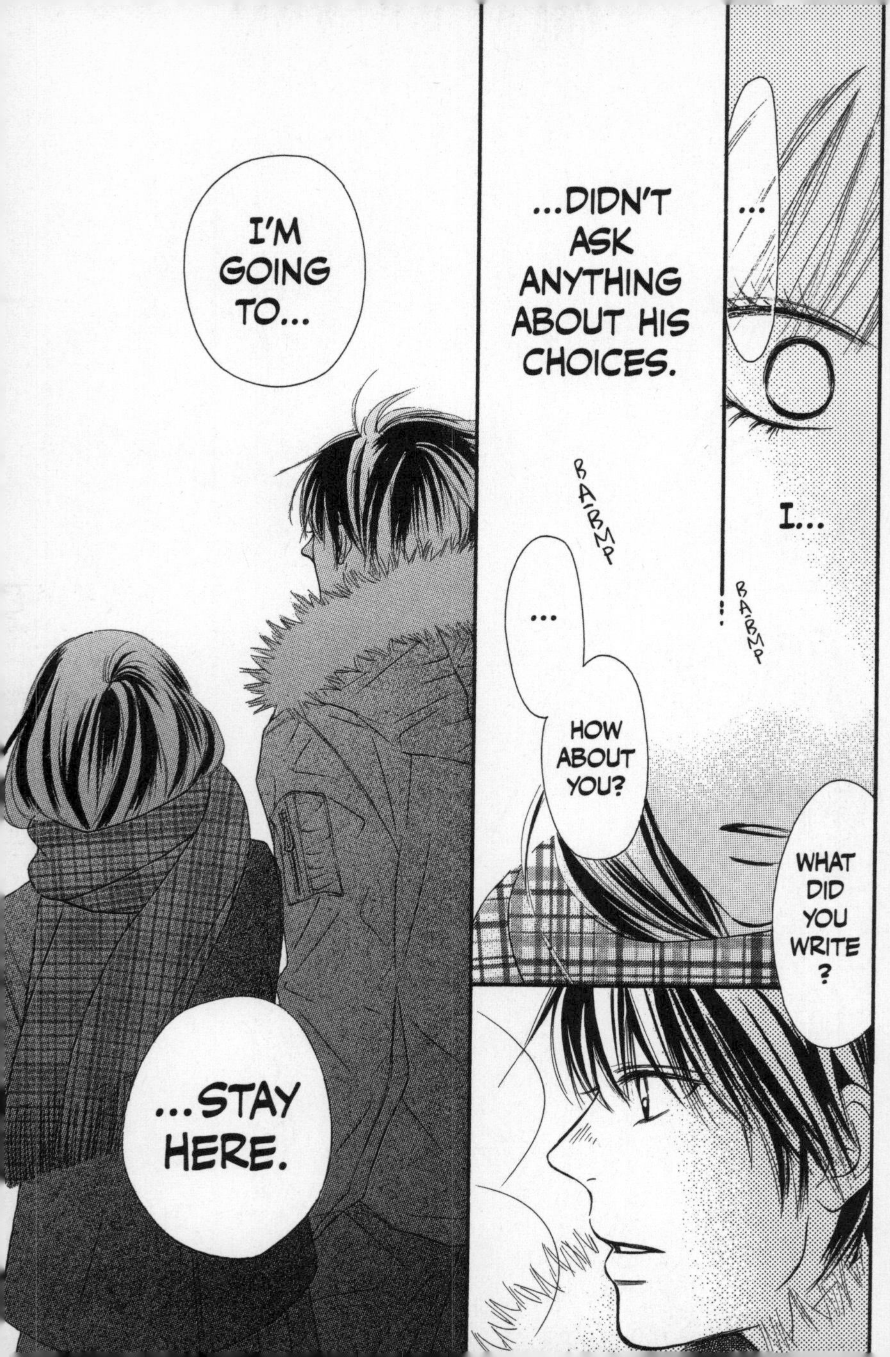
...
I...
BA-BMP
...DIDN'T ASK ANYTHING ABOUT HIS CHOICES.
BA-BMP
...
HOW ABOUT YOU?
WHAT DID YOU WRITE?
I'M GOING TO...
...STAY HERE.

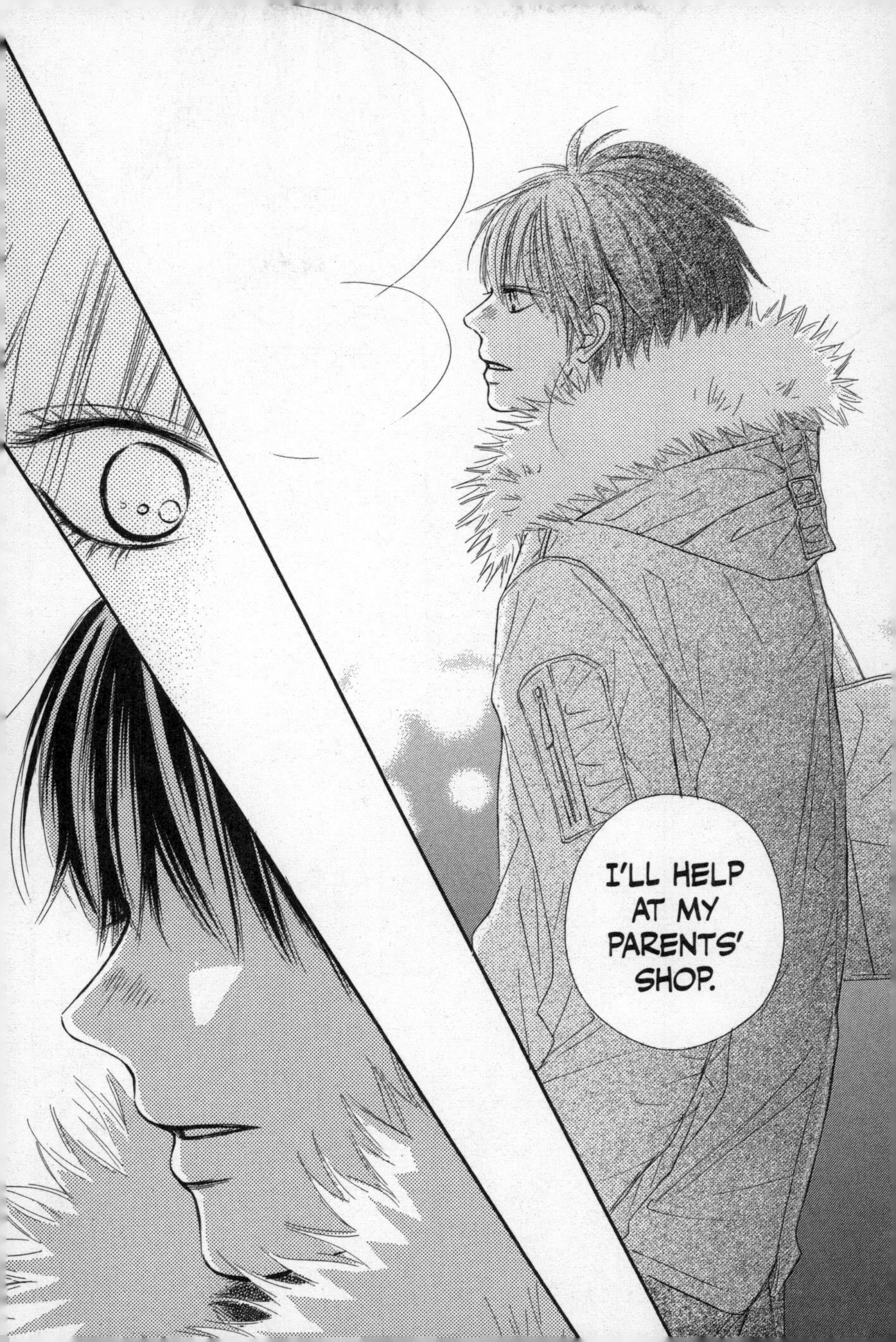
I'LL HELP AT MY PARENTS' SHOP.

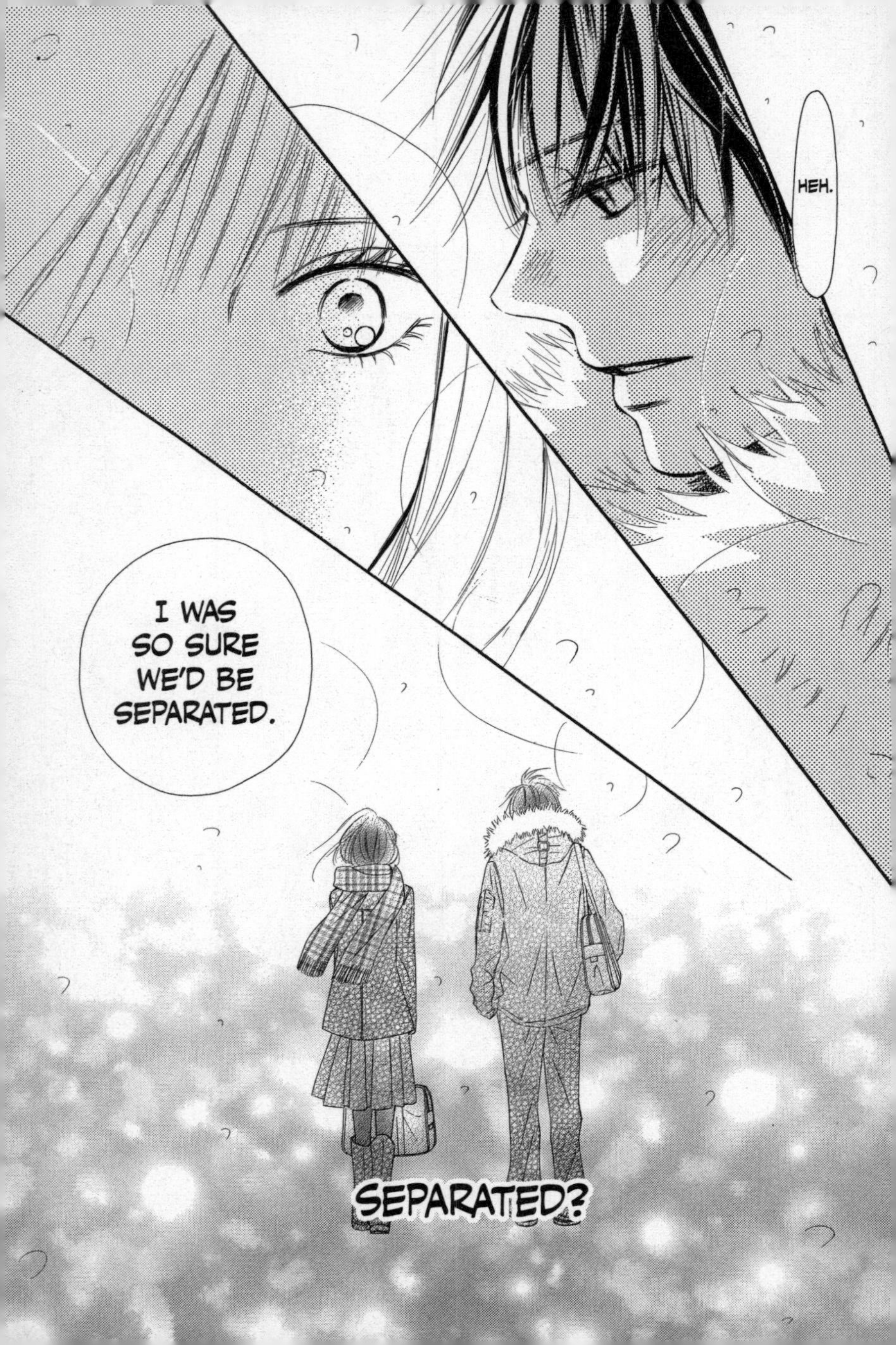
HEH.
I WAS SO SURE WE'D BE SEPARATED.
SEPARATED?

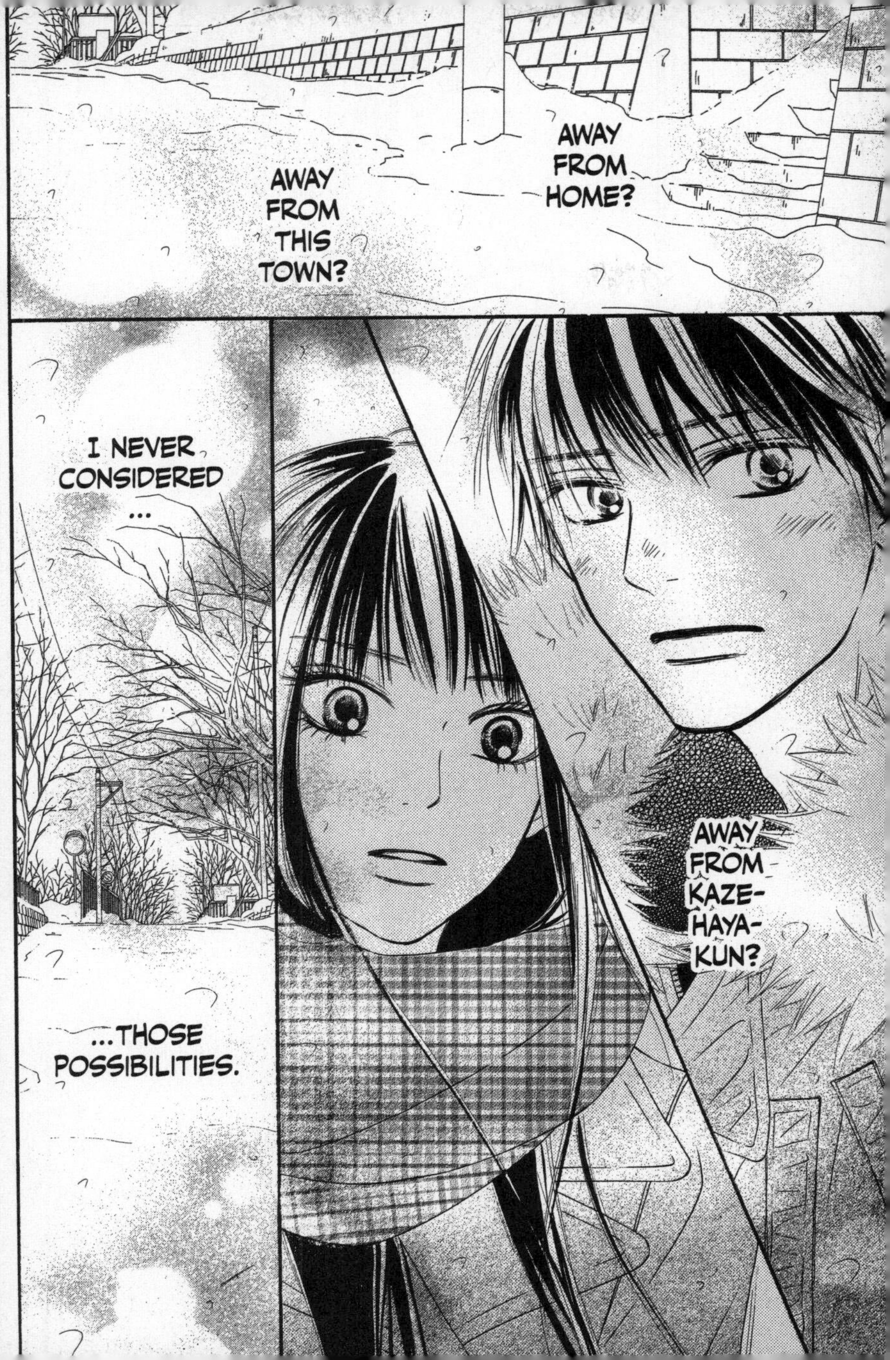
AWAY FROM HOME?
AWAY FROM THIS TOWN?
AWAY FROM KAZE-HAYA-KUN?
I NEVER CONSIDERED ...
...THOSE POSSIBILITIES.

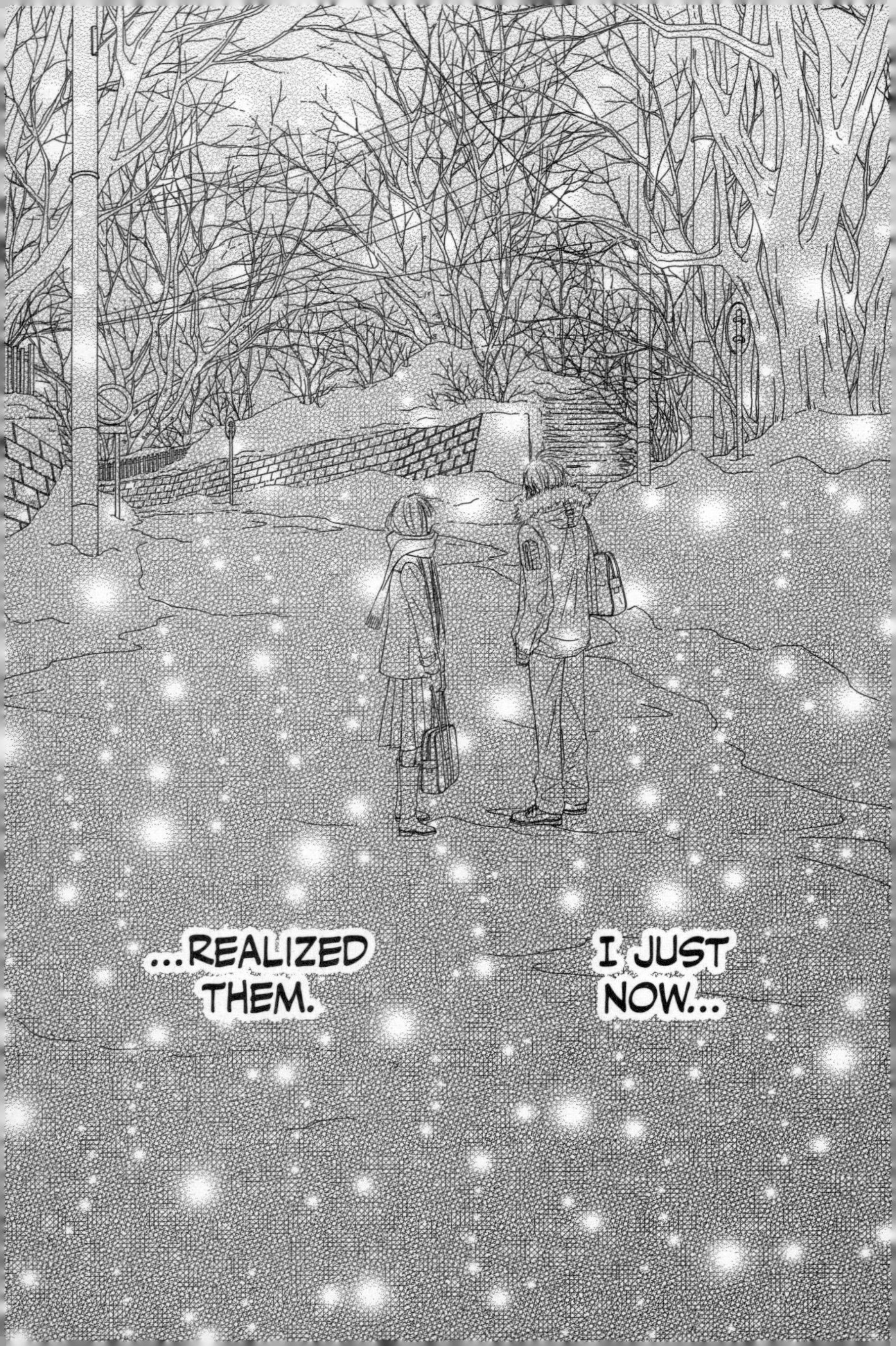
I JUST NOW...
...REALIZED THEM.

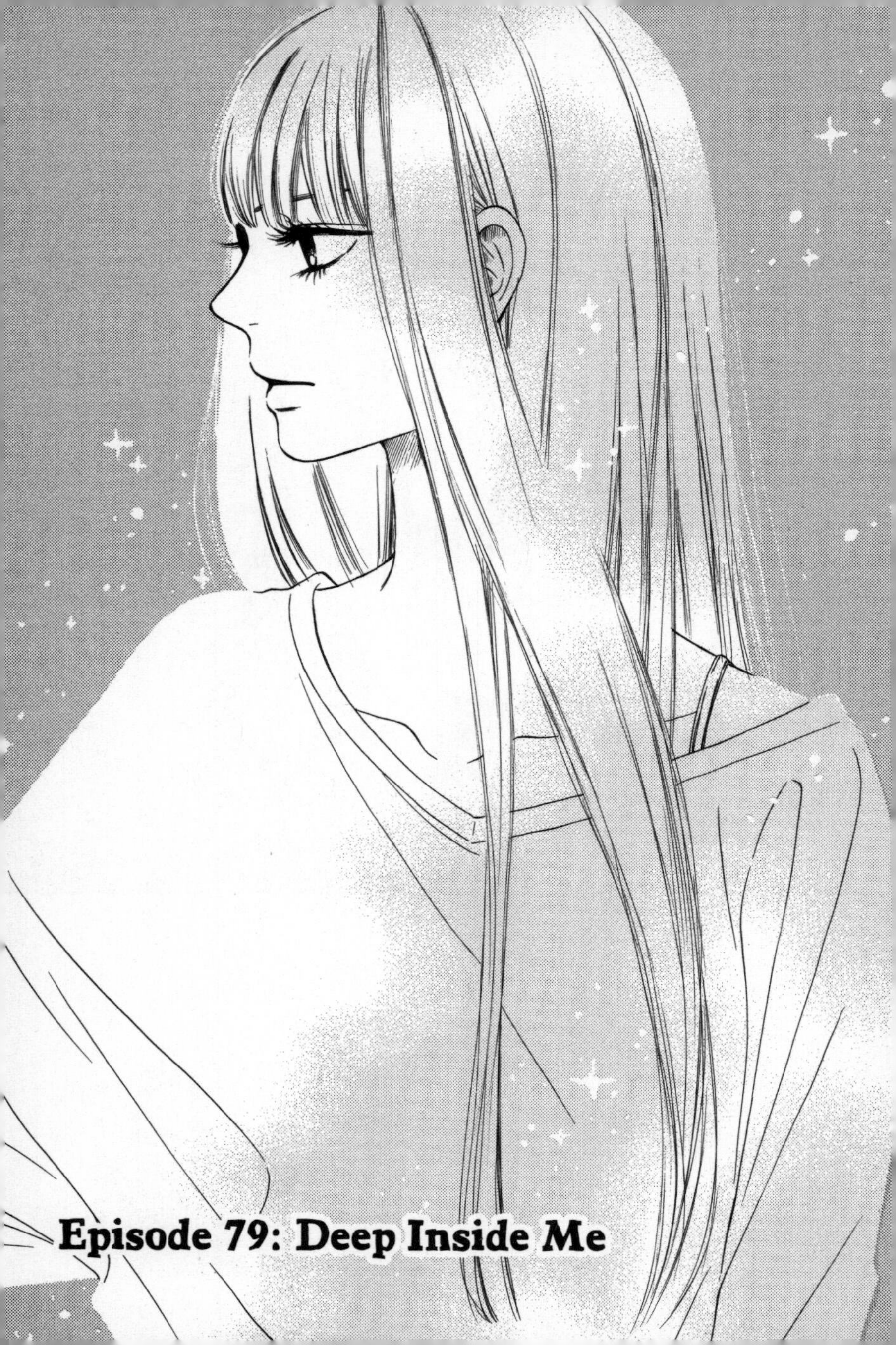

Episode 79: Deep Inside Me

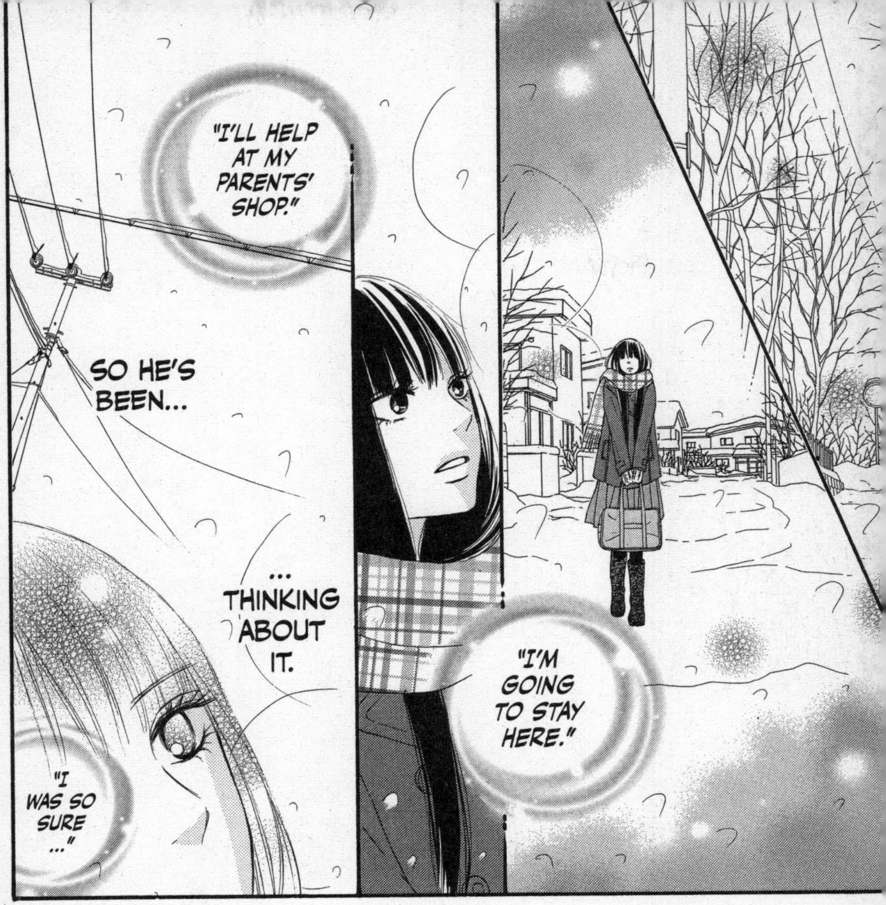
"I'M GOING TO STAY HERE."
"I'LL HELP AT MY PARENTS' SHOP."
SO HE'S BEEN...
... THINKING ABOUT IT.
"I WAS SO SURE ..."

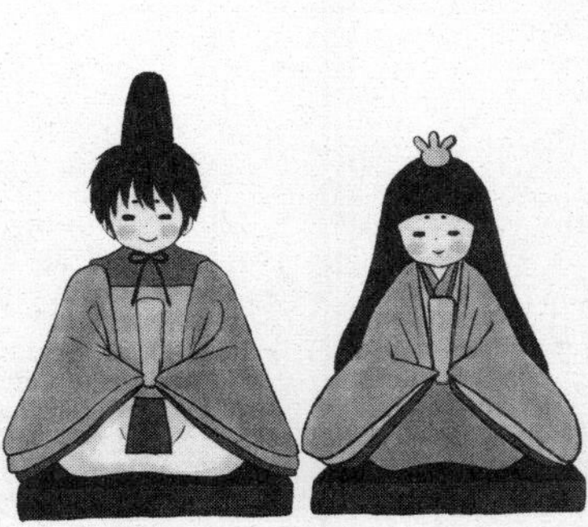

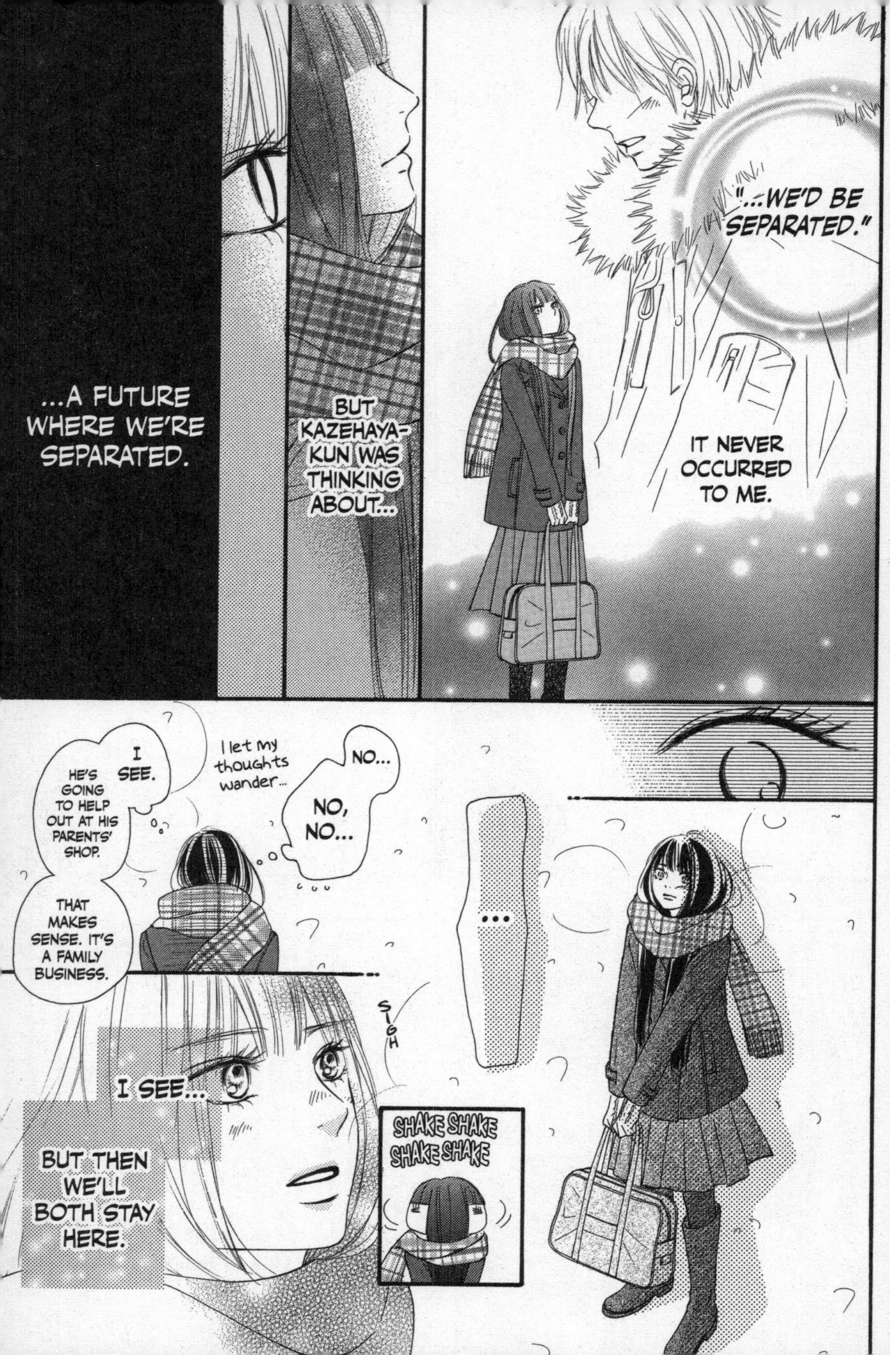
"...WE'D BE SEPARATED."
IT NEVER OCCURRED TO ME.
BUT KAZEHAYA-KUN WAS THINKING ABOUT...
...A FUTURE WHERE WE'RE SEPARATED.
...
NO...
NO, NO...
I let my thoughts wander...
I SEE.
HE'S GOING TO HELP OUT AT HIS PARENTS' SHOP.
THAT MAKES SENSE. IT'S A FAMILY BUSINESS.
SHAKE SHAKE SHAKE SHAKE
SIGH
I SEE...
BUT THEN WE'LL BOTH STAY HERE.

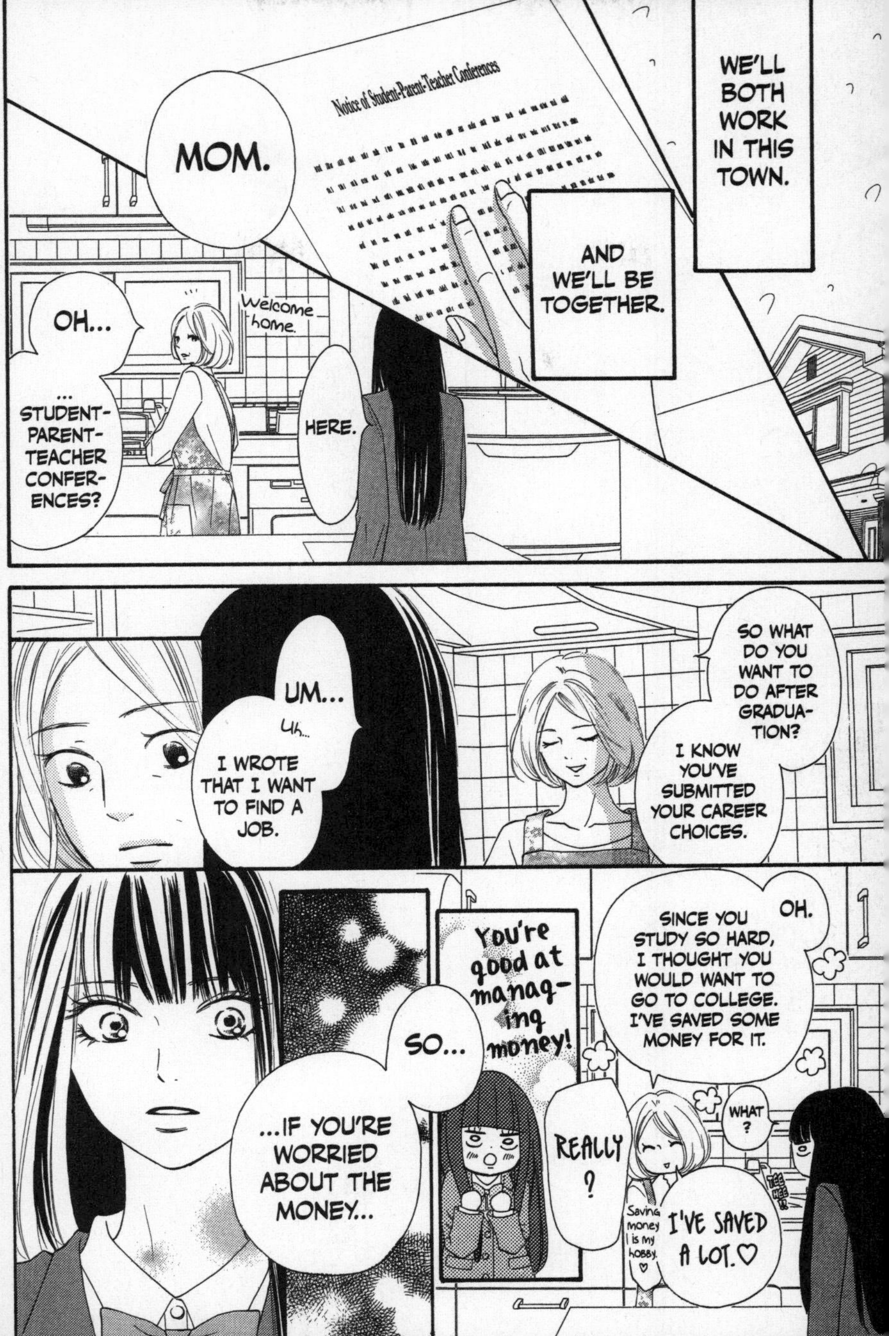

WE'LL BOTH WORK IN THIS TOWN.
AND WE'LL BE TOGETHER.
MOM.
Notice of Student-Parent-Teacher Conferences
Welcome home.
OH...
HERE.
...STUDENT-PARENT-TEACHER CONFER-ENCES?
SO WHAT DO YOU WANT TO DO AFTER GRADUA-TION?
I KNOW YOU'VE SUBMITTED YOUR CAREER CHOICES.
UM...
Uh...
I WROTE THAT I WANT TO FIND A JOB.
OH.
SINCE YOU STUDY SO HARD, I THOUGHT YOU WOULD WANT TO GO TO COLLEGE. I'VE SAVED SOME MONEY FOR IT.
WHAT?
I'VE SAVED A LOT.♡
Saving money is my hobby. ♡
REALLY?
You're good at manag-ing money!
SO...
...IF YOU'RE WORRIED ABOUT THE MONEY...

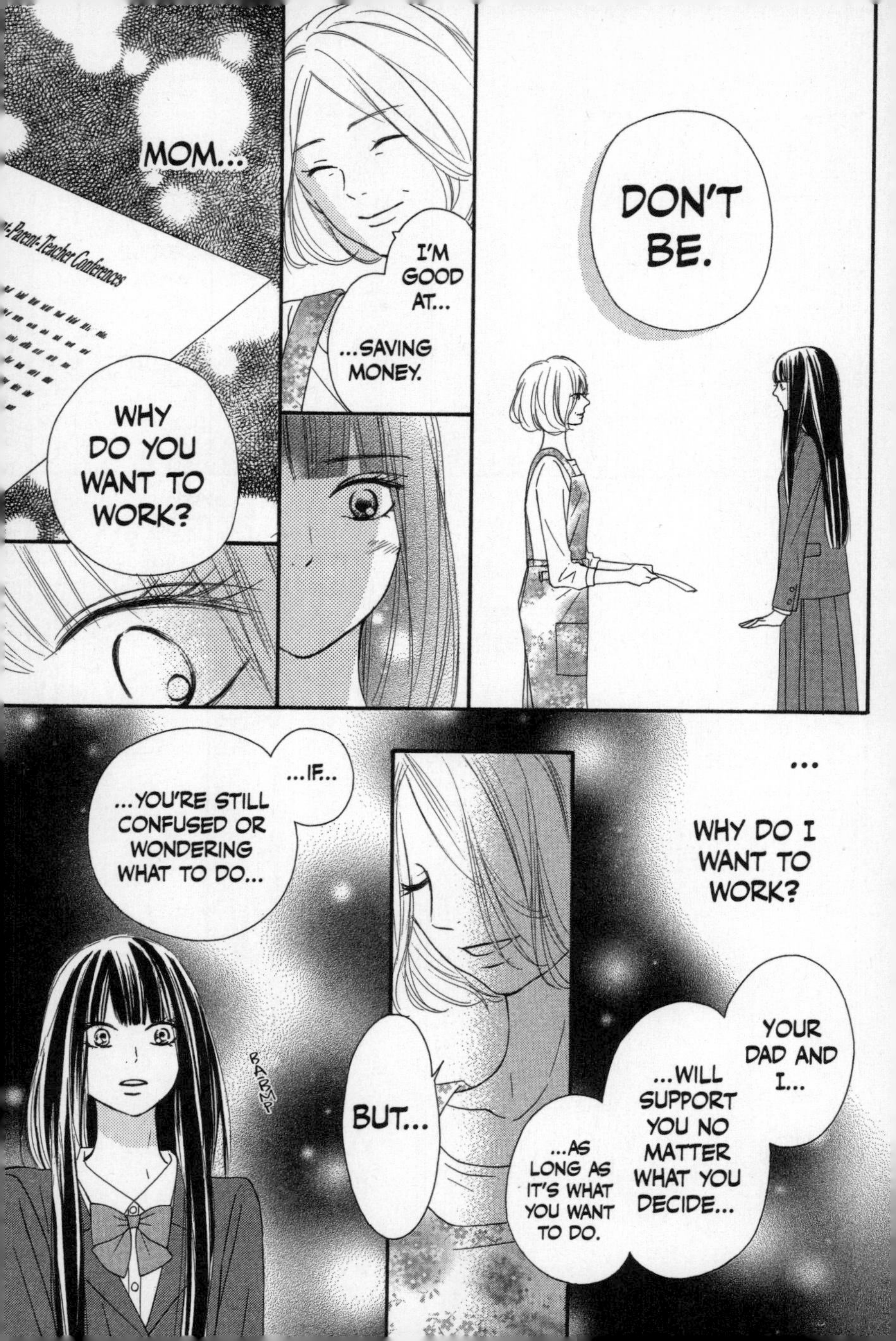
DON'T BE.
I'M GOOD AT...
...SAVING MONEY.
MOM...
Parent-Teacher Conferences
WHY DO YOU WANT TO WORK?
...
WHY DO I WANT TO WORK?
YOUR DAD AND I...
...WILL SUPPORT YOU NO MATTER WHAT YOU DECIDE...
...AS LONG AS IT'S WHAT YOU WANT TO DO.
BUT...
...IF...
...YOU'RE STILL CONFUSED OR WONDERING WHAT TO DO...
BA-BMP

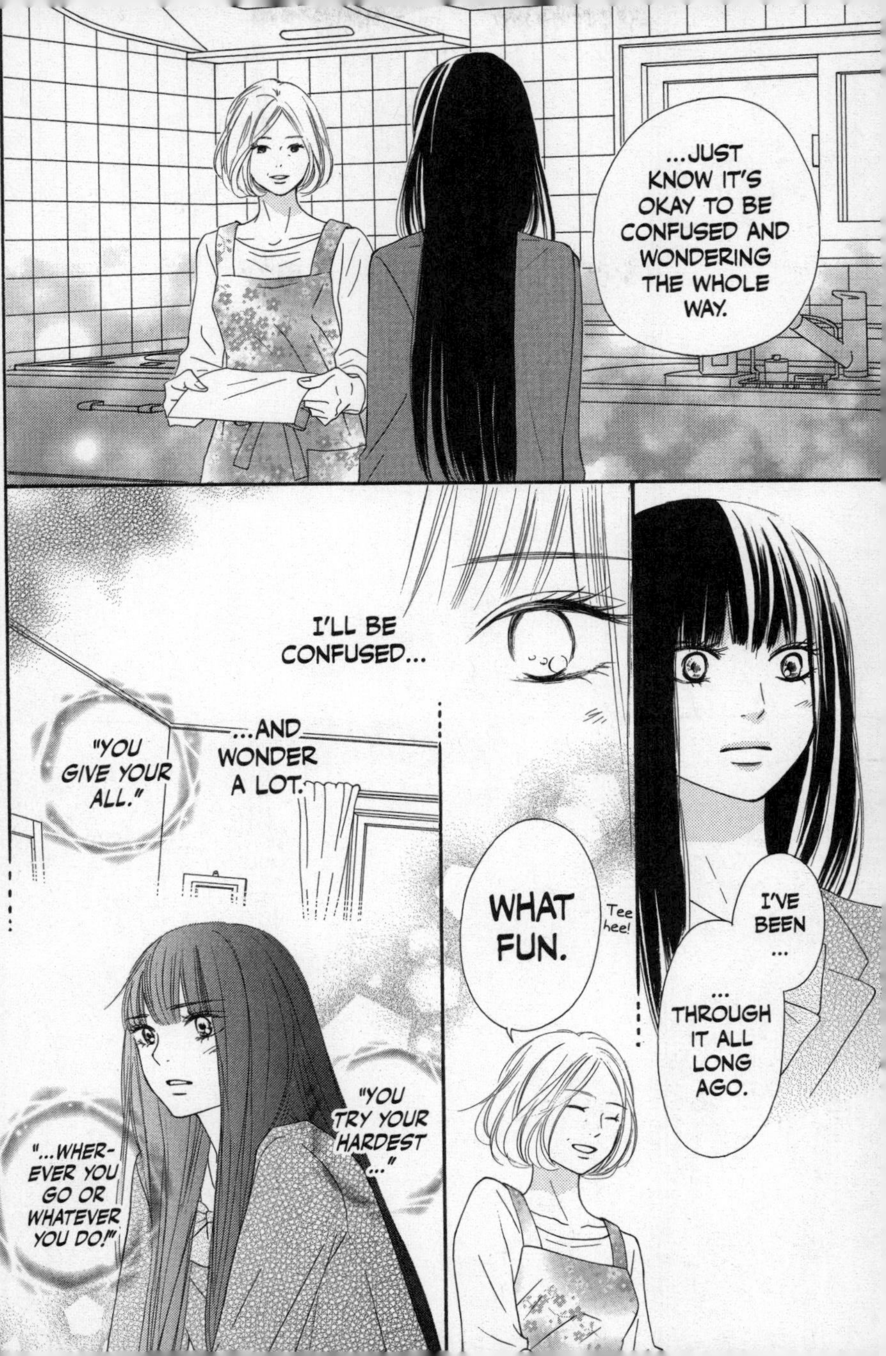
...JUST KNOW IT'S OKAY TO BE CONFUSED AND WONDERING THE WHOLE WAY.
I'VE BEEN ...
... THROUGH IT ALL LONG AGO.
WHAT FUN.
Tee hee!
I'LL BE CONFUSED...
...AND WONDER A LOT.
"YOU GIVE YOUR ALL."
"YOU TRY YOUR HARDEST ..."
"...WHEREVER YOU GO OR WHATEVER YOU DO!"

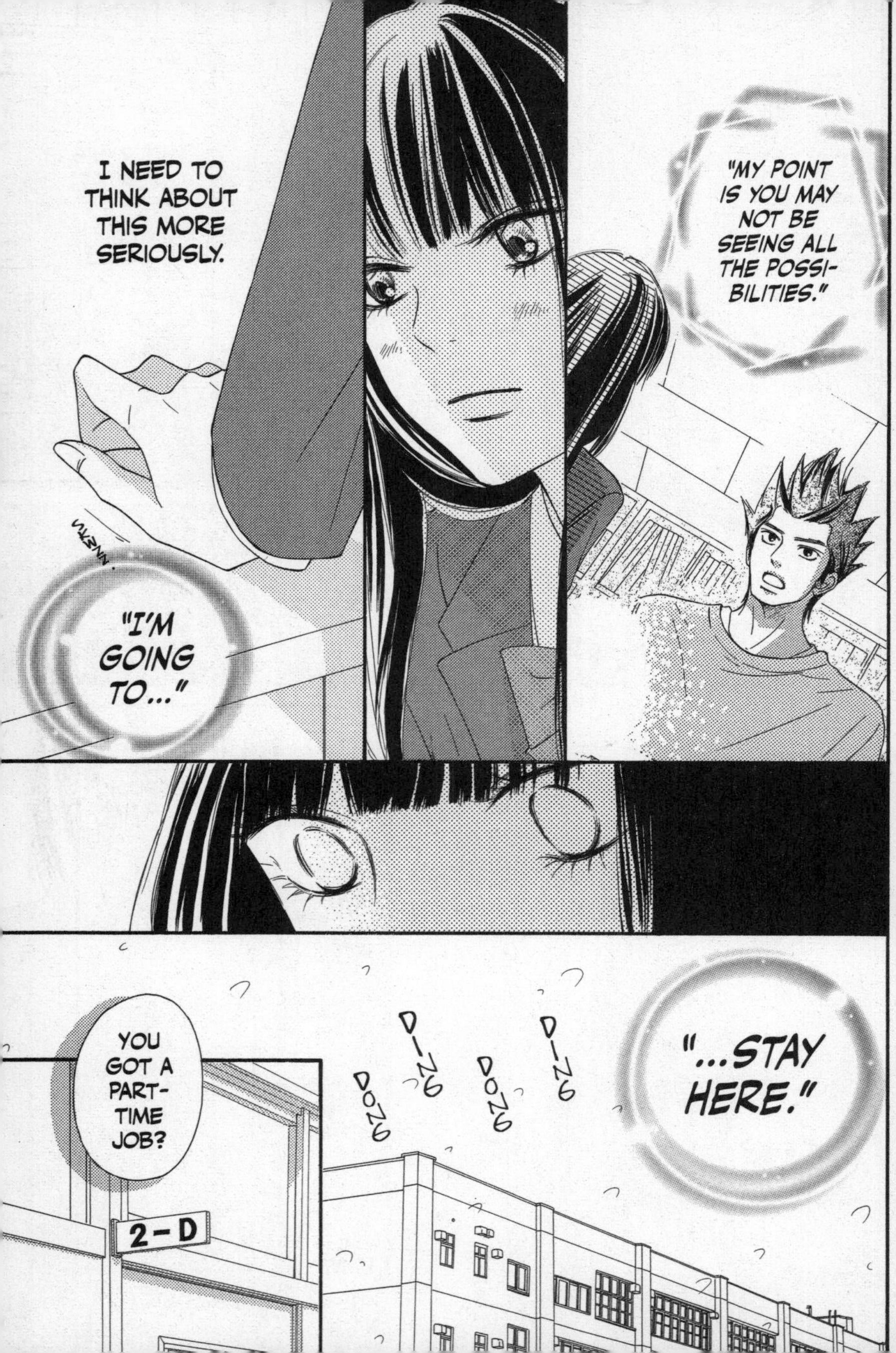
"MY POINT IS YOU MAY NOT BE SEEING ALL THE POSSI-BILITIES."
I NEED TO THINK ABOUT THIS MORE SERIOUSLY.
"I'M GOING TO..."
"...STAY HERE."
DING DONG
DING DONG
YOU GOT A PART-TIME JOB?
2-D

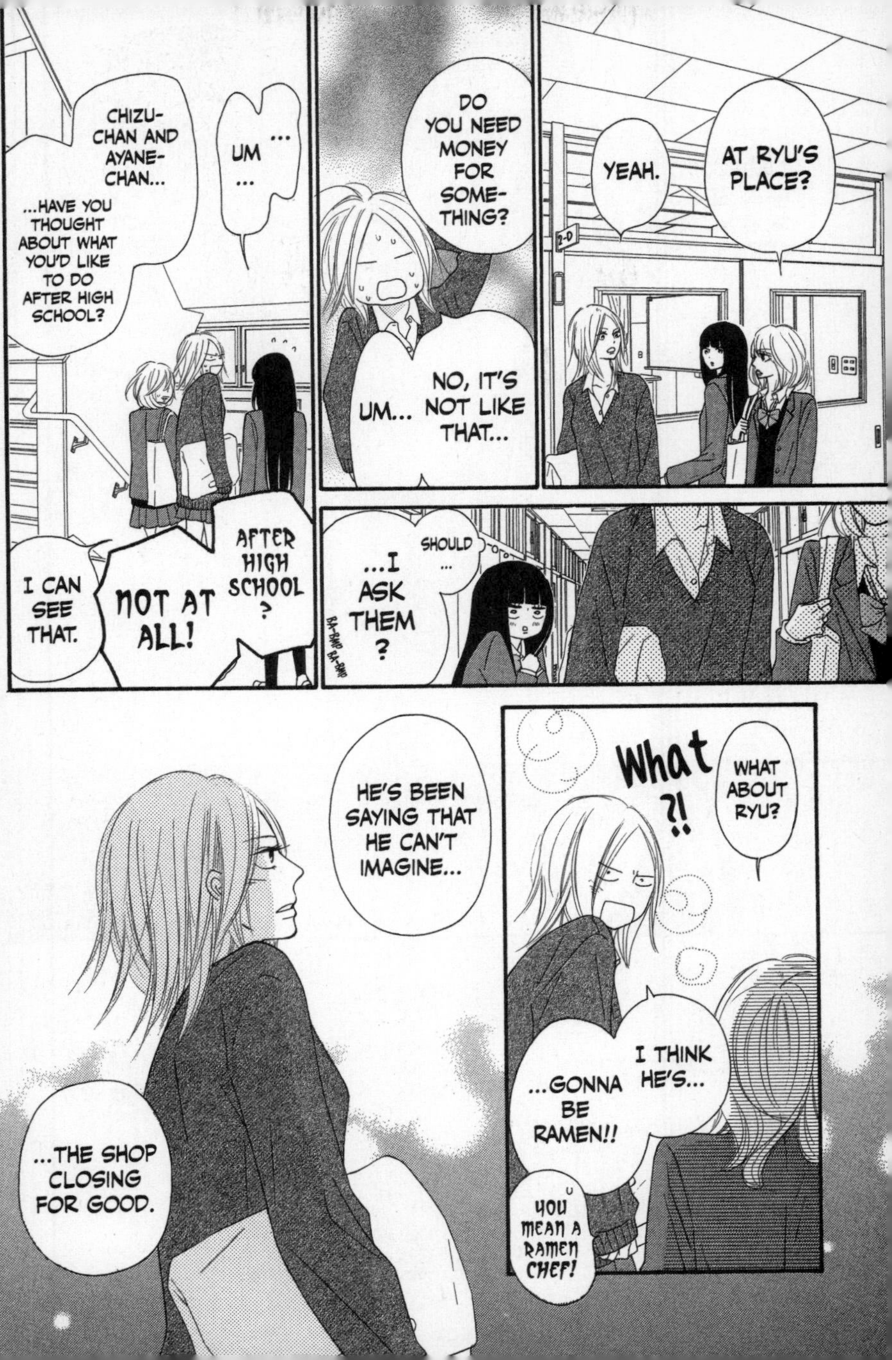

AT RYU'S PLACE?
YEAH.
DO YOU NEED MONEY FOR SOMETHING?
NO, IT'S NOT LIKE THAT...
UM...
SHOULD...
...I ASK THEM?
BA-BMP BA-BMP
UM... ...
CHIZU-CHAN AND AYANE-CHAN...
...HAVE YOU THOUGHT ABOUT WHAT YOU'D LIKE TO DO AFTER HIGH SCHOOL?
AFTER HIGH SCHOOL?
NOT AT ALL!
I CAN SEE THAT.
What?!
WHAT ABOUT RYU?
I THINK HE'S...
...GONNA BE RAMEN!!
YOU MEAN A RAMEN CHEF!
HE'S BEEN SAYING THAT HE CAN'T IMAGINE...
...THE SHOP CLOSING FOR GOOD.

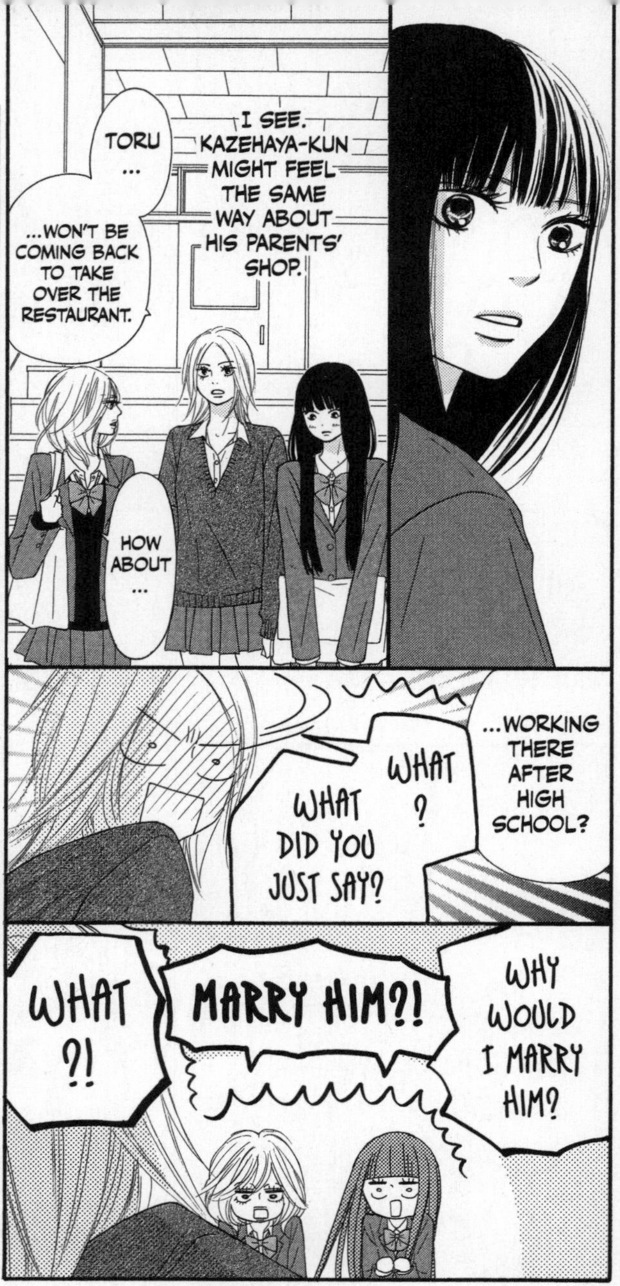
I SEE. KAZEHAYA-KUN MIGHT FEEL THE SAME WAY ABOUT HIS PARENTS' SHOP.
TORU ...
...WON'T BE COMING BACK TO TAKE OVER THE RESTAURANT.
HOW ABOUT ...
...WORKING THERE AFTER HIGH SCHOOL?
WHAT?
WHAT DID YOU JUST SAY?
WHY WOULD I MARRY HIM?
MARRY HIM?!
WHAT?!

KARUPIN on JAPAN 4

Huh? I didn't mean to write what I just did in the last comment. It sounded like I'm going to quit drawing manga. (I'm not quitting!)

For the graphic novel, I start by wondering which character I should put on the front cover, followed by what kind of flower should go on the spine. Then...

Oops!

Oh no...

I totally forgot to draw a picture for the back cover.

And, uh...when is the deadline?

Anyway, to those of you who will read Vol.20, see you then!

What is this craziness I'm feeling? It isn't necessary!

Karuho Shiina

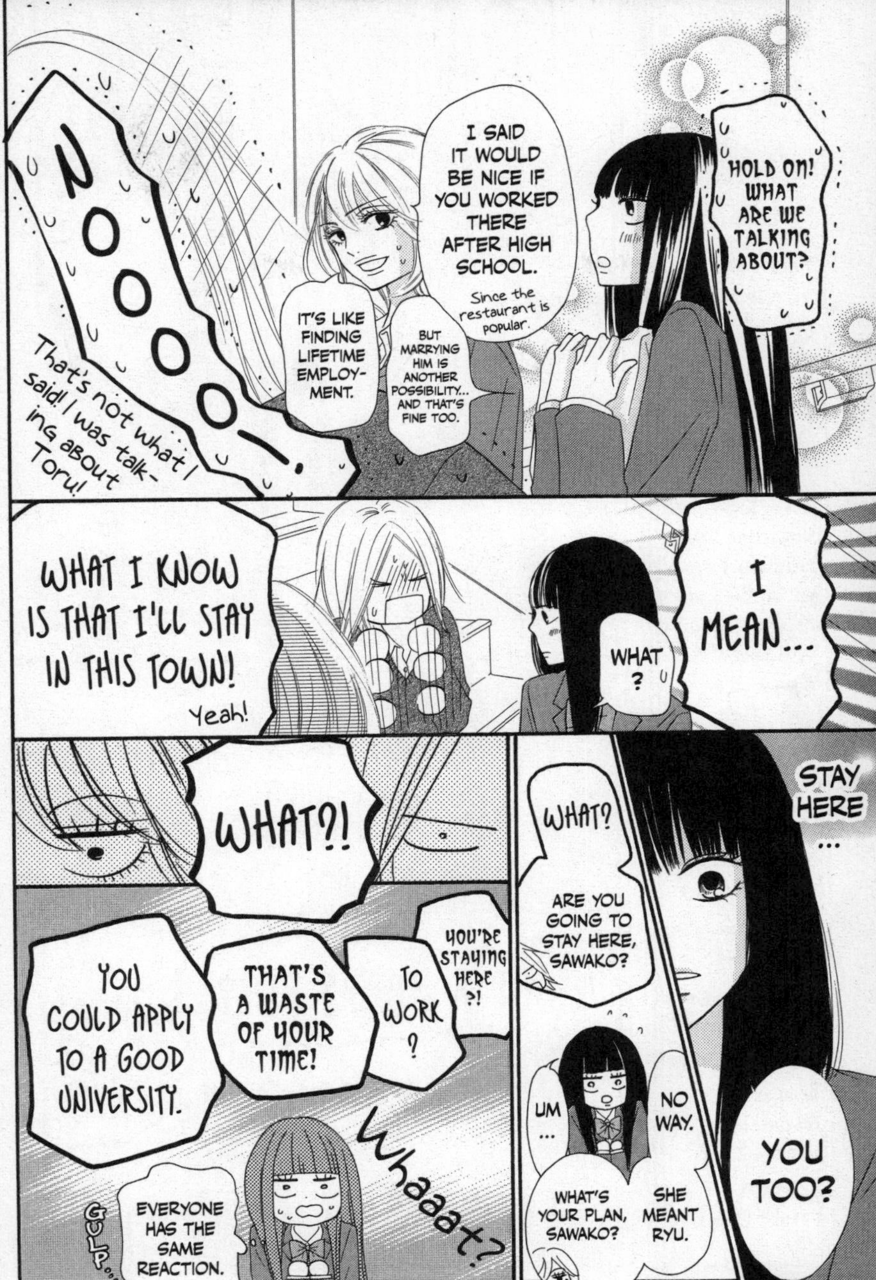
HOLD ON! WHAT ARE WE TALKING ABOUT?
I SAID IT WOULD BE NICE IF YOU WORKED THERE AFTER HIGH SCHOOL.
Since the restaurant is popular.
BUT MARRYING HIM IS ANOTHER POSSIBILITY... AND THAT'S FINE TOO.
IT'S LIKE FINDING LIFETIME EMPLOYMENT.
NOOOO—!
That's not what I said! I was talking about Toru!
I MEAN...
WHAT?
WHAT I KNOW IS THAT I'LL STAY IN THIS TOWN!
Yeah!
STAY HERE...
YOU TOO?
WHAT?
ARE YOU GOING TO STAY HERE, SAWAKO?
NO WAY.
UM...
SHE MEANT RYU.
WHAT'S YOUR PLAN, SAWAKO?
WHAT?!
YOU'RE STAYING HERE?!
TO WORK?
THAT'S A WASTE OF YOUR TIME!
YOU COULD APPLY TO A GOOD UNIVERSITY.
Whaaat?
EVERYONE HAS THE SAME REACTION.
GULP...

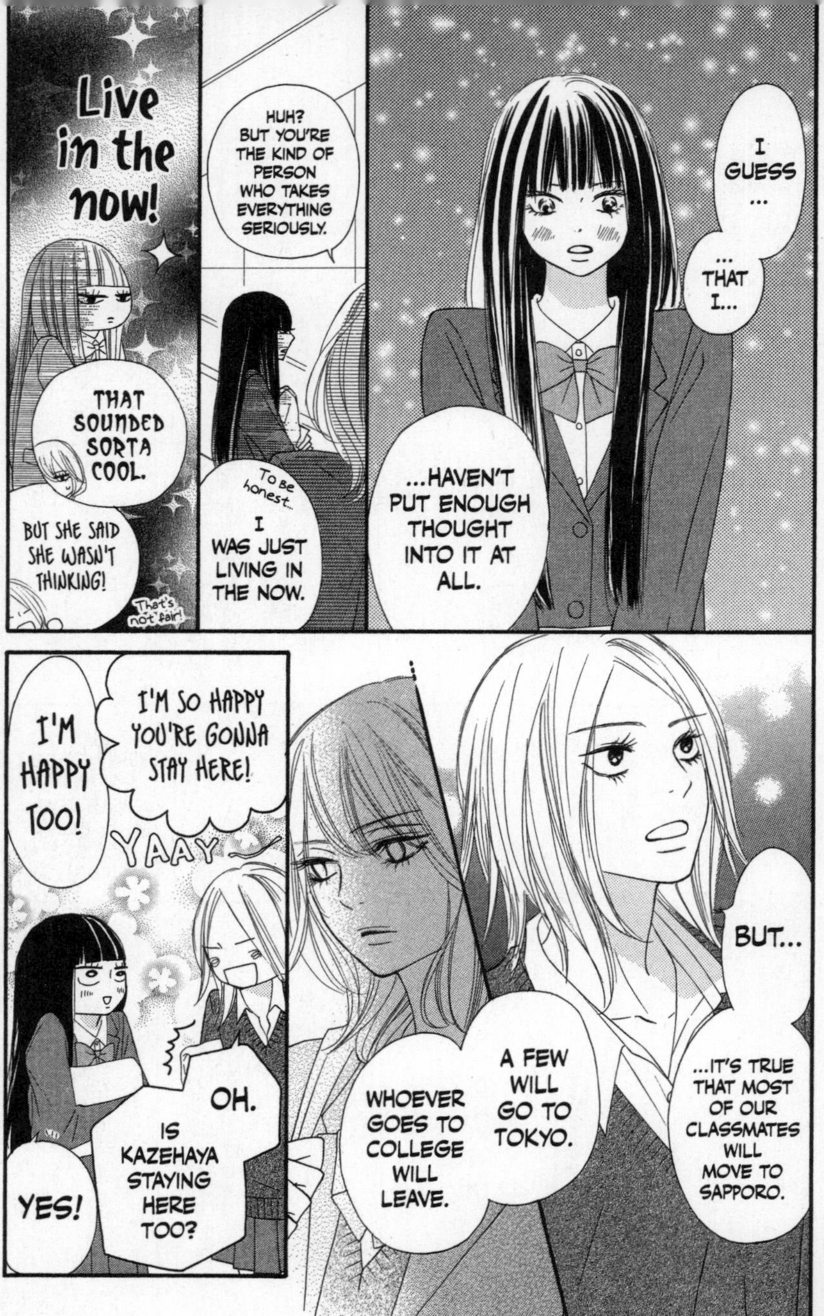
I GUESS...
...THAT I...
...HAVEN'T PUT ENOUGH THOUGHT INTO IT AT ALL.
HUH? BUT YOU'RE THE KIND OF PERSON WHO TAKES EVERYTHING SERIOUSLY.
To be honest...
I WAS JUST LIVING IN THE NOW.
Live in the now!
THAT SOUNDED SORTA COOL.
BUT SHE SAID SHE WASN'T THINKING!
That's not fair!
BUT...
...IT'S TRUE THAT MOST OF OUR CLASSMATES WILL MOVE TO SAPPORO.
A FEW WILL GO TO TOKYO.
WHOEVER GOES TO COLLEGE WILL LEAVE.
I'M SO HAPPY YOU'RE GONNA STAY HERE!
I'M HAPPY TOO!
YAAY
OH.
IS KAZEHAYA STAYING HERE TOO?
YES!

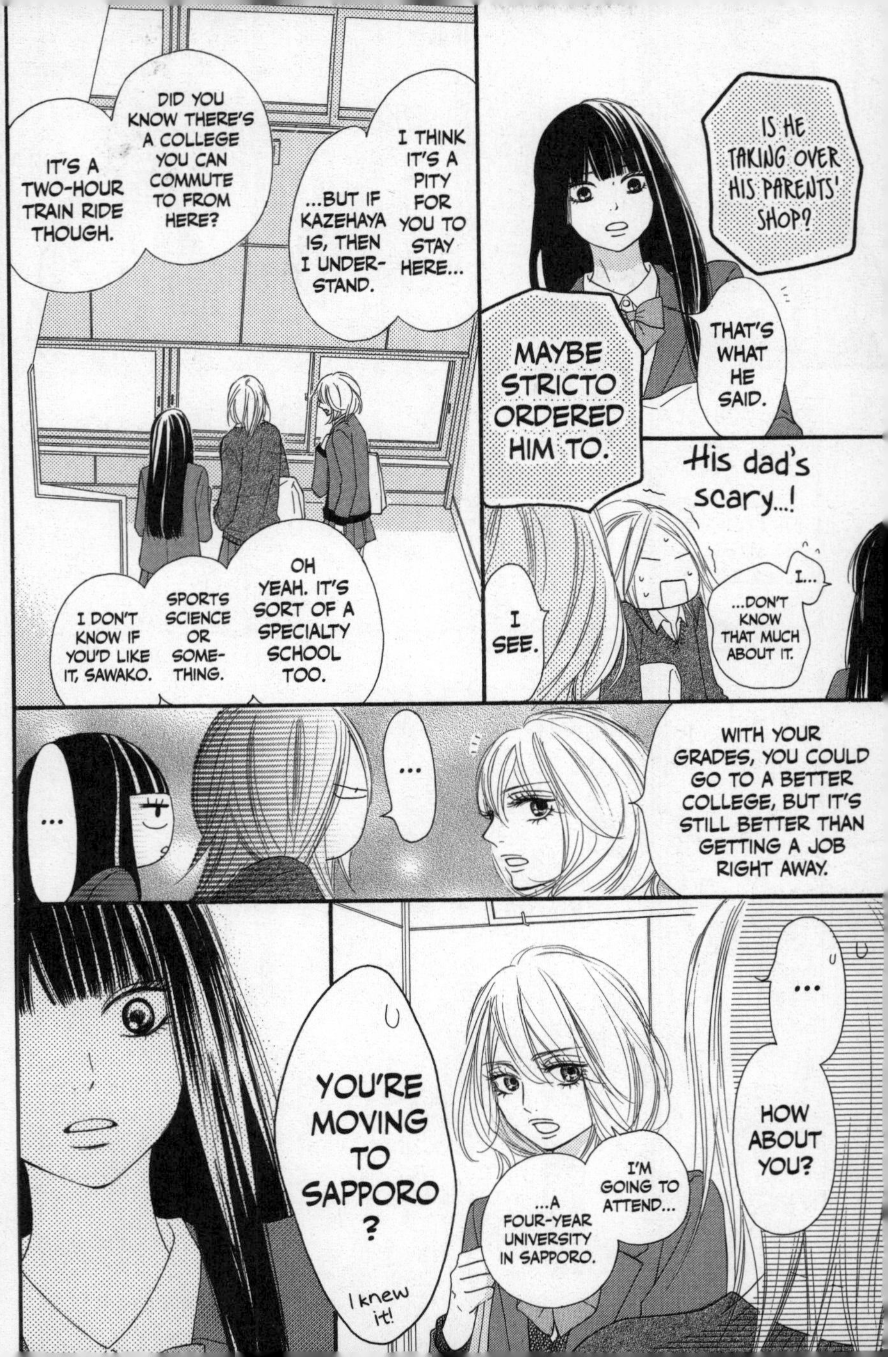
IS HE TAKING OVER HIS PARENTS' SHOP?
THAT'S WHAT HE SAID.
MAYBE STRICTO ORDERED HIM TO.
His dad's scary...!
I...
...DON'T KNOW THAT MUCH ABOUT IT.
I SEE.
I THINK IT'S A PITY FOR YOU TO STAY HERE...
...BUT IF KAZEHAYA IS, THEN I UNDERSTAND.
DID YOU KNOW THERE'S A COLLEGE YOU CAN COMMUTE TO FROM HERE?
IT'S A TWO-HOUR TRAIN RIDE THOUGH.
OH YEAH. IT'S SORT OF A SPECIALTY SCHOOL TOO.
SPORTS SCIENCE OR SOMETHING.
I DON'T KNOW IF YOU'D LIKE IT, SAWAKO.
WITH YOUR GRADES, YOU COULD GO TO A BETTER COLLEGE, BUT IT'S STILL BETTER THAN GETTING A JOB RIGHT AWAY.
...
...
...
HOW ABOUT YOU?
I'M GOING TO ATTEND...
...A FOUR-YEAR UNIVERSITY IN SAPPORO.
YOU'RE MOVING TO SAPPORO?
I knew it!

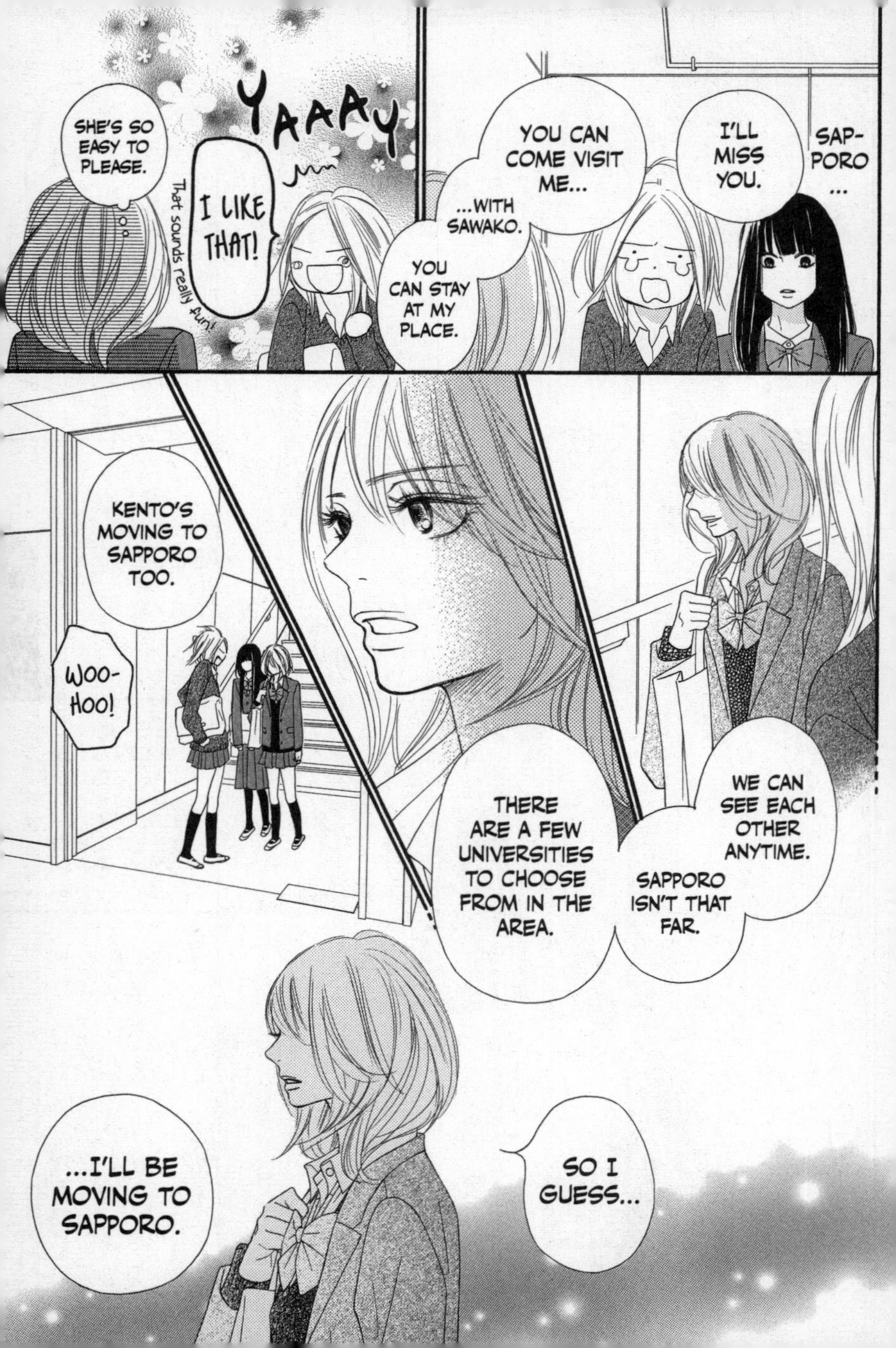
SAP-PORO...
I'LL MISS YOU.
YOU CAN COME VISIT ME...
...WITH SAWAKO.
YOU CAN STAY AT MY PLACE.
YAAAY
I LIKE THAT!
That sounds really fun!
SHE'S SO EASY TO PLEASE.
WE CAN SEE EACH OTHER ANYTIME.
SAPPORO ISN'T THAT FAR.
THERE ARE A FEW UNIVERSITIES TO CHOOSE FROM IN THE AREA.
KENTO'S MOVING TO SAPPORO TOO.
WOO-HOO!
SO I GUESS...
...I'LL BE MOVING TO SAPPORO.

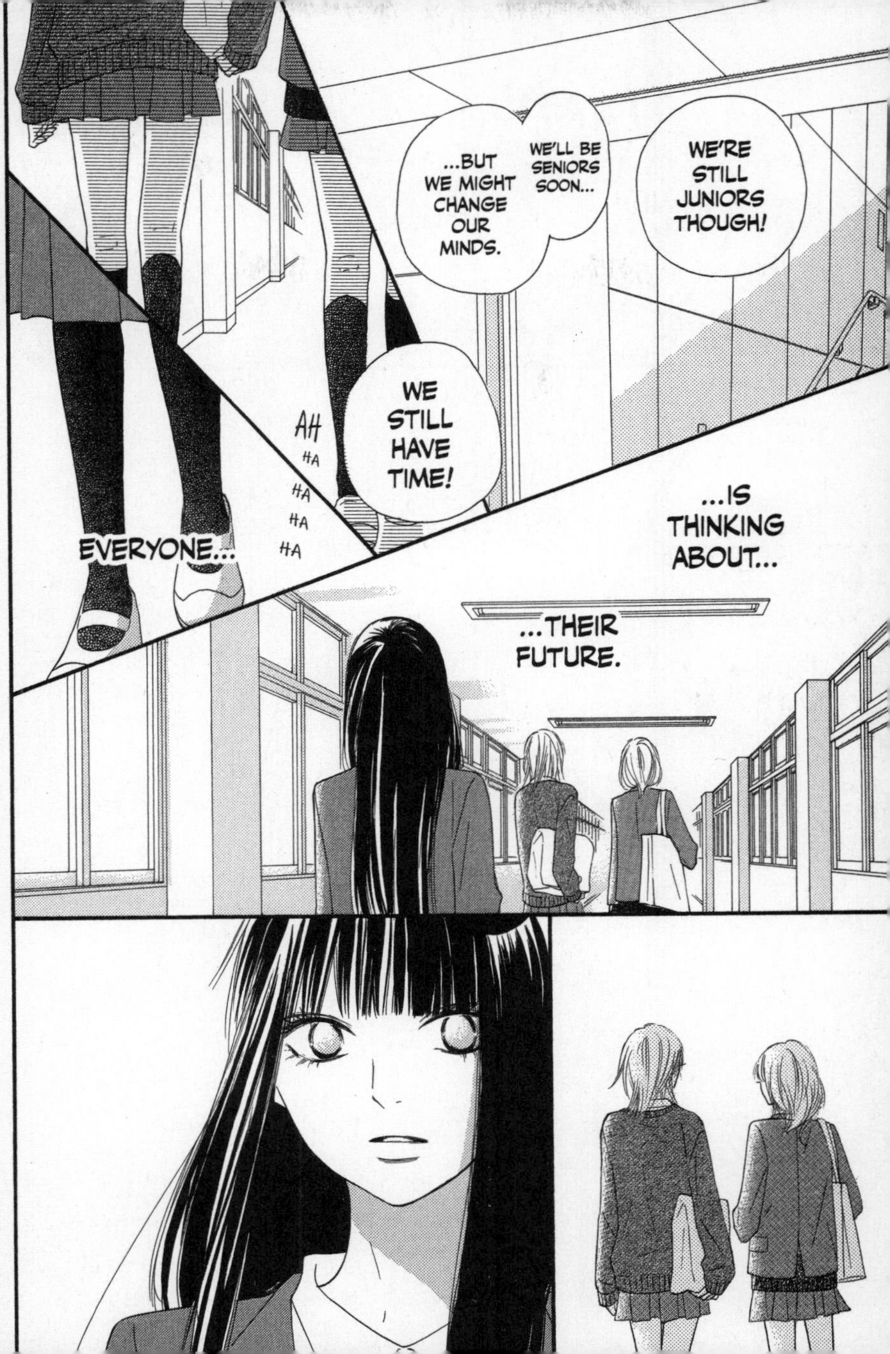
WE'RE STILL JUNIORS THOUGH!
WE'LL BE SENIORS SOON...
...BUT WE MIGHT CHANGE OUR MINDS.
WE STILL HAVE TIME!
AH HA HA HA HA
EVERYONE...
...IS THINKING ABOUT...
...THEIR FUTURE.

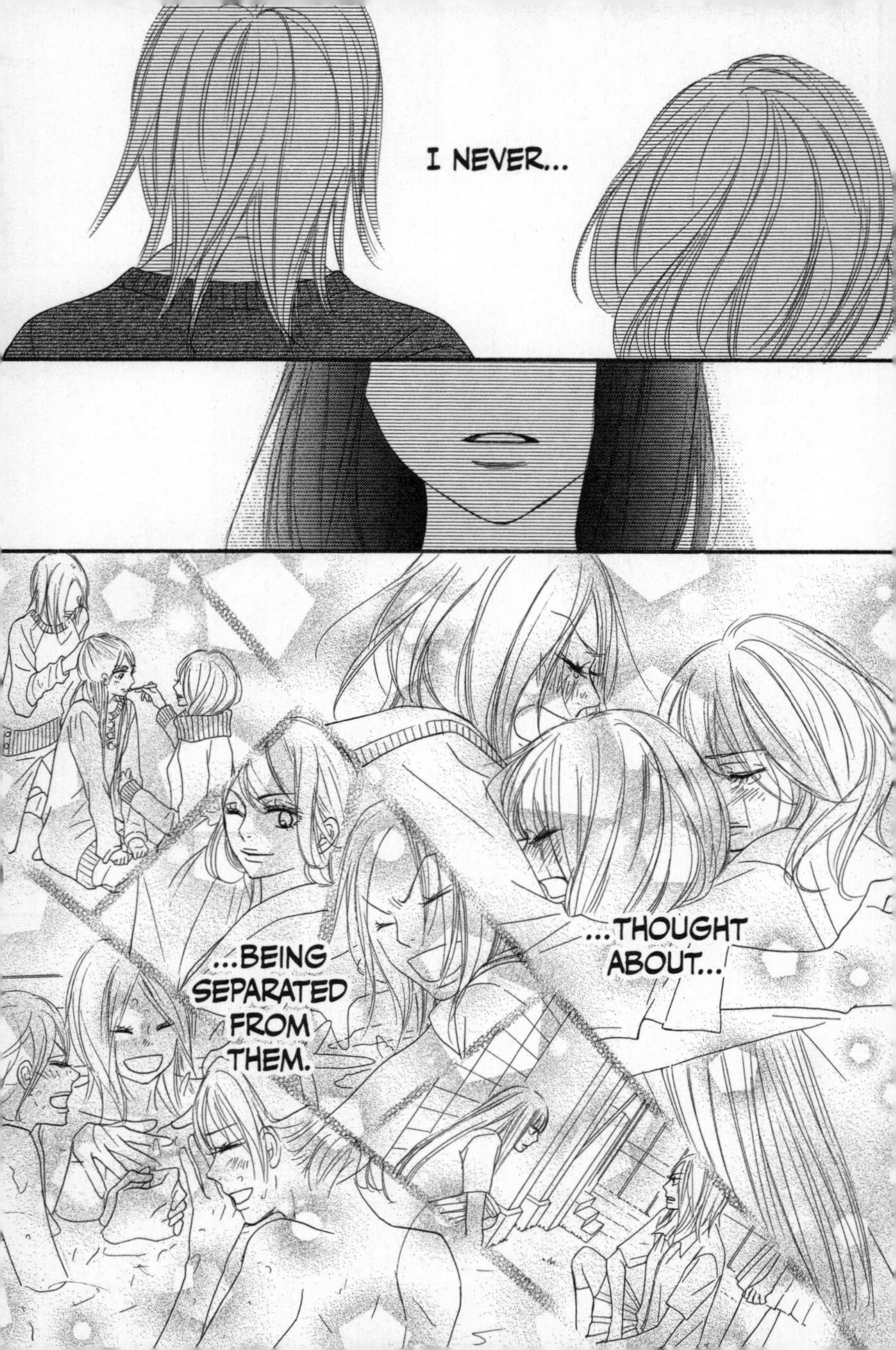
I NEVER...
...THOUGHT ABOUT...
...BEING SEPARATED FROM THEM.

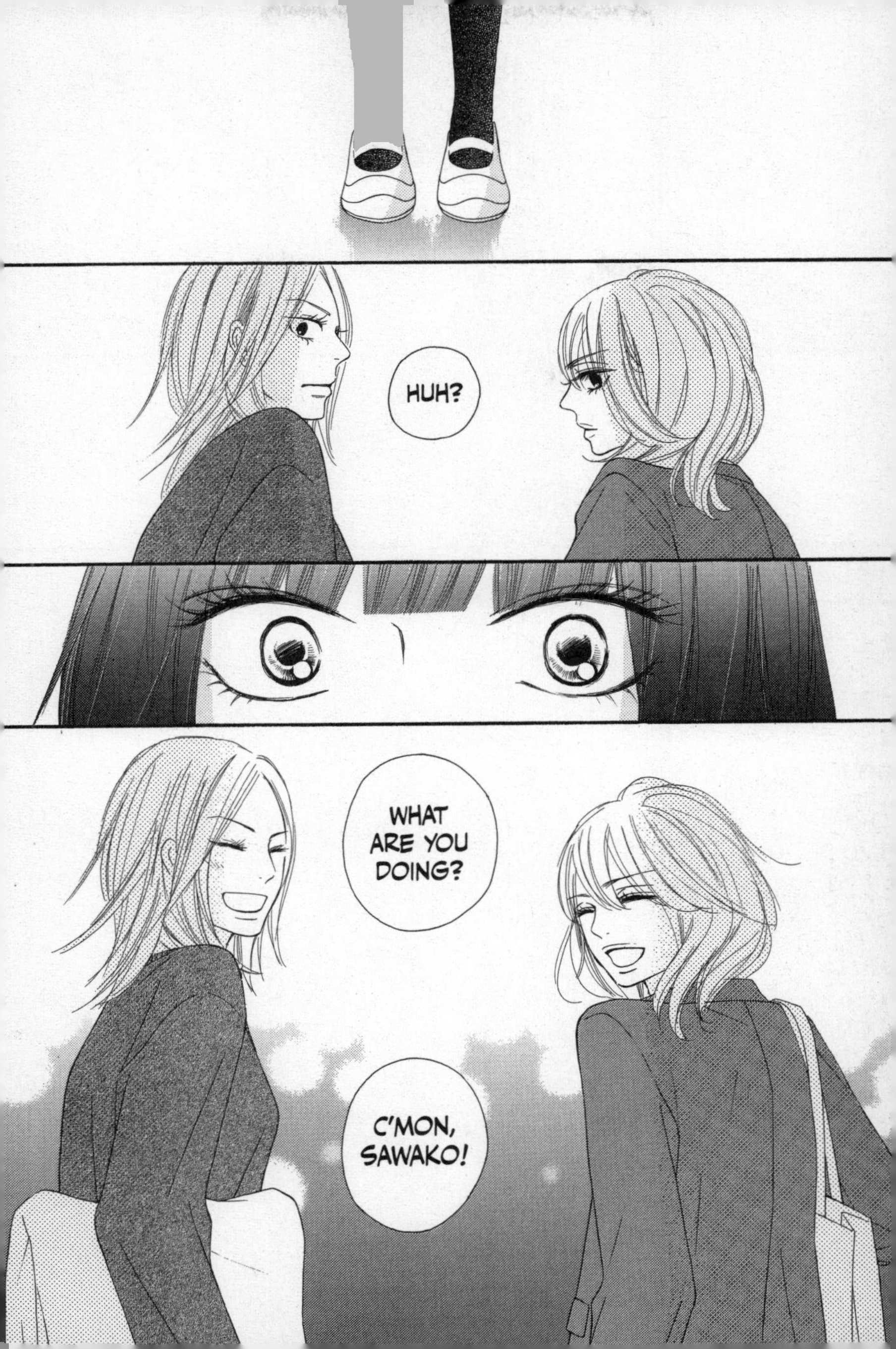
HUH?
WHAT ARE YOU DOING?
C'MON, SAWAKO!

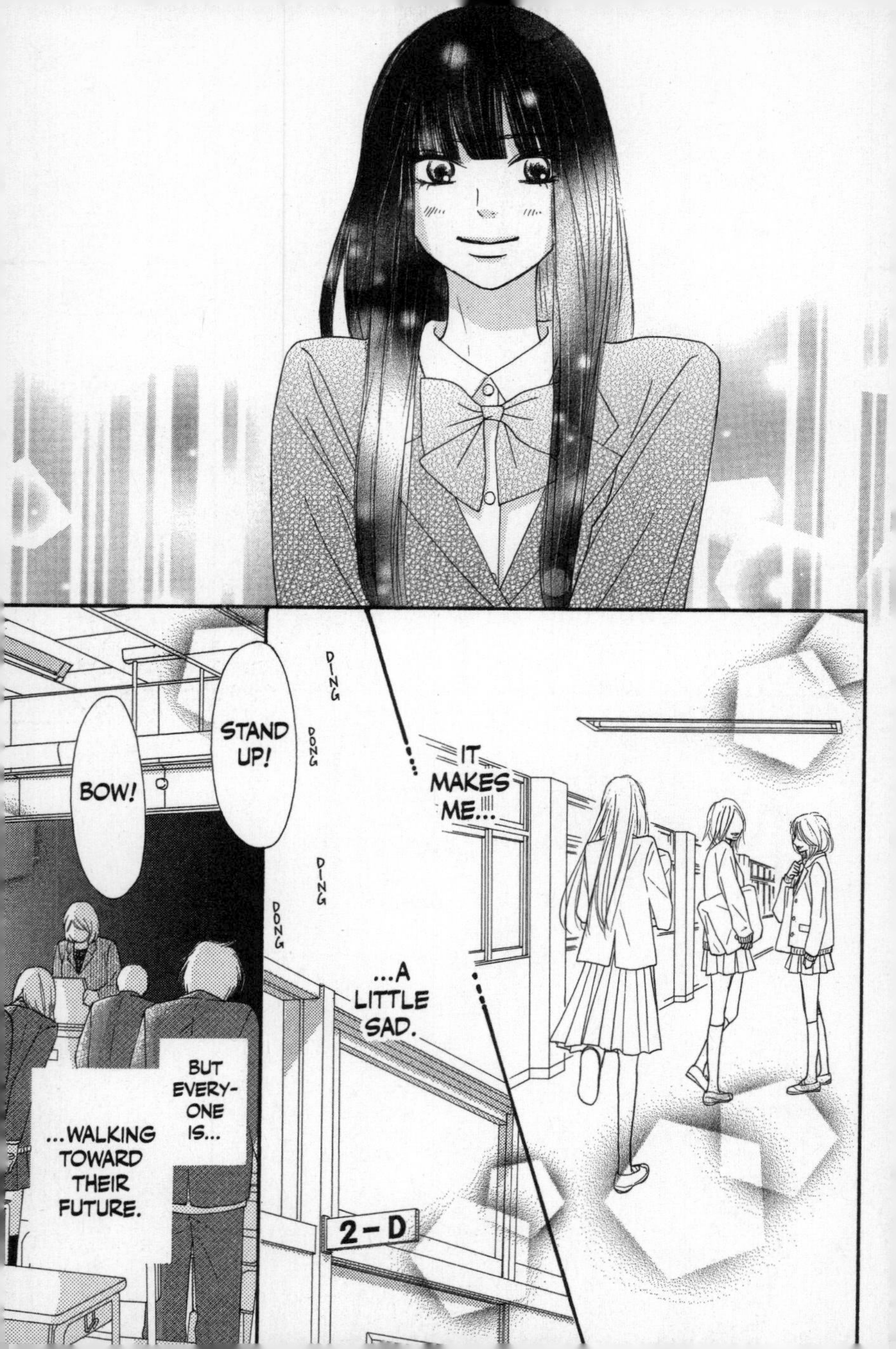
IT MAKES ME...
DING DONG
...A LITTLE SAD.
DING DONG
STAND UP!
BOW!
BUT EVERY-ONE IS...
...WALKING TOWARD THEIR FUTURE.
2-D

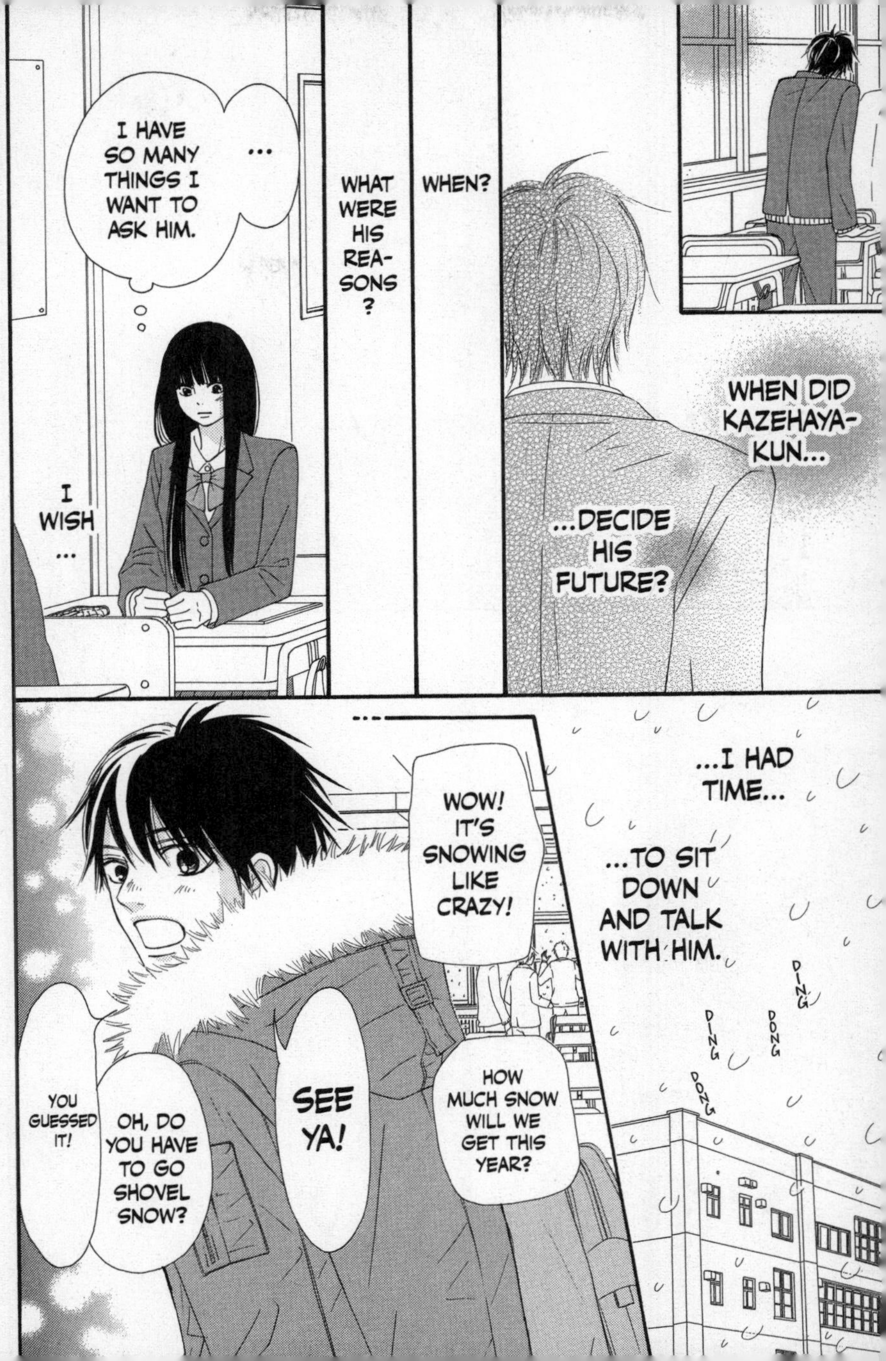

WHEN DID KAZEHAYA-KUN...
...DECIDE HIS FUTURE?
WHEN?
WHAT WERE HIS REASONS?
...
I HAVE SO MANY THINGS I WANT TO ASK HIM.
I WISH...
...I HAD TIME...
...TO SIT DOWN AND TALK WITH HIM.
DING DONG
DING DONG
WOW! IT'S SNOWING LIKE CRAZY!
HOW MUCH SNOW WILL WE GET THIS YEAR?
SEE YA!
OH, DO YOU HAVE TO GO SHOVEL SNOW?
YOU GUESSED IT!

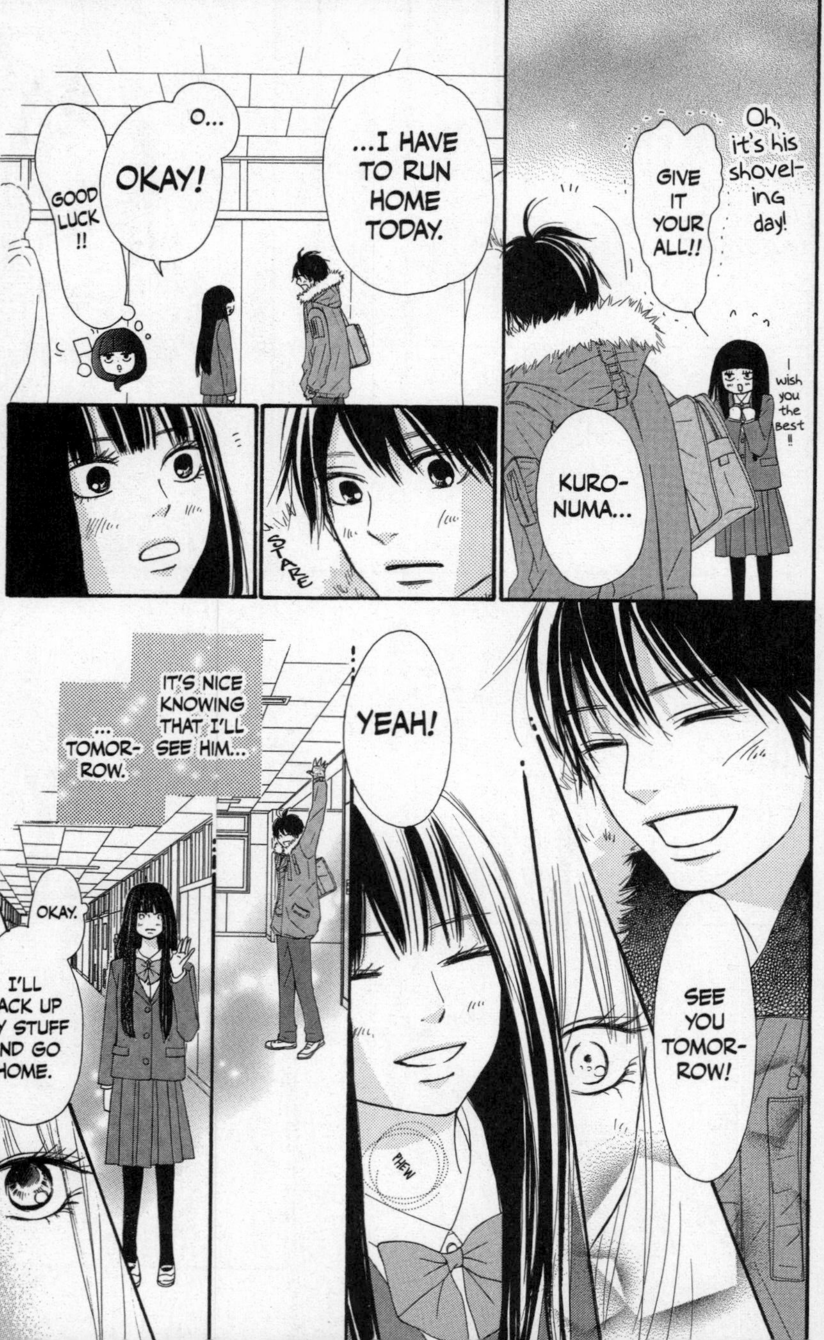
Oh, it's his shovel-ing day!
GIVE IT YOUR ALL!!
I wish you the Best!!
KURO-NUMA...
...I HAVE TO RUN HOME TODAY.
O...
OKAY!
GOOD LUCK!!
STARE
SEE YOU TOMOR-ROW!
YEAH!
PHEW
IT'S NICE KNOWING THAT I'LL SEE HIM...
... TOMOR-ROW.
OKAY.
I'LL PACK UP MY STUFF AND GO HOME.

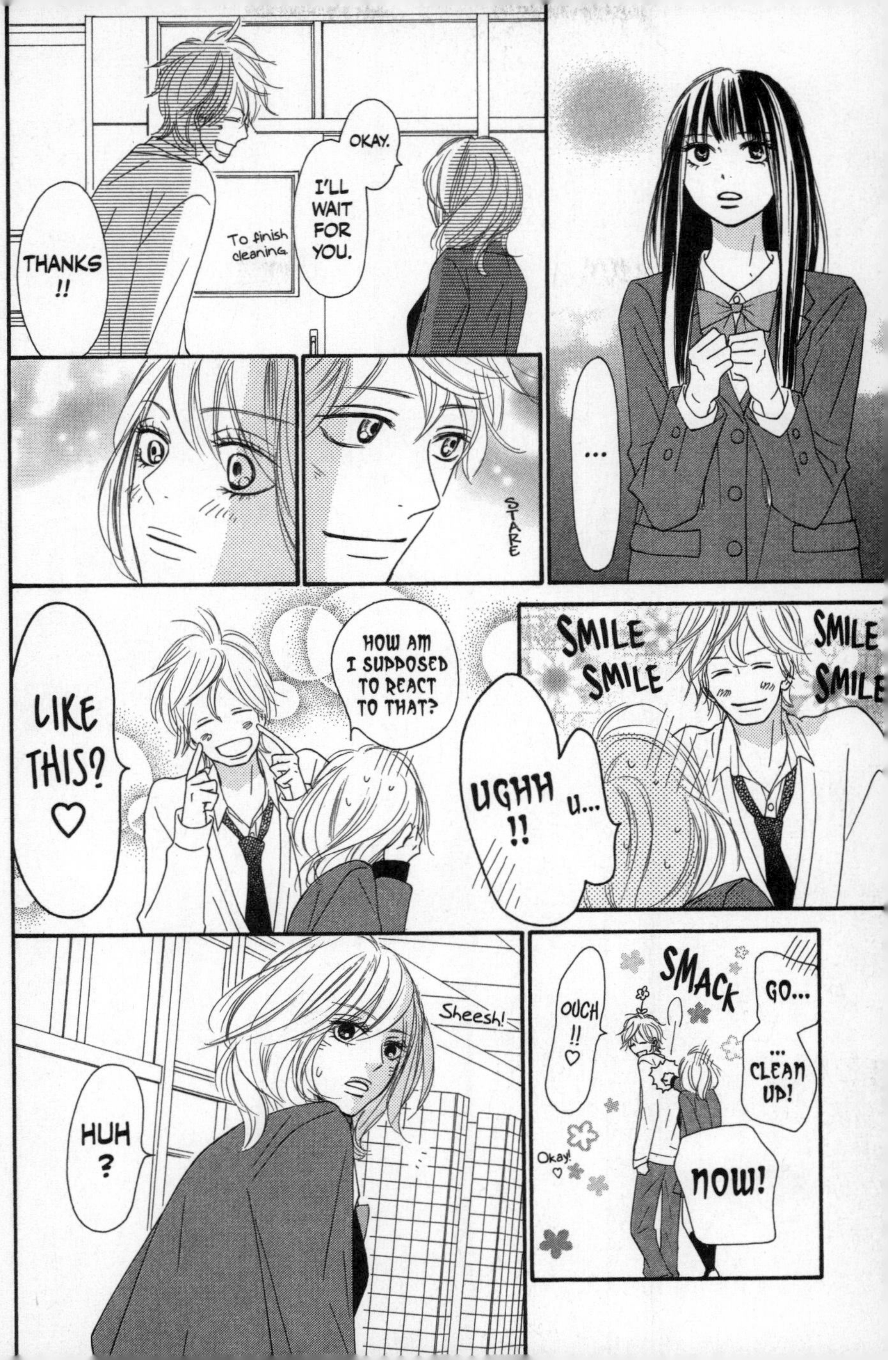
...
OKAY.
I'LL WAIT FOR YOU.
To finish cleaning.
THANKS!!
STARE
SMILE SMILE
SMILE SMILE
UGHH!!
u...
HOW AM I SUPPOSED TO REACT TO THAT?
LIKE THIS? ♡
GO... ...CLEAN UP!
NOW!
SMACK
OUCH!! ♡
Okay! ♡
Sheesh!
HUH?

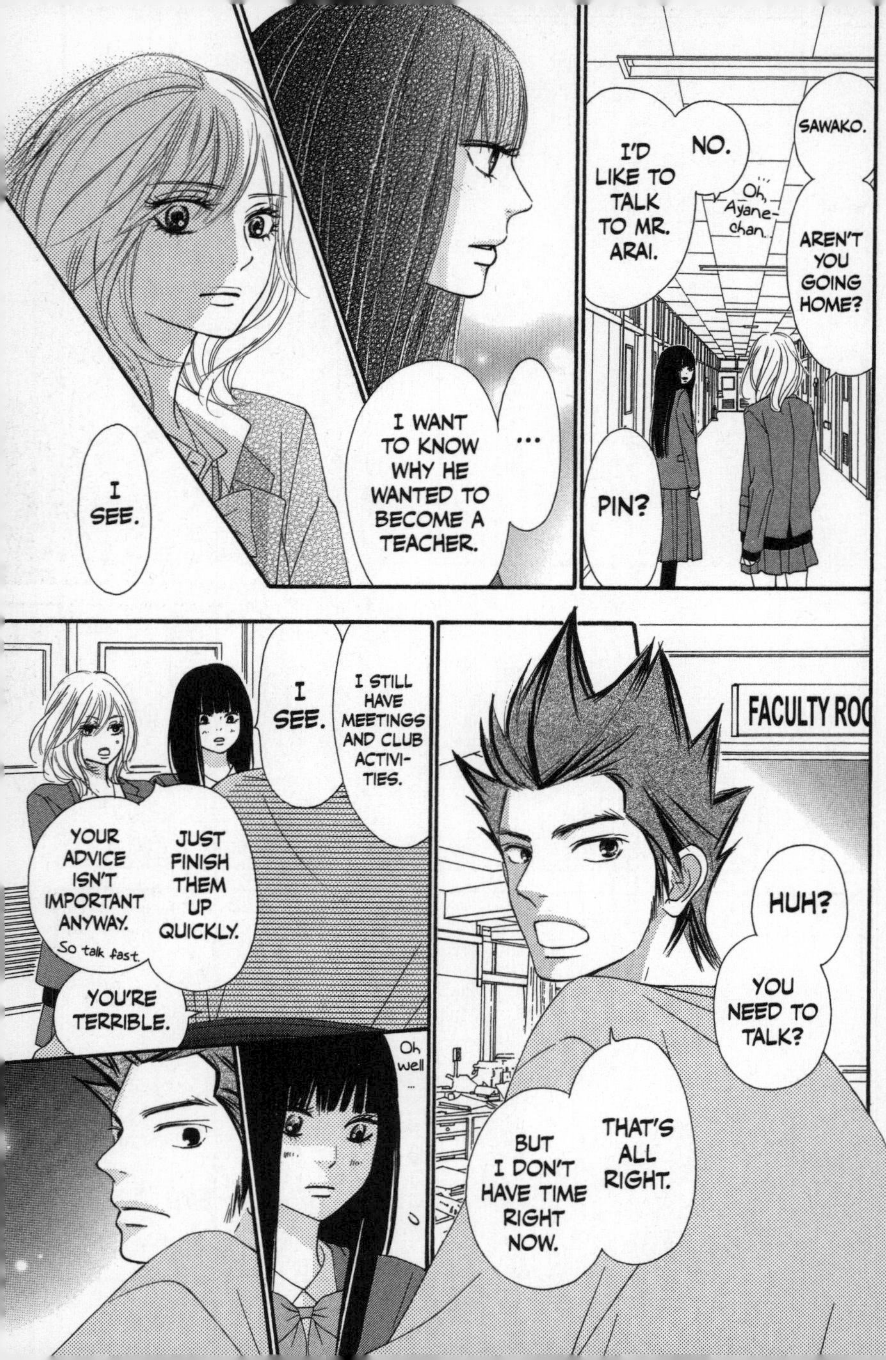
SAWAKO.
AREN'T YOU GOING HOME?
NO.
...Oh, Ayane-chan...
I'D LIKE TO TALK TO MR. ARAI.
PIN?
...
I WANT TO KNOW WHY HE WANTED TO BECOME A TEACHER.
I SEE.
FACULTY RO
HUH?
YOU NEED TO TALK?
THAT'S ALL RIGHT.
BUT I DON'T HAVE TIME RIGHT NOW.
I SEE.
I STILL HAVE MEETINGS AND CLUB ACTIVITIES.
JUST FINISH THEM UP QUICKLY.
YOUR ADVICE ISN'T IMPORTANT ANYWAY.
So talk fast.
YOU'RE TERRIBLE.
Oh well...

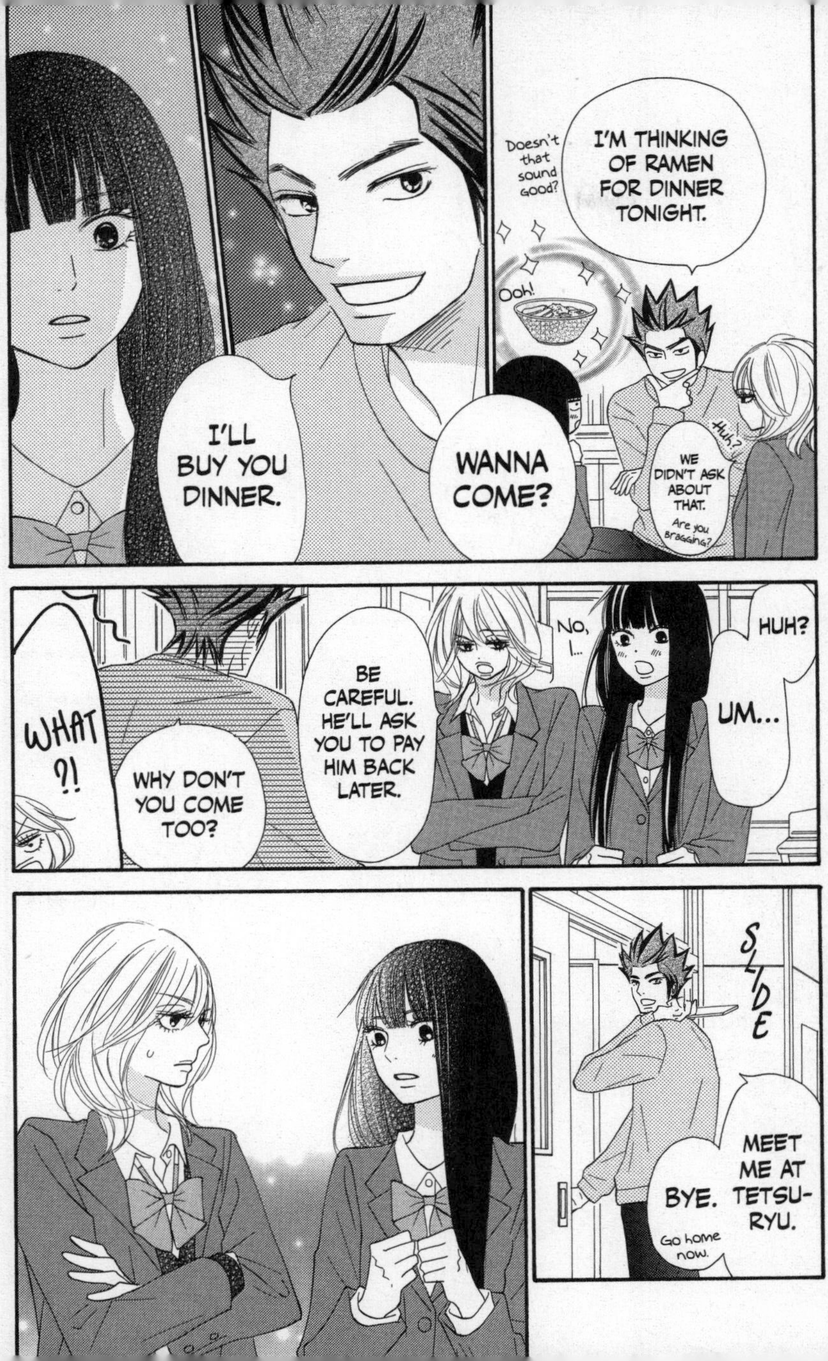
I'M THINKING OF RAMEN FOR DINNER TONIGHT.
Doesn't that sound good?
Ooh!
Huh?
WE DIDN'T ASK ABOUT THAT.
Are you bragging?
WANNA COME?
I'LL BUY YOU DINNER.
HUH?
UM...
No, I...
BE CAREFUL. HE'LL ASK YOU TO PAY HIM BACK LATER.
WHY DON'T YOU COME TOO?
WHAT ?!
SLIDE
MEET ME AT TETSU-RYU.
BYE.
Go home now.

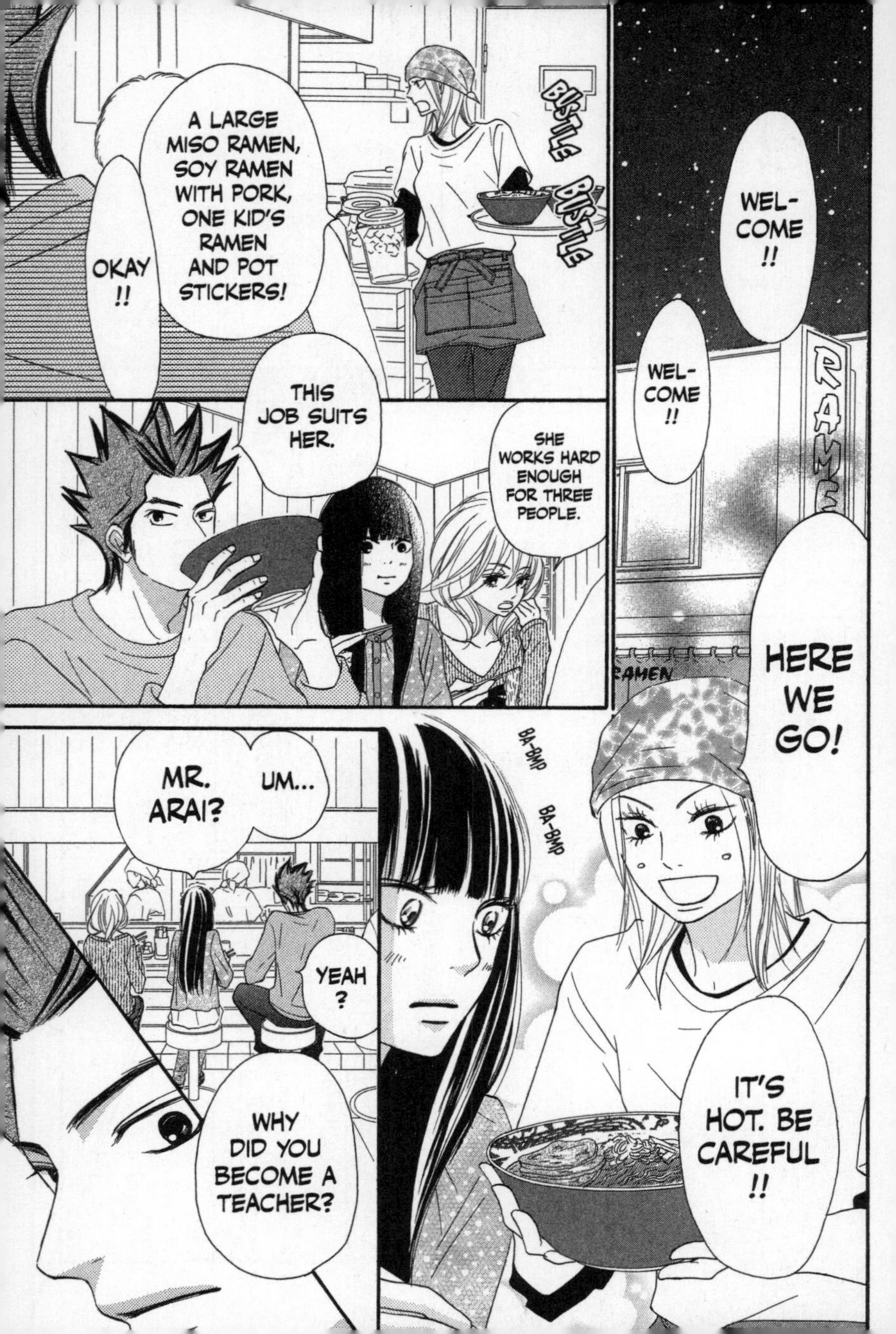
WEL-COME !!
WEL-COME !!
RAMEN
RAMEN
BUSTLE BUSTLE
A LARGE MISO RAMEN, SOY RAMEN WITH PORK, ONE KID'S RAMEN AND POT STICKERS!
OKAY !!
THIS JOB SUITS HER.
SHE WORKS HARD ENOUGH FOR THREE PEOPLE.
HERE WE GO!
BA-BMP
BA-BMP
IT'S HOT. BE CAREFUL !!
UM...
MR. ARAI?
YEAH ?
WHY DID YOU BECOME A TEACHER?

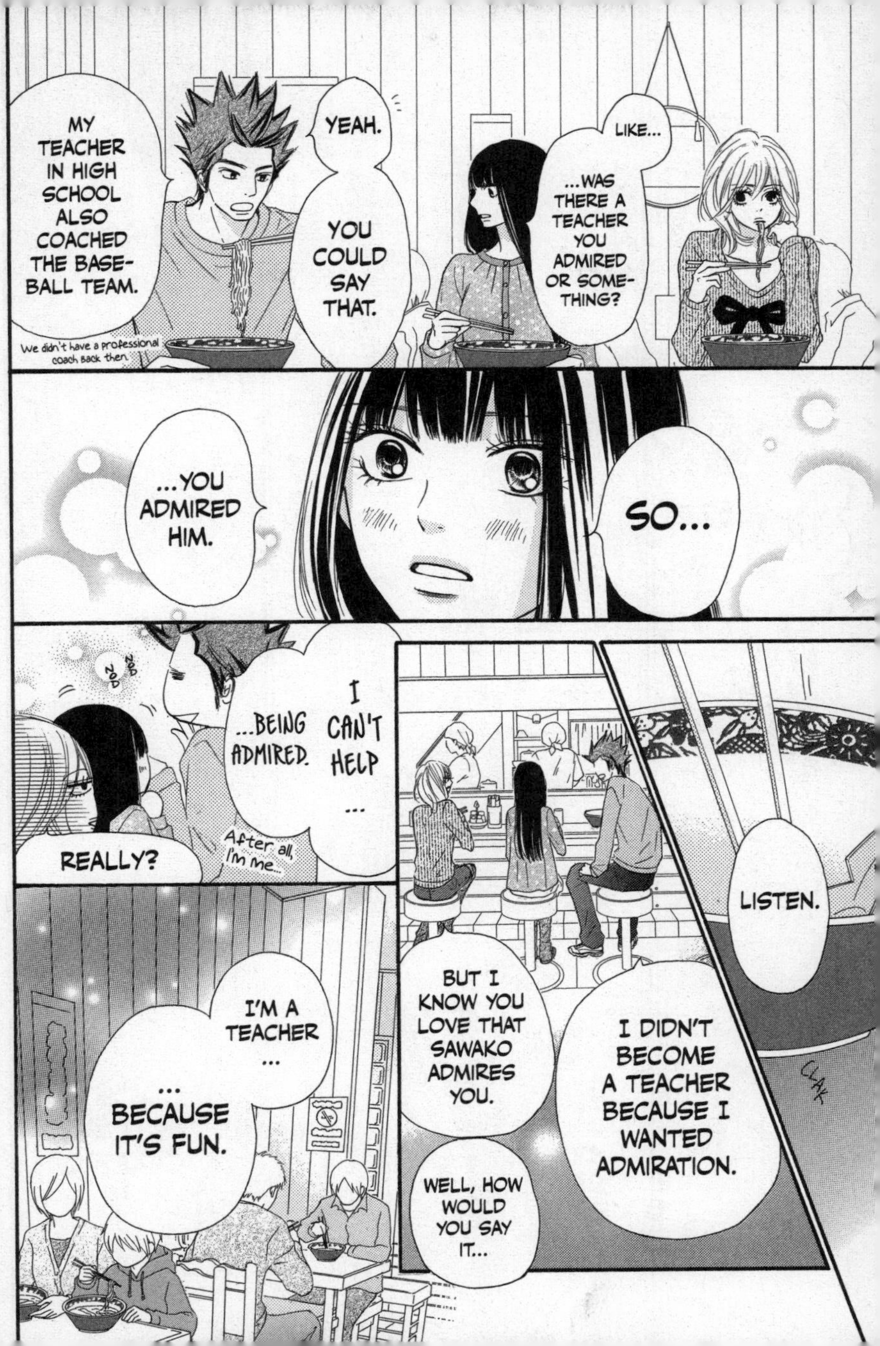
LIKE...
...WAS THERE A TEACHER YOU ADMIRED OR SOMETHING?
YEAH.
YOU COULD SAY THAT.
MY TEACHER IN HIGH SCHOOL ALSO COACHED THE BASE-BALL TEAM.
We didn't have a professional coach back then.
SO...
...YOU ADMIRED HIM.
LISTEN.
CLAK
I DIDN'T BECOME A TEACHER BECAUSE I WANTED ADMIRATION.
BUT I KNOW YOU LOVE THAT SAWAKO ADMIRES YOU.
WELL, HOW WOULD YOU SAY IT...
I CAN'T HELP ...
...BEING ADMIRED.
NOD NOD
After all, I'm me...
REALLY?
I'M A TEACHER ...
... BECAUSE IT'S FUN.

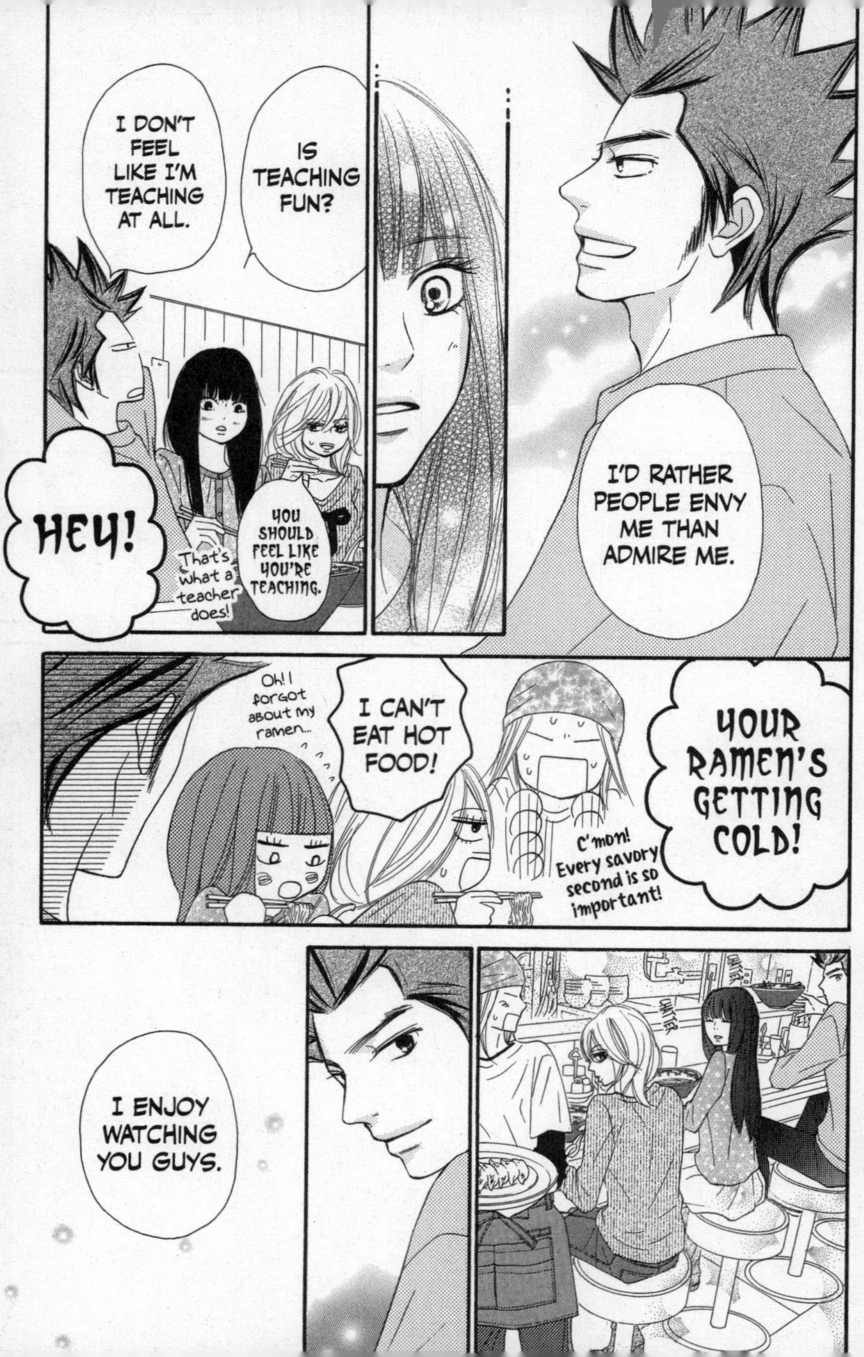
I'D RATHER PEOPLE ENVY ME THAN ADMIRE ME.
IS TEACHING FUN?
I DON'T FEEL LIKE I'M TEACHING AT ALL.
YOU SHOULD FEEL LIKE YOU'RE TEACHING.
HEY!
That's what a teacher does!
YOUR RAMEN'S GETTING COLD!
C'mon! Every savory second is so important!
I CAN'T EAT HOT FOOD!
Oh! I forgot about my ramen...
CHATTER
CHATTER
I ENJOY WATCHING YOU GUYS.

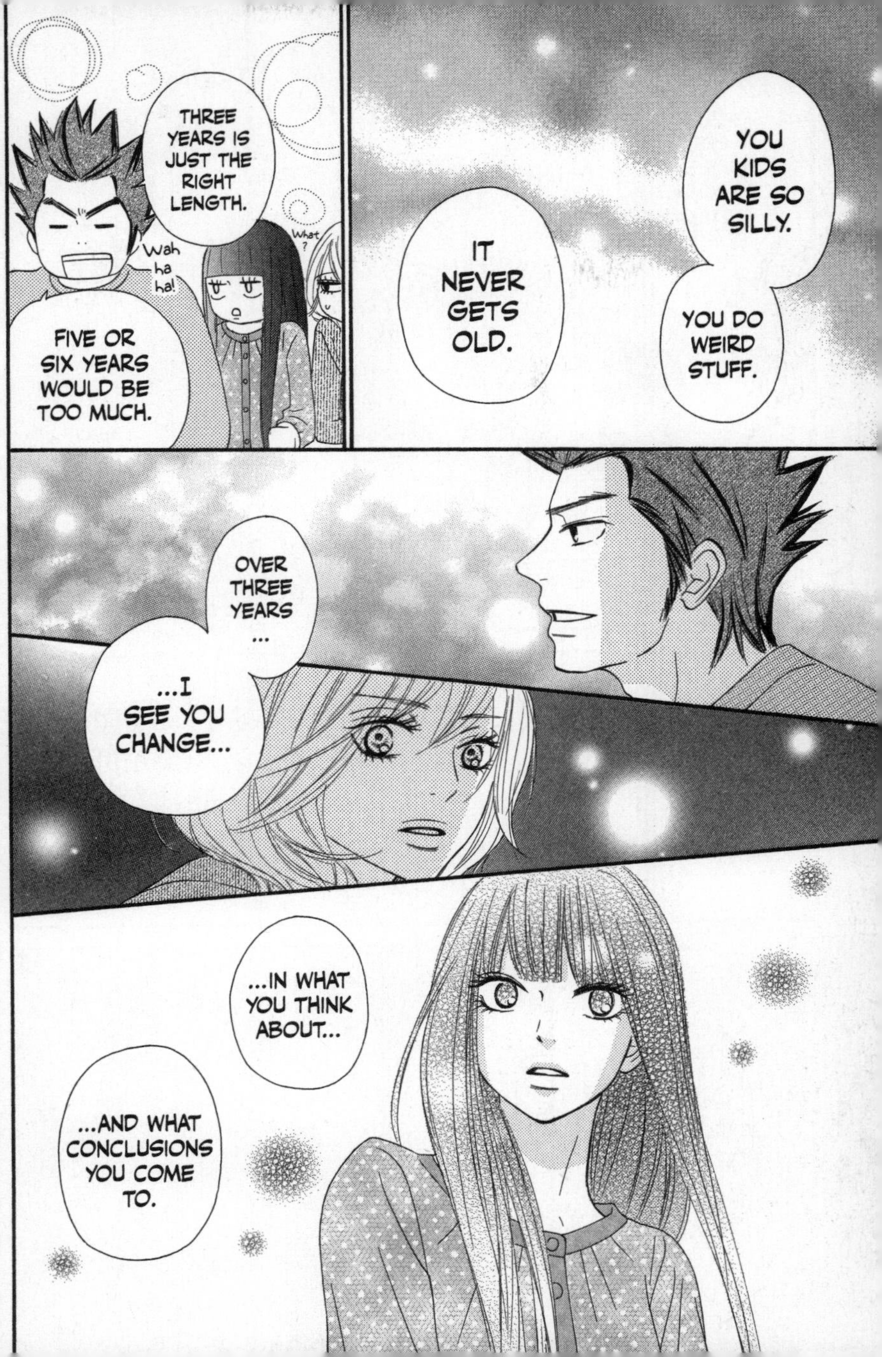
YOU KIDS ARE SO SILLY.
YOU DO WEIRD STUFF.
IT NEVER GETS OLD.
THREE YEARS IS JUST THE RIGHT LENGTH.
What?
Wah ha ha!
FIVE OR SIX YEARS WOULD BE TOO MUCH.
OVER THREE YEARS ...
...I SEE YOU CHANGE...
...IN WHAT YOU THINK ABOUT...
...AND WHAT CONCLUSIONS YOU COME TO.

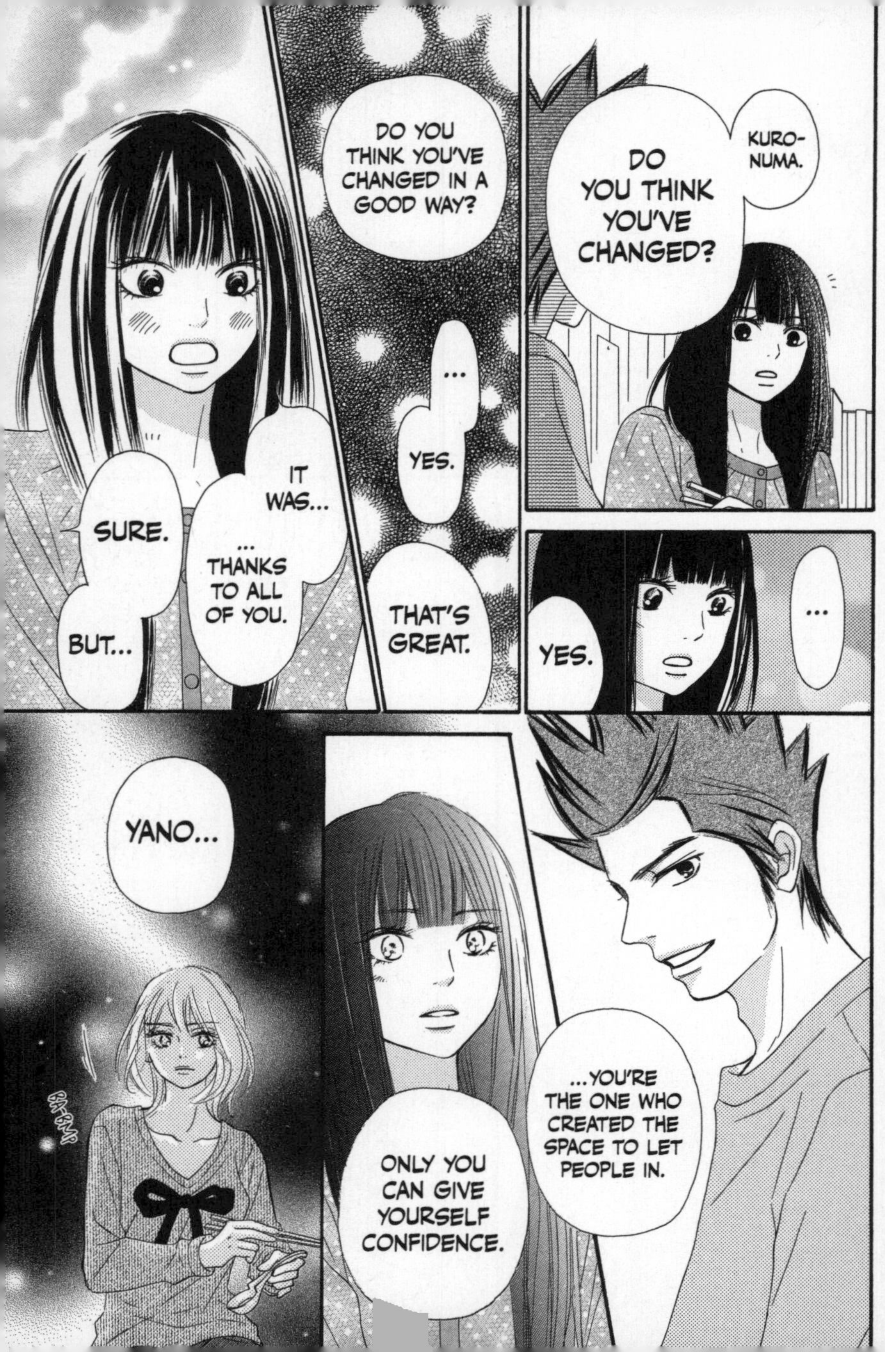
KURO-NUMA.
DO YOU THINK YOU'VE CHANGED?
...
YES.
DO YOU THINK YOU'VE CHANGED IN A GOOD WAY?
...
YES.
THAT'S GREAT.
SURE.
BUT...
IT WAS...
...THANKS TO ALL OF YOU.
...YOU'RE THE ONE WHO CREATED THE SPACE TO LET PEOPLE IN.
ONLY YOU CAN GIVE YOURSELF CONFIDENCE.
YANO...
BA-BMP

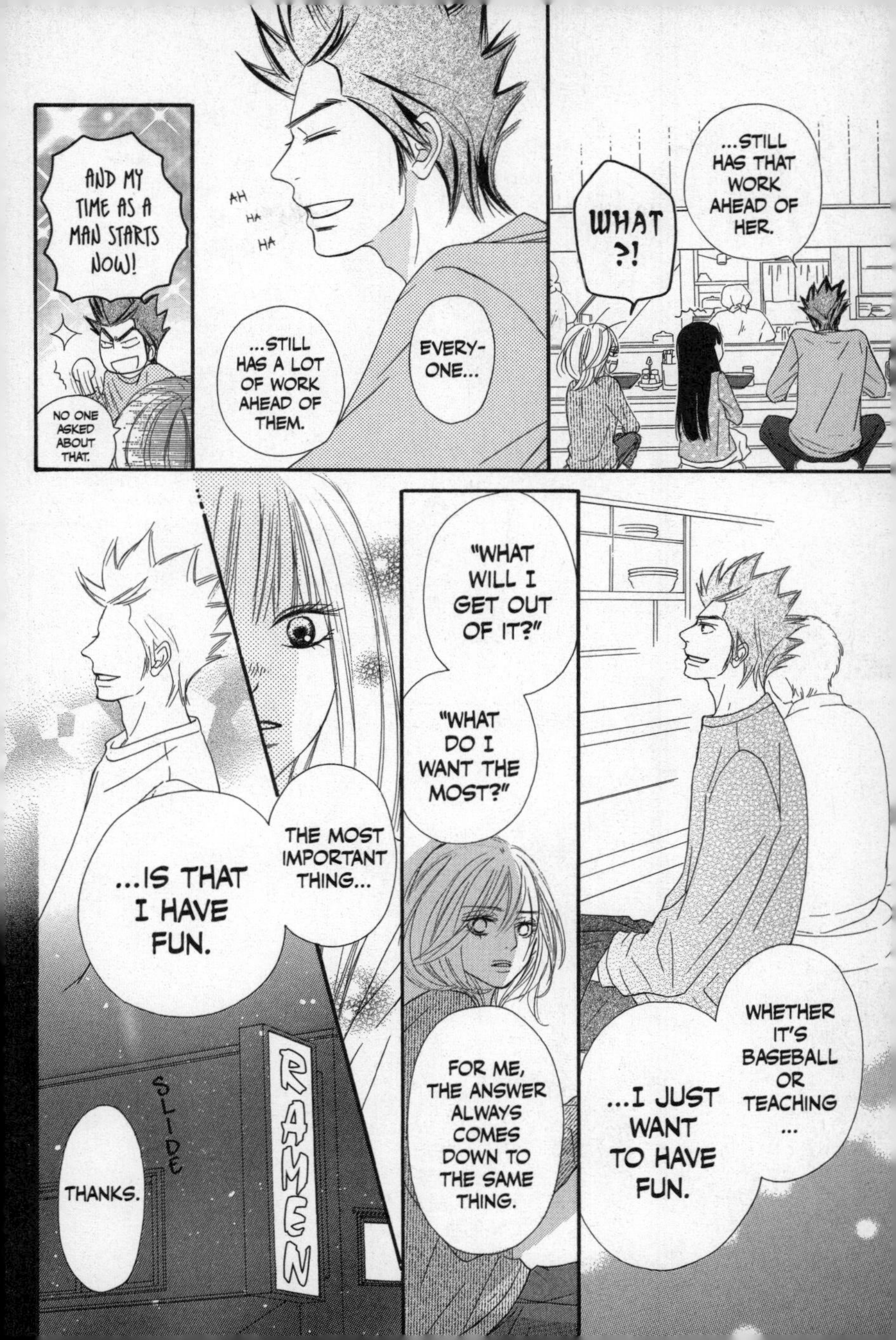
...STILL HAS THAT WORK AHEAD OF HER.
WHAT?!
EVERY-ONE...
...STILL HAS A LOT OF WORK AHEAD OF THEM.
AH HA HA
AND MY TIME AS A MAN STARTS NOW!
NO ONE ASKED ABOUT THAT.
"WHAT WILL I GET OUT OF IT?"
"WHAT DO I WANT THE MOST?"
WHETHER IT'S BASEBALL OR TEACHING...
...I JUST WANT TO HAVE FUN.
FOR ME, THE ANSWER ALWAYS COMES DOWN TO THE SAME THING.
THE MOST IMPORTANT THING...
...IS THAT I HAVE FUN.
RAMEN
SLIDE
THANKS.

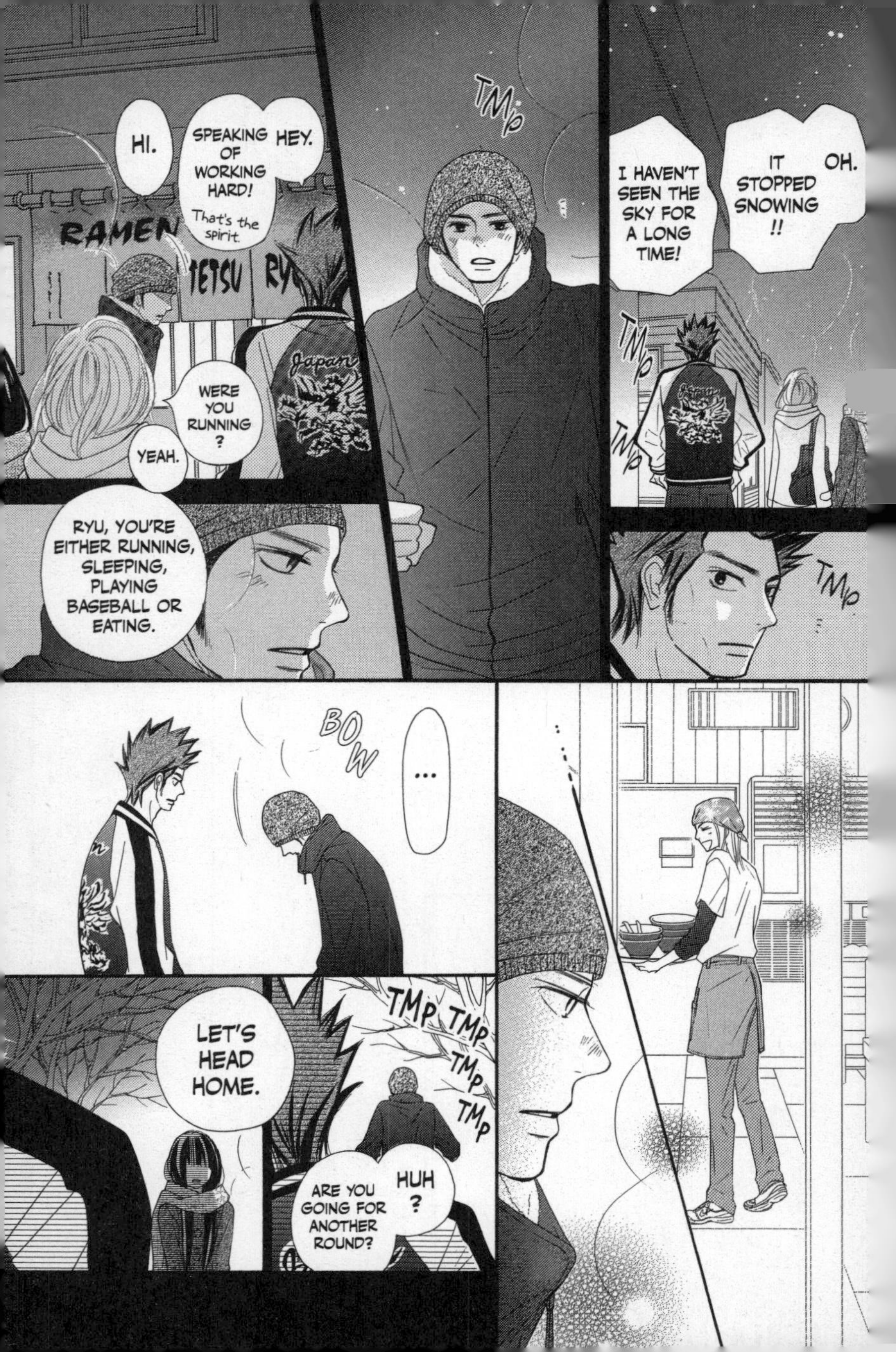
OH.
IT STOPPED SNOWING!!
I HAVEN'T SEEN THE SKY FOR A LONG TIME!
TMP
TMP
TMP
TMP
HEY.
SPEAKING OF WORKING HARD!
That's the spirit.
HI.
RAMEN
TETSU
RYU
WERE YOU RUNNING?
YEAH.
RYU, YOU'RE EITHER RUNNING, SLEEPING, PLAYING BASEBALL OR EATING.
BOW
...
TMP TMP TMP TMP
LET'S HEAD HOME.
HUH?
ARE YOU GOING FOR ANOTHER ROUND?

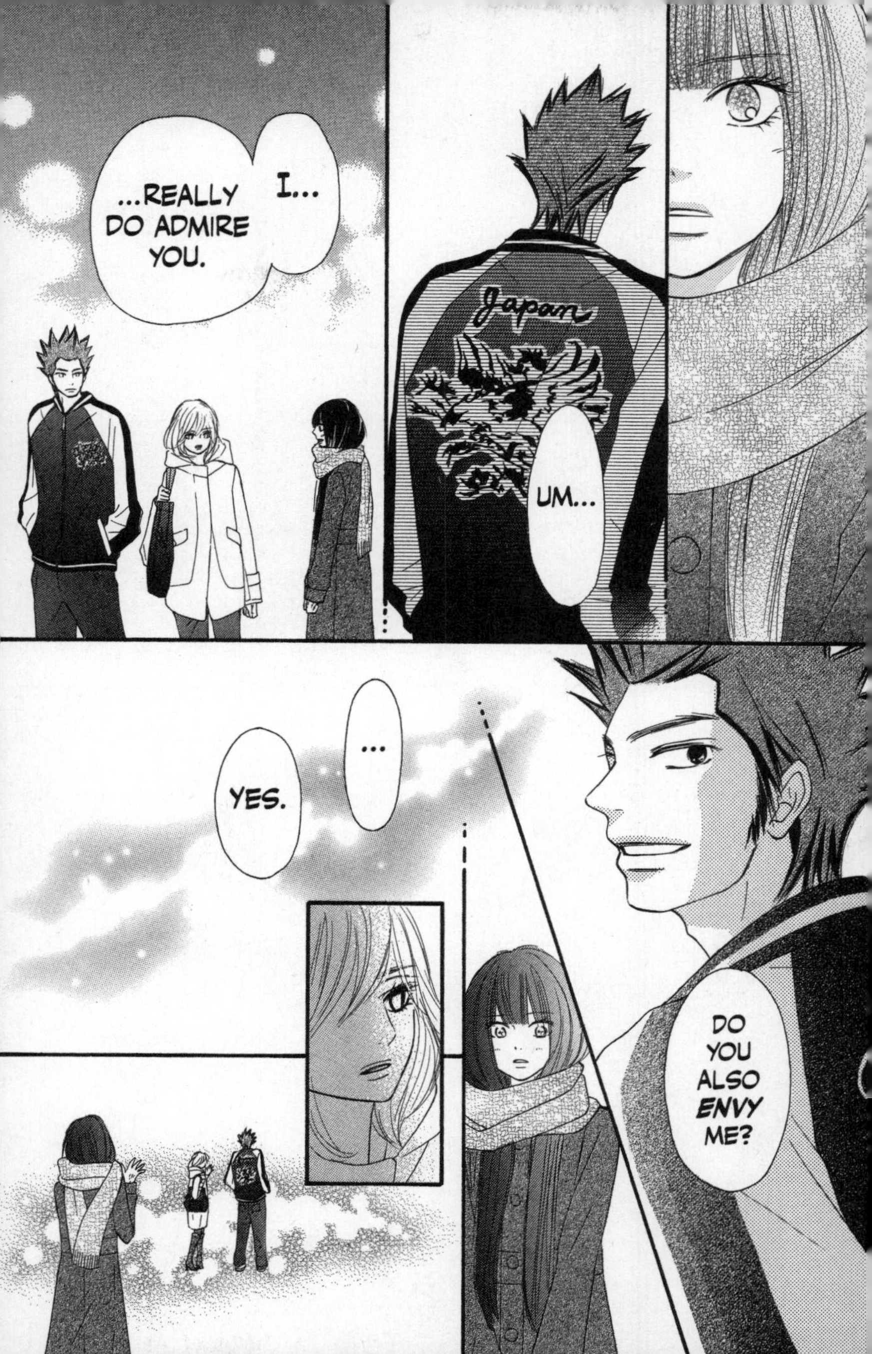
Japan
UM...
I...
...REALLY DO ADMIRE YOU.
DO YOU ALSO ENVY ME?
...
YES.

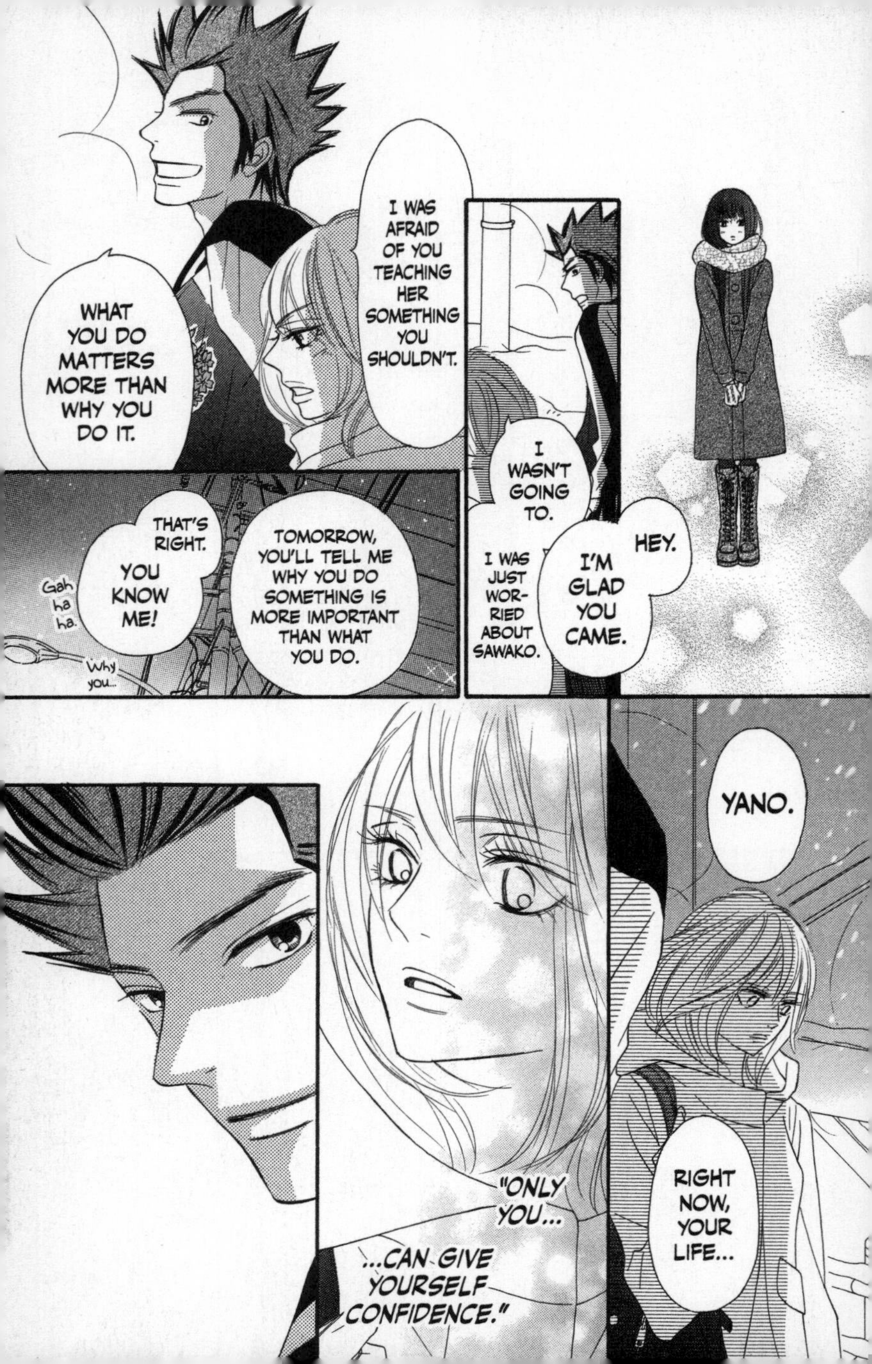
I WAS AFRAID OF YOU TEACHING HER SOMETHING YOU SHOULDN'T.
WHAT YOU DO MATTERS MORE THAN WHY YOU DO IT.
I WASN'T GOING TO.
I WAS JUST WORRIED ABOUT SAWAKO.
TOMORROW, YOU'LL TELL ME WHY YOU DO SOMETHING IS MORE IMPORTANT THAN WHAT YOU DO.
THAT'S RIGHT.
YOU KNOW ME!
Gah ha ha.
Why you...
HEY.
I'M GLAD YOU CAME.
YANO.
RIGHT NOW, YOUR LIFE...
"ONLY YOU...
...CAN GIVE YOURSELF CONFIDENCE."

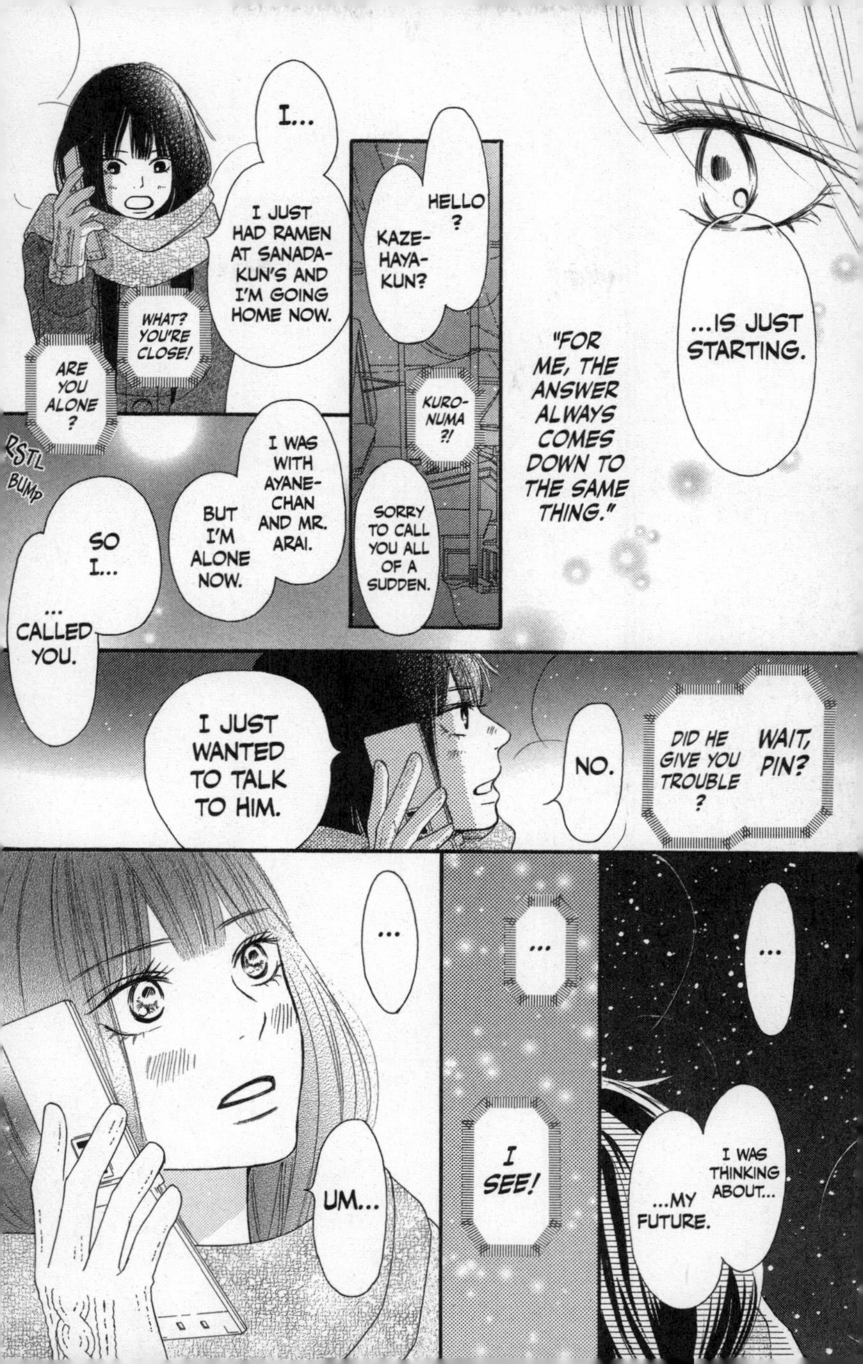
...IS JUST STARTING.
"FOR ME, THE ANSWER ALWAYS COMES DOWN TO THE SAME THING."
HELLO? KAZE-HAYA-KUN?
KURO-NUMA?!
SORRY TO CALL YOU ALL OF A SUDDEN.
I...
I JUST HAD RAMEN AT SANADA-KUN'S AND I'M GOING HOME NOW.
WHAT? YOU'RE CLOSE!
ARE YOU ALONE?
I WAS WITH AYANE-CHAN AND MR. ARAI.
BUT I'M ALONE NOW.
SO I...
RSTL
BUMP
...CALLED YOU.
WAIT, PIN?
DID HE GIVE YOU TROUBLE?
NO.
I JUST WANTED TO TALK TO HIM.
...
I WAS THINKING ABOUT...
...MY FUTURE.
...
I SEE!
...
UM...

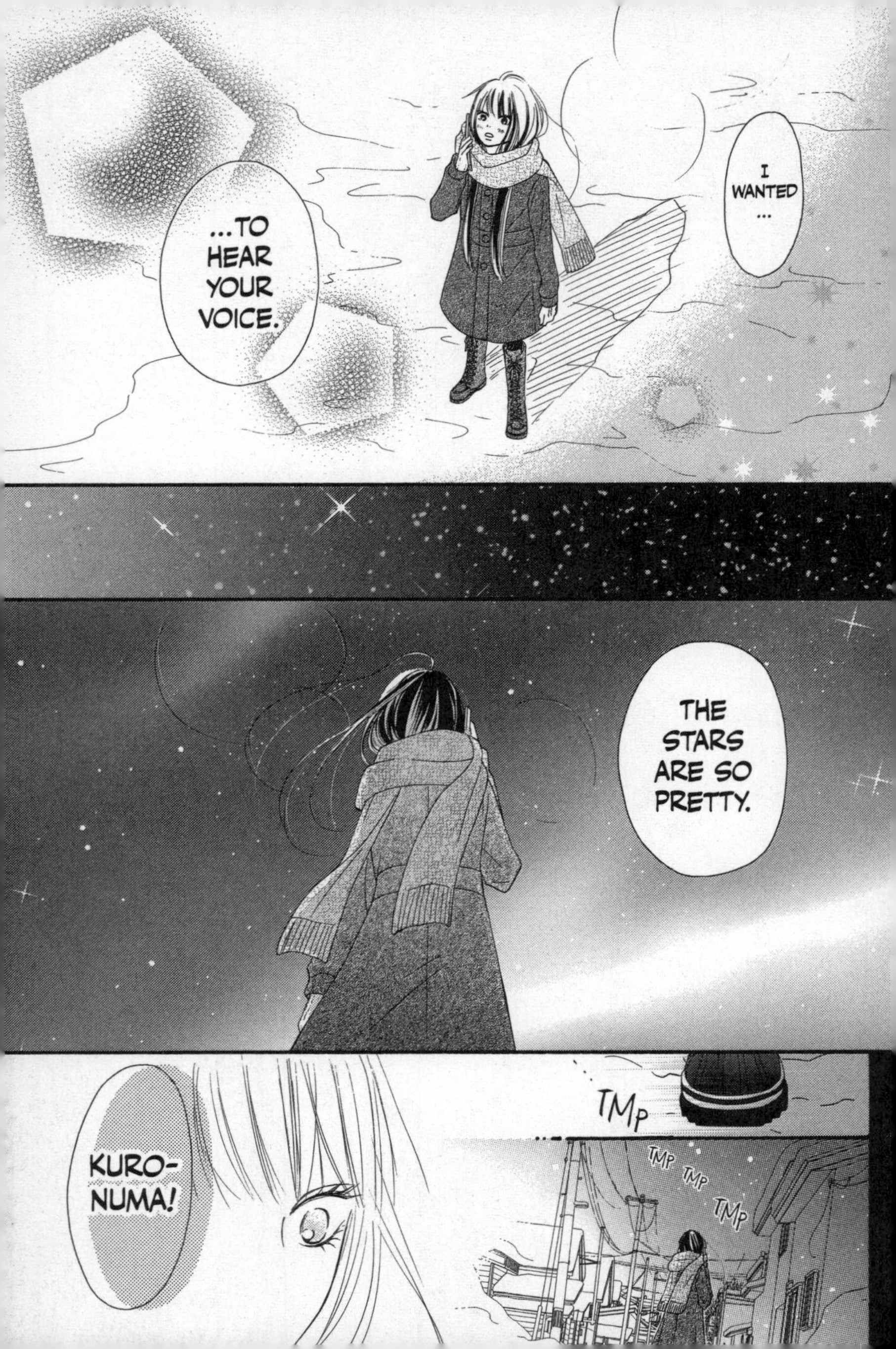
I WANTED...
...TO HEAR YOUR VOICE.
THE STARS ARE SO PRETTY.
TMP
TMP TMP TMP
KURO-NUMA!

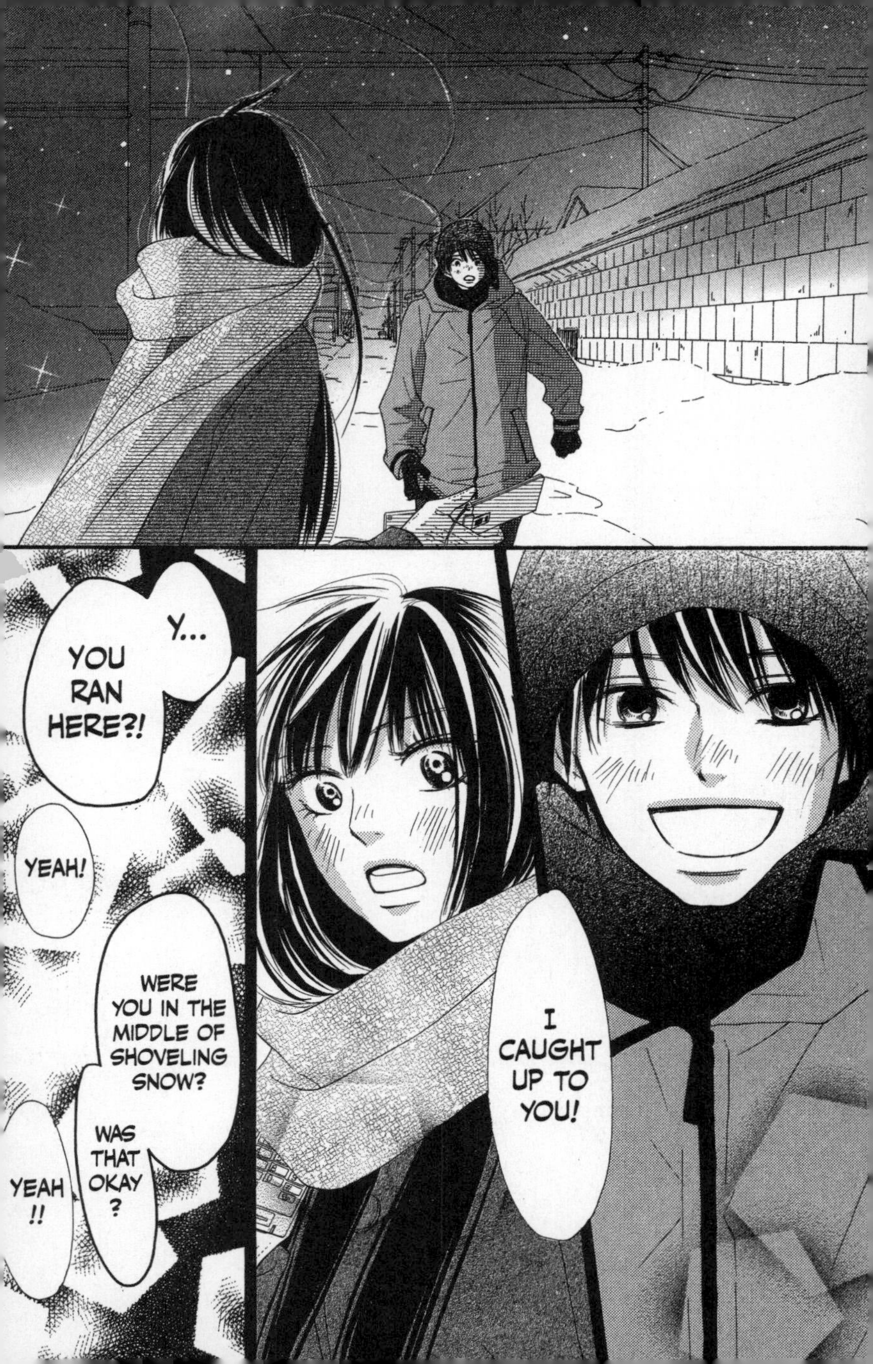
I CAUGHT UP TO YOU!
Y... YOU RAN HERE?!
YEAH!
WERE YOU IN THE MIDDLE OF SHOVELING SNOW?
WAS THAT OKAY?
YEAH!!

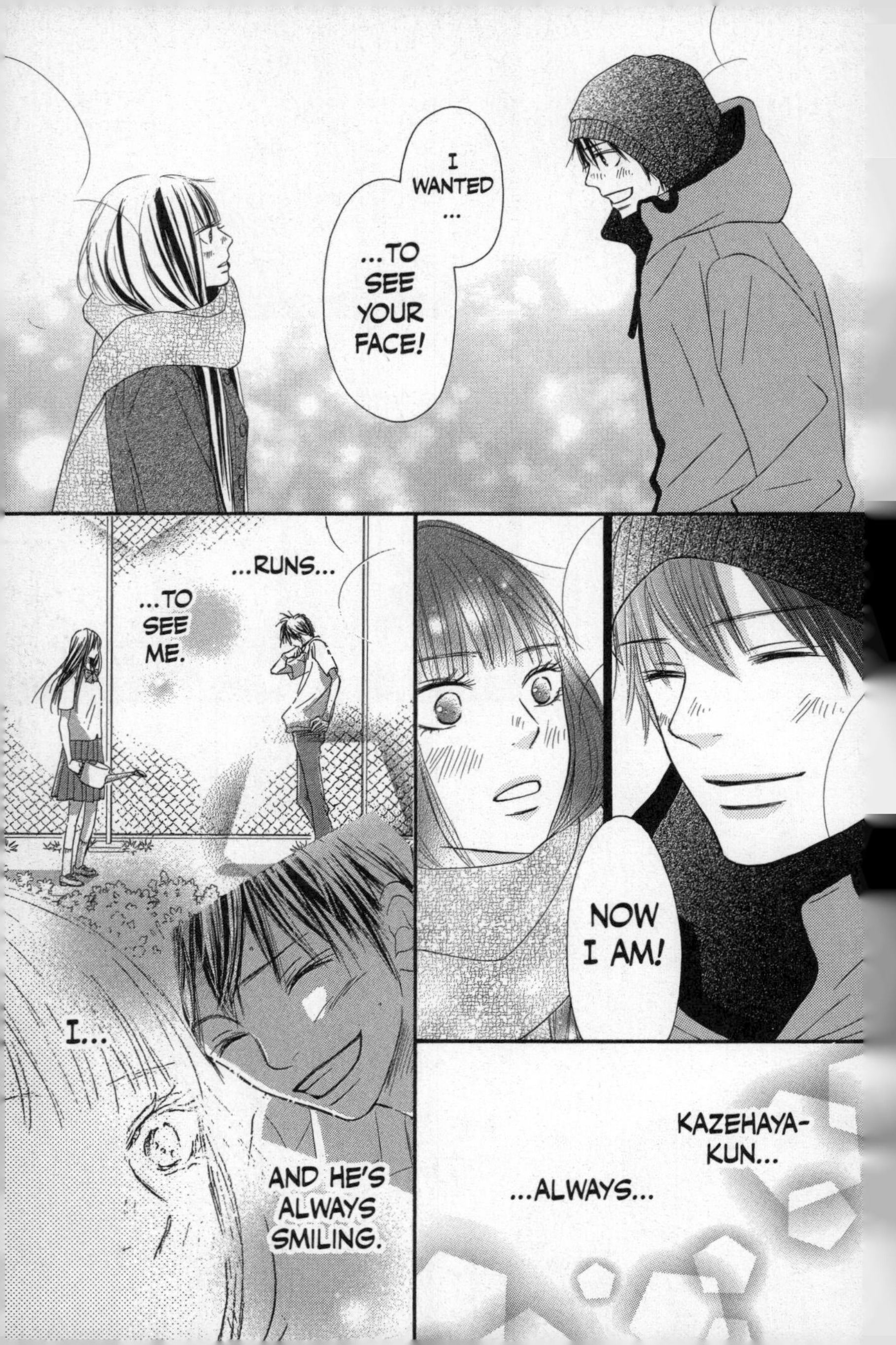
I WANTED ...
...TO SEE YOUR FACE!
NOW I AM!
KAZEHAYA-KUN...
...ALWAYS...
...RUNS...
...TO SEE ME.
I...
AND HE'S ALWAYS SMILING.

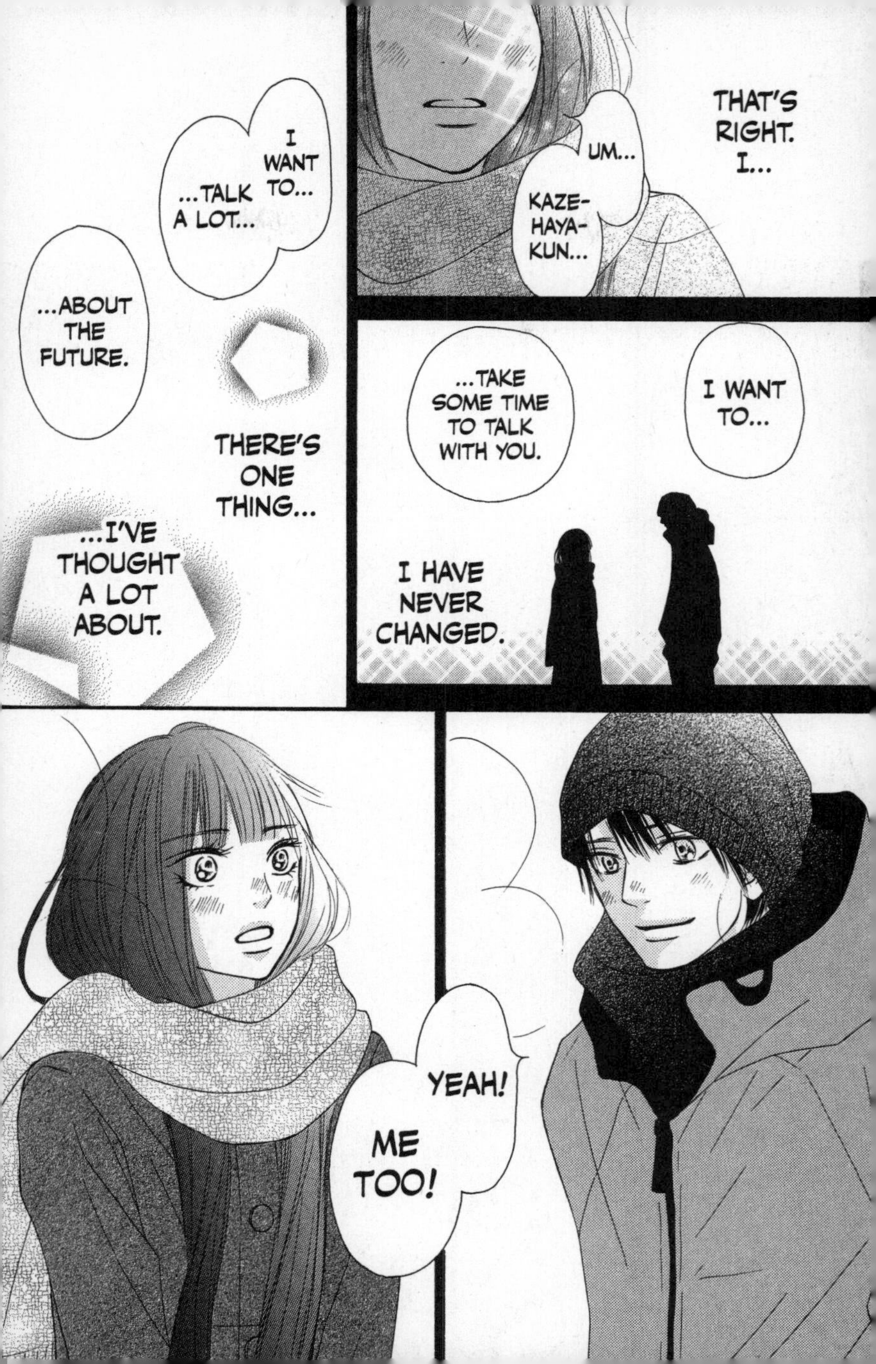
THAT'S RIGHT. I...
UM...
KAZE-HAYA-KUN...
I WANT TO...
...TAKE SOME TIME TO TALK WITH YOU.
I HAVE NEVER CHANGED.
I WANT TO...
...TALK A LOT...
...ABOUT THE FUTURE.
THERE'S ONE THING...
...I'VE THOUGHT A LOT ABOUT.
YEAH!
ME TOO!

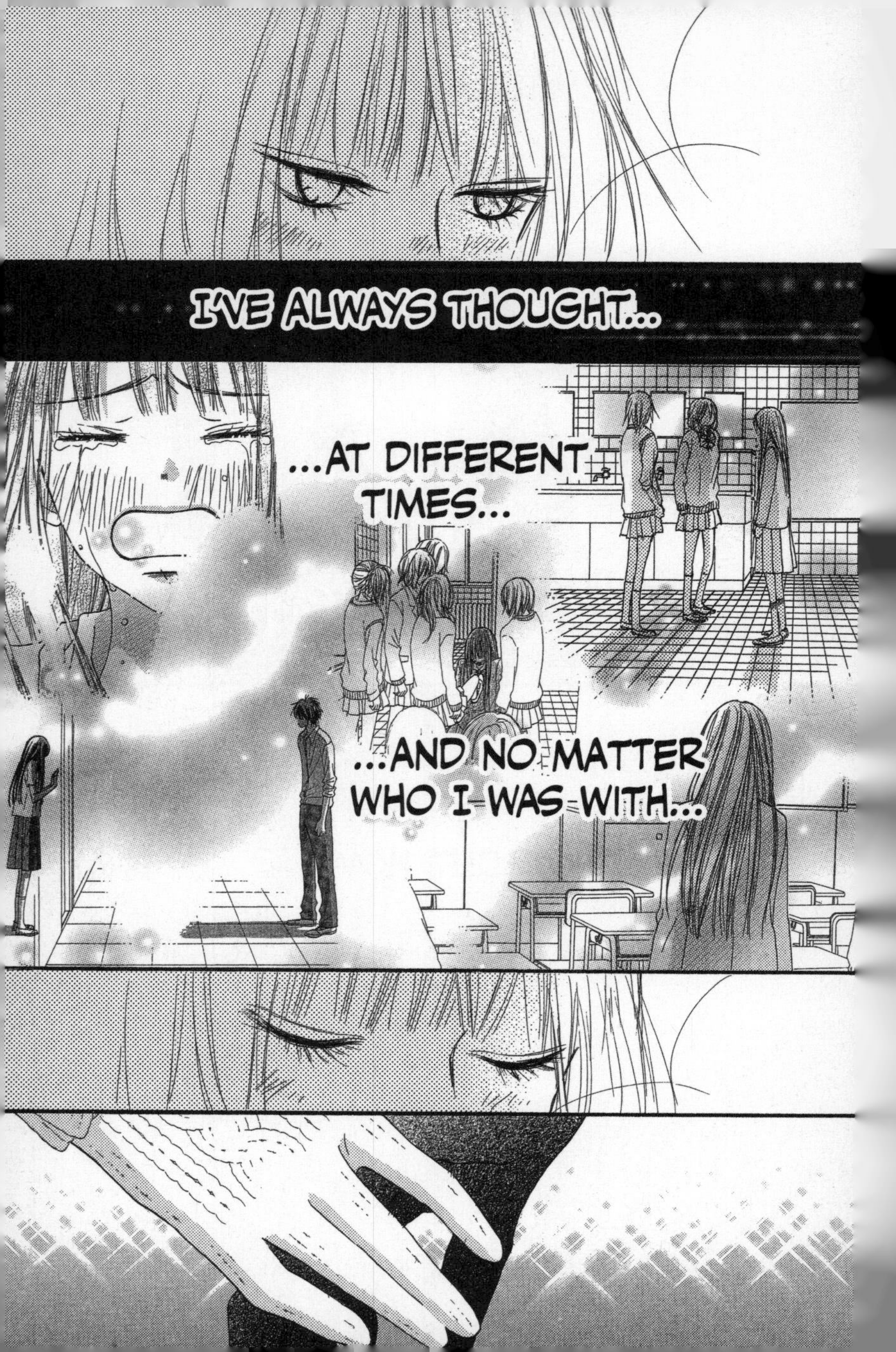
I'VE ALWAYS THOUGHT...
...AT DIFFERENT TIMES...
...AND NO MATTER WHO I WAS WITH...

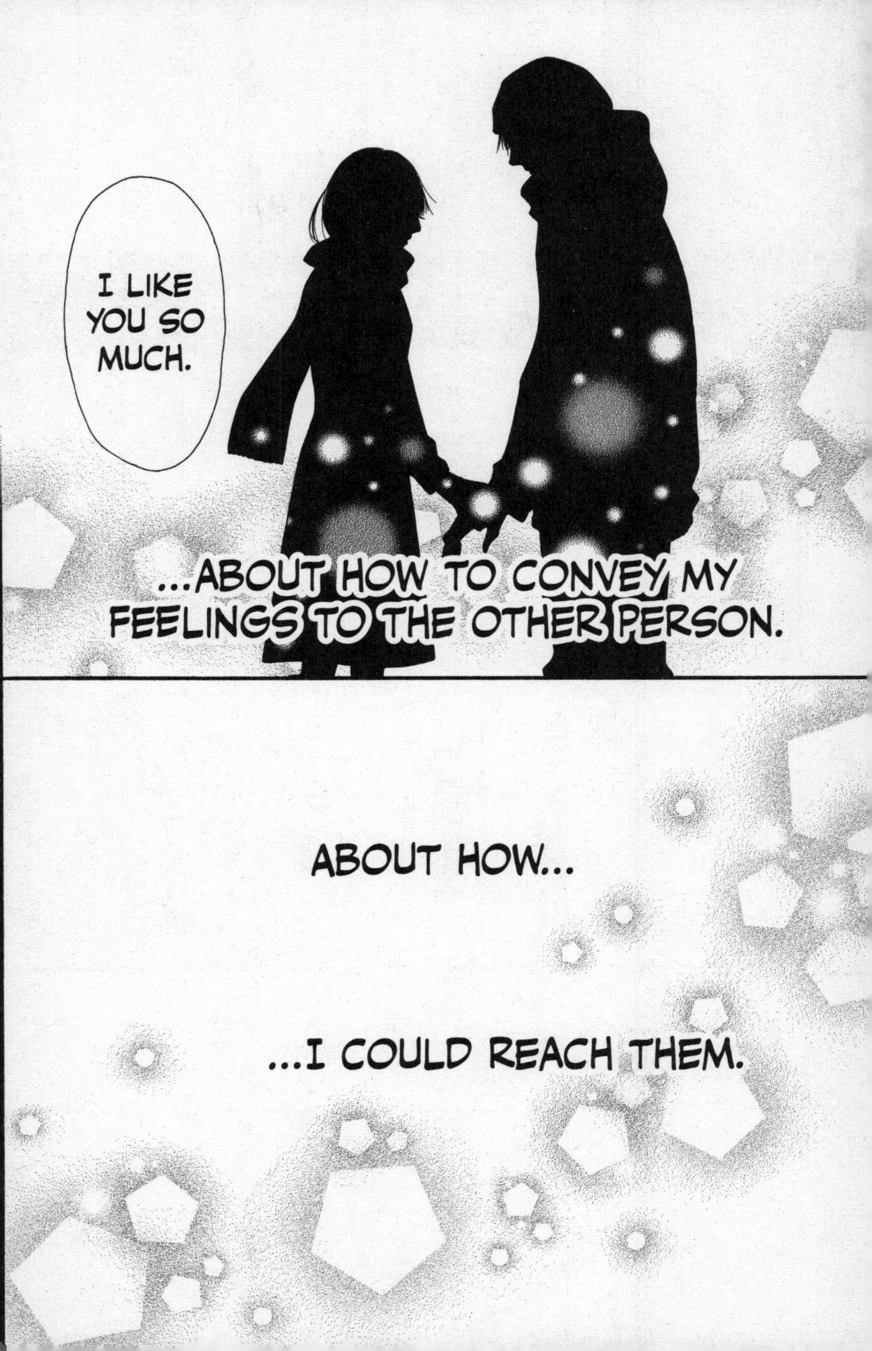
I LIKE YOU SO MUCH.
...ABOUT HOW TO CONVEY MY FEELINGS TO THE OTHER PERSON.
ABOUT HOW...
...I COULD REACH THEM.

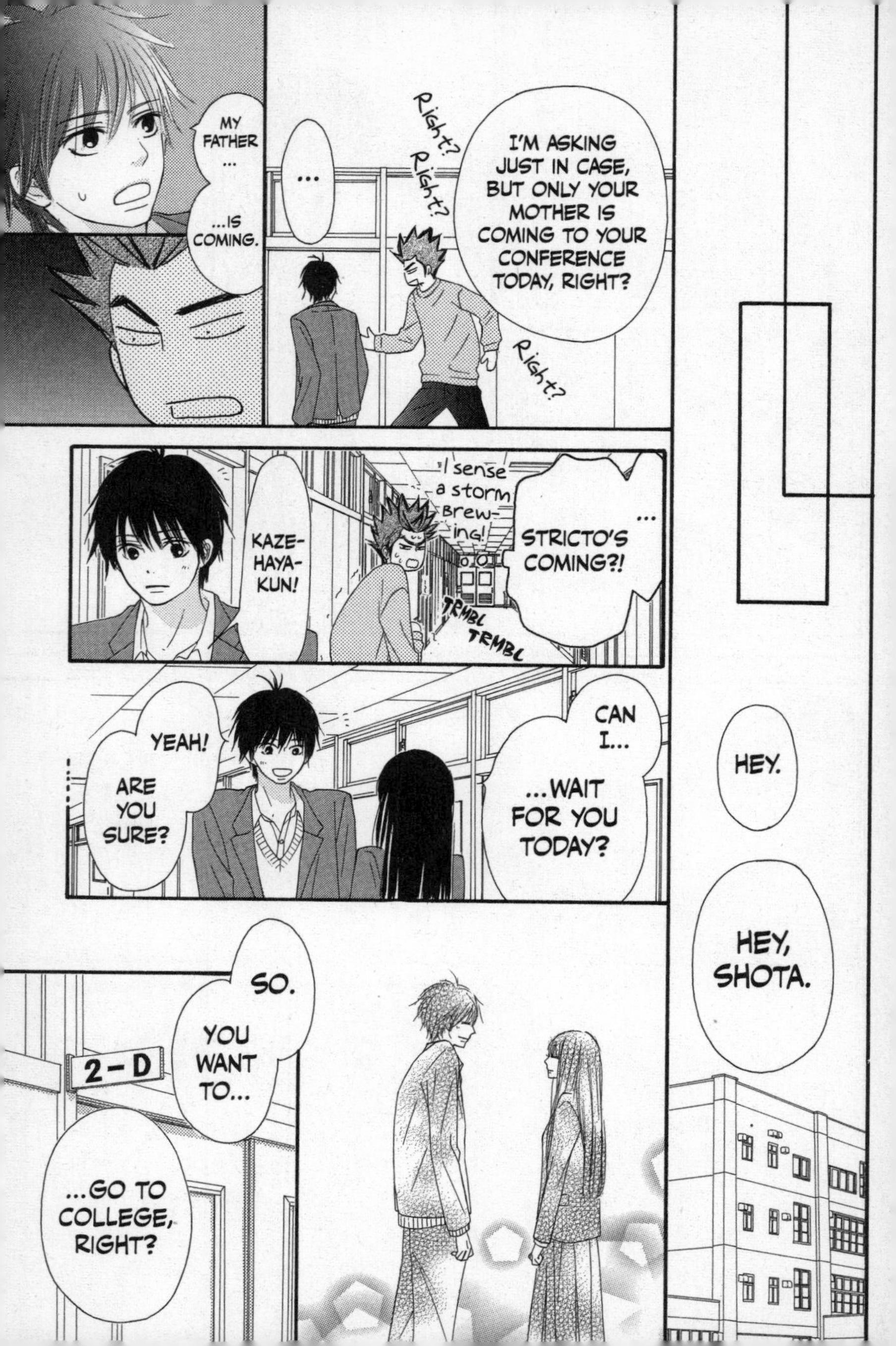
HEY.
HEY, SHOTA.
I'M ASKING JUST IN CASE, BUT ONLY YOUR MOTHER IS COMING TO YOUR CONFERENCE TODAY, RIGHT?
Right? Right?
Right?
...
MY FATHER ...
...IS COMING.
... STRICTO'S COMING?!
I sense a storm brew-ing!
TRMBL TRMBL
KAZE-HAYA-KUN!
CAN I...
...WAIT FOR YOU TODAY?
YEAH!
ARE YOU SURE?
SO.
YOU WANT TO...
...GO TO COLLEGE, RIGHT?
2-D

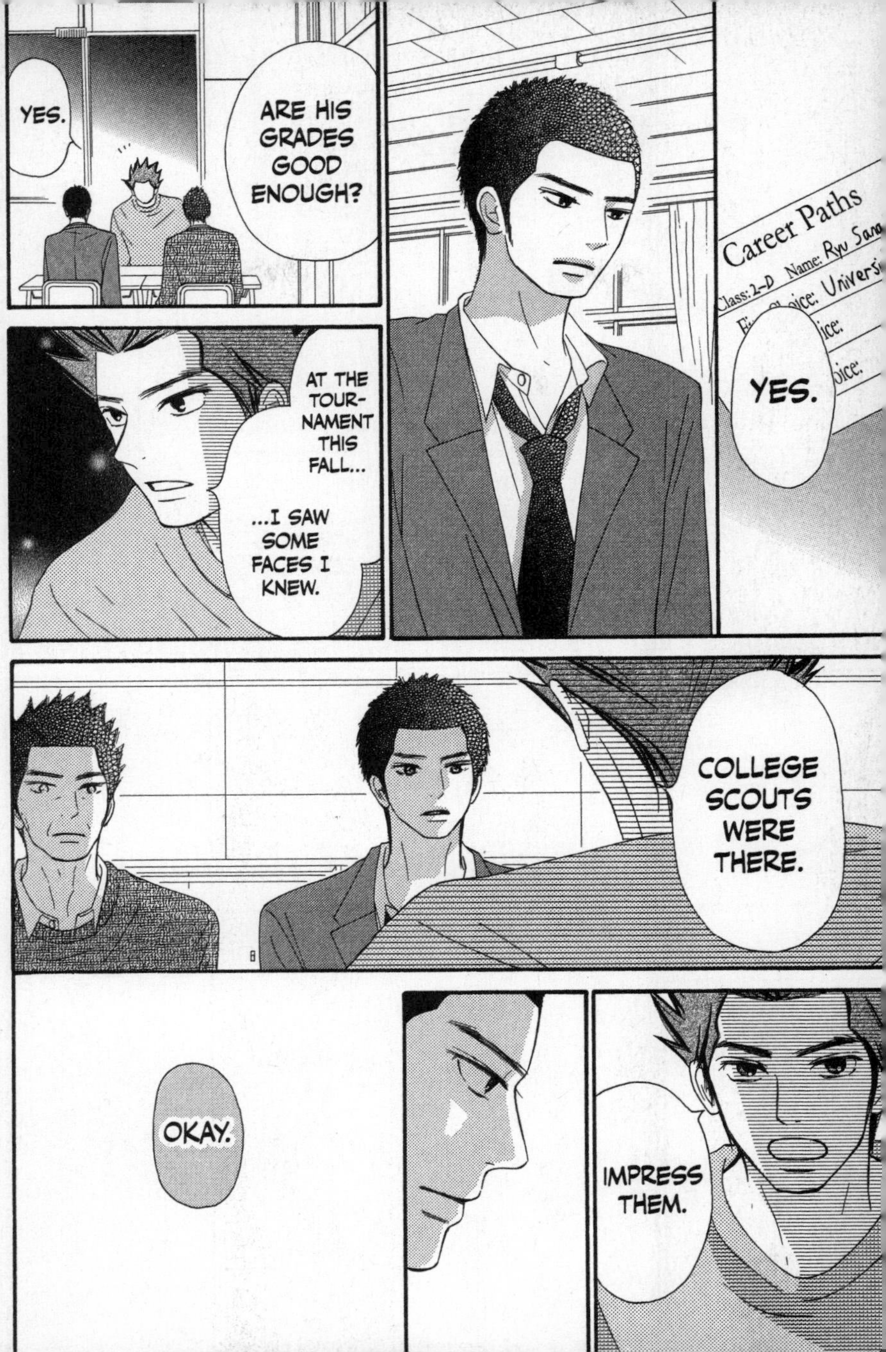
Career Paths
Class: 2-D Name: Ryu
YES.
ARE HIS GRADES GOOD ENOUGH?
YES.
AT THE TOURNAMENT THIS FALL...
...I SAW SOME FACES I KNEW.
COLLEGE SCOUTS WERE THERE.
IMPRESS THEM.
OKAY.

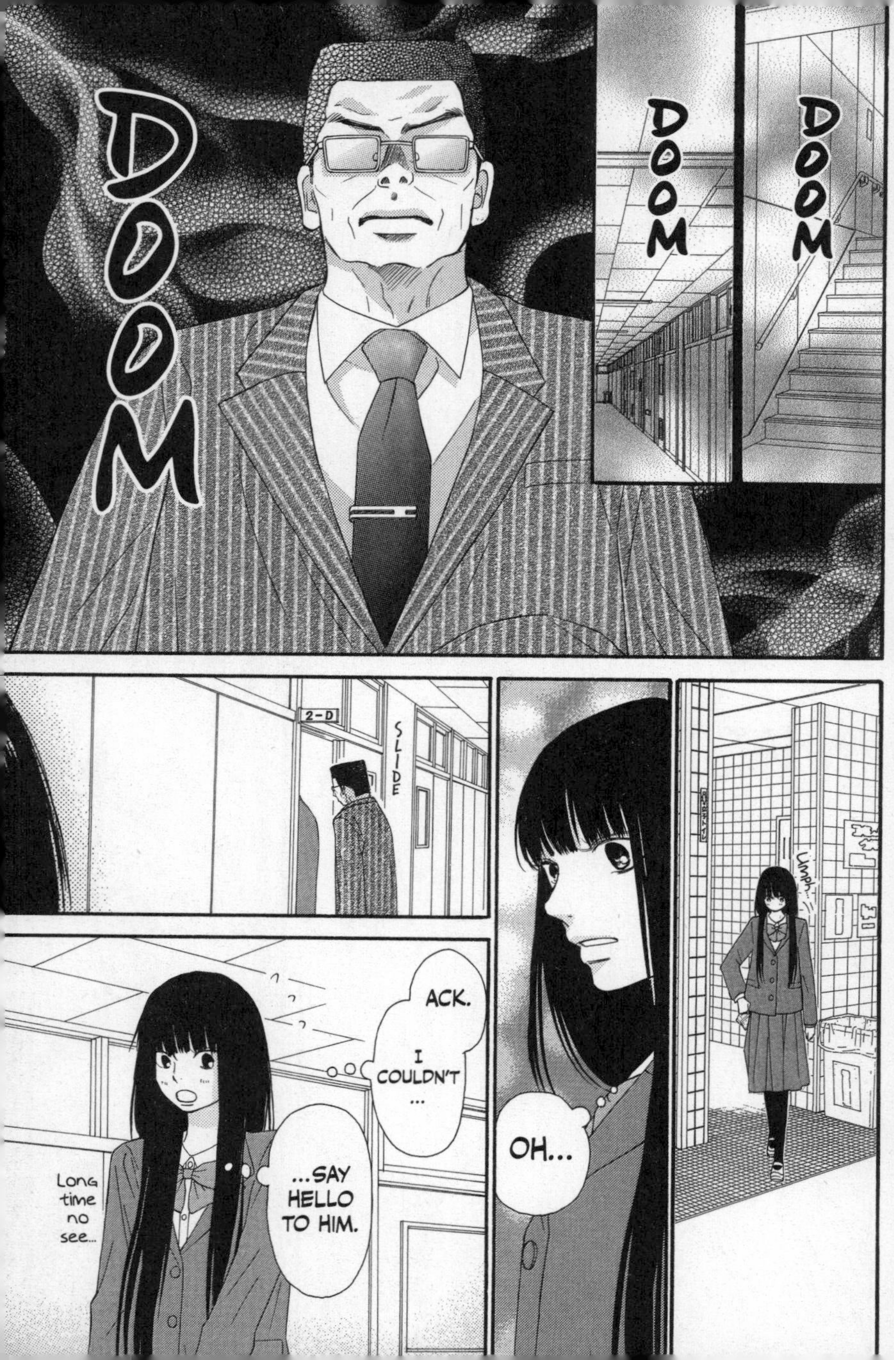
DOOM
DOOM
DOOM
Umph...
OH...
2-D
SLIDE
ACK.
I COULDN'T ...
...SAY HELLO TO HIM.
Long time no see...

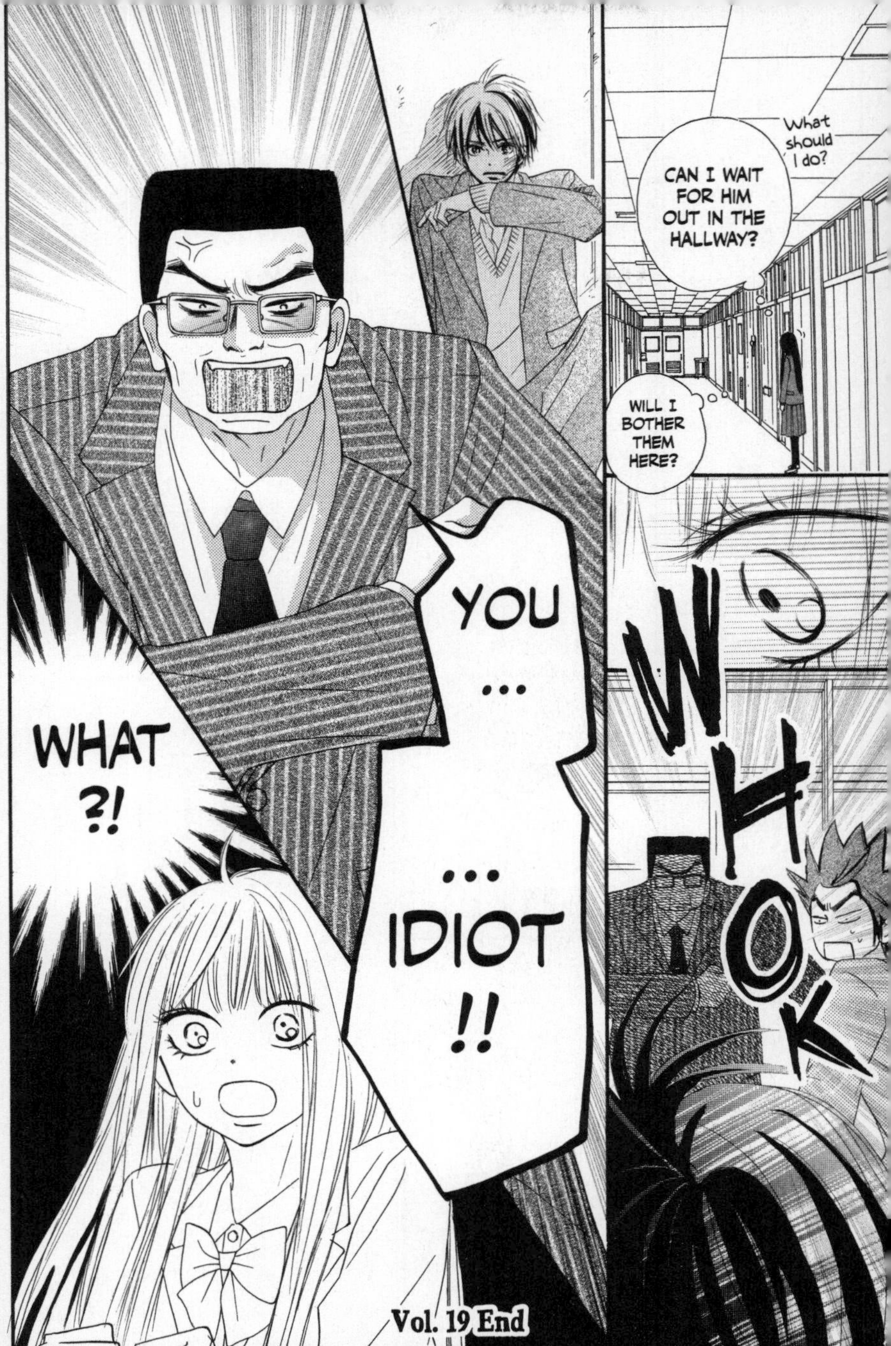
What should I do?
CAN I WAIT FOR HIM OUT IN THE HALLWAY?
WILL I BOTHER THEM HERE?
WHOK
YOU ... ... IDIOT!!
WHAT?!

Vol. 19 End

From me (the editor) to you (the reader).

Here are some Japanese culture explanations that will help you better understand the references in the *Kimi ni Todoke* world.

Honorifics:
When saying someone's name in Japanese, a suffix is often attached to indicate how familiar the speaker is with the person. Some are more polite and respectful, while others are endearing. Calling someone by just their first name is the most informal.
-kun is used for young men or boys, usually someone you are familiar with.
-chan is used for young women, girls or young children and can be used as a term of endearment.
-san is used for someone you respect or are not close to, or to be polite.

Page 15, road heating:
An underground heating system used to clear snow from roads.

Page 18, zoni:
A soup with rice cakes, often eaten on New Year's Day.

Page 26, *Kohaku*:
Kohaku Uta Gassen, or simply *Kohaku*, is a music program on New Year's Eve. Music artists are divided into red and white teams and compete for higher audience ratings.

Page 42, *Yukutoshi Kurutoshi*:
A television show after *Kohaku* only broadcast at midnight on New Year's Eve. It ushers out the old year and welcomes in the new year.

Page 62, soba:
Buckwheat noodles. A common dish on New Year's Eve. These are what Sawako made from scratch for her family.

Page 63, omikuji:
Paper fortunes sold at Shinto and Buddhist shrines.

Page 100, flowers sprouting out of your head:
A sign of "spring fever."

Page 109, college endorsement:
In Japan, colleges often have their own entrance examinations and essays, in addition to the general college entrance exam. Getting an endorsement from your high school and interviewing at the college of your choice bypasses the regular admissions process.